The Theory of Catering

RONALD KINTON

AND

VICTOR CESERANI

The School of Hotel Keeping
and Catering
Ealing Technical College

SECOND EDITION
Decimal and Metric

LONDON

EDWARD ARNOLD (PUBLISHERS) LTD

First Published 1964
Reprinted 1965
Reprinted 1967
Reprinted 1968 (twice)
Second Edition 1970
Reprinted 1970

Boards edition SBN 7131 1601 3
Limp edition SBN 7131 1602 1

Made and printed offset in Great Britain by
The Camelot Press Ltd., London and Southampton

Introduction

This book has been written to help meet the needs of students preparing for the examinations of the City and Guilds of London Institute Examinations, the Hotel and Catering Institute and the National Certificates.

It has not been our intention to write a comprehensive study, but rather to set out a simple outline; although some information has been included for reference purposes. Where further information may be required addresses and recommended books are listed at the end of each chapter.

We wish to stress the necessity for practical work to be closely related to theory and for theory subjects to be linked one with the other. We therefore make no apology for the repetition of essential facts in different chapters. Furthermore we do not consider diagrams, pictures, etc., are a satisfactory substitute for the real thing.

We express our sincere thanks to all the staff of the Hotel and Catering School, Ealing Technical College, for their assistance and encouragement. We are also grateful to Mr. A. Williams of the North Thames Gas Board for his assistance with the chapter on Gas, to the Sutton District Water Company on Water and to the Southern Electricity Board on Electricity.

We are grateful to the North Thames Gas Board and to Benham and Sons Ltd. for permission to reproduce photographs and to the Central Council for Health Education for allowing us to redraw their 'Germometer' card.

We also appreciate the guidance and assistance we have received from Edward Arnold (Publishers) Ltd.

R. K.

1964 V. C.

Introduction to the second edition

Teachers and students will be aware that this new edition is being published at a time when there is great discussion within the industry of the implications of the 1971 changeover to decimal currency and the adoption by Britain in 1975 of a metric system of measurement, the Systéme International d'Unites (SI).

Our enquiries have led us to the view that the new systems are more readily assimilable if the student is not given the old unit alongside the new one. For the most part, therefore, the text is completely metric. However, we have been obliged to leave the imperial units where manufacturers, suppliers or Trade Associations could not give us a definite indication of their intentions, for example in connection with the purchasing units of some commodities and the water capacity of immersion heaters. As soon as we have to hand complete information about the 'metric' intentions of the various sectors in the industry we will be revising this edition.

An Introduction to Decimalisation and Metrication has been added for this edition as an attempt to re-introduce students to working in decimals and to the fundamental workings of the Metric System. Students are recommended to turn to this section whenever they are unsure about the relative value of the new units.

Other amendments have been made to keep abreast of certain changes in examining techniques, and some additions have been made, e.g. speciality menus.

R. K.
V. C.

1970

Contents

Chapter		page
	Introduction to Decimalisation and Metrication	vii
1	SAFETY – FIRST AID – FIRE PRECAUTIONS – WORKING METHODS	1
2	HYGIENE: PERSONAL HYGIENE	9
	KITCHEN HYGIENE	15
	FOOD HYGIENE	19
3	*Services:* GAS	38
4	*Services:* ELECTRICITY	56
5	*Services:* WATER	75
6	KITCHEN EQUIPMENT	91
7	ELEMENTARY NUTRITION	105
8	COMMODITIES	129
9	PRESERVATION OF FOODS	238
10	STOREKEEPING	247
11	KITCHEN ORGANISATION	261
12	KITCHEN FRENCH	269
13	MENU PLANNING	296
14	FOOD BUYING	336
15	SERVICE OF FOOD	342
16	TYPES OF CATERING	346
17	EXAMINATIONS	362
	BIBLIOGRAPHY	369
	FURTHER INFORMATION—ADDRESSES	371
	INDEX	373

Celsius and Fahrenheit scales are shown on page xvi.

List of Colour Plates

		Facing page
1.	Shell-fish (molluscs)	110
2.	Shell-fish (crustaceans)	110
3.	Flat fish	143
4.	Flat fish	143
5	Round oily fish	206
6.	Round white fish	206
7.	Some other fish	239
8.	Carcase of lamb	239
9.	Joints of lamb	302
10.	Lamb prepared for cooking	302
11.	Game birds	335
12.	Vegetables	335

A Section of 8 pages of black and white photographs showing Kitchen Equipment appears between pages 62 and 63.

Introduction to Decimalisation and Metrication

WHAT ARE DECIMALS?

According to the dictionary, a decimal counting system is one which proceeds by tens 1, 10, 100, 1000, etc. Below one, fractions are expressed in tenths, hundredths, thousandths, etc., and written as 0·1, 0·01, 0·001.

Simple examples of using decimals when adding, subtracting, multiplying and dividing:

ADDITION

Add 12·13, 2·157 and 7·934

$$\begin{array}{rr} & 12{\cdot}13 \\ & 2{\cdot}157 \\ & 7{\cdot}934 \\ \hline \textit{Ans.} & 22{\cdot}221 \\ \hline \end{array}$$

Note that the decimal points are in a vertical line, including the decimal point in the total and that the working is the same as ordinary addition.

SUBTRACTION

Subtract 17·123 from 73·1

$$\begin{array}{rr} & 73{\cdot}1 \\ & 17{\cdot}123 \\ \hline \textit{Ans.} & 55{\cdot}977 \\ \hline \end{array}$$

DIVISION

Divide 0·004 by 0·02

Make the divisor 0·02 into a whole number 2

To do this the point is moved two places to the right. The same must be done to the dividend 0·004 which becomes 0·4 ∴ 0·4 divided by 2 = ·2

$$0{\cdot}02\overline{)0{\cdot}004} \text{ becomes } 2\overline{)0{\cdot}4}^{\;0{\cdot}2}$$

MULTIPLICATION

Multiply 1·345 by 4·38

```
         1·345
          4·38
       -------
       5380
        40350
        10760
       -------
Ans.   5·89110
```

Explanation: Multiply as with ordinary numbers, ignoring the decimal points for the time being, as shown.

1st line 1345 × 4(00), etc.
starting figure (0) is placed *beneath the 4*

2nd line 1345 × 3(0)
starting figure (5) is placed *beneath the 3*

3rd line 1345 × 8
starting figure (0) is placed *beneath the 8*

4th line (*a*) add lines 1, 2, 3 (these are called partial products) to give the figure 589110.

(*b*) Count the number of figures after the decimal point in each of the two numbers being multiplied, thus 1·345 (3 fig. after d.p.); 4·38 (2 fig. after d.p.); giving a total of *5* figures after the decimal points.

(*c*) Let the decimal point bounce *5* places from the right to left in our answer line, thus

5·89110 = 5·89110 *Ans.*

DECIMAL CURRENCY

The decimal currency system to be introduced into this country in 1971 is called the 'pound-new penny' system. The pound sterling will remain but is to be divided into 100 'new' pennies. (The word 'new' will be dropped as the old currency disappears.)

The new coins are

	old currency
½ new penny	1·2
1 ,, ,,	2·4
2 ,, pennies	4·8
5 ,, ,,	1s.
10 ,, ,,	2s.
50 ,, ,,	10s.

The £ sign for pounds (£40) and the p sign for new pence (50p) are to be used. The two signs must never be used together in the same expression. The £ should always appear when the decimal point is used, e.g. £11·98

e.g. 68p

(It is useful to remember that the new pence are percentages of £1, i.e. 50p is 50% of £1.)

When writing amounts in new pence the following methods are acceptable

95p	£0·95
5p	£0·05
½p	£0·00½

The nought should always appear in the first pound column, as £·95 could be misread as £95. Likewise two digits are used in the new pence column, as £0·5 could be read as 50 new pence or 5 new pence.

For general use the new halfpenny is expressed as a fraction, not as a third place of decimals and should be shown as 5½p or £0·05½.[1]

ADDITION OF NEW PENCE

12p + 73p + 21p + 5p

```
 12
 73 +
 21
  5
----
111p = £1·11 Ans.
```

After adding, count two places from the right (dividing by 100) and insert the decimal point, the figures to the left of the point are pounds and those to the right are new pence.

ADDITION OF POUNDS AND NEW PENCE

£1·58 + £12·50 + 7p

```
  £
  1·58
 12·50
 00·07
------
 14·15 = £14·15 Ans.
```

Note: The sum is headed by the £ sign only, usually situated over the first digit in the pounds column.

[1] In machine accounting the ½ penny will be shown as a 5 in the third place of decimals and the decimal point will appear on the line, e.g. £32.345 = £32·34½

SUBTRACTION

	£
Deduct 22p from £1	1·00
	0·22
	0·78 = £0·78 or
	78p *Ans.*

Whilst both old and new currencies are in operation it will be necessary to calculate using old and new coins, for example:

	£
12 × £1	12·00
15 × 10/- = 15 × 50p	7·50
5 × 50p	2·50
14 × 10p	1·40
6 × 2/- = 6 × 10p	0·60
7 × 5p	0·35
8 × 1/- = 8 × 5p	0·40
4 × 6d = 4 × 2½	0·10
3 × 3d = 9d*	0·04
7 × 2p	0·14
21 × 1p	0·21
15 × 1d = 1/3d*	0·06
7 × ½p	0·03½
	£25·33½

MULTIPLICATION

£1·92 × 5	1·92
	5
	9·60 = £9·60 *Ans.*

As there are two decimal figures after the point in the sum, there must be two decimal places in the answer.

Another example: 8¼ kg of smoked salmon at £1·75 per kg (8¼ = 8·25).

```
  8·25
  1·75
825 00
577 50
 41 25
144375
```

* See conversion table (page xi).

As there are four decimal places in the orginal numbers there must be four decimal places in the answer, which now reads 14·4375. The answer is in pounds and should be given correct to the second decimal place (correct to the nearest penny). *Ans.* £14·44

DIVISION

Make certain that the decimal point in the answer is immediately above the decimal point in the amount to be divided. *Example:* 24 people win £80·16 to be divided between them, how much does each receive?

```
      3·34
  24 |80·16
      72
      --
       81
       72
       --
        96
        96    Ans. £3·34 each
```

CONVERSION TABLE

Shillings	*New Pence*	*d*	p
20	100	12	5
19	95	11	4½
18	90	10 }	4
17	85	9 }	
16	80	8	3½
15	75	7	3
14	70	6	2½
13	65	5	2
12	60	4	1½
11	55	3 }	1
10	50	2 }	
9	45	1	½
8	40		
7	35		
6	30		
5	25		
4	20		
3	15		
2	10		
1	5		

A useful aid to converting old currency to decimal currency is to consider the shillings and pence as a whole number, ignoring the shilling sign, for example 4/6 = 46. If this number is then halved, giving 23 then 23p is a very close approximation. To convert decimal amounts to the old currency, multiply by 2; when the amount is more than one figure insert the shilling sign between the last two figures on the right, e.g. 23p × 2 = 46 4/6

Examples of simple short cuts:

(i) To find the cost of 38 articles at 9½p each
(38 × 10p) minus (38 × ½p)
that is 38 × 9½p = 380 − 19 = 361 = £3·61

(ii) To find the cost of 14 articles at 49p each
(14 × 50p) − 14p
that is 700 − 14 = 686 = £6·86

(iii) When considering discount for example:

1% discount of £1 equals 1p, therefore
5% discount of £110 equals 550p
550p = £5·50 deducted from £100 = £104·50

CHANGING TO THE METRIC SYSTEM

The metric system is a decimal system applied to measurement. It was devised by the French after the Revolution as an attempt to rationalise their counting methods. Gradually a place in the system has been found for every aspect of life which requires to be measured from quantities of flour to cosmic rays. The Systéme Internationale (SI), as it is now called, is being adopted by Britain.

There are six basic units

Quantity	*Basic Unit*	*Symbol*
length	metre	m
mass	kilogramme	kg
time	second	s
electric current	ampere	A
temperature	kelvin[1]	K
luminous intensity	candela	cd

and some of the supplementary units which concern the catering industry are

[1] Do not be put off by the Kelvin. 1 degree Kelvin = 1 degree Celsius (centigrade) 0°C is equal to 273·15° on the Kelvin scale). Celsius is the preferred term to centigrade and will be used throughout, and is written as 75°C.

power	watt	W
area	square metre	m^2
volume	cubic metre (litre)	m^3
pressure	newton per sq metre	N/m^2-
quantity of heat	joule	J
calorific value	joule	J/m^3
temperature	degree Celsius	deg C

As metric units are based on the number 10 their value must increase or decrease by tens. Whether measuring weight, capacity or length the multiples are expressed by the same prefix. Those which have relevance to the industry are

Prefix	*Symbol*	*Factor by which the Unit is multiplied*
mega	M	1 000 000
kilo	k	1 000
hecto[1]	h	100
deca[1]	da	10
deci[1]	d	0·1
centi[1]	c	0·01
milli	m	0·001

The following table shows these prefixes applied to the standard unit of length: the metre:

10 millimetres (mm)	=1 centimetre (cm)
10 centimetres (cm)	=1 decimetre (dm)
10 decimetres (dm)	=1 metre (m)
10 *metres*	=1 decametre (dam)
10 decametres (dam)	=1 hectometre (hm)
10 hectometres (hm)	=1 kilometre (km)

Thus there are 100 centimetres in 1 metre; 1000 metres in a kilometre, etc.

WORKING IN METRIC UNITS

Length

1 mm	=	0·039 inch
1 cm	=	0·394 inch
1 metre	=	39·37 inches or 1·09 yd
1 kilometre	=	0·62 or $\frac{5}{8}$ of a mile

[1] These prefixes are limited in practical use.

Length

1 yard	=	0·914 m
1 foot	=	0·304 m
1 inch	=	2·54 cm or 25·4 mm
$\frac{3}{4}$ inch	=	1·9 cm or 19·05 mm
$\frac{1}{2}$ inch	=	1·27 cm or 12·7 mm
$\frac{1}{4}$ inch	=	0·635 cm or 6·35 mm
$\frac{1}{8}$ inch	=	0·317 cm or 3·17 mm
$\frac{1}{10}$ inch	=	0·254 cm or 2·54 mm

The basic unit for measuring length is the metre. For short lengths the centimetre (0·01 of a metre) and millimetre (0·001 of a metre) are used; and for long distances the kilometre (1000 metres).

Weight

The gramme represents a very small mass and the kilogramme therefore is the most used unit. For small quantities, however, the gramme is suitable, for example 1 lb equals 453 grammes. Large weights are expressed in tonnes (*t*).

1 ton	=	1·016 tonne or 1016·05 kg			
1 cwt	=	50·8 kg			
1 stone	=	6·35 kg			
1 lb	=	453 grammes	1 kg	=	2·2 lb
1 oz	=	28·35 g	28·35 grammes	=	1 oz

(It is worth noting that 1 g is the weight of 1 cubic centimetre (1 cm³) of water.)

Capacity and Volume

The cubic metre, which is the basic unit for measuring capacity and volume, is too large for everyday use and therefore the litre which is 1/1000 or 0·001 of a cubic metre is used.

1 centilitre	=	0·07 gill	
1 decilitre	=	0·176 pint	
1 litre	=	1·76 pints	
1 decalitre	=	2·2 gallons	
1 gallon	=	4·546 litres	or 4·546 dm³
1 quart	=	1·136 litres	or 1·136 dm³
1 pint	=	0·568 litre	or 0·568 dm³
1 gill	=	0·142 litre	or 0·142 dm³ or 1·42 decilitre
1 fluid ounce	=	28·4 cm³	·28 decilitre

Temperature

The Celsius (centigrade) scale is being used in place of the Fahrenheit scale. To change from Fahrenheit to Celsius subtract 32, multiply by 5 and divide by 9. For example

$$\begin{array}{r} 212 \\ -\ 32 \\ \hline 180 \\ \times\ \ 5 \\ \div 9\ \overline{|900} = 100 \end{array} \qquad 212°F = 100°C.$$

For conversion of Celsius (centigrade) to Fahrenheit multiply by 9, divide by 5 and add 32.

Pressure

Pressure has so far been measured in pounds per square inch; in the metric system the expression for pressure is newtons per square metre, which is abbreviated to N/m^2

$$1\ lb/in^2$$
$$\text{one pound per square inch} = 6894{\cdot}76\ N/m^2$$

Newton (N) is the unit of force which when applied to 1 kilogramme of mass gives it acceleration of 1 metre per second.

Energy—heat

The terms Btu (British Thermal Unit) therm and calorie will be replaced by the joule (J) which is the unit for measuring energy and quantity of heat

1 therm = 105·506 MJ
1 Btu = 1·055 kJ

(For calorific value the term Jm^3 is used.)

METRIC EQUIVALENT

	Approximate equivalent	*Exact equivalent*
1 oz	30 gramme	28·3 gramme
2 oz	60 gramme	56·6 gramme
4 oz	120 gramme	113·2 gramme
6 oz	180 gramme	169·8 gramme
8 oz	¼ kg	227·0 gramme
12 oz	360 gramme	340·0 gramme
1 lb	½ kg	0·454 kg
1 stone	6 kg	6·35 kg
1 cwt	50 kg	50·8 kg

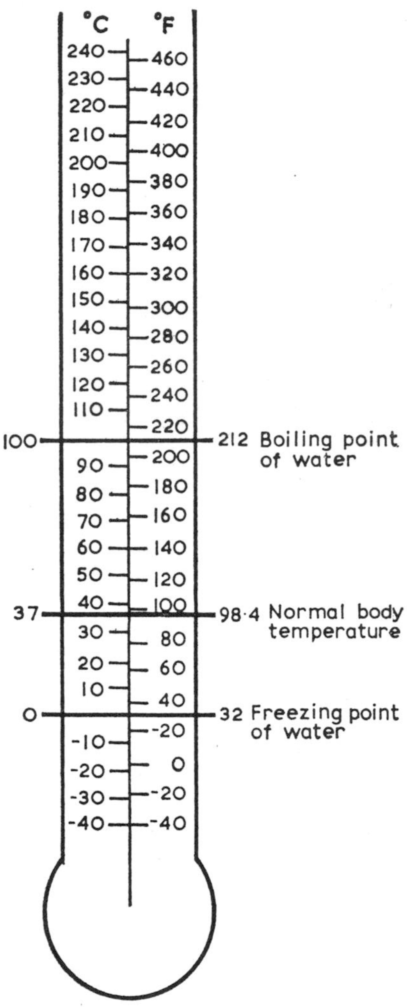

Fahrenheit and Celsius temperature scales.

METRIC EQUIVALENTS

	Approximate equivalent	*Exact equivalent*
1 gill	1/12 litre	0·1065 litre
½ gill	1/16 litre	0·071 litre
¾ pint	⅜ litre	0·426 litre
1 pint	½ litre	0·568 litre
1 quart	1 litre	1·136 litres
1 gallon	5 litres	4·543 litres
⅛ inch	3 mm	3·175 mm
¼ inch	½ cm	0·635 cm
½ inch	1 cm	1·27 cm
1 foot	3 dm	3·05 dm

1. Safety

It is essential that people working in the kitchen are capable of using the tools and equipment in a manner which will neither harm themselves nor those with whom they work. Moreover, they should be aware of the causes of accidents and be able to deal with any which occur.

Accidents are caused in various ways:

(*a*) excessive haste
(*b*) distraction
(*c*) failure to apply safety rules

It should be remembered that most accidents could be prevented.

(*a*) Excessive haste—the golden rule of the kitchen is 'never run' and this may be difficult to observe during a very busy service.

Excessive haste causes people to take chances which inevitably lead to mishaps.

(*b*) Distraction—accidents may be caused by not concentrating on the job in hand, through lack of interest, personal worry or distraction from someone else. The mind must always be kept on the work so as to reduce the number of accidents.

PREVENTION OF ACCIDENTS

It is the responsibility of everyone to observe the safety rules; in this way a great deal of pain and loss of time can be avoided.

PREVENTION OF CUTS AND SCRATCHES

KNIVES: These should never be misused and the following rules should always be observed:

1. The correct knife should be used for the appropriate job.
2. Knives must always be sharp and clean, a blunt knife is more likely to cause a cut owing to excessive pressure having to be used.
3. Handles should be free from grease.
4. When carrying knives, the points must be held downwards.
5. They should be placed flat on the board or table.
6. Knives should be wiped clean with the edge away from the hands.

CHOPPERS: These should be kept sharp and clean and when used care should be taken that no other knives, saws, hooks, etc., can be struck by the chopper, which could cause them to fly into the air. This applies also when using a large knife for chopping.

CUTTING BLADES ON MACHINES: Guards should always be in place when the machine is in use; they should not be tampered with nor should hands or fingers be inserted past the guards. Before the guards are removed for cleaning, the blade or blades must have stopped revolving.

When the guard is removed for cleaning, the blade should not be left unattended, in case someone should put a hand on it by accident. If the machine is electrically operated the plug should, when possible, be removed.

CUTS FROM MEAT AND FISH BONES

Jagged bones can cause cuts which may turn septic, particularly fish bones and the bones of a calf's head which has been opened to remove the brain. Cuts of this nature, however slight, should never be neglected. Frozen meat should not be boned out until it is completely thawed out, because it is difficult to handle, the hands become very cold and the knife slips easily.

PREVENTION OF BURNS AND SCALDS

A burn is caused by dry heat and a scald by wet heat, both can be very painful and have serious effects, and certain precautions should be taken to prevent them.

1. Sleeves of jackets and overalls should be rolled down and aprons worn at a sensible length so as to give adequate protection.
2. A good thick dry cloth (rubber) is most important, it should never be used wet on hot objects and is best folded to give greater protection. It should not be used if thin, torn or with holes.
3. Trays containing hot liquid, for example roast gravy, should be handled carefully, one hand on the side and the other on the end of the tray so as to balance it.
4. Hot pans brought out of the oven should have something white, e.g. a little flour, placed on the handle and lid as a warning that it is hot. This should be done as soon as the pan is taken out of the oven.
5. Handles of pans should not protrude over the edge of the stove as the pan may be knocked off the stove.
6. Large full pans should be carried correctly—that is to say, when there is only one handle the forearm should run along the full length of the handle and the other hand should be used to balance the pan where the handle joins the pan. This should prevent the contents from spilling.

7. Certain foods require extra care when heat is applied to them, as for example when a cold liquid is added to a hot roux or when adding cold water to boiling sugar when making caramel. Extra care should always be taken when boiling sugar.

8. Frying, especially deep frying, needs careful attention. When shallow or deep frying fish, for example, the fish should be put into the pan away from the person so that any splashes will do no harm. With deep frying, fritures should be moved with care and if possible only when the fat is cool. Fritures should not be more than two-thirds full. Wet foods should be drained and dried before being placed in the fat, and when foods are tipped out of the frying basket a spider should be at hand. Should the fat in the friture bubble over on to a gas stove then the gas taps should be turned off immediately. Fire blankets and fire extinguishers should be provided in every kitchen.

9. Steam causes scalds just as hot liquids do. It is important to be certain that before opening steamers the steam is turned off and when the steamer door is opened no one is in the way of the escaping steam. The steamer should be in proper working condition; the drain hole should always be clear. The door should not be opened immediately the steam is turned off; it is better to wait for about half a minute before doing so.

10. Scalds can also be caused by splashing when passing liquids through conical strainers, it is wise to keep the face well back so as to avoid getting splashed. This also applies when hot liquids are poured into containers.

MACHINERY

Accidents are easily caused by misuse of machines. These rules should always be put into practice.

1. The machine should be in correct running order before use.

2. The controls of the machine should be operated by the person using the machine. If two people are involved there is the danger that a misunderstanding can occur and the machine be switched on when the other person does not expect it.

3. Machine attachments should be correctly assembled and only the correct tools used to force food through mincers.

4. When using mixing machines the hands should not be placed inside the bowl until the blades, whisk or hook have stopped revolving. Failure to observe this rule may result in a broken arm.

5. Plugs should be removed from electric machines when they are being cleaned so that they cannot be accidently switched on.

EXPLOSIONS

The risk of explosion from gas is considerable. To avoid this occurring it is necessary to ensure that the gas is properly lit. On ranges with a pilot on the oven it is important to see that the main jet has ignited from the pilot. If the regulo is low sometimes the gas does not light at once, the gas collects and an explosion occurs. When lighting the tops of solid-top ranges it is wise not to place the centre ring back for a few minutes after the stove is lit as the gas may go out—gas then collects and an explosion can occur.

FLOORS

Accidents are also caused by grease and water being spilled on floors and not being cleaned up. It is most important that floors are always kept clean and clear, pots and pans, etc., should never be left on the floor, nor should oven doors be left open, because anyone carrying something large may not see the door, or anything on the floor and trip over.

Many people strain themselves by incorrectly lifting or attempting to lift items which are too heavy. Large stock pots, rondeaus, forequarters and hindquarters of beef for example should be lifted with care. Particular attention should be paid to the hooks in meat so that they do not injure anyone.

On no account should liquids be placed in containers on shelves above eye-level, especially when hot. They may be pulled down by someone else.

Safe kitchens are those which are well lit and well ventilated and where the staff take precautions to prevent accidents happening. When accidents do happen it is necessary to know something of First Aid.

FIRST AID

First Aid is concerned only with *first* aid, it is no substitute for attention by a trained person. If the injury is serious the injured person should be treated by a doctor or nurse as soon as possible.

SHOCK

The signs of shock are faintness, coldness, clammy skin and whiteness. It should be treated by keeping the person comfortable, laid down and warm. Cover the person with a blanket or clothing, but do not apply hot water bottles.

CUTS

All cuts should be covered immediately with a waterproof dressing, after the skin round the cut has been washed. When there is considerable bleeding it should be stopped as soon as possible. Bleeding may be controlled by direct pressure, by bandaging a dressing firmly on the cut. It may be possible to stop bleeding from a cut artery by pressing the artery with the thumb against the underlying bone.

Bleeding may also be controlled by applying pressure with a rubber bandage or pressure bandage on a limb between the cut and the heart for *no longer* than 15 MINUTES at a time.

FRACTURES

A person suffering from broken bones should not be moved until the injured part has been secured so that it cannot move.

BURNS AND SCALDS

If serious, the burn or scald should be covered with clean cloth and the person sent immediately to hospital.

If slight, plunge under cold running water to relieve pain, then apply a burn dressing and bandage, but avoid breaking any blisters.

ELECTRIC SHOCK

Switch off the current. If this is not possible free the person with something dry such as cloth, wood or rubber. If breathing has stopped, give artificial respiration and send for a doctor.

GASSING

Do not let the gassed person walk, but carry him into the fresh air. If breathing has stopped apply artificial respiration and send for a doctor.

ARTIFICIAL RESPIRATION

If breathing has stopped, artificial respiration must be started before any other treatment is given and continued until the person is breathing again.

Further information from the St. John Ambulance Association.

FIRE PRECAUTIONS

In the event of an outbreak of fire whether caused by electricity or gas, the supply to the stove must be turned off at once.

Should a pan of fat catch fire it should be extinguished by using a foam, carbon dioxide or a dry powder type of extinguisher or it may be smothered by using a fire blanket. On no account should water be used to extinguish burning fat. If fat has spilt on to the stove and is alight it usually goes out fairly quickly, provided the gas or electricity is turned off at once.

In the event of a person's clothes catching alight, then a fire blanket should be wrapped round the flames and the person rolled in the blanket on the floor to put out the flames.

Should a fire spread in a kitchen, doors and windows should be closed and fans turned off so as to confine the fire to a limited area and to prevent air entering, so helping to extinguish the fire. A fire should not be allowed to get out of control before the fire brigade is called and it is important to make certain that people in the vicinity are warned of the fire.

CHOICE OF FIRE EXTINGUISHER

Type of fire risk	*Type of extinguisher*
1. Fires involving wood, paper fabrics or similar materials requiring cooling or quenching.	*Water CO_2* (carbon dioxide) Operated by piercing a gas cylinder, the gas then forces the water out. When *hoses* are used for fighting a fire the hose should be connected to the mains water supply. *Soda-Acid* Made in several sizes. Contain a canister of bicarbonate of soda and a bottle of dilute sulphuric acid. The acid is contained in a glass phial which when broken reacts with the bicarbonate of soda and forces water out of the nozzle.
2. Fire involving flammable liquids petrols, oils, greases, fats requiring rapid action.	*Foam* Contains a small canister within a large one, both containing different chemicals which when mixed form foam. This is forced out of the canister and forms a blanket, so preventing air reaching the fire and thus causing it to go out.

3. Fires involving live electrical apparatus.	A non-conducting extinguishing agent must be used. *Dry powder* *Co² (gas)*

Each extinguisher should be fixed on a suitable bracket, be properly maintained and always available for use, and immediately refilled after use. It is important that staff learn how to use them.

For further advice, consult the Fire Prevention Branch of the Fire Brigade and for a list of approved extinguishers apply to the Fire Officers' Committee.

WORKING METHODS

To avoid wastage of time, labour and materials, careful thought and study of many practical jobs can often help to make the job more efficient in many ways. This is called Work Study and when sensibly applied to a practical situation the result is usually a saving of time, labour and materials.

SIMPLE EXAMPLES

Planning and Equipment

In the planning of the layout of equipment for a kitchen, a careful study should be made not only of where the equipment is to be fixed but also of the movement of the staff who will be using the equipment. In the following examples of bad planning it will be seen that time must be wasted through unnecessary walking by the staff.

To cut down on the walking the following arrangement would be more suitable:

Table⟶Grill⟶Service   Sink⟷Table⟷Stove

Crumbing of Foodstuffs

When, for example, croquette potatoes are made the work should flow smoothly.

Mixture (duchess mixture) ⟶ Flour ⟶ Eggwash ⟶ Breadcrumbs ⟶ Tray for finished items

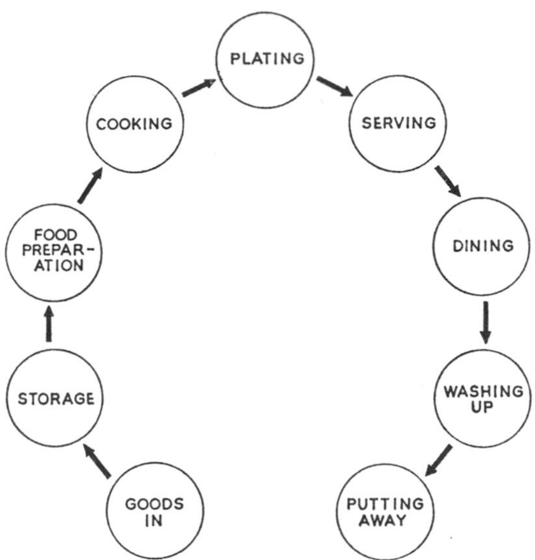

An example of planning the flow of work.

Preparing Beans

When preparing French beans they should all be topped and tailed, then cut—not topping, tailing and cutting each bean separately.

Cutting of Foods

When cutting food, articles to be cut should be on the left of the chopping board (for right-handed people), drawn with the left hand to the centre of the board, cut and pushed to the right. This should be a continuous, smoothly flowing process.

Food is often wasted by using bad working methods. For example: when preparing spinach, to tip a whole box of spinach into the sink of water, then pick off the stalks so that they drop back on to the unpicked spinach will always result in waste. This is a bad practice used by careless cooks because three-quarters of the way through the job the contents of the sink (including an amount of good spinach) is thrown away. This can happen in the preparation of other vegetables such as sprouts, potatoes, carrots.

These are just a few examples of how planning and working methodically can save time, energy and materials.

For further information see chapter 2 of *Quantity Food Production*, Kotschevar, McCutchan.

2. *Hygiene*

PERSONAL HYGIENE

Germs or bacteria are to be found in and on the body and they can be transferred on to anything with which the body comes in contact. Personal cleanliness is essential to prevent germs getting on to food.

Personal Cleanliness

Self-respect is necessary in every food-handler because a pride in one's appearance promotes a high standard of cleanliness and physical fitness. Persons suffering from ill-health or who are not clean about themselves should not handle food.

Bathing

Regular bathing at least once a week is essential, otherwise germs can be transferred on to the clothes and so on to food. If possible a daily bath or shower is ideal, but if this is not possible a thorough wash is satisfactory.

Hands

Hands must be thoroughly washed frequently; particularly after using the toilet, before commencing work and during the handling of food.

They should be washed in hot water with the aid of a brush and soap, rinsed, and dried on a *clean* towel, suitable paper towel or by hand hot-air drier. Hands and finger-nails if not kept clean can be a great source of danger as they can so easily transfer harmful bacteria on to the food.

Rings, watches and jewellery should not be worn where food is handled. Particles of food may be caught under a ring, and germs could multiply there until they are transferred into food.

Watches (apart from the fact that steam ruins them) should not be worn, because foodstuffs, e.g. salads and cabbage, which have to be plunged into plenty of water may not be properly washed because a watch is worn.

Jewellery should not be worn, since it may fall off into food (unknown to the wearer).

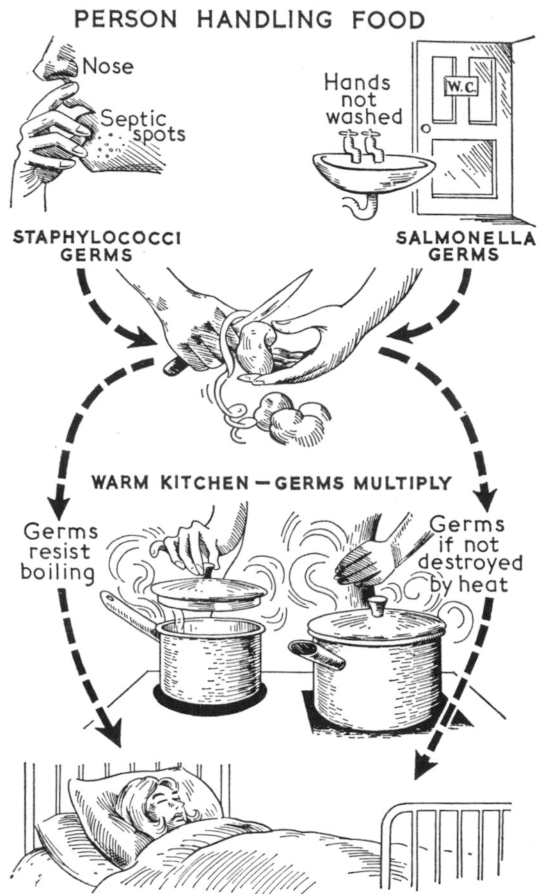

How food poisoning may be caused by a person handling food.

Finger-nails

These should always be kept clean and short as dirt can easily lodge under the nail and be dislodged when, for example, making pastry, so introducing bacteria into food. Nails should be cleaned with a nail-brush.

Hair

Hair should be washed regularly and kept covered where food is being handled. Hair which is not cared for is likely to come out or shed dandruff which may fall into food. Men's hair should be kept short as it is easier to keep clean; it also looks neater. Women's hair should be covered as much as possible. The hair should never be scratched, combed or touched in the kitchen, as germs could be transferred via the hands to the food.

Nose

The nose should not be touched when food is being handled. If a handkerchief is used, the hands should be washed afterwards. Ideally, paper handkerchiefs should be used and then destroyed, the hands being washed afterwards. The nose is an area where there are vast numbers of harmful bacteria; it is therefore very important that neither food, people nor working surfaces are sneezed over, so spreading germs.

Mouth

There are many germs in the area of the mouth, therefore the mouth or lips should not be touched by the hands or utensils which may come into contact with food. No cooking utensils should be used for tasting food, nor should fingers be used for this purpose as germs may be transferred to food. A clean teaspoon should be used for tasting, and washed well afterwards.

Coughing over foods and working areas should be avoided as germs are spread long distances if not trapped in a handkerchief.

Ears

The ear-holes should not be handled whilst in the kitchen as, again, germs can be transferred.

Teeth

Sound teeth are essential to good health. They should be kept clean and visits to the dentist should be regular so that teeth can be kept in good repair.

Feet

As food-handlers are standing for many hours, care of the feet is important. They should be washed regularly and the toe-nails kept short and clean. Tired feet can cause general tiredness which leads to carelessness, and this results in a lowering of the standards of hygiene.

Cuts, Burns, Sores, etc.

It is particularly important to keep all cuts, burns, scratches and similar openings of the skin covered with a waterproof dressing. Where the skin is septic, as with certain cuts, spots, sores, carbuncles, there are vast numbers of harmful bacteria which must not be permitted to get on food; in most cases people suffering in this way should not handle food.

Cosmetics

Cosmetics, if used by food-handlers, should be used in moderation, they should not be put on in the kitchen and the hands should be washed well afterwards. Cosmetics should be put on a clean skin, not used to cover up dirt.

Smoking

Smoking must never take place where there is food, because when a cigarette is taken from the mouth, germs from the mouth can be transferred to the fingers and so on to food. When the cigarette is put down the end which has been in the mouth can transfer germs on to working surfaces. Ash on food is most objectionable and it should be remembered that smoking where there is food is an offence against the law.

Spitting

Spitting should never occur, because germs can be spread by this objectionable habit.

Clothing and Cloths (*Rubbers*)—see also page 13

Clean whites (protective clothing) and clean underclothes should be worn at all times. Dirty clothes enable germs to multiply and if dirty clothing comes into contact with food the food may be contaminated. Cloths (rubbers) used for holding hot dishes should also be kept clean as the cloths are used in many ways such as wiping knives, wiping dishes and pans. All these uses could convey germs on to food.

Outdoor clothing and other clothing which has been taken off before wearing whites, should be kept in a locker away from the kitchen.

GENERAL HEALTH AND FITNESS

The maintenance of good health is essential to prevent the introduction of germs into the kitchen. To keep physically fit, adequate rest, exercise, fresh air and a wholesome diet are essential.

Sleep and Relaxation

Persons employed in the kitchen require adequate sleep and relaxation as they are on the move all the time, often in a hot atmosphere where the tempo of work may be very fast. Frequently, the hours are long or extended over a long period of time, as with split duty, or they may extend into the night. In off-duty periods it may be wise to obtain some relaxation and rest rather than spend all the time energetically. The amount of sleep and rest required depends on each person's needs and the variation between one person and the next is considerable.

Exercise and Fresh Air

People working in conditions of nervous tension, rush, heat and odd hours need a change of environment and particularly fresh air. Swimming, walking or cycling in the country may be suitable ways of obtaining both exercise and fresh air.

Wholesome Food and Pure Water

A well-balanced diet, correctly cooked, and pure water will assist in keeping kitchen personnel fit. The habit of 'picking' (eating small pieces of food whilst working) is bad, it spoils the appetite and does not allow the stomach to rest.

Meals should be taken regularly, long periods without food are also bad for the stomach. Pure water is ideal for replacing liquid lost by perspiring in a hot kitchen.

Worry

If possible it is best not to worry, as worrying causes a great deal of ill-health. The catering industry like most others has its worrying times and it is well to remember that not only does the job suffer, but health also, if this state of mind is not kept under control.

CLOTHING IN THE KITCHEN

It is of considerable importance that people working in the kitchen should wear suitable clothing and footwear. Suitable clothing must be:

1. Protective
2. Washable
3. Suitable colour
4. Light in weight and comfortable
5. Strong
6. Absorbent

1. *Protective*

Clothes worn in the kitchen must protect the body from excessive heat. For this reason chefs' jackets are double-breasted and have long sleeves; they are to protect the chest and arms from the heat of the stove and to prevent hot foods or liquids burning or scalding the body.

Aprons. These are designed to protect the body from being scalded or burned and particularly to protect the legs from any liquids which may be spilled; for this reason the apron should be of sufficient length to protect the legs.

Chef's Hat. This is designed to enable air to circulate on top of the head, and can help to prevent baldness. The main purpose of the hat is to prevent loose hairs from dropping into food and to absorb perspiration on the forehead.

Footwear. This should be stout and kept in good repair so as to protect and support the feet. As the kitchen staff are on their feet for many hours, boots for men give added support and will be found most satisfactory.

2. *Washable*

The clothing should be of a washable material as many changes of clothing are required.

3. *Colour*

Clothing which is white is readily seen when soiled and needs to be changed, and there is a tendency to work more cleanly when wearing 'whites'. Chef's trousers of blue and white check are a practical colour but require frequent changing.

4. *Light and Comfortable*

Clothing must be light in weight and comfortable, not tight. Heavy clothing would be uncomfortable and a heavy hat in the heat of the kitchen would cause headaches.

5. *Strong*

Clothes worn in the kitchen must be strong to withstand hard wear and frequent washing.

6. *Absorbent*

Working over a hot stove causes people to perspire; this perspiration should be absorbed, and for this reason underclothes should be worn. The hat absorbs perspiration and the neckerchief is used to prevent perspiration from running down the body, for wiping the face and also to protect the neck, which is easily affected by draughts.

SUMMARY OF PERSONAL HYGIENE

The practice of clean habits in the kitchen is the only way to achieve a satisfactory standard of hygiene, these habits are listed below:

Hands must be washed frequently and always after using the toilet. Food should be handled as little as possible.

Bathing must occur frequently.

Hair must be kept clean and covered in the kitchen; it should not be combed or handled near food.

Nose and mouth should not be touched with the hands.

Cough or sneeze in a handkerchief not over food.

Jewellery, rings and watches should not be worn.

Smoking, spitting and snuff-taking must not occur where there is food.

Cuts and burns should be covered with a waterproof dressing.

Clean clothing should be worn and only clean cloths used.

Foods should be tasted with a clean teaspoon.

Tables should not be sat on.

Unless fit, kitchen personnel should not handle food.

KITCHEN HYGIENE

Neglect in the care and cleaning of any part of the premises and equipment could lead to a risk of food infection. Kitchen hygiene is of very great importance:

(*a*) to those who work in the kitchen, because clean working conditions are more agreeable to work in than dirty conditions;

(*b*) to the owners, because custom should increase when the public know the kitchen is clean;

(*c*) to the customer—no one should want to eat food prepared in a dirty kitchen.

KITCHEN PREMISES

Ventilation

Adequate ventilation must be provided so that fumes from stoves are taken out of the kitchen, and stale air in the stores, larder, stillroom, etc., is extracted. This is usually effected by erecting hoods over stoves and using extractor fans.

Hoods and fans must be kept clean; grease and dirt is drawn up by the fan and if it accumulates it can drop on to food. Windows used for ventilation should be screened to prevent entry of dust, insects and birds.

Lighting

Good lighting is necessary so that people working in the kitchen do not strain their eyes. Natural lighting is preferable to artificial lighting. Good lighting is also necessary to enable the staff to see into corners so that the kitchen can be properly cleaned.

Plumbing

Adequate supplies of hot and cold water must be available for keeping the kitchen clean, cleaning equipment and for staff use. For certain cleaning hot water is essential, and the means of heating water must be capable of meeting the requirements of the establishment.

There must be suitable provision of toilets which must not be in direct contact with any rooms in which food is prepared.

Hand-washing facilities (separate from food preparation sinks) must also be available.

Cleaning of Toilets and Sinks

Toilets must never be cleaned by food-handlers. Sinks and hand basins should be cleaned with an abrasive and thoroughly rinsed.

Floors

Kitchen floors have to withstand a considerable amount of wear and tear therefore they must be:

(*a*) hardwearing
(*b*) capable of being easily cleaned
(*c*) smooth, but not slippery
(*d*) even
(*e*) without cracks or open joints
(*f*) impervious (non-absorbent)

Quarry tile floors, properly laid, are suitable for kitchens, since they fulfil the above requirements.

Cleaning—floors are swept, washed with very hot detergent water and then dried. This can be done by machine or by hand.

Walls

Walls should be strong, smooth, impervious, washable and light in colour. The joint between the wall and floor should be rounded for ease of cleaning. Tiling is the best wall surface because it is easily cleaned and requires no further maintenance.

Cleaning—clean with hot detergent water and dry.

Ceilings

Ceilings must be free from cracks and flaking. They should not be able to harbour dirt.

Doors and Windows

Doors and windows should fit correctly and be clean. The glass should be clean inside and out so as to admit maximum light.

Food Lifts

Lifts should be kept very clean and no particles of food should be allowed to accumulate as lift shafts are ideal places for rats to gain access into kitchens.

HYGIENE OF KITCHEN EQUIPMENT

(also see Chapter 6)

Kitchen equipment should be so designed that it can be:

(*a*) cleaned easily
(*b*) readily inspected to see that it is clean

Failure to maintain equipment and utensils hygienically and in good repair may cause food poisoning.

Material used in the construction of equipment must be

hard so that it does not absorb food materials
smooth so as to be easily cleaned
resistant to rust
resistant to chipping

Equipment must not be made from toxic materials, for example lead, and food must be protected from lubricants.

Easily cleaned equipment is free from unnecessary ridges, screws, ornamentation, dents, crevices inside square corners, and has large smooth areas. Articles of equipment which are difficult to clean—for example, mincers, sieves and strainers—are items where particles of food can lodge so allowing germs to multiply and contaminate food when the utensil is next used.

NORMAL CLEANING OF MATERIALS

Metal. As a rule all metal equipment should be cleaned immediately after use.

(*a*) *Portable items.* Remove food particles and grease. Wash by immersion in hot detergent water. Thoroughly clean with a hard bristle brush or soak till this is possible. Rinse in water 77°C.

(*b*) *Fixed items.* Remove all food and grease with a stiff brush or soak with a wet cloth, using hot detergent water. Thoroughly clean with hot detergent water. Rinse with clean water. Dry with a clean cloth.

Abrasives should only be used in moderation as their constant scratching of the surface makes it more difficult to clean the article next time.

Marble. Scrub with a bristle brush and hot water and then dry.

Wood. Scrub with a bristle brush and hot detergent water, rinse and dry.

Plastic. Wash in reasonably hot water.

China, Earthenware. Avoid extremes of heat and do not clean with an abrasive. Wash in hot water and rinse in very hot water.

Copper. Remove as much food as possible. Soak. Wash in hot detergent water with the aid of a brush. Clean the outside with a paste made of sand, vinegar and flour. Wash well. Rinse and dry.

Aluminium. Do not wash in water containing soda as the protective film which prevents corrosion may be damaged. When water is boiled in an aluminium pan a black stain results, this can be removed by using an acid food, e.g. rhubarb. To clean, remove food particles. Soak. Wash in hot detergent water. Clean with steel wool or abrasive. Rinse and dry.

Stainless steel. Stainless steel is easy to clean. Soak in hot detergent water. Clean with a brush. Rinse and dry.

Tin. Tin which is used to line pots and pans should be soaked, washed in detergent water, rinsed and dried. Tinned utensils where thin sheet steel has a thin coating of tin must be thoroughly dried, otherwise they are likely to rust.

Zinc. This is used to coat storage bins of galvanised iron and it should not be cleaned with a harsh abrasive.

Vitreous enamel. Clean with a damp cloth and dry. Avoid using abrasives.

Equipment requiring particular care in cleaning (sieves, conical strainers, mincers, graters).

Extra attention must be paid to these items, because food particles clog the holes. The holes can be cleaned by using the force of water from the tap, by using a bristle brush and by moving the article, particularly a sieve, up and down in the sink, so causing water to pass through the mesh.

Whisks must be thoroughly cleaned where the wires cross at the end opposite the handle as food can lodge between the wires. The handle of the whisk must also be kept clean.

Saws and choppers, Mandolins. These items should be cleaned in hot detergent water, dried and greased slightly.

Tammy cloths, muslins and piping bags. After use they should be emptied, food particles scraped out, scrubbed carefully and boiled. They should then be rinsed and allowed to dry.

Certain piping bags made of plastic should be washed in very hot water and dried. Nylon piping bags should be boiled.

CLEANING OF LARGE ELECTRICAL EQUIPMENT
(*Mincers, Mixers, Choppers, Slicers, etc.*)

1. Switch off the machine and remove the electric plug.
2. Remove particles of food with a cloth, palette knife, needle or brush.
3. Thoroughly clean with very hot detergent water all removable and fixed parts. Pay particular attention to threads and plates with holes on mincers.
4. Rinse thoroughly.
5. Dry and reassemble.
6. Whilst cleaning see that exposed blades are not left uncovered or unguarded and that the guards are replaced when cleaning is completed.
7. Any specific maker's instruction should be observed.
8. Test that the machine is properly assembled by plugging in and switching on.

FOOD HYGIENE

The most succulent mouth-watering dish into which has gone all the skill and art of the world's best chefs, using the finest possible ingredients, may look, taste and smell superb, yet be unsafe, even dangerous to eat because of harmful bacteria.

It is of the utmost importance that everyone who handles food, or who works in a place where food is handled, should know that food must be both clean and safe. Hygiene is the study of health and the prevention of disease, and because of the dangers of food poisoning, hygiene requires particular attention from everyone in the catering industy.

There are germs everywhere, particularly in and on our bodies; some of these germs if transferred to food can cause illness and in some cases death. These germs are so small they cannot be seen by the naked eye, yet food which looks clean and does not smell or taste bad may be dangerous to eat if harmful germs have contaminated it.

The duty of every person concerned with food is to prevent contamination of food by germs and to prevent these germs or bacteria from multiplying.

Food-handlers must know the Food Hygiene Regulations but no matter how much is written or read about food hygiene the practice of hygienic habits by people who handle food is the only way to safe food.

FOOD POISONING

Fourteen thousand people each year have been found by doctors to be suffering from food poisoning. This is the average number of notified cases for the last ten years, and there are thousands more who have not notified their doctor, but have suffered from food poisoning. This appalling amount of ill-health could be prevented. Failure to prevent it may be due to:

(*a*) Ignorance of the rules of hygiene.
(*b*) Carelessness, thoughtlessness or neglect.
(*c*) Poor standards of equipment or facilities to maintain hygienic standards.
(*d*) Accident.

Food Poisoning can be prevented by:

1. High standards of personal hygiene.
2. Attention to physical fitness.
3. Maintaining good clean working conditions.
4. Maintaining equipment in good repair and in clean condition.
5. Adequate provision of cleaning facilities and cleaning equipment.
6. Correct storage of foodstuffs at the right temperature.
7. Correct reheating of food.
8. Quick cooling of foods prior to storage.
9. Protection of foods from vermin and insects.
10. Hygienic washing up procedure.
11. Food-handlers knowing how food poisoning is caused.
12. Food-handlers not only knowing but carrying out procedures to prevent food poisoning.

Food Poisoning—What it is

Food poisoning can be defined as an illness characterised by stomach pains and diarrhoea and usually vomiting, developing within 1–36 hours after eating the affected food.

Causes of Food Poisoning

Food poisoning results when harmful foods are eaten. They may be harmful because

(*a*) *chemicals* have entered foods accidentally during the growth, preparation or cooking of the food;
(*b*) *germs* have entered the food from humans, animals or other sources and the bacteria themselves, or the toxins (poisons) produced in the food by certain bacteria, have caused the foods to be harmful. By far the greatest number of cases of food poisoning is caused by harmful bacteria.

Chemical Food Poisoning

Certain chemicals may accidentally enter food and cause food poisoning.

Arsenic is used to spray fruit during growth, and occasionally fruit has been affected by this poison.

Lead poisoning can occur from using water that has been in contact with lead pipes and then drunk or used for cooking.

Antimony or *zinc.* Acid foods if stored or cooked in poor quality enamelled or galvanised containers can also cause poisoning.

Copper pans should be correctly tinned and never used for storing foods, particularly acid foods, as copper can be affected by them.

Certain plants are poisonous—for example, poisonous mushrooms or fungi. Rhubard leaves and the parts of potatoes which are exposed to the sun above the surface of the soil are also poisonous.

Prevention of Chemical Food Poisoning

Chemical food poisoning can be prevented by

(*a*) Using correctly maintained and suitable kitchen utensils;
(*b*) Obtaining foodstuffs from reliable sources;
(*c*) Care in the use of rat poison, etc.

Bacterial Food Poisoning

Food contaminated by bacteria (germs) is by far the most common cause of food poisoning.

BACTERIA

Bacteria are minute, single-celled organisms which can only be seen under a microscope. They are everywhere in our surroundings, and as most bacteria cannot move by themselves they are transferred to something by coming into direct contact with it.

Some bacteria form spores which can withstand high temperatures for long periods of time (even 6 hours) and on return to favourable conditions they continue to live normally.

Some bacteria produce toxins outside their bodies so that they mix with the food; the food itself is then poisonous and symptoms are almost immediate, usually vomiting.

Other bacteria produce toxins in their bodies which are not released until the bacteria die. Symptoms are delayed until the germs have multiplied and died in sufficient numbers to cause illness.

Certain bacteria produce toxins which are resistant to heat; foods in which this toxin has been produced may still cause illness, even though the food is heated to boiling-point and boiled for half an hour. Some bacteria will grow in the absence of air, others need it.

Bacteria multiply by dividing in two, under suitable conditions, once every 20 minutes. Therefore one bacterium could multiply in 10–12 hours to between 500 million and 1000 million bacteria.

Not all bacteria are harmful, some are useful—for example, those used in cheese production.

Some bacteria which are conveyed by food cause diseases other than food poisoning. These include typhoid, paratyphoid, dysentery, scarlet fever. In these cases the bacteria do not multiply in the food, they are only carried by it and the disease is known as a food-borne disease. With bacterial food poisoning the bacteria multiply in the food.

The time between eating the contaminated food (ingestion) to the beginning of the symptoms of the illness (onset) depends on the type of bacteria which have caused the illness.

CONDITIONS FAVOURABLE TO BACTERIA

For the multiplication of bacteria certain conditions are necessary:

1. FOOD of the right kind.
2. TEMPERATURE must be suitable.
3. MOISTURE must be adequate.
4. TIME must elapse.

Germs multiply on or in moist foods in a warm temperature if left for a period of time.

Food

Most foods are easily contaminated; those less likely to cause food poisoning have a high concentration of vinegar, sugar or salt.

Foods most easily contaminated. The following foods are particularly susceptible to the growth of bacteria because of their composition. Extra care must be taken to prevent them from being contaminated.

1. Stock, sauces, gravies, soups.
2. Meat and meat products (sausages, pies, cold meats).
3. Milk and milk products.
4. Egg and egg products.
5. All foods which are handled.
6. All foods which are reheated.

Temperature

Bacteria multiply rapidly at body temperature, 37°C. They grow between temperatures of 20 and 43° C. This is a similar heat to a badly ventilated kitchen and for this reason foods should not be kept in the kitchen. They should be kept in the larder or refrigerator. Lukewarm water is an ideal heat for bacteria to grow in. Washing-up must not take place in warm water as bacteria are not killed and the conditions are ideal for their growth, therefore pots and pans, crockery and cutlery may become contaminated.

Boiling will kill bacteria in a few minutes, but to destroy toxins boiling for a half-hour is necessary. To kill heat-resistant spores, 4–5 hours' boiling is required. It is important to remember that it is necessary not only to heat foods to a sufficiently high temperature but also for a sufficient length of time to be sure of safe food. Extra care should be taken in warm weather to store foods at low temperatures and to reheat thoroughly foods which cannot be boiled.

Bacteria are not killed by cold, although they do not multiply at low temperatures; they lie dormant for long periods. If foods have been contaminated before being made cold, on raising the temperature the bacteria will multiply. Foods which have been taken out of the refrigerator, kept in a warm kitchen and returned to the refrigerator for use later on may well be contaminated.

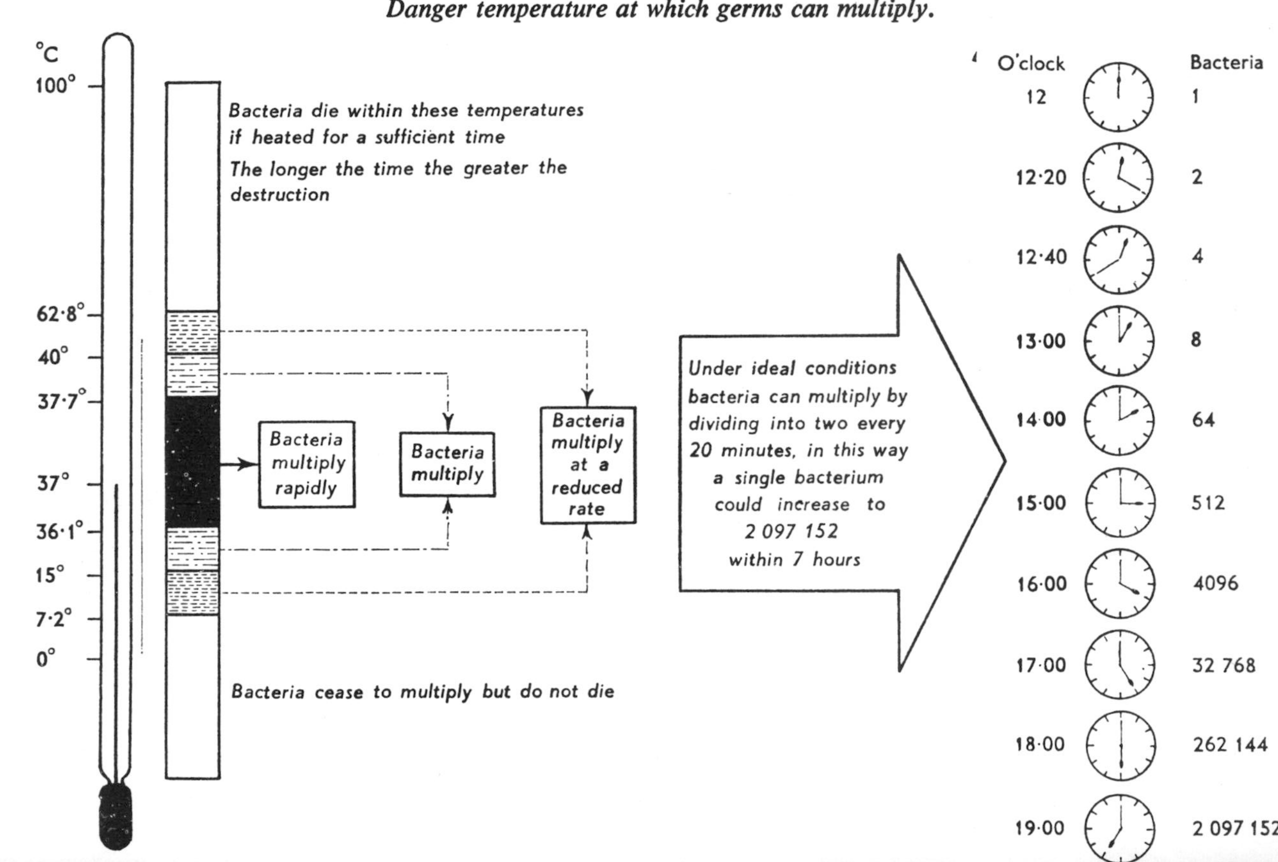
Danger temperature at which germs can multiply.
°C
100°
62·8°
40°
37·7°
37°
36·1°
15°
7·2°
0°
Bacteria die within these temperatures if heated for a sufficient time
The longer the time the greater the destruction
Bacteria multiply rapidly
Bacteria multiply
Bacteria multiply at a reduced rate
Bacteria cease to multiply but do not die
Under ideal conditions bacteria can multiply by dividing into two every 20 minutes, in this way a single bacterium could increase to 2 097 152 within 7 hours
O'clock
12
12·20
12·40
13·00
14·00
15·00
16·00
17·00
18·00
19·00
Bacteria
1
2
4
8
64
512
4096
32 768
262 144
2 097 152

Moisture

Bacteria require moisture for growth, they cannot multiply on dry food. Ideal foods for their growth are jellies, custards, creams, sauces, etc.

Time

Under ideal conditions one bacterium divides into two every twenty minutes, in 5–6 hours millions of bacteria will have been produced. Small numbers of bacteria may have little effect, but in a comparatively short time sufficient numbers can be produced to cause food poisoning. Particular care therefore is required with foods stored overnight especially if adequate refrigerated space is not available.

TYPES OF FOOD POISONING BACTERIA

The most usual types of food poisoning bacteria are

1. The Salmonella group (cause food poisoning by living bacteria).
2. Staphylococci (cause food poisoning by poisons (toxins) of the bacteria).
3. *Clostridium Welchii* and similar organisms (cause food poisoning by large numbers of bacteria).

Salmonella Group

These bacteria are present in the intestines; they are excreted, and anything coming into contact directly or indirectly with the excreta may be contaminated. Infected excreta from man or animals may contaminate rivers and water supplies which may cause further infection. Salmonella infection is the result of man or animals eating food contaminated by salmonella infected excreta originating from man or animals, so completing a circle of infection. For example, when flies land on the excreta of a dog which has eaten infected dog-meat and the flies then go on to food, the people who eat the contaminated food suffer from food poisoning.

Foods affected by the Salmonella Group. Those most affected are eggs, meat, poultry, and desiccated coconut. Contamination can be caused by:

1. Insects and vermin, because salmonellae are spread by droppings, fur, feet, hairs, etc.
2. The food itself may be infected (as with duck eggs).

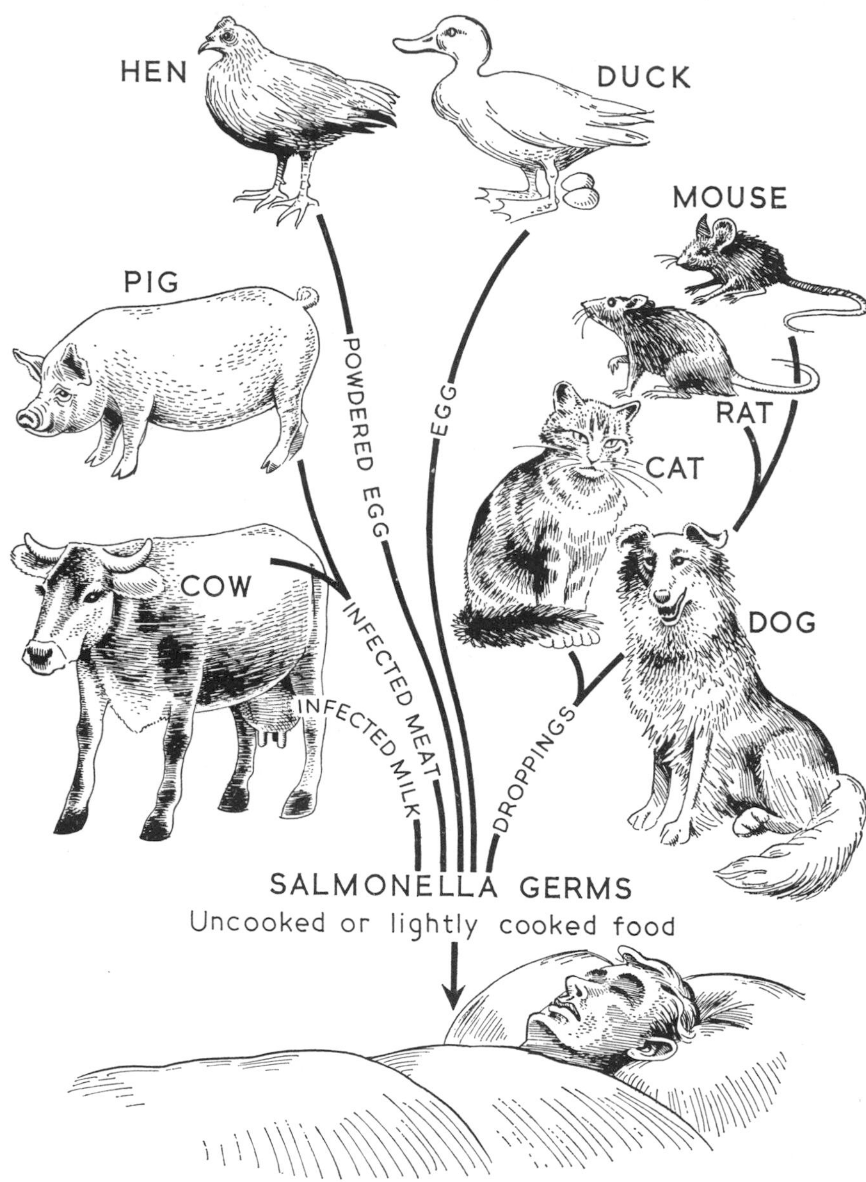

Foods contaminated by salmonella germs if uncooked or lightly cooked may result in food poisoning.

3. By cross contamination—for example, if a chicken is drawn on a board and the board is not properly cleaned before another food (for example, cold meat), is cut on the board.

4. The food could be infected by a human being who has the disease or who is a carrier (a person who does not suffer from food poisoning, but who carries and passes on the germs to others).

Staphylococci

These germs are present on human hands and other parts of the skin, or sores, spots, etc., and in the nose and throat.

Foods affected by Staphylococci. Foods which have been handled are often contaminated because the hands have been infected from the nose or throat, cuts, etc. Brawn, pressed beef, pies, custards are foods frequently contaminated because they are ideal foods for the multiplication of bacteria.

Clostridium Welchii

These bacteria are distributed from the intestines of humans and animals and are found in the soil.

Foods affected by Clostridium Welchii. Raw meat is the main source of these bacteria, the spores of which survive light cooking.

Clostridium Botulinus is another type of bacteria which causes food poisoning which is rare in this country.

SOURCES OF INFECTION

Food-poisoning bacteria live in

(*a*) the soil;
(*b*) humans—intestines, nose, throat, skin, cuts, sores, spots, etc.;
(*c*) animals, insects and birds—intestines and skin, etc.

Prevention of Food Poisoning from Bacteria

To prevent food poisoning everyone concerned with food must

(*a*) prevent bacteria from multiplying;
(*b*) prevent bacteria from spreading from place to place.

This means harmful bacteria must be isolated, the route of infection must be broken and conditions favourable to their growth eliminated. The conditions favourable to their growth—heat, time, moisture and a suitable food on which to grow—have been explained. It is also necessary to prevent harmful bacteria being brought into premises or getting on to food. This is achieved by a high standard of hygiene of personnel, premises, equipment and food-handling.

SPREAD OF INFECTION

(*a*) Human—coughing, sneezing, by the hands.
(*b*) Animal, insects, birds—droppings, hair, etc.
(*c*) Inanimate objects—towels, dishcloths, knives, boards.

Human

People who are feeling ill, suffering from diarrhoea, vomiting, sore throat or head cold must not handle food.

As soon as a person becomes aware that he or she is suffering from, or is a carrier of, typhoid or paratyphoid fever or salmonella or staphylococcal infection likely to cause food poisoning or dysentery, the person responsible for the premises must be informed. He must then inform the Medical Officer for Health.

Standards of personal hygiene should be high (see section on personal hygiene, page 9).

Animal

Vermin, insects, domestic animals and birds can bring infection into food premises.

Rats and mice are a dangerous source of food infection because they carry harmful bacteria on themselves and in their droppings. Rats infest sewers and drains and since excreta is a main source of food-poisoning bacteria, it is therefore possible for any surface touched by rats to be contaminated.

Rats and mice frequent warm dark corners and are found in lift shafts, meter cupboards, lofts, openings in walls where pipes enter, under low shelves and on high shelves. They enter premises through any holes, defective drains, open doorways, in sacks of foodstuffs or even in a load of coke.

Signs to look for are droppings, smears, holes, runways, gnawing marks, grease marks on skirting boards and above pipes, paw foot-marks, damage to stock and also rat odour.

Rats spoil ten times as much food as they eat and there are at least as many rats as human beings. They are very prolific, averaging ten babies per litter and six litters per year so that under ideal conditions it is possible for one pair of rats to increase to 350 million in three years. To prevent infestation from rats and mice the following measures should be taken:

(*a*) Food stocks should be moved and examined to see that no rats or mice have entered the store-room.

(*b*) No scraps of food should be left lying about.
(*c*) Dustbins and swillbins should be covered with tight fitting lids.
(*d*) No rubbish should be allowed to accumulate outside the building.
(*e*) Buildings must be kept in good repair.
(*f*) Premises must be kept clean.

If the premises have become infested with rats or mice the Public Health Inspector should be contacted.

Insect Infection

House flies are the foremost of the insects which spread infection. Flies alight on filth and contaminate their legs, wings and bodies with harmful bacteria, and deposit these on the next object on which they settle; this may well be food. They also contaminate food with their excreta and saliva.

To control flies, the best way is to eliminate their breeding-place. As they breed in rubbish and in warm, moist places, dustbins in summer are ideal breeding grounds, therefore:

(*a*) Dustbins and swill-bins must be kept covered at all times with tight fitting lids.
(*b*) The bins must be kept clean.
(*c*) Ideally, dustbins and swill-bins should not be kept. Rubbish should be burnt immediately if it cannot be disposed of through a waste-master.
(*d*) Paper bins which are destroyed with the rubbish are preferable to other types of bin.

Other ways to control flies are

(*a*) Screen windows to keep flies out of kitchens.
(*b*) Use paints which contain an insecticide.
(*c*) Use sprays to kill flies (only where there is no food).

Cockroaches. Cockroaches like warm, moist, dark places. They leave their droppings and a liquid which gives off a nauseating odour. They can carry harmful bacteria on their bodies and deposit them on anything with which they come into contact.

Silverfish. These small silver-coloured insects feed on, amongst other things, starchy foods and are found on moist surfaces.

Beetles. Beetles are found in warm places and can also carry harmful germs from place to place.

Insects are destroyed by using an insecticide, and it is usual to employ people familiar with this work.

Cats and Dogs

Domestic pets should not be permitted in kitchens or on food premises as they carry harmful bacteria on their coats and are not always clean in their habits. Cats are useful to control rats and mice, but they should not be allowed to go into places where food is prepared.

Birds

Entry of birds through windows should be prevented as food and surfaces on which food is prepared may be contaminated by droppings.

Dust

Dust contains bacteria, therefore it should not be allowed to settle on food or surfaces used for food. Kitchen premises should be kept clean, then no dust will accumulate. Hands should be cleaned after handling dirty vegetables.

WASHING UP

The correct cleaning of all the equipment used for the serving and cooking of food is of vital importance to prevent multiplication of bacteria. This cleaning is divided into the pan wash (plonge) or scullery and the china wash-up.

Scullery

For the effective washing up of pots and pans and other kitchen equipment the following method of work should be observed.

1. Pans should be scraped and all food particles placed in a bin.
2. Hot pans should be allowed to cool before being plunged into water.
3. Pans which have food stuck to them, should be allowed to soak (starchy foods, such as porridge and potatoes, are best soaked in cold water).
4. Frying-pans should be thoroughly wiped with a clean cloth, they should not be washed unless absolutely necessary.
5. Trays and tins used for pastry work should be thoroughly cleaned with a dry cloth, while warm.
6. Pots, pans and other equipment should be washed and cleaned with a stiff bristle brush, steel wool or similar article, in hot detergent water.
7. The washing-up water must be changed frequently, it must be kept both clean and hot.

8. The cleaned items should be rinsed in very hot clean water to sterilise.

9. Pans, etc., which have been sterilised (minimum temperature 82°C) dry quickly; if it has not been possible to rinse in very hot water they should be dried with a clean cloth.

10. Equipment should be stored on clean racks, pans should be stacked upside down.

China Wash-up

The washing up of crockery and cutlery may be by hand or machine.

Handwashing

1. Remove scraps from plates with a scraper or by hand.
2. Wash in water at 60°C containing a detergent.
3. Place in wire baskets and immerse them into water at 82°C for at least two minutes.
4. The hot utensils will air-dry without the use of a drying cloth.
5. Both the washing and sterilising water must be kept clean and at the correct temperature.

Machine washing-up. There are several types of machines which wash and sterilise crockery. In the more modern machines the detergent is automatically fed into the machine which has continuous operation. To be effective the temperature of the water must be high enough to kill any harmful bacteria and the articles passing through the machine must be subjected to the water for sufficient time to enable the detergent water to thoroughly cleanse all the items. The detergent used must be of the correct amount and strength to be effective.

Where brushes are used they must be kept free from food particles.

Hygienic Storage

One of the most important ways to prevent contamination of food is the correct storage of food (see also chapter on storekeeping, page 247).

Foodstuffs of all kinds should be kept covered as much as possible to prevent infection from dust and flies.

Foods should be kept in a refrigerated cold room or refrigerator where possible.

Hot foods which have to go into a refrigerator must be cooled quickly. This can be done by dividing large quantities of food into smaller containers, by cooling in a draught of air using fans or by raising the container and placing an article underneath, for example a triangle or weight, so that air can circulate, or by placing the container in a sink with running cold water. If large quantities of food, for example minced beef, are left in one container the outside cools but the centre is still warm. When reheated the time taken to bring such a large quantity to the boil is sufficient to allow the bacteria to continue to multiply. If the food is not boiled long enough food poisoning can occur (see Temperature, page 24).

Particular care must be taken to store foods correctly in the warmer months; food not refrigerated in hot weather does not cool completely and, furthermore, flies and bluebottles are numerous in the summer.

FOODS WHICH REQUIRE SPECIAL ATTENTION

Meat

1. All made-up dishes, such as cottage pie, need extra care. They must be very thoroughly cooked.
2. Reheated meat dishes must be thoroughly reheated.
3. Pork must be well cooked (this is because pork is frequently affected by trichinosis which is a disease caused by a worm).
4. Poultry which is drawn in the kitchen should be cleaned carefully; boards, tables and knives must be thoroughly cleaned afterwards, otherwise there is a danger of contamination from excreta.
5. Meat should be handled as little as possible. Minced and cut up meats are more likely to become contaminated because of infection from the food-handler. Boned and rolled joints require extra care in cooking as inside surfaces may have been contaminated.
6. Sausages should be cooked right through.
7. Tinned hams are lightly cooked, therefore they must be stored in a refrigerator.

Fish

Fish is usually washed, cooked and eaten fresh and is not often a cause of food poisoning, except in reheated fish dishes.

Care must be taken to reheat thoroughly such dishes as fish cakes, fish pie, coquille de poisson, etc.

Some fish, such as oysters and mussels, have caused food poisoning because they have been bred in water which has been polluted by sewage. They are today purified before being sold. All shell fish should be used fresh. If bought alive, there is no doubt as to their freshness.

Eggs

Unless dried, hens' eggs do not cause food poisoning, but ducks' eggs should be used with caution and must be thoroughly cooked. Dried eggs if used should be reconstituted and used right away, not left in this condition in a warm kitchen as they may have been contaminated in processing. Hollandaise sauce which is made with eggs is an example of a food which should not be kept in a warm kitchen for long. If not used in the morning it should not be used for the evening service.

Milk

Milk when used in custards, trifles, puddings, etc., unless eaten soon after preparation should be treated with care. If required for the following day these dishes must be refrigerated.

Watercress and Other Green Salad

Watercress must be thoroughly washed, as it grows in water which could be contaminated by animals. All green salads and other foods eaten raw should be well washed.

Synthetic Cream

Synthetic cream can be a cause of food poisoning if allowed to remain in warm conditions for long periods. It is easily contaminated by handling.

Coconut

Desiccated coconut has been a cause of food poisoning, and if used in cooking it must be well cooked. It is not advisable to use it as a cake decoration on cream.

Gravies, soups and sauces also require particular care.

FOOD-BORNE DISEASES

Typhoid and paratyphoid are diseases caused by harmful bacteria carried in food or water. Scarlet fever, tuberculosis and dysentery may be caused by drinking milk which has not been pasteurised.

To prevent diseases being spread by food and water the following measures should be taken.

1. Water supplies must be purefied.
2. Milk and milk products should be pasteurised.
3. Carriers should be excluded from food preparation rooms.

THE FOOD HYGIENE REGULATIONS

These regulations should be known and complied with by all people concerned with the handling of food. A copy of the full regulations can be obtained from H.M. Stationery Office and an abstract can be obtained which gives the main points of the full regulations.

These points are as follows:

EQUIPMENT must be kept clean and in good condition.

PERSONAL REQUIREMENTS

1. All parts of the person liable to come into contact with food must be kept as clean as possible.

2 All clothing must be kept as clean as possible.

3. All cuts or abrasions must be covered with a waterproof dressing.

4. Spitting is forbidden.

5. Smoking and the use of snuff are forbidden in a food room or where there is food.

6. As soon as a person is aware that he is suffering from or is a carrier of such infections as typhoid, paratyphoid, dysentery, salmonella or staphylococcal infection he must notify his employer who must notify the Medical Officer of Health.

REQUIREMENTS FOR FOOD PREMISES

Toilets

1. These must be clean, well lighted and ventilated.

2. No food room shall contain or directly communicate with a toilet.

3. A notice requesting people to wash their hands after using the toilet must be displayed in a prominent place.

4. The ventilation of the soil drainage must not be in a food room.

5. The water supply to a food room and toilet is only permitted through an efficient flushing cistern.

Washing Facilities

1. Hand basins and an adequate supply of hot water must be provided.

2. Supplies of soap, nail-brushes and clean towels must be available by the hand basins.

First Aid

Bandages, dressings and antiseptics must be provided in a readily accessible position.

Lockers

Sufficient lockers must be available for outdoor clothes.

Lighting and Ventilation

Food rooms must be suitably lighted and ventilated.

Sleeping Room

Rooms in which food is prepared must not be slept in. Sleeping rooms must not communicate with a food room.

Refuse

Refuse must not be allowed to accumulate in a food room.

Buildings

The structure of food rooms must be kept in good repair to enable them to be cleaned and to prevent entry of rats, mice, etc.

Food Temperatures

All foods must be kept in a cool larder or at a temperature where micro-organisms will be killed. Foods should not be kept at a temperature of 7°C–62°C.

Storage

Foods should not be placed in a yard, etc., lower than 20 cm unless properly protected.

PENALTIES

Any person guilty of an offence shall be liable to a fine not exceeding £100 or to a term of imprisonment not exceeding three months or both.

SUMMARY OF FOOD HYGIENE

Dangers to Food

Chemical (copper, lead, etc.).
Plant (toadstools).
Bacteria (cause of most cases of food poisoning).

Bacteria

Almost everywhere.
Must be magnified 500–1000 times to be seen.
Multiply by dividing in two every 20 minutes.

Sources of Food-poisoning Bacteria

Human—nose, throat, excreta, spots, cuts, etc.
Animal—excreta.
Foodstuffs—meat, eggs, milk, from animal carriers.

Method of Spread of Bacteria

Human—cough, sneezes, hands.
Animal—excreta (rats, mice, cows, pets, etc.), infected carcasses.
Insects—flies, cockroaches.
Other means—equipment, china, towels.

Factors Essential for Bacterial Growth

Temperature.
Time.
Moisture.
Suitable food.

Method of Control of Bacterial Growth

Heat—Sterilisation.
Pasteurisation 63°C—65°C for ½ hour or 72°C for 15 seconds.
Cooking.
Cold—Refrigeration.
Deep freeze.

Foods Commonly causing Food Poisoning

Made-up meat dishes.
Trifles, custards, synthetic cream.
Sauces.
Left-over foods.

Prevention of Food Poisoning

Care of Person. 1. Washing of hands. 2. Handle food as little as possible. 3. Cover cuts and burns with waterproof dressing. 4. Clean clothes and clean habits.

Care of food. 1. Keep food cold during storage. 2. Cook meat and duck eggs thoroughly. 3. Cook and eat foods same day. 'Warmed-up' foods must be thoroughly reheated. 4. Protect foods from flies, rats, mice, etc.

Care of environment. 1. Provide spacious well-lighted and well-ventilated premises. 2. Adequate wash and cleaning facilities. 3. Ample cold storage. 4. Suitable washing-up facilities.

FURTHER INFORMATION MAY BE HAD FROM:

Central Council for Health Education, Tavistock House North, Tavistock Square, London, W.C.1.

Royal Society of Health, 90 Buckingham Palace Road, London, S.W.1.

Royal Institute of Public Health and Hygiene, 28 Portland Place, London, W.1.

Food Hygiene Laboratory, Central Public Health Laboratory, Colindale, London, N.W.9.

Local Public Health Departments.

RECOMMENDED BOOKS

Betty C. Hobbs, *Food Poisoning and Food Hygiene*. (Arnold.)
Food Hygiene Regulations. (H.M. Stationery Office.)
Food Hygiene Codes of Practice. (H.M. Stationery Office.)
Hygienic Food Handling. (St. John Ambulance Association.)
Clean Catering. (H.M. Stationery Office.)

3. *Services: Gas*

Services is the study of gas, water and electricity, each of which is a complicated specialist subject. A simple study can be made, however, which is a help to the student in understanding how important a part all three play in the catering industry.

TRANSFERENCE OF HEAT

This is carried out by one of three methods: Conduction, Convection, Radiation.

Conduction is the travelling of heat through a solid, or from one solid to another, provided they are in contact, e.g. a poker in a fire or a saucepanful of water on a hot-plate.

Good conductors of heat are all metals.

Bad conductors of heat are cork, plastics, china, wood, string, cotton, and these are used in the manufacture of certain articles or parts of articles which require to be kept cool, e.g. pot triangles, dry oven cloths.

Convection is the passage of heat through liquids and gases, e.g. a saucepanful of water being heated, the water at the bottom becomes heated first and then because it is lighter rises to the top and the heavier cold water takes its place at the bottom, e.g. an Ideal boiler.

Hot-water radiators, so called, should be called convectors.

Radiation is the method by which heat travels from a hot object

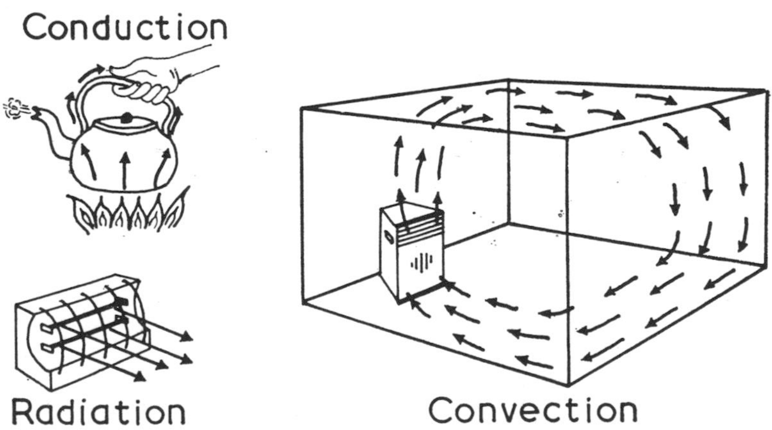

Three ways in which heat is transferred.

in straight rays as does light. Any object in the path of the rays becomes heated, e.g. grilling, coal-fire, electric fire.

An example illustrating the use of the three terms could be a saucepan of water on an open coal fire:

Fire to metal	—	radiation
Metal to water	—	conduction
Heating of the water	—	convection

Gas is produced from coal by the following process:

1. In a retort house coal is heated to produce crude gas.
2. In a condenser the crude gas is cooled to atmospheric pressure and some impurities deposited.
3. The crude gas is passed through an Electro-detarrer to remove remaining tar.
4. The gas is then passed through a Scrubber which removes ammonia.
5. Then through a Purifier.
6. Then through a Benzol Recovery Plant where the gas is sprayed with oil in order to remove benzol.
7. The gas then passes through a Station Meter which measures the gas output.
8. Then to a Gasholder for storage.
9. The gas then goes to a Gas Drying Plant where water is removed.
10. Gas output is controlled by the Governor House which maintains gas at constant pressure for the consumer.
11. The gas then goes into the street mains and so into houses and establishments.

Sea gas or natural gas is also available.

THE PROPERTIES OF COAL-GAS

1. Poisonous—coal gas before being burnt is poisonous and contains carbon monoxide.
2. Characteristic smell—the strong overpowering smell of gas could be removed during manufacture, but is retained so that escaping gas can be detected.
3. Gas is lighter than air.
4. Gas will burn. Oxygen is necessary for the combustion of coal gas. One volume of gas requires one volume of oxygen. Air contains four parts of nitrogen to one part of oxygen, therefore one volume of gas requires five volumes of air.

The reasons for converting coal to gas are for cleanliness and economy; the majority of the heat and by-products of coal are lost in smoke as can be seen in the following example:

Heat Value

$\frac{1}{2}$ kg coal gives approx. 2600 units of heat when heated. When converted, $\frac{1}{2}$ kg coal gives approx. 4450 units (gas). Gas is more labour-saving and easier to control and no storage space is required.

Gas passes through mains into houses and establishments through a gas meter which at present records the amount used in cubic feet. (It will be recorded in cubic metres (cm^3) under the metric system.)

CALCULATION OF GAS BILLS (AT PRESENT)

1. The Gas Board states the calorific value (C.V.) of the gas in British Thermal Units per cubic foot, i.e. 500 B.Th.U.'s/ft^3.

To find how many B.Th.U.'s have been used, multiply the consumption in ft^3 by the C.V.

2. Gas is charged per therm. 1 therm = 100 000 B.Th.U.'s, therefore divide the B.Th.U.'s consumed by 100 000 to find the number of therms.

3. Supposing 1 therm costs 7p the calculation of the bill is as follows:

previous reading = 42 600 ft^3
present reading = 44 600 ft^3
consumption = 2000 ft^3
C.V. = 500
price per therm = 7p

Therefore cost $= \frac{2000 \times 500}{100\,000} \times 7 = 70\text{p}$ (£0.70)

CALCULATION OF GAS BILLS UNDER THE METRIC SYSTEM

Calorific Value is measured in joules per cubic metre (J/m^3). The joule is *the* unit of energy in the metric system and in this context is used to measure *heat* energy.

1 therm equals approx. 105 506 000 joules, but as this would require calculating in too large numbers our gas bills will probably be calculated in units of 100 Megajoules (Mega = million). 100 MJ is approximately equal to one therm.

A calculation might be as follows:

previous reading = 470 m^3
present reading = 520 m^3
Therefore consumption = 50 m^3
C.V. (Stated by the Gas Board in Megajoules per cubic metre) = 22 (MJ/m^3)

Cost at 7p per 100 MJ $= \frac{50 \times 22}{100} \times 7 = 77\text{p}$ (£0.77)

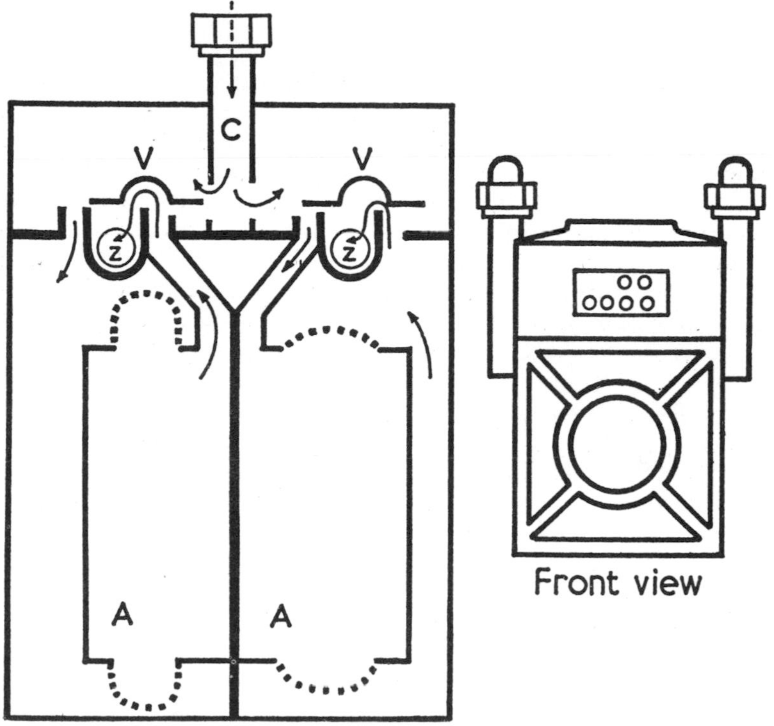

The gas meter.

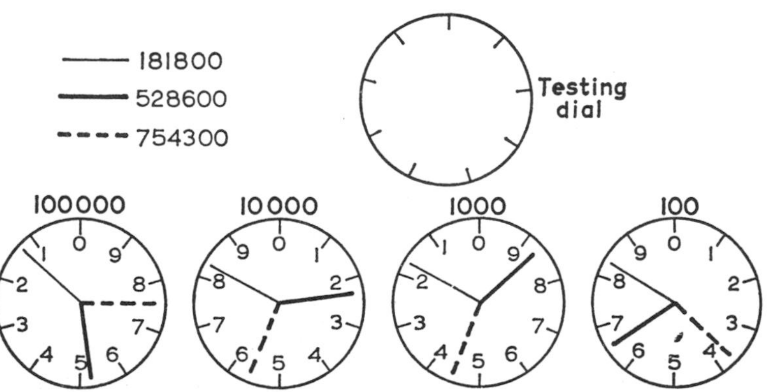

Reading the gas meter (three examples shown).

THE GAS METER

How it works

The gas meter is an intricate and accurate machine. It is divided into three parts: the upper part contains the gas inlets and outlets and the sliding valves *V* which work in with the bellows *A*; the two lower parts each contain a bellows made of a special skin (the dotted line shows the skin). When the gas is turned on it flows into the meter via the main inlet *C*, passes through the valves and so alternately into the inside and outside respectively of the bellows. As it goes in and out by the 'breathing' bellows it is mechanically measured and passes out of the ports marked *Z*. The measured volume is recorded on the dials on the front. The arrows show flow of gas.

Rules for reading the Gas Meter at present

Note—the testing dial is used for testing purposes only.

1. Notice number of cu. ft. which each dial represents.
2. Read from left to right or from highest to lowest; record each dial in turn. (If it points to a number, record it; between two numbers, record the lowest one; between 0 and 9, record 9; between 0 and 1 record 0.)
3. Add number of noughts according to last dial.

THERE ARE TWO METHODS BY WHICH GAS IS BURNED

1. By ignition at the burner head, when the oxygen needed for combustion is obtained from the surrounding atmosphere.
2. By ignition at the burner head when part of the air is mixed with gas beforehand. This is known as primary air and trapped in a vent in the burner itself.

The first method is known as the non-aerated or neat or luminous flame. It has the merit of not lighting back, having a measure of 'fixed' gas rating, and is of value when a high gas rate is required in a restricted space within an appliance. It has the limitation of 'sooting' a surface if contact is made.

The second is known as the aerated or bunsen flame. It has the advantage of being able to come into contact with cooking-pot surfaces without sooting, provided that the gas/air mixture is reasonably adjusted. *N.B.*—The restriction of primary air to a bunsen burner will turn it into a non-aerated flame.

For these reasons non-aerated burners are used when surface contact cannot occur and aerated burners when contact can and often must occur.

There is actually a third method of burning gas, and of recent years this has been applied to large-scale catering cooking ranges.

It is by the ignition of gas at a burner head using no primary air, but by issuing at a gas rate of 40–60 cubic feet (11–17 cubic metres) per hour, thereby causing a velocity which entrains air en route from burner head to the whole length of the flame; this may be some 30–48 cm in length. No 'sooting' takes place when the flame is at its medium to maximum rating, but can occur at very low rates. At this low rate contact with a surface is unlikely and the 'disadvantage' can be ignored.

The burner is used for heating the solid plate tops of cooking ranges, and has the merit of still higher temperatures at the centre of the 'bull's eye' (650°C) with low maintenance costs.

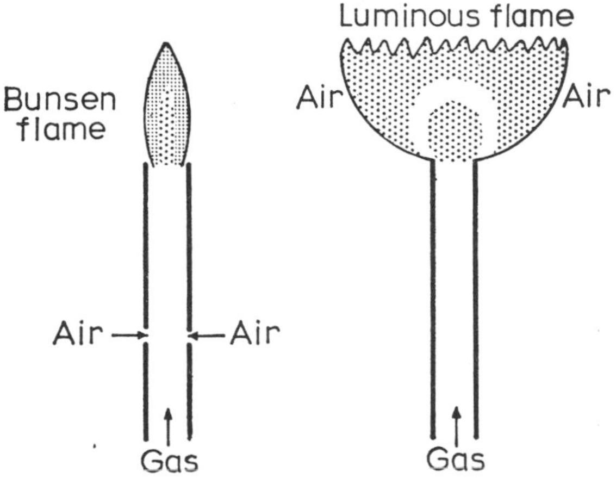

The two kinds of gas flame.

USAGE OF THE VARIOUS TYPES OF BURNERS

Non-aerated: Water heaters of all types. Deep-frying ranges. Pastry ovens and ovens that are heated from without (known as indirect fired ovens). Hotcupboards. Water boilers.

Aerated: Cooking ovens when burners are within the oven (known as direct fired ovens). Hot-plate or boiling tops of cooking ranges. Steaming ovens. Grills and salamanders. Boiling pans. Bain Marie. Stockpot stoves.

Non-aerated—Velocity: Solid top stoves.

STRIKING BACK OR LIGHTING BACK

This applies only to aerated type burners and is caused by the gas being ignited at the air vent hole of the burner, causing the flame at the burner head to be luminous with disturbed combustion.

Causes of Lighting Back

1. Incorrect lighting by placing igniter flame (match, taper, gas pilot or lighter) too close to the burner.
2. Fierce draught acting on burner adjustment.
3. Incorrect gas/air adjustment.
4. Dirty burners causing gas starvation at gas/air adjustment.
5. Rough interior of burner tube.

The items 3, 4 and 5 can be corrected by local Gas Board staff or manufacturers' staff.

THERMOSTATS

The rod type thermostat can be made to be more responsive in action by the use of a Relay Valve. This, in fact, makes the gradual

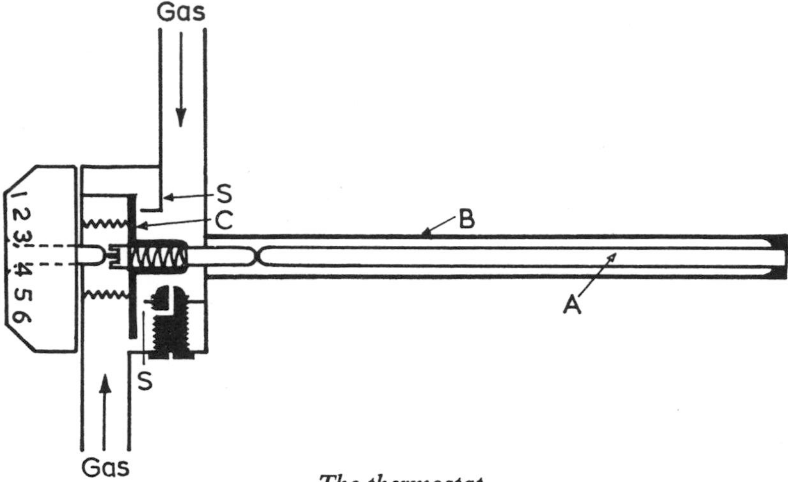

The thermostat.

acting thermostat almost snap action in performance. The relay valve is simple in design and from the external appearance like a pressure governor—it is different in function. In simple terms the valve holds the gas at full rate until the thermostat has reached the point of determined temperature—a gas weep pipe which connects the relay valve and thermostat and is burnt at the burner itself is the deciding factor in the action. When this is cut off or open by the thermostat, the weight of the valve controls the gas flow. Hence the gas is up and down in a short time, responding sensitively.

The thermostat is a simple device for controlling the temperature in cooker ovens and some water heaters. Its action depends upon the fact that some metals expand more than others when heated.

The brass tube B in the diagram encloses a rod A, made of special steel, to which is attached a valve C. The valve C regulates the amount of gas flowing to the burner.

When gas is burning, the brass tube becomes heated and as it expands it carries with it the inner rod A, which expands very little, and brings the valve head C closer to its seating S, thus reducing the flow of gas. Should the air in the oven or the water in the heater cool down, the brass tube becomes less hot, contracts a little, and moves the valve C slightly away from its seating and so allows more gas to pass to the burner until once again the proper temperature is reached.

BRITISH STANDARD SPECIFICATION FOR GAS-HEATED CATERING EQUIPMENT

This British Standard was prepared under the authority of the Gas Industry Standards Committee, as a result of requests received from the Interdepartmental Committee of the Ministry of Fuel and Power, and was originally published in 1954. It has now been completely revised.

The standards of performance laid down will help to ensure that the appliances are safe and will give good service, although it is necessary to point out that compliance with this British Standard does not of itself guarantee that satisfactory service will be attained. Conditions of use vary greatly and it is necessary to relate the standards of performance to the actual use to which the appliance will be subjected during its life. Experience has shown that even detailed testing of samples by laboratories equipped for the purpose and staffed by personnel in touch with user requirements must be supplemented by practical experience. The local gas undertaking can supply details of gas quality, will have access to facilities for carrying out all tests specified in this standard and will frequently be concerned with the fitting and maintenance of the equipment.

Particular attention is drawn to the necessity for regular inspection and maintenance of catering equipment, particularly of safety devices, in order that they may be relied upon to give adequate service to the user. This specification covers:

1. Ovens
2. Boiling burners
3. Grills
4. Deep fryers
5. Steamers
6. Boiling pans
7. Bulk water boilers

8. Automatic boiling water equipment
9. General requirements

The manufacturing requirements of equipment are l id down and in addition combustion, fire safety, stability and safety in use, and condition applicable to the use of governors, thermostats, flame failure devices.

The Gas Council issue each year an approved list of catering equipment covering some 700 appliances all of which have satisfied the requirements of the British Standard Specification.

PRESSURE GOVERNORS

The purpose of the constant pressure governor is to maintain a constant pressure at its outlet, irrespective of any normal pressure fluctuating at its inlet.

Pressure governors are fitted to most catering appliances, particularly to those that have fixed injectors (see section on burners) and those that have burners that are enclosed and concealed from visual observation.

Constant pressure may be fitted to the outlet of the gas meter to give a constant pressure to all gas-heated equipment.

Individual control is to be preferred.

The governors are made in a variety of designs and gas ratings to suit all equipment.

A Simple Description of the Action of a Constant Pressure Governor is:

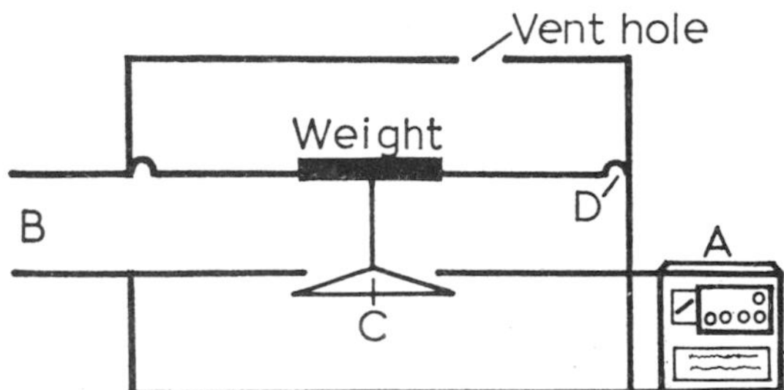

Gas meters at A.

It moves towards the outlet B via a conical shaped valve C which moves towards or from a gap according to the diaphragm D to which it is attached.

This diaphragm is adjusted by weights that are placed on top: the less the weight loading, the lower the pressure at the outlet (because the valve moves up to partially close the gap); the greater the weight the higher the pressure exerted at the outlet, because the valve moves down and opens up the area of the gap.

THE INSTANTANEOUS WATER HEATER—SINK

SETTING 'BOILING'

When the pointer of the temperature control' 'A' is turned to 'Boiling, the channels 1 and 2 are closed. Turning on the hot water tap 'B' allows the main stream of water to flow through the water governor 'C' and the feed pipe 'D' to the heating chamber 'E'. An additional small quantity flows through a venturi 'F', creating the pressure difference needed to open the gas valve 'G', and is added to the water in the heating chamber by means of the pipe 'H'. Gas passes to the main burner where it is ignited by the pilot flame. The flow rate being small, the water boils in the heating chamber and is delivered through a swivel spout 'I'.

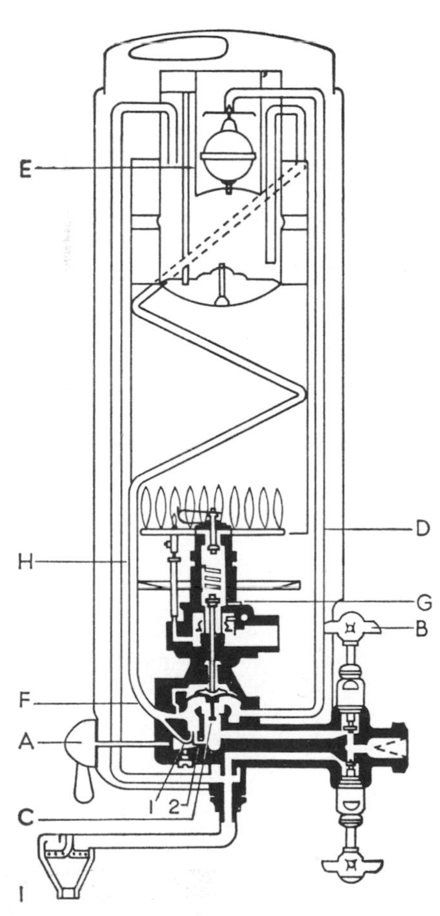

SETTING 'HOT'

On this setting, channel 1 opens, allowing some water to by-pass the venturi, and the increased flow rate reduces the temperature of the water to 'hot'.

SETTING 'WARM'

On this setting, channel 2 also opens so that some water can by-pass the water governor. The flow rate, being further increased, produces warm water.

THE INSTANTANEOUS WATER HEATER—MULTIPOINT

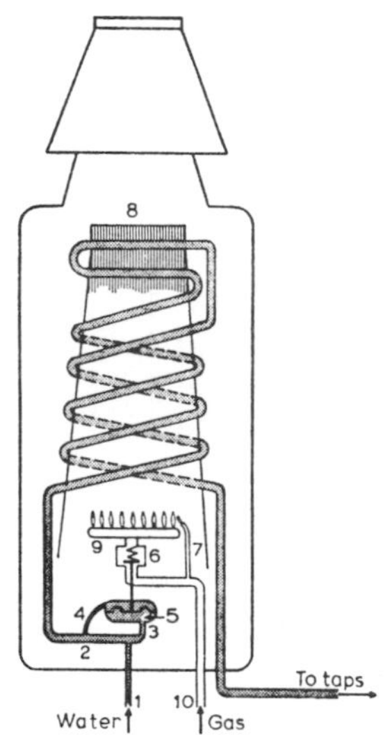

The diagram shows the working of a multipoint gas water heater. When a hot tap is turned on, the cold water flows in at 1 and passed through a venturi tube 2, thus creating a differential pressure across a flexible diaphragm 5 through pipes 3 and 4. This moves the diaphragm, which is fixed to a spring loaded valve 6, and allows gas to flow up the gas pipe 10 to the burners 9 where the pilot flame 7 ignites it. The cold water flows up to the finned heat exchanger 8 where it is heated on its way to the open hot tap. When the hot tap is closed, water ceases to flow and valve 6 closes completely, owing to the action of the spring, and so shuts off the gas supply to the burners.

THE STORAGE WATER HEATER

As hot water is drawn from the storage container through the pipe A, it is replaced by cold water flowing in through the inlet B. This water then passes down through the return pipe C into the heating unit, and thence back to storage through the flow pipe D. As the entire contents get hot, the thermostat E expands and gradually and automatically reduces the gas flow to the burner, to a rate sufficiently low to keep the water hot. This rate is kept at a minimum by the lagging of the installation. For convenience in fixing, the storage container and heating unit may be obtained one above the other, as shown, or side by side.

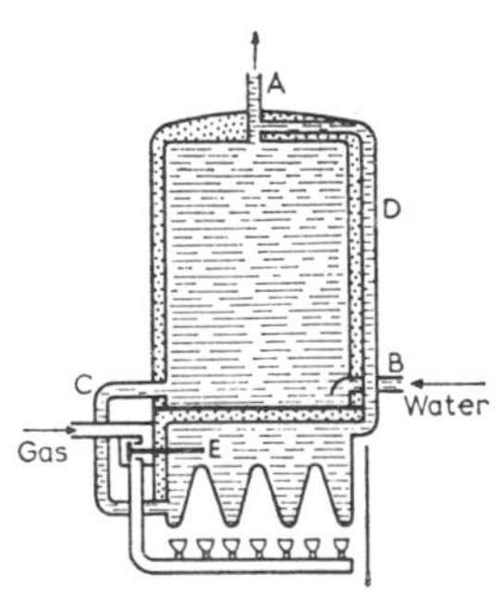

THE DIRECT AND INDIRECT HOT WATER SYSTEMS

Diagrams 1 and 2 show how water flows in domestic hot water systems. A is the cold water pipe feeding cistern B. From cistern B cold water flows down into lagged hot water storage tank C.

In Diagram 1, the tank C gets its hot water *directly* from the gas circulator D.

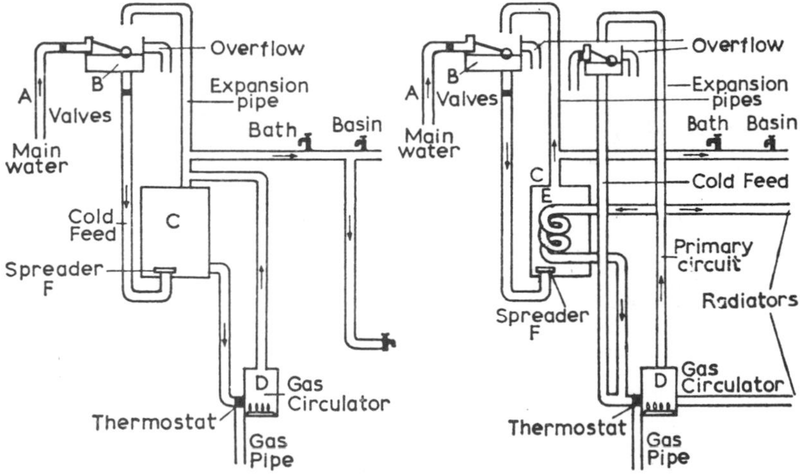

In diagram 2, the same applies but the water in C is heated *indirectly* by coil E which is filled with hot water from D.

Indirect systems are installed where radiators for heating are also fitted. Radiator temperatures may be anything up to 82°C and, as hard water scale forms rapidly above 60°C, the same water must be used the whole time in the radiator circuit (i.e. after the first deposition of scale no further scale occurs). A branch off this indirect circuit heats the hot water; otherwise drawing off hot water would rob the radiator circuit.

When a hot tap is turned on, hot water is forced out of tank C (by pressure from the cold water cistern) into the pipes that lead to the various hot taps. The spreader F minimises the mixing of cold water with the hot water already in the tank C. Arrows show the flow of water. (*The drawings are diagrammatic only and do not show the various components drawn to scale.*)

THE GAS ROOM HEATER

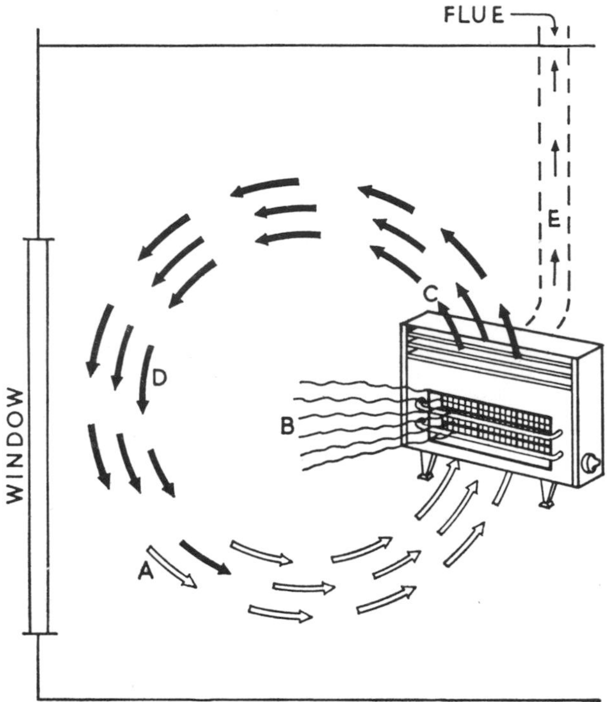

When a gas room heater is burning it creates no smoke and causes an up-draught in the flue or chimney which induces more fresh air into the room: thus a gas heater ventilates a room as well as warms it. The latest type of heater gives out radiant heat *plus* convected warmth: this means the heater warms people and objects directly with radiant heat B like that of the sun; at the same time cool air A is drawn in at louvres below the heater, passes behind it and comes out into the room as warmed air C D from louvres above the heater. The vitiated air E is removed up the flue with the products of combustion.

THE GAS COOKER

The drawing shows a side view of a popular type gas cooker, with gas pipes omitted. When burner A is lighted the heat rises (as shown by arrows), causes thermostat B to expand (automatically controlling the gas supply) and then flows round the oven and out of vent C.

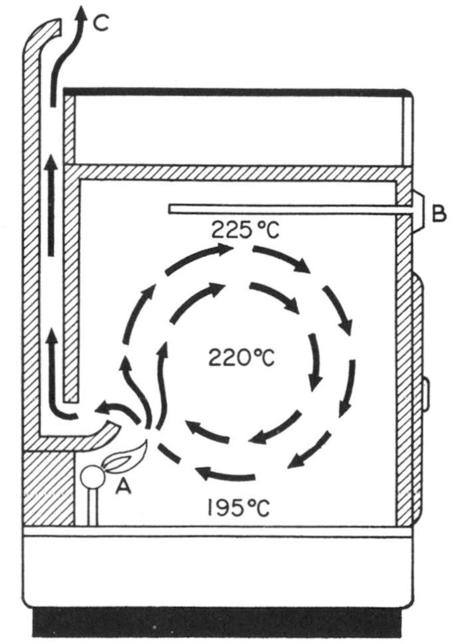

With the thermostat at a medium setting, the temperature in the upper part of the oven is about 225° C; in the middle of the oven it is 220°C, but about 195°C. at the bottom (temperatures measured with special thermometers). The upper two-thirds of the lighted oven are therefore hotter than the third at the bottom. This enables dishes requiring different temperatures to be cooked in the oven at the same time.

THE GAS REFRIGERATOR

The simple principle on which gas refrigeration is based is that when a liquid evaporates it draws heat from its surroundings. A solution of ammonia in water is heated in the boiler by a small gas flame and the ammonia gas driven off is condensed to liquid ammonia in the air cooled condenser. This is led into the evaporator with some hydrogen and begins to evaporate. In evaporating, heat is absorbed and refrigeration produced.

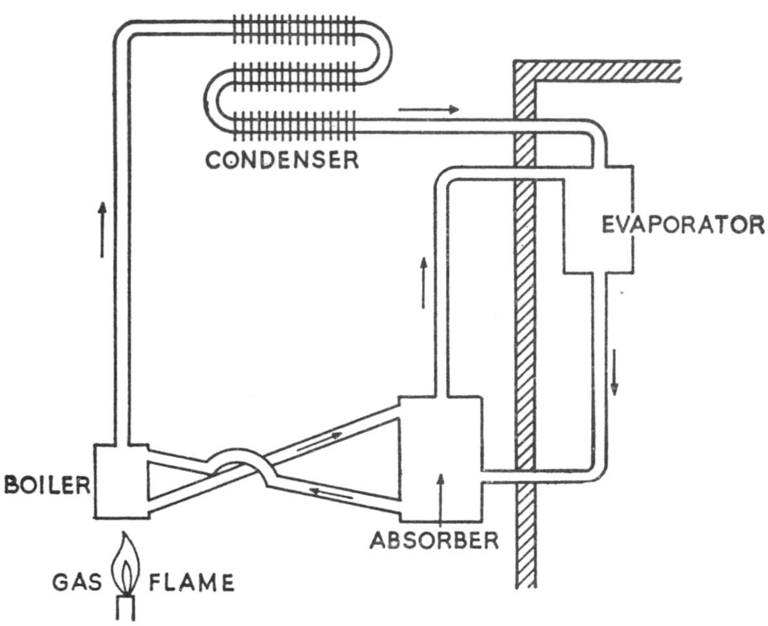

The gases produced are then led to the absorber and the ammonia absorbed by some weak liquid trickling down the absorber. The strong ammonia solution produced is then driven back into the boiler, while the hydrogen gas which is not absorbed is led into the evaporator.

The weak liquid trickling down the absorber is provided from the boiler.

In this way a complete cycle is obtained and refrigeration produced by heating only.

There are no moving parts at all.

The amount of heating is automatically controlled by a thermostat inside the refrigerator.

WARM AIR HEATING

Fanned warm air heating comes from an appliance consisting basically of a burner and heat exchanger, in a mild steel casing, through which a fan blows warm air. Such heaters can be fitted in either new or existing premises though installation is easier when the building is being erected.

There are two types of systems. In a 'selective heating' system the gas heater is housed in a central cupboard and connected by short lengths of ducting to registers fitted flush with wall in rooms adjacent to the cupboard.

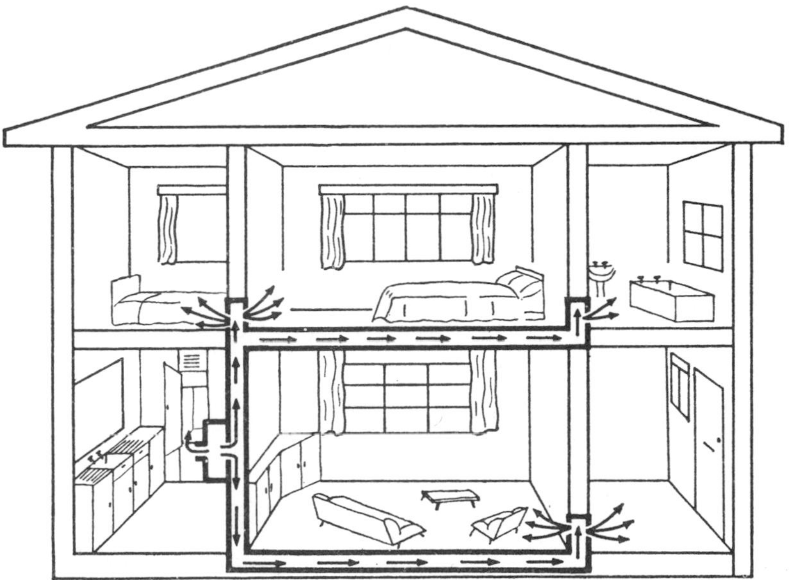

By opening or shutting the registers, which are louvres with closure plates, the warm air can be directed into any one room to provide full heating or into two or three rooms for background heating.

In 'whole house' systems, a larger gas air heater conveys warm air to all rooms at the same time through ducting. The registers in unoccupied rooms can be closed, if required.

In both systems the registers are fitted at low level to provide an even room temperature. Through grilles at high level in the rooms, air is returned to the heater compartment for rewarming and recirculation.

Automatic control of the system can be achieved by installing a room thermostat with clock control.

COMBINED SMALL BORE CENTRAL HEATING AND HOT WATER

Older central heating systems had rather large pipes and the water circulated because hot water rises when it is heated: the force causing the water to circulate was very small and so large pipes had to be used to make as little resistance as possible to the water circulation.

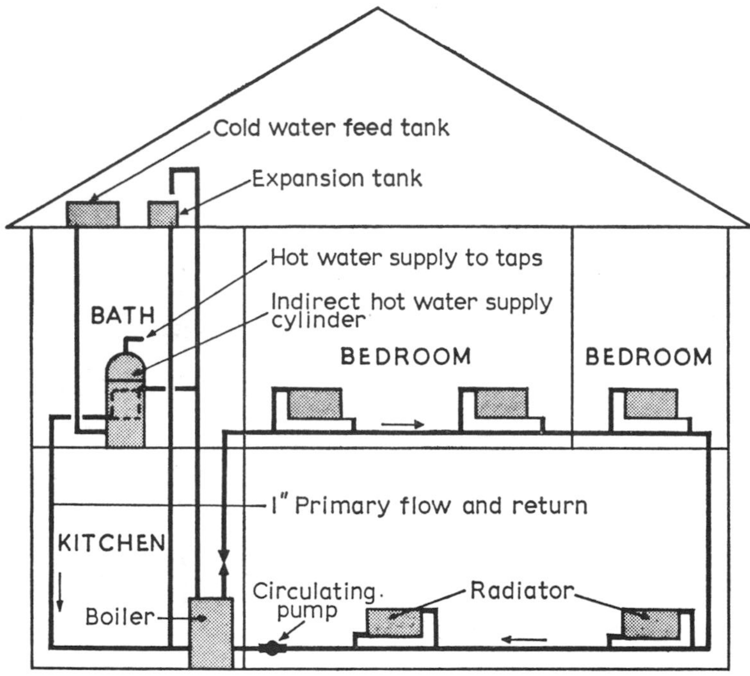

Now that small silent circulating pumps needing practically no attention are available, which provide a much greater circulating force, it is possible to reduce the size of the piping connecting the radiators; 1·27 cm diameter copper piping is usually used. This is easy to install and the additional circulating power that the pump provides allows the installer a much freer hand in planning his pipe runs. This makes installation easier in existing houses without a lot of mess and having to knock large holes in walls. A special drill is used for making a neat hole right in the corner through walls and ceilings for the 1·27 cm piping. When the piping is painted it hardly shows at all.

With an automatic gas-fired boiler and styled pressed steel radiators in various colours, we have the perfect central heating system.

BACKGROUND HEATING

Background heating can be produced by a flueless or balanced flue gas convector heater: both types warm the air which then circulates through the room. The low gas rate of the convector heater makes a flue unnecessary in an average sized room; with a balanced flue heater the

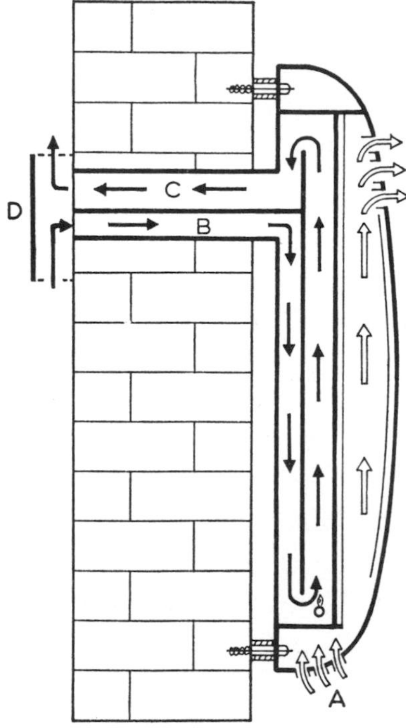

products of combustion do not enter the room. In the diagram shown above of this type of heater, air from the room A enters the heater at the base, is warmed and discharged into the room through the grille in the outer casing. The balanced flue itself consists of two main parts: the duct **B** for the incoming air necessary for combustion, and the flueway **C** through which the products of combustion are carried to the open air **D.**

Further information may be obtained from the Gas Council or local Gas Board.

4. Services: Electricity

GENERATION OF ELECTRICITY

If a coil of wire is joined at both ends to another length of wire and a magnet is passed rapidly backwards and forwards through the coil a current of electricity is produced. In the electricity generating stations the magnets may be moved by turbines driven either by steam pressure or by water power and harnessed to drive the generators.

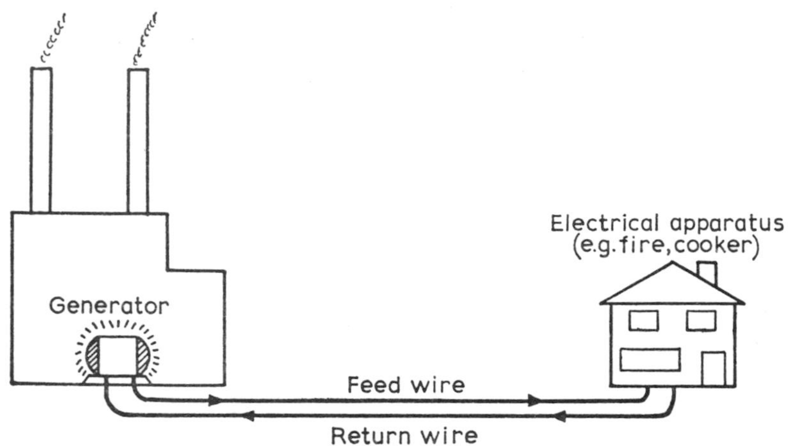

Electricity supply from producer to consumer.

There are two kinds of electric current:

direct (D.C.)
alternating (A.C.)

The one most produced is A.C. (alternate current); it is then carried by cables through grids and transformers to local substations. The consumer takes his supply of electricity from the substation.

Electricity must have a complete circuit from the source of supply through the load, e.g. an appliance back to the source of supply or it will cease to flow. Some substances are conductors of electricity—some are insulators.

All substances allow electricity to pass through them. Those which allow electricity to flow freely are known as *conductors*, e.g., metals, carbon, tap water, damp earth. Those which do not allow electricity to flow freely are known as *insulators*, e.g. glass, porcelain, wood, rubber, leather, plastic, stone. A substance's ability to be a good insulator depends on many things, such as its working temperature, the dampness of the surrounding air and its age. So when equipment is designed, an insulator is chosen so that it does not deteriorate after prolonged use under the conditions in which it is used.

Anyone who has received an electric shock will know that the human body also conducts electricity.

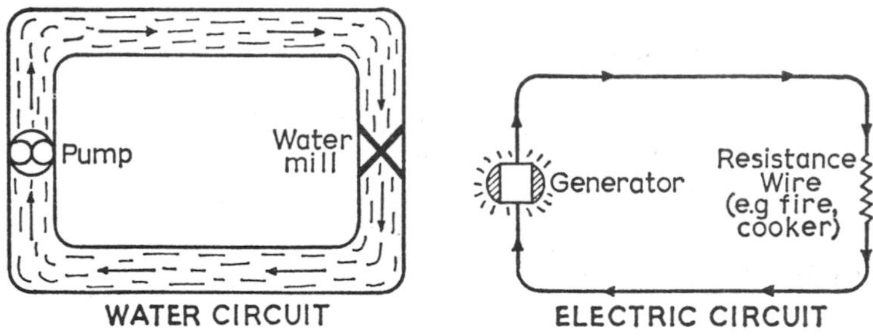

Examples of water circuit and electric circuit.

ELECTRICAL TERMS

Watts—measure power—that is, the rate at which any electric appliance is using electric current.

E.g. 60-watt lamp
1000 watts = 1 kilowatt (kW)

To find the number of watts (wattage or loading) measure amperes × volts.

Example: The wattage is often referred to as loading. Calculate the loading of an iron on 240-volt supply when a current of 2 amperes is flowing:

$$W = A \times V = 2 \times 240 = 480 \text{ watts}$$

Volts—measure pressure of flow. Comparing electricity to water, 'voltage' corresponds to pounds per square inch of a water supply. Before electricity can flow through a wire the electrical pressure at one end of the wire must be greater than at the other end. 240 volts is a common measure in domestic use, but this does vary from district to district. Knowledge of the district voltage is essential.

Amperes—measure the rate of flow of a current, and can be estimated by dividing the 'watts' by the 'volts'.

Units—is the term used to indicate the amount used and is shown on electricity bills. A typical charge is 0.7p for every (*kW*) 1000 watts of electricity switched on for one hour.

Ohms—measure the resistance of the wires to the passage of electricity and is comparable with the friction offered by a water pipe to water flowing through it.

'Ohm's Law' on which the science of electricity is founded is as follows:

$$\text{Amperes} = \frac{\text{Volts}}{\text{Ohms}} \qquad \text{Volts} = \text{Amperes} \times \text{Ohms} \qquad \text{Ohms} = \frac{\text{Volts}}{\text{Amperes}}$$

Examples:

If the voltage = 250
amperes = 5
wattage = V × A = 250 × 5 = 1250 watts
If the voltage = 110
amperes = 10
wattage = 1100 watts

To find the voltage, divide the watts by amperes

$$V = \frac{W}{A}$$

wattage = 2000
amperes = 10

$$\therefore \text{voltage} = \frac{W}{A} = \frac{2{,}000}{10} = 200 \text{ volts}$$

wattage = 10
amperes = $\frac{1}{2}$

$$\therefore \text{voltage} = \frac{10}{\frac{1}{2}} = \frac{10}{1} \times \frac{2}{1} = 20 \text{ volts}$$

$$\text{Amperes} = \frac{\text{Watts}}{\text{Volts}}$$

wattage = 1000
volts = 5

$$\therefore \text{amperes} = \frac{W}{V} = \frac{1000}{5} = 200 \text{ amperes}$$

A building has a load of 200 60-watt lamps. What current is required to supply the building if it is connected to a 240-volt supply?

W = 200 × 60 = 12000
V = 240

$$A = \frac{W}{V} = \frac{12000}{240} = 50 \text{ amperes}$$

Find the current flowing through a 100-watt lamp connected to a 250-volt supply

$$A = \frac{W}{V} = \frac{100}{250} = \frac{2}{5} = 0{\cdot}4 \text{ amperes}$$

Therefore a 2 A plug could be safely used.

What ampere plug would be necessary for four 100-watt lamps using 240 volts?

$$A = \frac{W}{V} = \frac{400}{240} = 1\tfrac{2}{3} \text{ A}$$

Therefore a 2 A plug could be safely used.

$$\text{Amperes} = \frac{\text{Volts}}{\text{Ohms}}$$

If the voltage is 230 and the resistance *R* (ohms) is 10 the socket outlet is able to supply 23 amperes.

$$\frac{V}{R} = A = \frac{230}{10} = 23 \text{ A}$$

If the voltage is 240 and the resistance is 24 ohms the socket outlet is able to supply 10 amperes.

$$\frac{V}{R} = A = \frac{240}{24} = 10 \text{ A}$$

If the resistance (R) is 25 ohms and the amperage is 5 the voltage is 125.

$$R \times A = V = 25 \times 5 = 125 \text{ volts}$$

If the resistance is 10 ohms and the amperage is 50 the voltage is 500.

$$R \times A = V = 10 \times 50 = 500 \text{ volts}$$

To find the resistance of, and the current flowing through, a 60-watt lamp connected to a 230-volt supply.

$$A = \frac{W}{V} = \frac{60}{230} = \frac{6}{23} \text{ A}$$

$$R = \frac{V}{A} = \frac{230 \times 23}{6} = \frac{5290}{6} = 881\tfrac{2}{3} \text{ ohms}$$

What is the current passing through a 100-watt lamp (*a*) on a 100-volt supply; (*b*) on a 200-volt supply?

$$(a)\ A=\frac{W}{V}=\frac{100}{100}=1\ A$$

$$(b)\ A=\frac{W}{V}=\frac{100}{200}=\tfrac{1}{2}\ A$$

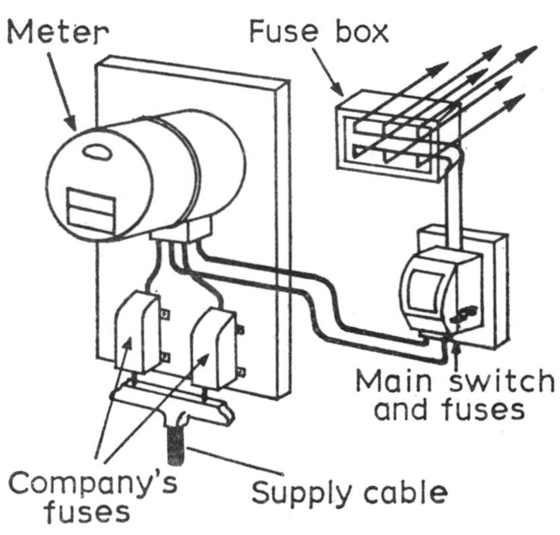

Supply-cable connection.

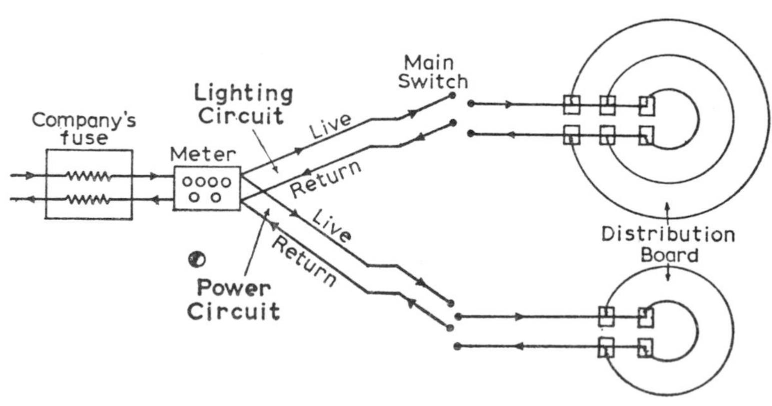

Lighting and power circuit.

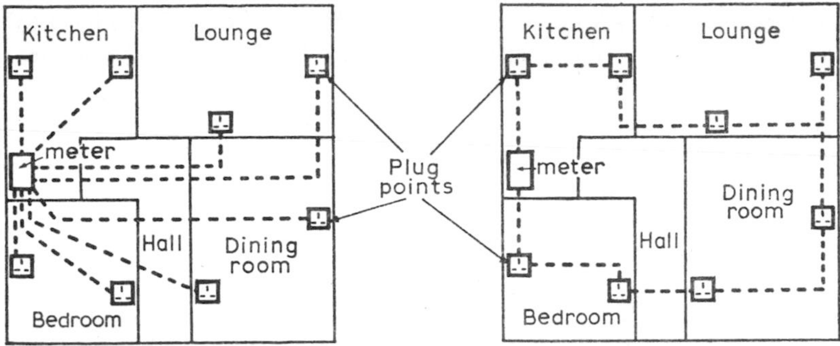

Comparison of ordinary wiring and ring circuit.

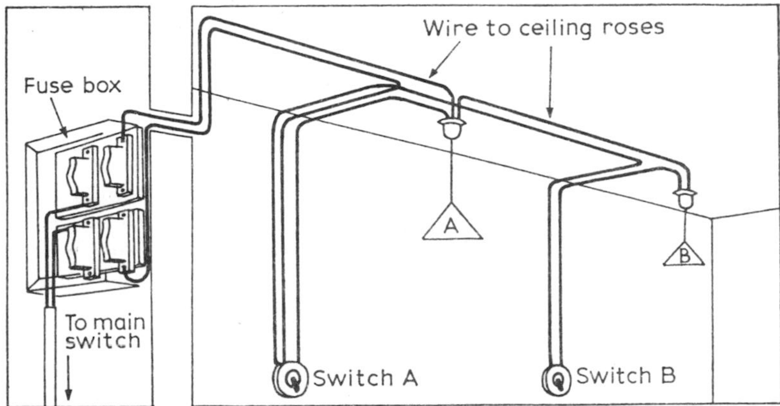

Wiring of separate circuits (note that A and B lamps are controlled by separate switches).

ELECTRICAL INSTALLATION

House installation—the Company's fuse is sealed so that the householder cannot open it and it belongs to the company. It is designed to limit the total current taken for the whole house.

Meter—records the amount of electricity used in kilowatt hours. If lighting and heating are charged at different rates there must be two meters.

Main switch—to cut off entire lighting or power circuit.

Distribution board (Consumer Unit)—divided into sub-circuits, each sub-circuit has its own fuse. In many cases, as a safety device, the main switch and distribution board are combined so that it is impossible to remove the fuse without switching off electricity.

Meter reading—the method for reading is the same as for the gas meter (see p. 40), except on the fourth dial where there is no need to add any noughts. The last two dials are 1/10 and 1/100 and are shown after a decimal point.

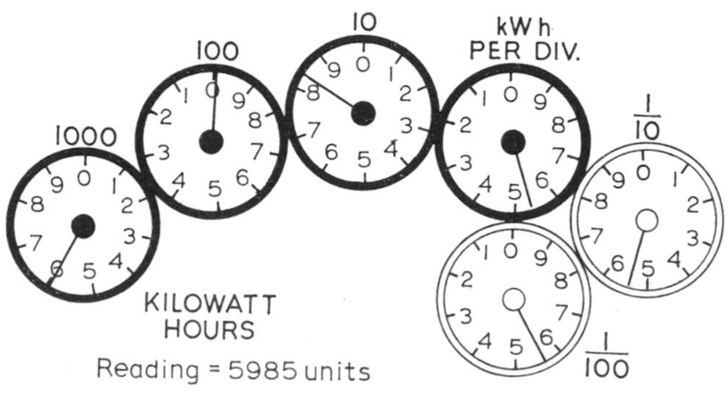

The electricity meter.

THE RING-CIRCUIT SYSTEM

This is a comparatively new means of wiring a house without a great deal of expense. The old method of wiring a house was to wire each socket on a separate length of cable connected to the fuse-board. Even if two sockets were situated fairly close together, each had a separate length of cable. This was obviously expensive. The new system, called ring circuit, overcomes this. Only one length of cable is used, and this is taken through each room of the house in turn, feeding every socket on the way. (The fixed lighting, of course, is on a separate circuit of its own.) When the cable has passed through all the rooms it returns to the fuse-board, completing the ring. The fuse at the fuse-board is chosen to protect the cable forming the ring circuit and is usually not greater than 30 amperes. All the sockets on the ring circuit are the same size, so that any appliance can be plugged into any socket. The plugs are 13 A pattern and have rectangular pins. Each plug is fitted with a cartridge fuse to protect the appliance. If the fuse blows, only that appliance is affected. A new fuse can be fitted simply by unscrewing the plug; there is no need to switch off the main supply.

There are standard fuse sizes—

2 A for appliances up to 480 watts
5 A for appliances up to 1200 watts
10 A for appliances up to 2400 watts
13 A for appliances up to 3000 watts

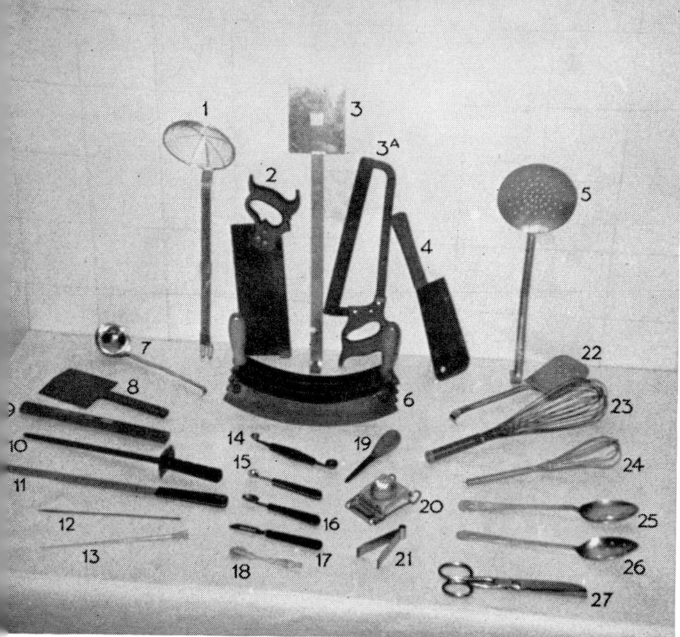

1. Spider
2. Saw Tenon
3. Iron Spatule
3A. Butcher's Saw
4. Chopper
5. Skimmer
6. Four-bladed Chopper
7. Ladle
8. Cutlet Bat
9. Ruler
10. Steel
11. Carving Knife
12. Trussing Needle
13. Larding Needle
14, 15 *and* 16. Parisienne Cutters
17. Vegetable Peeler
18. Pastry Wheel
19. Oyster Knife
20. Egg Slicer
21. Pastry Nippers
22. Fish Slice
23. Balloon Whisk
24. Small Whisk
25. Metal Spoon
26. Perforated Spoon
27. Fish Scissors

1. Examples of Small Equipment.

2. Examples of Equipment which are difficult to clean.

1. Ricer (Potato Masher)—un Passe-purée
2. Tammy Cloth—une Etamine
3. Mouli—Moulin à Légumes
4. Sieve—un Tamis
5. Muslin—une Mousseline
6. Conical Strainer (Fine)—un Chinois Fin
7. Conical Strainer (Coarse)—un Chinois Gros
8. Colander—une Passoire
9. Jelly Bag
10. Mincer Attachments
11. Ruler (shown to indicate size of equipment)

1. Salmon Kettle—une Saumonière
2. Savarin Mould—un Moule à Savarin
3. Sugar Boiler—un Poêlon
4. Charlotte Moule—un Moule à Charlotte
5. Dariol Mould—un Mould à Dariole
6. Small Saucepan—une Russe
7. Copper Bowl—une Bassine en Cuivre
8. Pomme Anna Mould—une Casserole à Pomme Anna
9. Braising Pan—une Braisière
10. Sauté Pan—un Plat à Sauter
11. Sauteuse—une Sauteuse
12. Ruler

3. Examples of Copper Equipment.

4. Examples of Wooden Equipment.

1. Chopping Board
2. Sieve
3. Rolling Pin
4. Salt Box
5. Mandolin
6. Ruler
7. Wooden Spoon
8. Spatule
9. Triangle
10. Mushroom

1. Friture—une Friture
2. Oval Drainer
3. Baking Sheet—une Plaque à Pâtisserie
4. Baking Tray
5. Double Grill Wires—une Grill à Poisson
6. Grater
7. Pancake Pan—une Poêle à Crêpe
8. Omelet Pan—une Poêle à L'Omelette
9. Frying Pan—une Poêle
10. Frying Basket—un Panier à Friture
11. Boat shape Mould—un moule à Barquette
12. Tartlet Mould—un Moule à Tartlette
13. Flan Ring—un Moule à Flan
14. Raised Pie Mould—un Moule à Pate
15. Cooling Wire
16. Ruler

5. Examples of Metal Equipment.

6. Examples of Electrical Equipment.

1. Electric Mixer-mincer
2. Gravity Feed Slicer
3. Bowl Chopper

4 *and* 5. Mincer Attachments

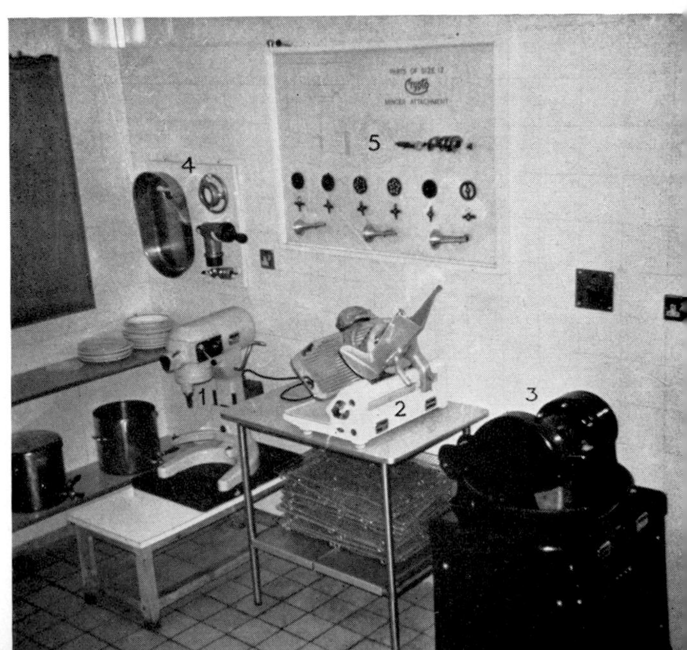

1. Tray
2. Whisking Bowl
3. Basin
4. Saucepan
5. Mandolin
6. Braising Pan
7. Stockpot
8. Bowl
9. Ruler

7. Examples of Stainless Steel Equipment.

8. Examples of Aluminium Equipment.

1. Turbot Kettle—Turbotière
2. Saucepan
3. Braising Pan
4. Saucepan

5 *and* 6. Bains-marie

7. Ruler

9. Examples of China and Earthenware.

1. Casserole
2. Earthenware Dish
3. Ravier
4. Bowl
5. Soufflé Dish
6. Egg Cocotte
7. Ruler
8. Pie Dish
9. Sole Dish

10 *and* 11. Egg Dishes

12. Basin

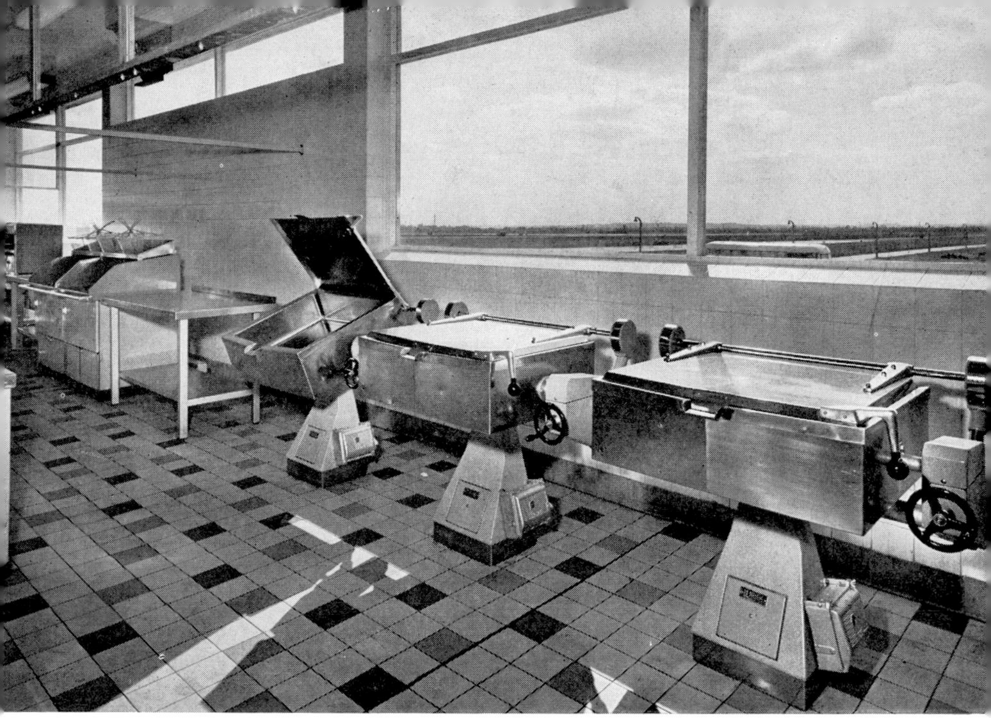

10. Shallow Tilting Pans at B.E.A. Flight Catering Base, London Airport.

11. Pastry Ovens and Boiling Pans at Bowmaker Ltd, Bournemouth.

12. A Solid-top Range including a Deep Fat-fryer, Steam Oven and in a works canteen

13. Still Room and Pastry Service to the Public Restaurant of Rackams (Harrods) Ltd Birmingham.

14. Large Equipment: Steaming Ovens and Boiling pans at Shenley Hospital, St. Albans.

15. Large Equipment: Gas Range, Under-fired Grill and Stockpot Stove.

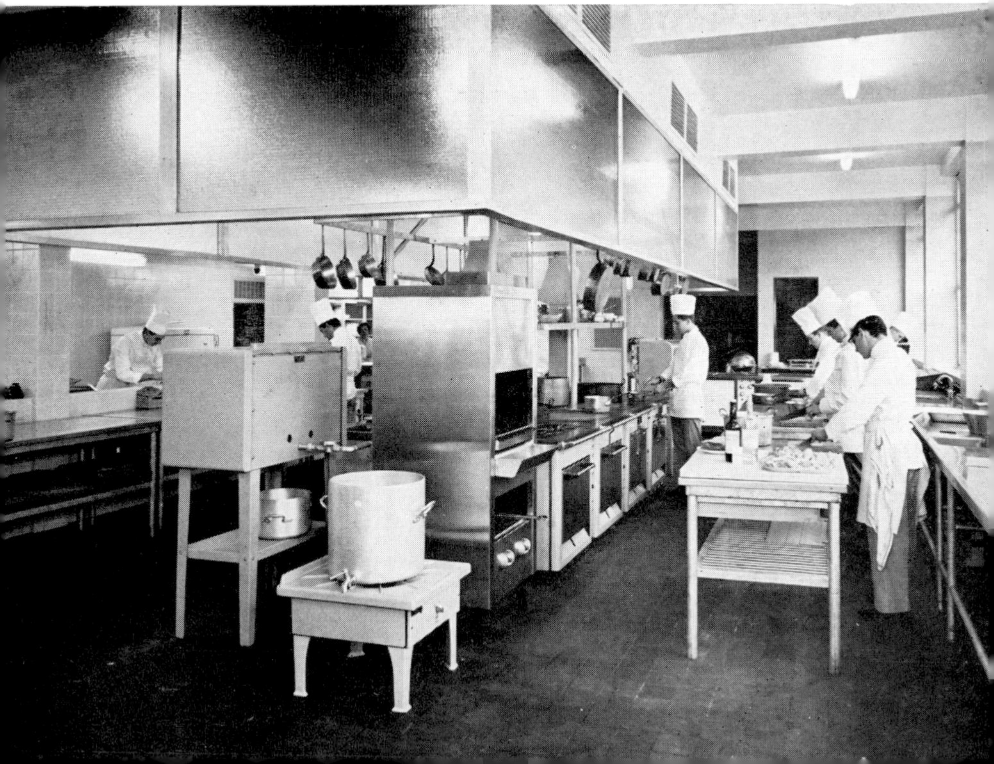

CONVECTION OVENS

Forced air convection ovens are a recent innovation in the Catering Industry and are made in a number of sizes, varying from large double deck units suitable for use in large kitchens to small capacity cookers (photo (a)) for inclusion in back bar units and smaller kitchens.

They are extremely efficient in operation, both from the point of view of running costs, capacity and evenness of colouring. They are obtainable both for gas and electric heating.

A convection oven works on the following principles. The heat produced in the cooker is blown round the shelves by a fan, and recirculates it around the food continuously, allowing lower cooking temperatures to be used, and resulting in less shrinkage of food and faster cooking times.

HIGH COMPRESSION STEAMING

Another piece of modern equipment specially designed for bulk and convenience cooking is the High Compression Steamer.

The one illustrated (photo (c)) can take for example a load of 7·5 kilos of Frozen cut Green Beans and cook them in 3 minutes. These steamers drastically cut cooking times and labour costs.

MICROWAVE/CONVECTION COOKING

A pure microwave oven does not colour food, so that two distinct operations are required in prime cooking, that of colouring before or after exposure to microwaves.

A recent development however combines the speed of microwaves with the conventional finish by the convected hot air in one oven (photo (b)), so that complete prime cooking processes, such as roasting, grilling and baking, can be carried out in one operation. This means that many items can be fully cooked from fresh or refrigerated in a few minutes.

In addition to using the microwave and convection heating combined for cooking, either may be used on its own, either as a microwave oven for reheating purposes, or as a convection cooker.

ELECTRIC SWITCHES

Purpose—to complete an electric circuit when the switch is closed (ON position) so that a current can flow and to break the circuit when the switch is opened (OFF position) so that the current is interrupted.

Two types of switch are in common use, namely single pole and double pole switches.

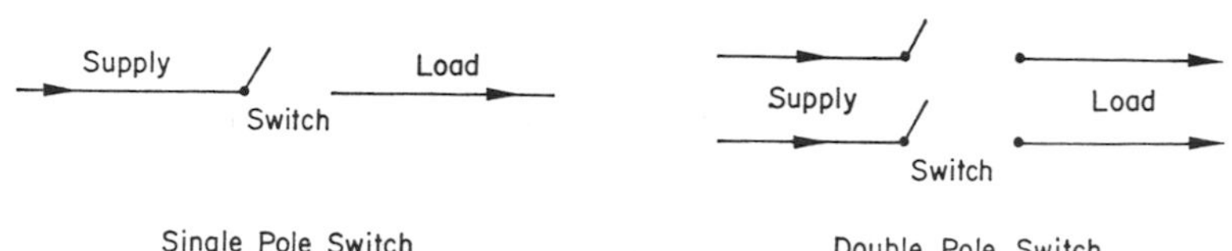

Single Pole Switch　　　Double Pole Switch

Single Pole Switch: A switch, usually with two terminals, which causes one break in the circuit when the switch is turned off. It must always be connected in the live side of the supply (the conductor with the red or brown coloured insulation).

Double Pole Switch: A switch, usually with four terminals, which causes two breaks in the circuit, one in either conductor of the supply. Both poles are operated from the same mechanism. A double pole switch is usually used as a 'Master' switch disconnecting the ring from the mains supply.

Many types of switch are available covering a wide range of applications and a switch must be chosen according to its duty. The main things to look for are the current and voltage ratings of the switch and compare them with the load of the circuit which they will be expected to control. Both ratings should be the same or larger.

FUSES

The fuse in an electrical circuit acts as a safety device. Fuse wire is obtainable in varying thicknesses, usually 5, 10, 15 amperes, and for general purposes should be used as follows:

Lighting circuits — maximum of 5 amperes.
Power circuits — maximum of 10 or 15 amperes.

If more than the maximum amount of current passes through the circuit the wires will get hot, the insulation may burn, and there may be a fire.

The fuse consists of a short length of wire within the circuit and is of such a thickness that it will melt if more than the maximum amount of current flows through it, so breaking the circuit. This is known as a blown fuse.

The fuse should always be connected in the live side of the supply. No fuse should ever be connected in the neutral side.

Causes of a Blown Fuse

A. Too many appliances plugged into a circuit.

E.g. A 3-kW fire; 750-watt kettle; 750-watt iron plugged into a power circuit 15 A; voltage 240.

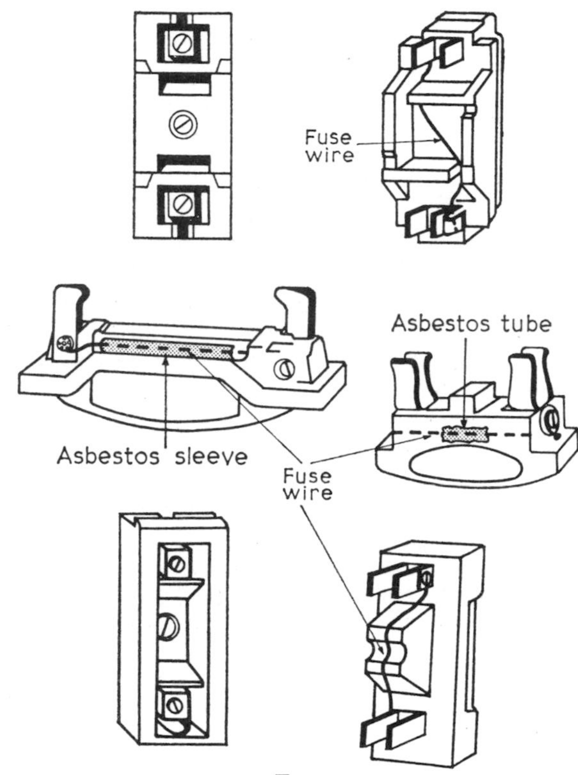

Fuses.

To find the current flowing through the three appliances:

$$W = V \times A$$

therefore $A = \frac{W}{V}$

$$= \frac{4500}{240} = 18\tfrac{3}{4}\ A$$

therefore Current $= 18\frac{3}{4}$ amperes.

Therefore a greater amount of current than 15 A is flowing, and consequently the fuse will blow and the circuit will be broken.

B. Plugging a power appliance into a lighting circuit.

E.g. A 2-kW fire plugged into a circuit designed to carry 5 amperes, voltage 240.

To find the current flow:

$$\text{Current flow} = \frac{W}{V} \text{ amperes}$$

$$= \frac{2000}{240} = 8\tfrac{1}{3} \text{ amperes}$$

therefore Current $= 8\frac{1}{3}$ amperes

Therefore the fuse will blow. It also causes a strain on the flex.

C. Short circuit due to insulation failure.

Means that lead and return wires touch and therefore current does not reach the appliance. Often due to wear of wire insulation.

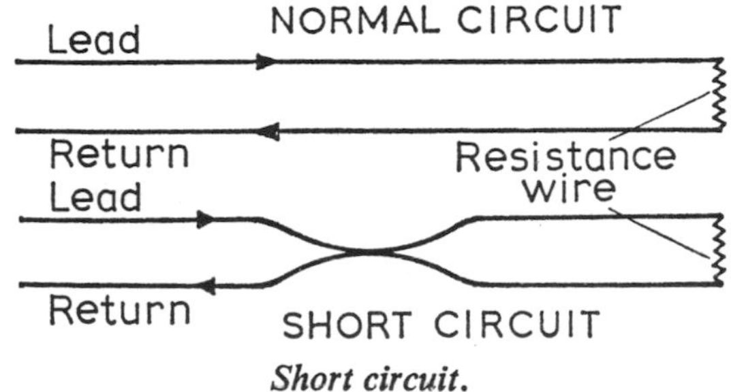

Short circuit.

Repair of Fuses

1. Turn off the main switch.
2. Find the fuse that has blown—this may be known beforehand; if not, try each one in turn.
3. Remove broken fuse wire.
4. Replace with new fuse wire of the correct size (5, 10, 13 or 15 amperes).
5. Before replacing the repaired fuse and before switching on, find the cause of the old fuse wire melting; check all connections and the leads.

PLUGS AND SOCKETS

1. Purpose—to enable portable appliances to be plugged into the electric circuit. In some cases a switch is also included in the socket.
2. Usual sizes—5, 10, 13 and 15 A, to suit appliance (13 A plugs are always 3-pin and used for ring circuit only).

3. Designs—2- and 3-pin. Any appliance provided with an earth connection should never be plugged in to a 2-pin socket outlet.

4. **Earthing—safety device to reduce** shock.

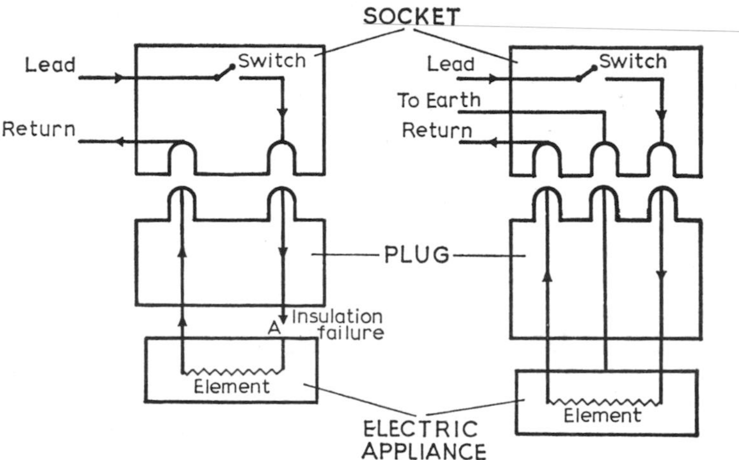

Plugs and sockets.

If there should be an insulation failure (e.g. Point A) the metal frame of the appliance would carry the current. If touched, the person who did it would receive a shock and the current would pass to earth. To prevent this a 3-pin plug and socket should be used and the wiring is arranged as follows:

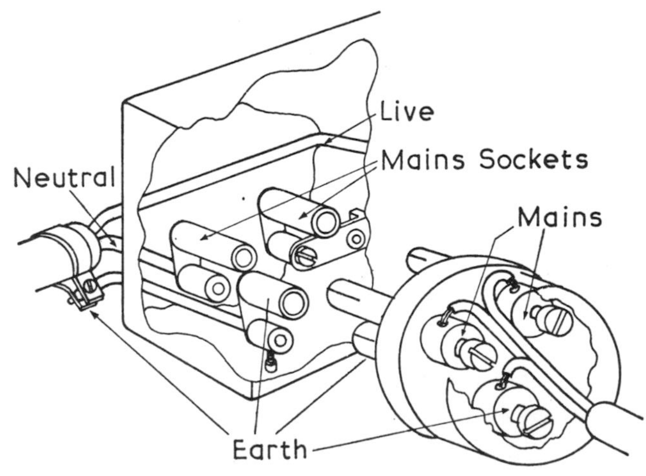

Three-pin plug and socket.

If the frame becomes live, current will pass through earth wire and not via the person touching it.

Sometimes sockets are fitted with a safety locking device, so that a plug cannot be removed if the current is still on, or vice-versa.

The Wiring of Plugs

1. Remove the outer insulation for about 3·8 cm–5 cm, thus leaving three coloured wires exposed. Bind the top of insulation with insulating tape or rubber.

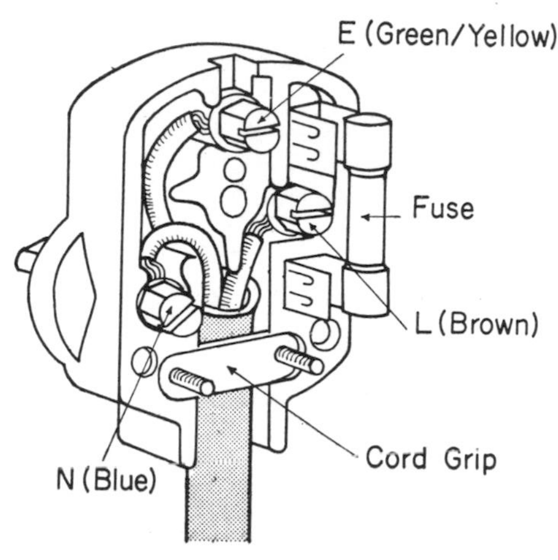

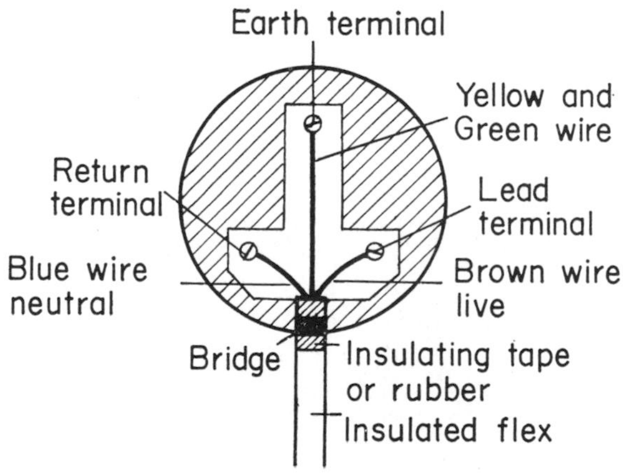

Wiring of three-pin plug.

2. If the plug has a bridge, fix the flex with this.

3. Measure each wire—cut it off at a length which will allow it to go round the terminal. The last portion of the wire only is cleared of rubber insulation.

4. Wind uncovered wire in clockwise direction around terminal and tighten screw.

5. Replace the casing of the plug.

ELECTRIC COOKERS

The Oven. As for a gas cooker it has double walls and door, the space between being lagged or filled with air.

There are a variety of positions for the heating elements—sides, top and bottom.

The boiling plates. The totally enclosed type is insulated with magnesium oxide, a heat conductor. An average loading is approximately 1800 W.

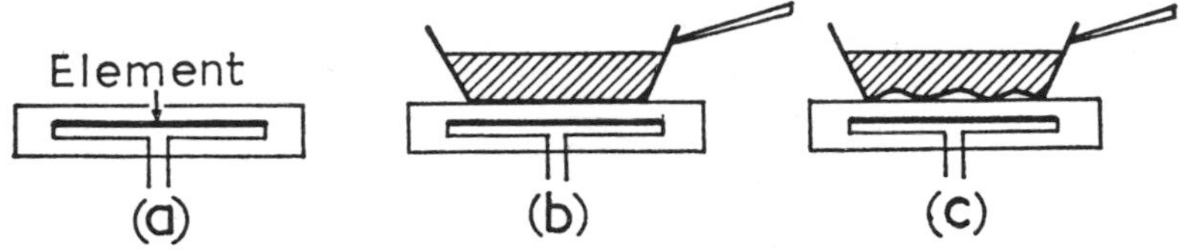

Electric boiling plates: (a) *Element inside plate.* (b) *Correct type of pan.* (c) *Incorrect type of pan giving inefficient conduction of heat.*

The grill boiler has an average loading of 1800 W, and may be used as a grill or by inserting a plate underneath, used as a boiling plate. The sheathed wire type has an average loading of 1800 W.

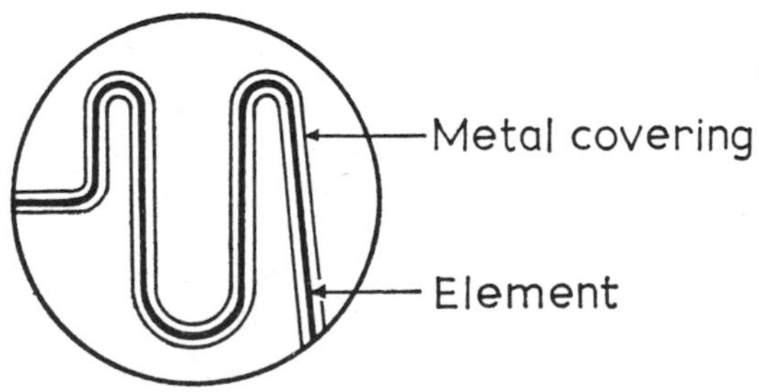

Sheathed wire type of boiling plate.

Loading: e.g. Boiling plate 1800 W
Grill boiler 1800 W
Oven 1400 W
Total = 5000 W or 5 kW

Voltage is 230

$$\text{Therefore } \frac{W}{V} = \frac{5000}{230} \text{ A}$$

$$C = \frac{5000}{230} = 21{\cdot}7 \text{ A}$$

Thus, if boiling plates and oven are put on at the same time, a current of 21·7 amperes will flow, and therefore a cooker must have its own wiring and fuses to carry the heavier current. The usual size fuse is 30 amperes.

The main switch is a double pole switch—that is, it breaks the live and neutral conductors simultaneously and it often has a light when it is turned on. The box cannot be opened without first turning off the main switch. Very often there is a 15 A point for an electric kettle.

Heat control—oven and boiling plates. Thermostatic control is similar to that in use as gas cookers. See page 44.

ELECTRIC WATER HEATING

This can be carried out in a variety of ways.

1. Electric kettles—have an immersion heater fitted into them and are constructed in the same way as the portable ones. Most kettles contain a safety device, if the kettle boils dry the current is automatically switched off. Average loading 500–1800 W. An electric kettle should not be filled while it is plugged in.

2. Immersion heater fitted into an existing hot water tank. Usual loading, 20–25 gallons, 2–3 kW.

Immersion heaters fitted into existing water tanks.

The Electric Circulator

This is similar to gas circulator. It heats up water in small quantities in a short time.

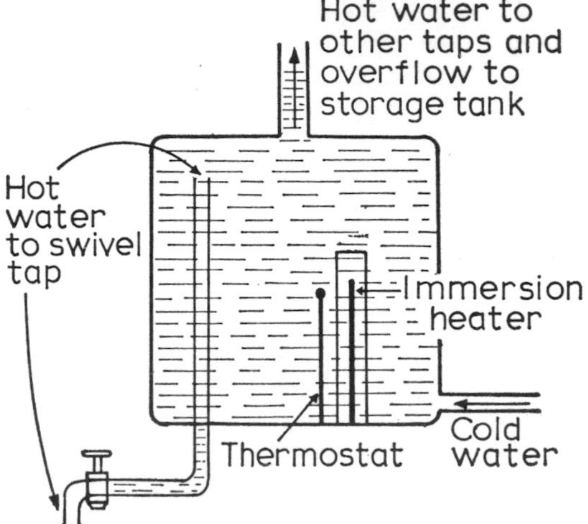

Electric water circulator with thermostat and draw-off tap.

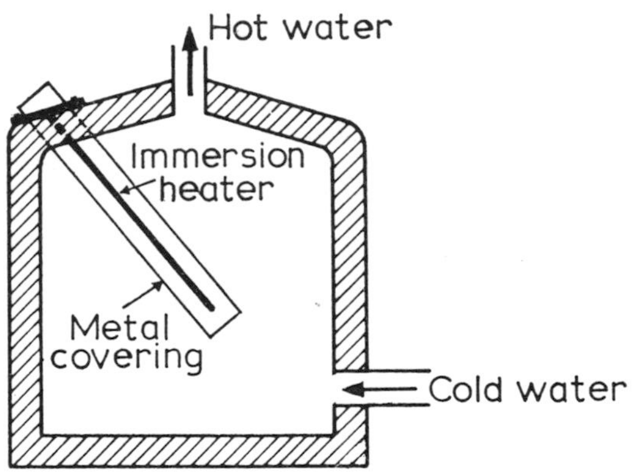

Electric circulation.

The cold water comes in at the bottom and the water nearest the heater is heated very quickly. This can be controlled by a thermostat or three heat control.

$1\frac{1}{2}$-, 3- and 5-gallon heater	= 750 W.	12-gallon heater	= 1·2 kW.
15-gallon heater	= 1·5 kW.	20-gallon heater	= 2 kW.
30-gallon heater	= 2·5 kW.	40-60-gallon heater	= 3 kW.

REFRIGERATION

HOW REFRIGERATION WORKS

Cold is the absence of heat and to make things cold it is necessary to remove the heat it contains, this is the function of a refrigerator. To make a food cold something which is colder is used to draw the heat from the food. To do this a refrigerant is used, for example ammonia.

Water boils at 100°C, but other substances will boil at a temperature below the freezing point of water. Ammonia boils at −33°C below zero. However much the heat is increased the temperature of water cannot be increased. If ammonia is placed in a refrigerator the ammonia absorbs the heat from the cabinet until a temperature of 100°C below zero is achieved in the cabinet. Like the water which cannot be heated more than 100°C because the water pulls the heat out of the flame so the ammonia draws the heat out of the cabinet.

If ice blocks are used to cool a refrigerator cabinet, the melting ice, in the form of water, does the cooling by drawing off the heat; with ammonia the heat is drawn off by the vapours. This is expensive if the vapours are lost, therefore they are changed back into a liquid and used again; to do this it is necessary to condense the vapours.

It should be remembered that when liquids boil they soak up heat without getting any warmer, and produce vapour.

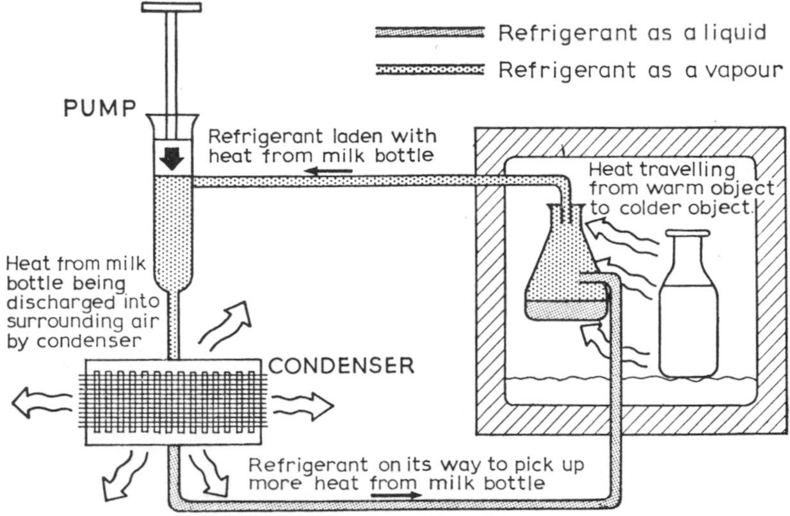

How refrigeration works.

COMPRESSION TYPE REFRIGERATOR

The compression type refrigerator works on the principle described. The three main parts are:

1. *The evaporator* inside the cabinet where the refrigerant boils and changes into a vapour and absorbs the heat.

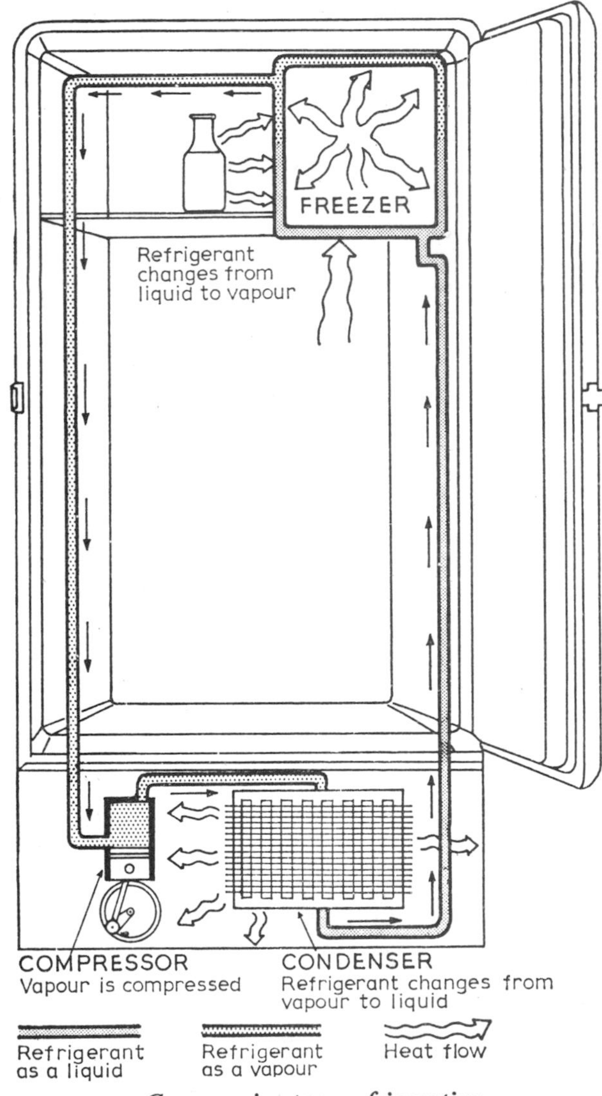

Compression type refrigeration.

2. *The compressor* which puts pressure on the refrigerant so that it can get rid of its heat. To enable the compressor to work, it is necessary to have an electric motor to operate the compressor or pump.

3. *The condenser* which helps to discharge the heat.

ABSORPTION TYPE REFRIGERATOR

This type of refrigerator does not have any moving parts as no compressor is used. A solution of ammonia gas in water is the refrigerant. The gas is given off from the solution when it is heated by an electrical element or gas flame. The ammonia gas passes to the condenser where it is liquefied. The liquefied ammonia passes to the evaporator with some hydrogen, where it expands and draws the heat from the cabinet. The gases produced pass to the absorber, where they mix with water and become a solution again. The solution returns to be heated again while the hydrogen goes to the evaporator.

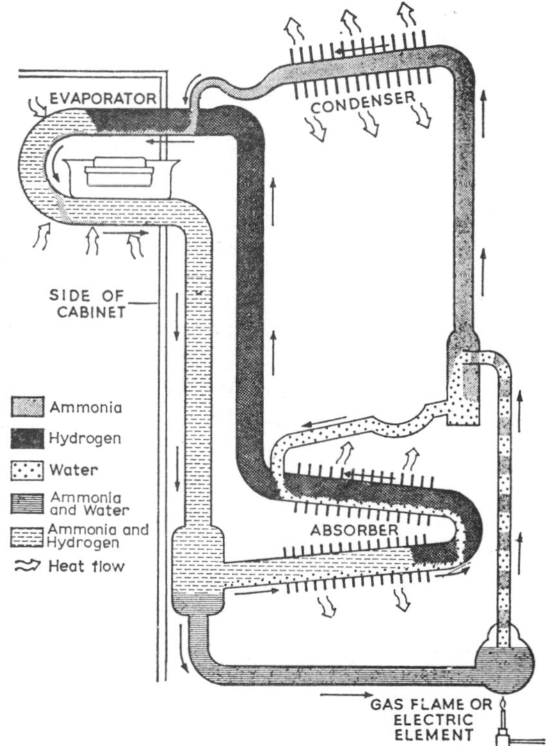

Absorption type refrigeration.

REFRIGERANTS

A refrigerant must have a boiling point below the temperature at which ice forms and it should be non-corrosive and non-explosive. Substances such as sulphur-dioxide, methyl-chloride and dichloro-difluoromethane are used as refrigerants.

THE CABINET

This must be well insulated to prevent entry of heat from outside. In modern refrigerators, insulations such as expanded polystyrene and foamed polyurethane are used extensively.

COLD ROOMS, CHILL ROOMS, DEEP-FREEZE CABINETS AND COMPARTMENTS

In large establishments it is necessary to have refrigerated space at different temperatures. The cold rooms may be divided into separate rooms; one for chill temperature for storing salads, fruits, certain cheeses; one for meats, poultry, game and tinned food which have to be refrigerated; one for deep-frozen foods. Frequently, the cold-room storage is designed so that after proceeding from the chill room into the cold room the deep freeze compartment is reached. Refrigerated cabinets, thermostatically controlled to various desired temperatures, are also used in large larders. Deep-freeze cabinets are used where a walk-in deep-freeze section is not required and they maintain a temperature of −17°C −15°C. Deep-freeze cabinets require defrosting twice a year.

FURTHER INFORMATION ON ELECTRICAL DEVELOPMENT

Consult The Electricity Council, The Electric Catering Centre, 45 St. Martins Lane, London, W.C.2, or the Electrical Association for Women, 25 Foubert Place, London, W.1. For reading, consult Gladwell, *Practical Maintenance and Equipment* (Barrie andRockliff).

5. Services: Water

By law, water authorities are required to provide a supply of clean, wholesome water—that is, water free from: visible suspended matter; odour and taste; all bacteria which are likely to cause disease; mineral matter injurious to health.

Water is obtained from the following sources: rainfall which is collected in the following ways: natural lakes; rivers; artificial reservoirs; underground lakes; wells; springs.

Water is collected in storage reservoirs and is then given several cleansing processes before being piped to the consumer.

1. As storage reservoirs are deep, much suspected matter settles to the bottom of the water.
2. The water passes through two filters, one designed to remove all solid matter (leaves, twigs, etc.) and the second to remove fine suspended particles and bacteria.
3. Water is then impregnated with chlorine to remove and kill off all disease bearing bacteria.
4. The water then rests in order to give the chlorine time to react fully.
5. Water is then run to a pumping station where it is forced out into the street mains.

HARD WATER

In certain districts water is hard and as this may be detrimental to water pipes, the use of a water softener is sometimes recommended.

Causes of Hardness

1. Temporary hardness is due to the natural presence of calcium or magnesium bicarbonates dissolved in the water. This can be removed by boiling, but the vessel in which it boils becomes coated with 'fur'. Fur can be removed from kettles by commercial products or by boiling vinegar in the kettle and then boiling with clean water. It can be removed from pipes and boilers by a plumber who will pass a strong acid through them.
2. Sulphates or chlorides of calcium and magnesium, when dissolved into the water as it trickles through the earth, is called permanent hardness. This is much more difficult to remove than temporary hardness. Hardness may be removed from water by the following methods:

(*a*) Soap added to water—the first amount softens the water and any more added will form a lather.

Disadvantages: (*a*) uneconomical; (*b*) scum forms, therefore unsuitable for washing.

(*b*) Soda—cheap, quite effective. The correct amount roughly should be added, e.g. London water with 16° of hardness requires 28·39 g soda to 45·4 litres of water. When using soda and soap together the soda should be added first and allowed to dissolve so that it softens the water.

(*c*) Ammonia solution—works in the same way as soda.

These methods will remove temporary hardness as well as permanent hardness.

(*d*) Use of a water softener—called the base exchange method.

A water softener is an apparatus which by a chemical action can take some of the hardness out of water. After a certain period of time if this action is to be maintained the water softener has to be re-generated. Re-generation means adding a fresh substance to the water softener in order to continue the chemical action. When the whole of the water supply is softened, the drinking tap is usually placed on the pipe before it passes through the softener, so that the drinking water is not treated.

HOUSEHOLD COLD WATER SYSTEM (SUPPLY)

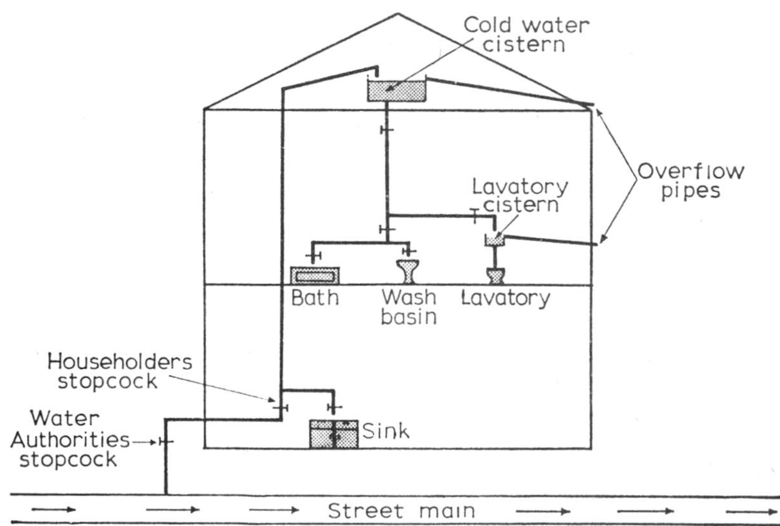

Cold water system.

The tap supply to the sink brings water directly from the main, therefore it is suitable for drinking.

The Water Board's stopcock is situated generally outside the house and can be operated by the householder.

The householder's stopcock is usually found inside the house. There are usually other stopcocks throughout the house enabling water supplies at different points to be cut off.

If the ball-cocks failed to function, the water would flow out through the overflow pipe.

There is not always a cold water cistern. The entire supply sometimes comes direct from the main.

THE COLD WATER CISTERN

Purpose

To provide an emergency water supply should the main supply be turned off, or lowered.

In the average house there is usually a day's supply in the cistern, provided the water is carefully used. (Where the main supply has to be pumped (does not rely on gravity) houses are always supplied with a cold water cistern.)

Disadvantages

Possible contamination of the water through being stored in a cistern, although modern cisterns are now covered and the chances of contamination are less.

Position

It must be above the level of all taps; the higher the cistern is placed, the greater the pressure of water then supplied to the taps. The pressure depends upon the distance between the cistern and the taps.

Construction

A modern cistern is usually made of galvanised steel (it also could be made of wood or slate, lined with copper, lead or zinc). It should have a lid to keep the water clean, and this should be easily removed for repair purposes. It has to have an overflow pipe at the top in case anything should go wrong with the ball-valve. The cistern should be lagged with sacking, or a wooden casing with sawdust or cork between the casing and the cistern, if it is in an exposed position.

Ball valve

The purpose of this is to keep the cistern filled with a supply of water.

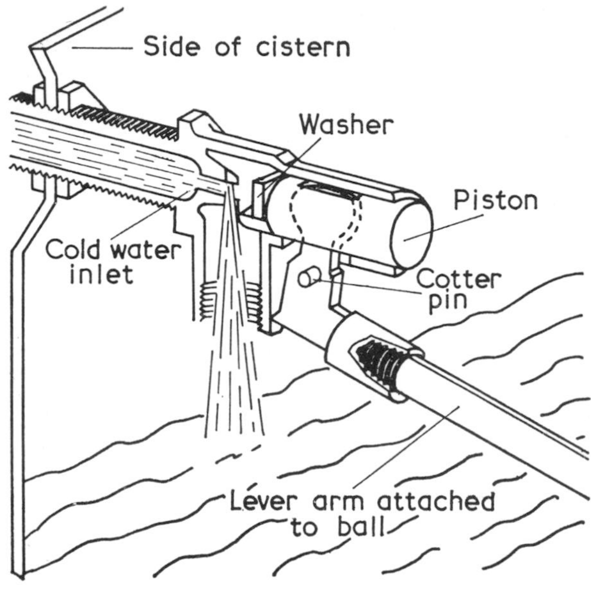

Operation of the Ball-valve.

When the cistern is full the washer is pressed firmly against the water entrance. Sufficient pressure is maintained by the rod (which connects the lever and the ball) being of adequate length. As the water level in the cistern drops the ball lowers and opens the valve.

Faults likely to occur

1. The ball may become punctured and therefore will drop to the bottom of the cistern and the valve will remain open.
2. Piston may be seized up in either position. To repair, turn off water at main, take valve to pieces and clean the piston, then replace.
3. Washer may wear out.

FLUSHING CISTERNS

Flushing cisterns should be so designed that they will discharge two gallons of water in five seconds.

In the diagram on page 79, the cistern is full and the level of the water is just below the level of the flush-pipe. The bell is at its lowest level. When the lever is pulled, the bell is raised and the water inside the bell is drawn up so that it is now above the level of the flush-pipe.

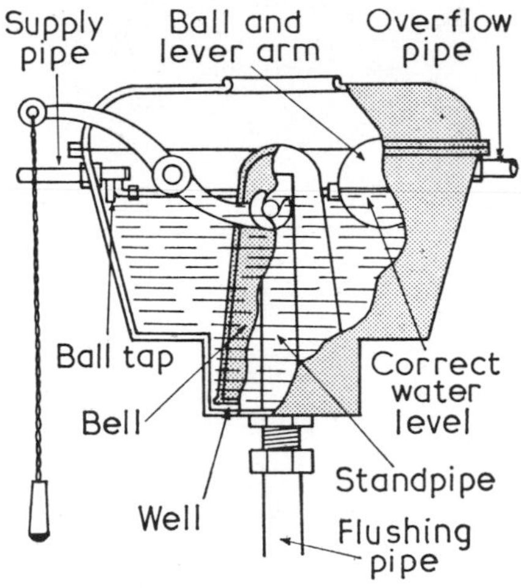

Flushing system.

The water then flows down the flush-pipe, pushing down the air which is there. This continues until the cistern is emptied. At the same time the ball is dropping with the level of the water and the ball-valve opens and the cistern begins to fill again. When the cistern is emptied the bell will drop to its original position.

There are other flushing systems working on a syphonic action.

THE WATER TAP

It will be found that after studying the appearance and function of various components, most repairs to a tap will be comparatively simple.

There are many sizes of washers, and two types: leather for cold water, rubber for hot water.

The dome is merely a decorative cover to the tap.

Rewashering of a Tap (see page 80)

1. Turn off the water supply to the tap.

2. Turn the tap on fully (*a*) to make sure the water is turned off (*b*) to allow space for the dome to be lifted.

3. Unscrew the dome, if any, and lift as high as possible.

4. Unscrew the nut by gripping it at point A and remove from tap. If the washer plate is fixed to the spindle it will lift out with it, if not, remove it separately.

5. Remove old washer by nut B and replace it with a new washer.

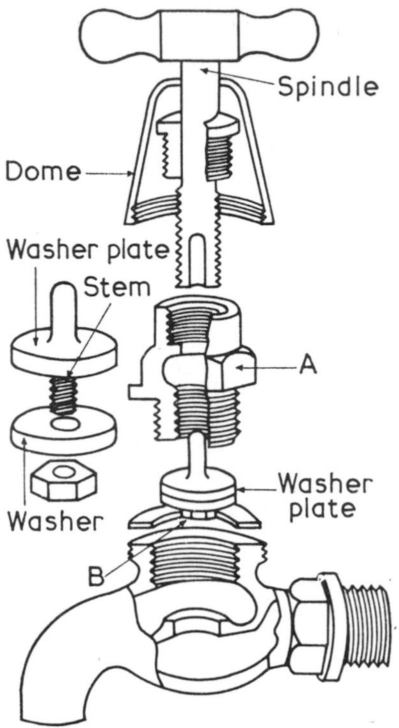

Tap components.

6. Reassemble the tap and turn on water supply to test that the new washer is working efficiently.

Stopcock (*Stop-valve*)

This works and is constructed in exactly the same way as the tap but just stops the water supply.

The Supatap

This is a more modern type of tap which has the big advantage that a new washer may be fitted in a minute or so without tools and without shutting off the water supply or draining the system.

HOT WATER SYSTEMS

METHODS OF HEATING WATER

1. Boiler (*a*) Gas circulator—indirect system, see page 81; (*b*) solid fuel boiler; (*c*) fire back boiler.
2. Storage heater—gas or electricity.

3. Immersion heater—electricity.

4. Instantaneous heater—usually fired by gas as electricity is not suitable.

Boiler Method

The water flows from the cistern into the bottom of the storage tank, and then into the bottom of the boiler. When it is heated it

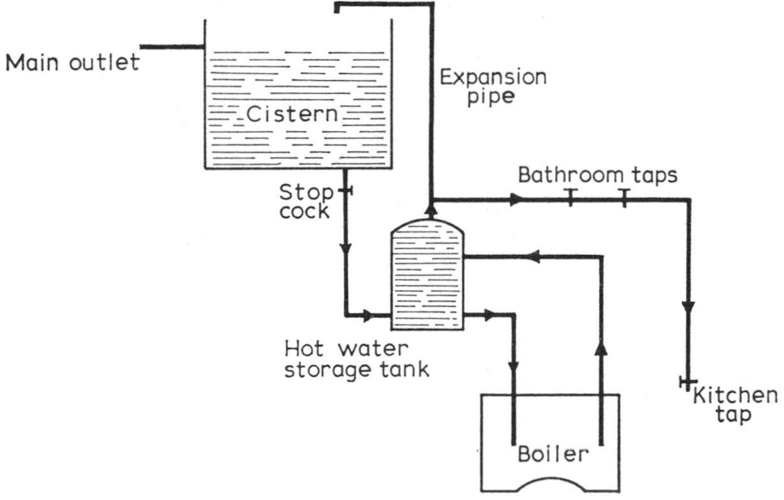

Hot water system (boiler method).

flows into the top of the storage tank and is kept there until it is drawn off to any of the hot water taps. If the water boiled in the storage tank and the taps were turned off, there would probably be an explosion, therefore there is an expansion pipe which leads from the storage tank back to the cistern. The boiler can be either a solid fuel or gas circulator. The storage tank should be lagged to prevent loss of heat, and therefore wastage of fuel.

Storage Water Heater

This type of gas heater, if it is to supply all the hot water taps, is usually of approximately 90 litres capacity in the average-sized house.

This type of storage heater can also be fitted individually over sinks and has a capacity of 7½–10 litres. Both types are thermostatically controlled. They can also be heated by electricity—see notes on electricity.

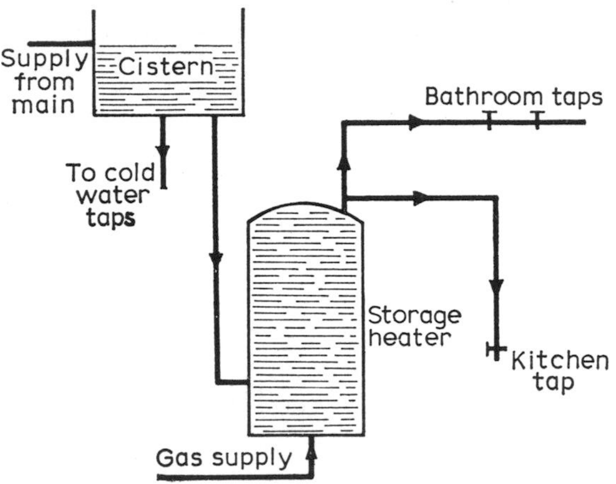

Hot water system with storage heater.

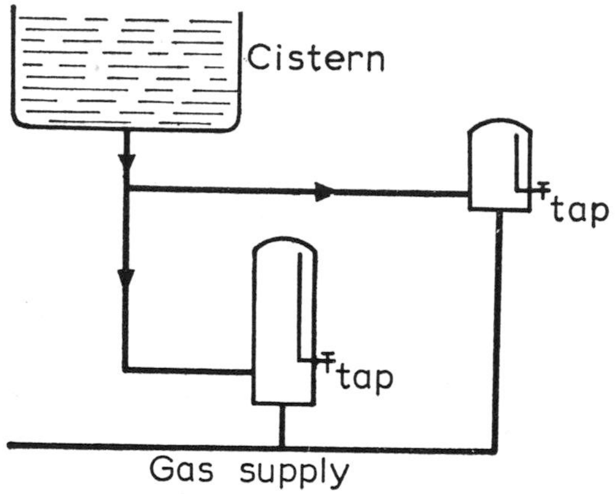

Water heater over individual sinks.

Gas Instantaneous Heater, Multipoint Type

This type of heater can supply several taps, and is generally situated in the kitchen. This heater usually depends on the pressure of the head of water for the pressure of gas. If the pressure of the water is low, the gas pressure will also be low, therefore the water should be drawn straight from the main.

Immersion Heater

This diagram shows that it is fitted into the existing tank (hot water). It can be used by itself or in conjunction with the boiler.

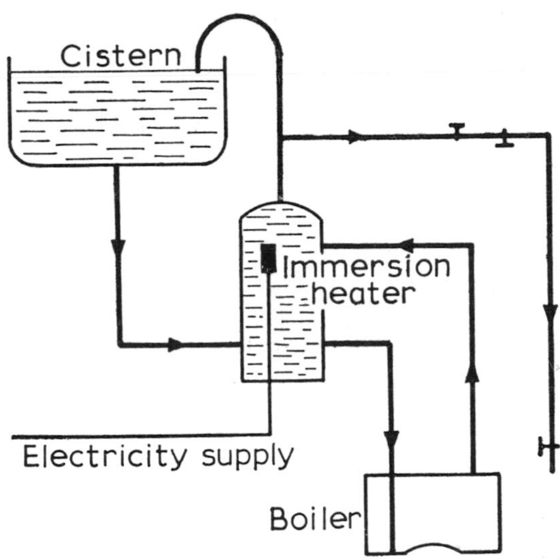

Water heated by immersion heater and boiler.

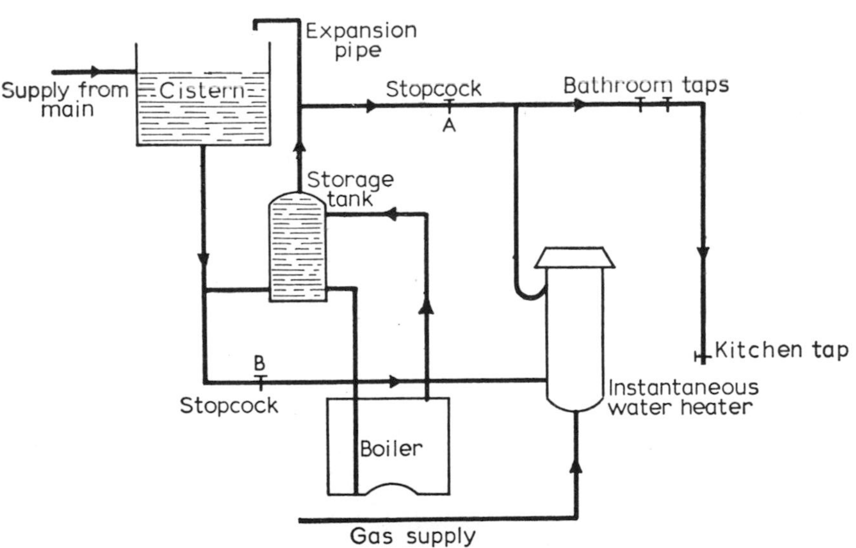

Gas instantaneous heater. Multipoint type.

DRAINAGE OF WATER

Drain pipes should be large enough to suit their purpose. Normal ones, approximately 8·89 cm—10·16 cm. Those for machines (potato peelers, etc.) are larger, approximately 6 inches. Any pipe leading from any appliance (tap, lavatory, etc.) to the drain must have a water seal to retain a certain amount of water in the pipe to prevent any unpleasant smells coming up the pipe and into the room.

Types of water seals: U-bend; S-bend; trap.

Water seals can be emptied by evaporation or by syphonage when two or more appliances are placed one above the other: e.g. hand basins on different floors.

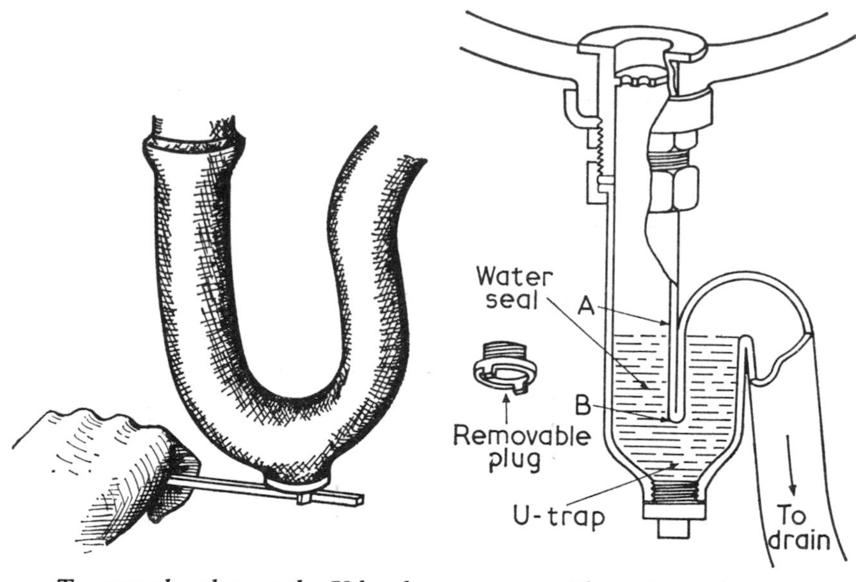

To open the plug on the U-bend a bar may be used.

The water seal.

A to B must not be less than 3·8 cm to be able to do its purpose. The seal is the most likely place to become blocked in the pipe. If this happens use a rubber water plunger to try to push the water through, but if this fails, the nut at the bottom should be removed, the water drained off and the solid matter removed with a piece of wire. There is also a more modern seal, made of plastic—detachable and pliable (reference—*Clean Catering* (H.M.S.O.)). The inside

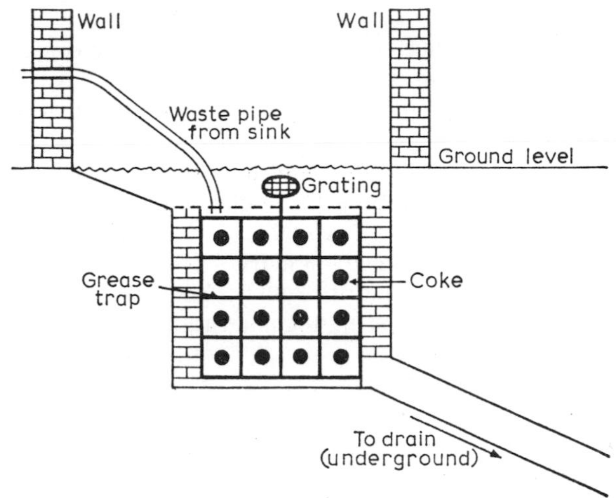

The grease trap.

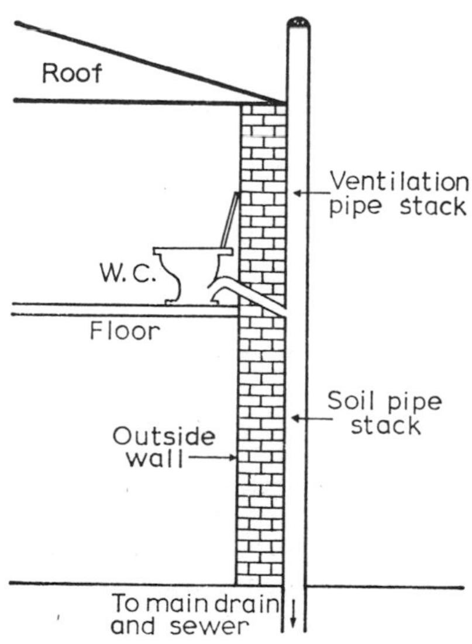

The soil pipe.

surface is very smooth, therefore there is no danger of dirt becoming stuck.

The *gully* receives the drain-pipes from baths, basins and sinks and also rain water from roof gutters.

If any solids pass the water seal, they are collected in the gulley and can be cleaned out.

Grease trap. Underneath the grating, there is a wire-mesh box which contains some loosely packed coke, which collects the grease and allows the water to pass through.

The gulley must be cleaned regularly—the grating removed and scrubbed and also just inside the gulley. The grease trap should be replenished with fresh coke at regular intervals. A bucket of hot water should be finally poured down the gulley. Disinfectants should be used after cleaning only.

The *soil pipe* is the waste pipe from the lavatory pan which goes directly below the ground to the drains. The top must extend above the level of any windows.

FREEZING OF PIPES

Freezing. The reason for pipes bursting when they freeze, is that water expands when frozen. If expansion takes place along the length

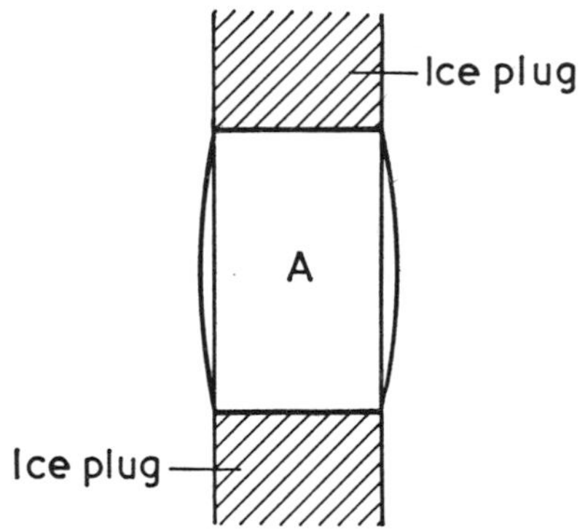

Freezing of water in pipes.

of the pipe, there will probably be no harm done, but if ice plugs form either side of A the pipe will bulge.

Precautions:

1. Lag all pipes.
2. Keep temperatures above 0°C.

Methods of thawing pipes:

1. Wrap a cloth around the frozen part, and pour hot water over it.
2. A blow lamp should only be used by a plumber or experienced person.
3. An oil stove placed near the frozen part to raise the temperature of the air.
4. If a waste pipe is frozen, pour hot water down it.

For burst pipes:

1. Turn off the main tap.
2. Turn off the stopcock between cistern and main pipe.
3. Open all taps, allow the water to escape.
4. Send for a plumber.

COMPARISON OF FUELS

Many factors need to be taken into consideration in the comparison of fuels. For example, the cheapest fuel to buy may not be the cheapest to burn. When comparing electricity with coal, the initial cost of electricity will be much higher, but when considering coal, one has to think of the storage space required, the cost of labour to move it, the cost of labour to clean the dirt it causes, etc.

A list of advantages and disadvantages of each fuel helps to make comparisons.

GAS COOKING

Advantages

1. Convenient, labour saving.
2. Free from smoke and dirt.
3. Easily controlled with immediate full heat and the flames are visible.
4. Special utensils are not required.
5. No fuel storage required.

Disadvantages

1. Some heat is lost into the kitchen.
2. Regular cleaning is necessary for efficiency.

ELECTRIC COOKING

Advantages

1. Clean to use and maintain.
2. Easily controlled and labour saving.
3. A good working atmosphere for kitchen staff as no oxygen is required to burn electricity.
4. Little heat is lost.
5. No fuel storage is required.

Disadvantages

1. Time is taken to heat up.
2. High initial cost of equipment and maintenance costs
3. Special utensils are required.

STEAM COOKING

Advantages

1. Low fuel cost.
2. Good heat for boiling liquids.
3. Low maintenance costs.

Disadvantages

1. Methods of cooking are limited.
2. High initial cost of installation.

SOLID FUEL COOKING

Advantages

1. Fuel cost is low on comparison.
2. Low maintenance costs.

Disadvantages

1. Cannot meet all cooking requirements
2. Storage of fuel.
3. Dirt and dust from fuel.
4. Labour costs to move fuel.
5. Difficulty of control of heat.

OIL COOKING

Advantages

1. Oil when bought in bulk is cheap.
2. Clean and convenient.
3. Labour saving.

Disadvantages

1. Need for large storage tanks.
2. Sources of supply may be affected.

THE STORAGE SPACE REQUIRED BY VARIOUS FUELS (METRIC)

Oil	per tonne 11 m^3 storage space
Anthracite	per tonne 13 m^3 storage space
Coal	per tonne 14 m^3 storage space
Coke	per tonne 26 m^3 storage space

Gas and electricity do not require storage space; this advantage is paid for by higher initial cost.

COMPARATIVE FUEL COSTS

1 therm = 100 000 British Thermal Units (B.Th.Us.).

A B.Th.U. is a measure of heat, the amount of heat required to raise 1 lb of water by 1°F.

Coke

If coke costs £10 per ton = 50p per cwt.

Therefore 1 lb. costs 0·5p.

Coke produces 12 000 B.Th.Us. per lb.

Therefore 1 Therm costs $\frac{0\cdot5 \times 100\,000}{12\,000} = 4\cdot2$p

A useful therm is the amount of heat put to good use. Coke is calculated to be 60% efficient.

Therefore a useful therm costs $\frac{4\cdot2 \times 100}{60} = 7$p.

Gas

An average cost could be 8p per therm.

Gas is calculated to be 80% efficient.

Therefore a useful therm costs $\frac{8 \times 100}{80}$ 10p.

If gas costs 10p per therm a useful therm costs $\frac{10 \times 100}{80} = 12\cdot5$p (12½p).

Electricity

1 unit of electricity produces 3 412 B.Th.Us.

1 unit of electricity costs approximately ½p.

Electricity is calculated to be 100% efficient.

Therefore 1 therm costs $\frac{0\cdot5 \times 100\,000}{3412} = 10\cdot5$p (10½p)

Oil

If oil costs 7½p per gallon (approx. 250 gallons = 1 ton).
1 gallon produces 165 000 B.Th.Us.
Oil is calculated to be 75% efficient.

Therefore 1 therm costs $\frac{7{\cdot}5 \times 100\,000}{165\,000} = 4{\cdot}5$

1 useful therm $= \frac{4{\cdot}5 \times 100}{75} = 6\text{p}$

RECOMMENDED BOOK

Gladwell, *Practical Maintenance and Equipment* (Barrie & Rockliff)

6. *Kitchen Equipment*

Kitchen equipment is expensive. In order to justify the expense it is essential that maximum use is made of it, which can only be achieved if all the equipment works efficiently and this depends on care and maintenance. It follows that the routine use, care and cleaning of all items of equipment is important, and this should be appreciated and understood.

Kitchen equipment may be divided into three categories:

1. Large equipment—ranges, steamers, boiling pans, fish-fryers, sinks, tables, etc.
2. Mechanical equipment—peelers, mincers, mixers, refrigerators, dishwashers, etc.
3. Utensils and small equipment—pots, pans, whisks, bowls, spoons, etc.

Manufacturers of large and mechanical kitchen equipment issue instructions on how to keep their apparatus in efficient working order, and it is the responsibility of everyone using the equipment to follow these instructions which should be displayed in a prominent place near the machines.

Arrangements should be made with the local gas company for regular checks and servicing of gas-operated equipment. Similar arrangements should be made with the electricity company in respect of electrical equipment. It is a good plan to keep a log-book of all equipment, showing where each item is located, when servicing takes place, noting any defects that arise, and instructing the fitter who may have carried out any work on the equipment to sign the log-book and to indicate exactly what has been done.

LARGE EQUIPMENT

STOVES

A large variety of stoves is available fired by gas, electricity, solid fuel or oil.

Solid tops should be washed clean, or wiped clean with a pad of sacking. When cool the stove tops can be more thoroughly cleaned by washing and using an abrasive. Emery paper can also be used if necessary. After any kind of cleaning a solid top should always be lightly greased.

On the open type of stove all the bars and racks should be removed, immersed in hot water with a detergent, scrubbed clean, dried and put back in place on the stove. All gas jets should then be lit to check that none are blocked. All enamel parts of stoves should be cleaned while warm with hot detergent water, rinsed and dried.

The insides of ovens and oven racks should be cleaned while slightly warm, using detergent water and a mild abrasive if necessary. In cases of extreme dirt or grease being baked on to the stove or oven a caustic jelly may be used, but thorough rinsing must take place afterwards.

Oven doors should not be slammed as this is liable to cause damage.

The unnecessary lighting or the lighting of ovens too early can cause wastage of fuel which is a waste of money. This is a bad habit common in many kitchens.

When a solid top gas range is lit, the centre ring should be removed, but it should be replaced after approximately 5 minutes, otherwise unnecessary heat is lost.

STEAMERS

Steaming ovens that work from a main steam supply need little maintenance. The door controls should be greased occasionally. This type of equipment is usually fitted with a gauge which registers the amount of steam pressure being supplied (usually 689·47 N/m^2), also an overflow valve which gives a warning whistle if the pressure is allowed to rise to a dangerous level. It is essential that both the gauge and valve are checked by a qualified engineer to ensure that they are working correctly.

If the steaming ovens are operated by gas or electricity then an automatic water supply by ball-valve, to ensure a constant level in the generating tank, is provided. It is necessary to see that the tap controlling the supply of water to the ball-valve is working correctly, also that the ball-valve arm and ball-valve washer are both in efficient working order. If these precautions are not observed there is the danger of the generating tank burning dry and becoming damaged as a result.

The steamer trays and runners should be washed in hot detergent water and then rinsed. The water supply should be turned off and the water drained from the generating chamber. The whole of the inside of the steamer should be cleaned with detergent water and rinsed. The water supply should then be turned on and the ball-valve arm checked to see that it is moving freely.

Steamer doors should be left open slightly when not in use to allow air to circulate.

Boiling Pans

Many types are available in different metals—aluminium, stainless steel, etc., in various sizes, 10, 15, 20, 30 and 40 litre capacity, and they may be heated by gas or electricity or from the main steam supply. As they are used for boiling or stewing large quantities of food it is important that they do not allow the food to burn, for this reason the steam jacket type boiler is the most suitable. Many of these are fitted with a tilting device to facilitate the emptying of the contents.

After use, the boiling pan and lid should be thoroughly washed with mild detergent solution and then well rinsed. The tilting apparatus should be greased occasionally and checked to see that it tilts easily. If gas fired the gas jets and pilot should be inspected to ensure correct working. If a pressure gauge and safety valve are fitted these should be checked to see that they are working correctly.

DEEP FAT-FRYERS

These are among the items of equipment which are used extensively in many catering establishments. The unskilled or careless worker can cause money to be lost by food or fat being spoilt through misuse of a deep fat-fryer.

Older types are fired by solid fuel; more modern fryers are heated by gas or electricity; most incorporate a thermostatic control in order to save fuel and prevent overheating. A development is the 'cool zone'; this is where the heating elements are at the sides of the fryer, but the lower part is kept at a reduced temperature. This stops particles that may fall off food being fried from dropping to the bottom of the fryer, burning and so spoiling other foods being cooked. This form of heating also saves fat.

Deep fat-fryers should be cleaned daily after use by:

1. Turning off the heat and allowing the fat to cool.
2. Draining off and straining the fat.
3. Closing the stopcock, filling the fryer with hot water containing detergent and boiling for 10–15 minutes.
4. Draining off the detergent water, refilling with clean water plus $\frac{1}{8}$ litre of vinegar per 5 litres of water and reboiling for 10–15 minutes.
5. Draining off the water, drying the fryer, closing the stopcock and refilling with clean fat.

HOT-CUPBOARDS AND BAINS-MARIE

Hot-cupboards (commonly referred to in the trade as the hot-plate) are used for heating plates and serving dishes and for keeping food hot. Care should be taken to see that the amount of heat fed into the hot-cupboard is controlled at a reasonable temperature. This is important, otherwise the plates and food will either be too hot or too cold and this could obviously affect the efficiency of the service. A temperature of 60C°–76°C. is suitable for hot-cupboards and a thermostat is a help in maintaining this.

Hot-cupboards may be heated by steam, gas or electricity. The doors should slide easily, and occasional greasing may be necessary. The tops of most hot-cupboards are used as serving counters and should be heated to a higher temperature than the inside. These tops are usually made of stainless steel and should be cleaned thoroughly after each service.

Bains-marie are open wells of water used for keeping foods hot, and are available in many designs, some of which are incorporated into hot-cupboards, some in serving counters, and there is a type which is fitted at the end of a cooking range. They may be heated by steam, gas or electricity and sufficient heat to boil the water in the bain-marie should be available. Care should be taken to see that a bain-marie is never allowed to burn dry when the heat is turned on. After use the heat should be turned off, the water drained off and the bain-marie cleaned inside and outside with hot detergent water, rinsed and dried. Any drain-off tap should then be closed.

GRILLS AND SALAMANDERS

The salamander or grill heated from above probably causes more wastage of fuel than any other item of kitchen equipment through being allowed to burn unnecessarily for long unused periods. Most salamanders have more than one set of heating elements or jets and it is not always necessary to have them all turned on full.

Salamanders are heated by gas or electricity and there is a type fired by gas which has incorporated an electrically driven fan. This combination gives an exceptionally fierce heat and is suitable for a very fast trade where a lot of food may have to be placed under a salamander in a short space of time.

Salamander bars and draining trays should be cleaned regularly with hot water containing a grease solvent such as soda. After rinsing they should be replaced and the salamander lit for a few minutes to dry the bars.

For under-fired grills to work efficiently they must be capable of cooking food quickly and should reach a high temperature 15–20 minutes after lighting, and the heat should be turned off immediately after use. When the bars are cool they should be removed and washed in hot water containing a grease solvent, rinsed, dried and replaced on the grill. Care should be taken with the fire bricks if they are used for lining the grill as they are easily broken.

CONTACT GRILLS

These are sometimes referred to as double-sided or infra-grills, have two heating surfaces arranged facing each other. The food to be cooked is placed on one surface and is then covered by the second. These grills are electrically heated and are capable of cooking certain foods very quickly. Because of this, extra care is needed, particularly when cooks are using this type of grill for the first time.

FRY PLATES, GRIDDLE PLATES

These are solid metal plates heated from below. They are used for cooking individual portions of meat, eggs, bacon, etc. They can be heated quickly to a high temperature and are suitable for rapid and continuous cooking. When cooking is first commenced on the griddle plates, a light film of oil should be applied to the food and the griddle plate to prevent sticking.

SINKS

Different materials are used for sinks according to the purpose for which they are intended.

(*a*) Heavy galvanised iron for heavy pot wash.

(*b*) Teak or other hardwood for glass or china wash. (If hardwood sinks are left unused for long periods of time they should be filled with cold water to prevent shrinkage of the timber.)

(*c*) Stainless steel for general purposes.

(*d*) Glazed earthenware for general light purposes.

Sinks, drainers, waste and overflow outlets should be cleaned and rinsed after use.

TABLES

Wooden tables should be scrubbed clean with hot soda water, rinsed and wiped as dry as possible to avoid warping.

Formica or stainless steel topped tables should be washed with hot detergent water, rinsed with hot water and dried.

Marble slabs should be scrubbed with hot water and rinsed. All excess moisture should be removed with a clean dry cloth.

No cutting or chopping should be allowed on table tops, chopping boards should be used.

Hot pans should not be put on tables, triangles must be used to protect the table surface.

The legs and racks or shelves of tables are cleaned with hot detergent water and then dried. Wooden table legs require scrubbing.

BUTCHER'S BLOCK

A scraper should be used to keep the block clean.

After scraping, the block should be sprinkled with a few handfuls of common salt in order to absorb any moisture which may have penetrated during the day.

Do not use water or liquids for cleaning unless absolutely necessary as water will be absorbed into the wood and cause swelling.

STORAGE RACKS

All types of racks should be emptied and scrubbed or washed periodically.

MECHANICAL EQUIPMENT

When a new item of equipment is installed it should be tested by a qualified fitter before being used by catering staff. The manufacturer's instructions must be displayed in a prominent place near the machine. The manufacturer's advice regarding servicing should be followed and a record book kept showing when and what maintenance the machine is receiving.

Before cleaning, the machine should be switched off and the plug removed from the socket.

POTATO-PEELERS

1. Potatoes should be free of earth and stones before loading into the machine.
2. Before any potatoes are loaded the water spray should be turned on and the abrasive plate set in motion.
3. The interior should be cleaned out daily and the abrasive plate removed to ensure that small particles are not lodged below.
4. The peel trap should be emptied as frequently as required.
5. The waste outlet should be kept free from obstruction.

REFRIGERATORS (*See also* pages 52, 71–74.)

In order to maintain a refrigerator at peak efficiency the following points should be observed:

1. Defrost weekly. The control should be turned to defrost; the racks should be emptied and racks and interior surfaces washed, rinsed and dried.

If the refrigerator is not defrosted regularly excess frost accumulates on the cooling system, acts as an insulator and causes the refrigerator motor to work longer than is necessary, thus shortening the life of the components.

2. The door or doors should be kept closed as much as possible, otherwise if too much warm air is allowed to enter, the refrigerator plant overworks and excess frost can accumulate on the cooling system.

3. Food should be stored sensibly and in such a way that the cold air can circulate all round. Excessive packing of food into a refrigerator should be avoided.

4. A qualified service engineer should be called in at the first sign of any defect in the machinery operating a refrigerator.

FOOD-MIXER

This is an important labour-saving, electrically operated piece of equipment used for many purposes, for example mixing pastry, cakes, mashing potatoes, beating egg whites, mayonnaise, cream, mincing or chopping meat and vegetables.

1. It should be lubricated frequently in accordance with manufacturer's instructions.

2. The motor should not be overloaded. Overloading can be caused by obstruction to the rotary components. For example, if dried bread is being passed through the mincer attachment without sufficient care the rotary cog can become so clogged with bread that it is unable to move. If the motor is allowed to run damage can be caused to the machine.

3. All components as well as the main machine should be thoroughly washed and dried. Care should be taken to see that no rust occurs on any part. The mincer attachment knife and plates will rust if not given sufficient care.

FOOD-SLICERS AND CHOPPERS

Food-slicers are obtainable both manually and electrically operated. They are labour-saving devices which can be dangerous if not operated with care. Because of this the working instructions should be placed in a prominent position near the machine.

1. Care should be taken that no material likely to damage the blades is included in the food to be sliced or chopped. It is easy for a careless worker to overlook a piece of bone which, if allowed to come into contact with the cutting blade, could cause severe damage.

2. Each section in contact with food should be cleaned and carefully dried after use.

3. The blade or blades should be sharpened regularly.

4. Moving parts should be lubricated, but oil must not come into contact with the food.

5. Extra care must be taken when blades are exposed.

CHIPPER (HAND OR ELECTRIC)

The manual type should be washed and dried after use. Care should be taken with the interior of the blades, they should be cleaned with a folded cloth. When chipping potatoes, pressure should be applied gradually to prevent damage to the cutting blades which can be caused by violent jerking.

The electric chipper should be thoroughly cleaned and dried after use, particular attention being paid to those parts which come into contact with food. Care should be taken that no obstruction prevents the motor from operating at its normal speed. Moving parts should be lubricated according to the maker's instructions.

MASHER (HAND OR ELECTRIC)

The hand type should be washed immediately after use, then rinsed and dried.

The electric masher should have the removal sections and the main machine washed and dried after use, extra care being taken over those parts which come into contact with food. The same care should be taken as with electric chippers regarding obstruction and lubrication.

WATER BOILING APPLIANCES FOR TEA- AND COFFEE-MAKING

There are two main groups of water boilers: bulk boilers from which boiling water can only be drawn when all the contents have boiled and automatic boilers which provide a continuous flow of boiling water.

BULK BOILERS

These are generally used when large quantities of boiling water are required at a given time. They should be kept scrupulously clean, covered with the correct lid to prevent anything falling in and when not used for some time they should be left filled with clean cold water.

AUTOMATIC BOILERS

These boilers have automatic waterfeeds and can give freshly boiled water at intervals. It is important to see that the water supply is efficiently maintained, otherwise there is a danger of the boiler burning dry and being damaged.

PRESSURE BOILERS

This is the type that operates many still sets, consisting of steam heating milk boilers and pressure boiler providing boiling water.

Care should be taken with the pilot light to see that it is working efficiently. As with all gas-fired equipment it is essential that regular inspection and maintenance is carried out by gas company fitters.

COFFEE AND MILK HEATERS

Water jacket boilers are made for the storage of hot coffee and hot milk with draw-off taps from the storage chamber. Inner linings may be of glazed earthenware, stainless steel or heat resistant glass. It is very important that the storage chambers are thoroughly cleaned with hot water after each use and then left full of clean cold water. The draw-off taps should be cleaned through regularly with a special brush.

DISHWASHING MACHINES

For hygienic washing up the generally recognised requirements are a good supply of hot water at a temperature of 60°C for general cleansing followed by a sterilising rinse at a temperature of at least one minute at 82°C.

Dishwashing machines take over an arduous job and save a lot of time and labour, ensuring that a good supply of clean, sterilised crockery is available.

There are three main types:

1. *Spray types* in which the dishes are placed in racks which slide into the machines where they are subjected to a spray of hot detergent water at 48°C–60°C from above and below.

The racks move on to the next section where they are rinsed by a fresh hot shower at 82°C. At this temperature they are sterilised, and on passing out into the air they dry off quickly.

2. *Brush type machines* use revolving brushes for the scrubbing of each article in hot detergent water, the articles are then rinsed and sterilised in another compartment.

3. *Agitator water machines* in which baskets of dishes are immersed in deep tanks and the cleaning is performed by the mechanical agitation of the hot detergent water. The loaded baskets are then given a sterilising rinse in another compartment.

Dishwashing machines are costly and it is essential that the manufacturer's instructions with regard to use and maintenance are followed at all times.

FOOD WASTE DISPOSERS are operated by electricity and take all manner of rubbish, including bones, fat, scraps and vegetable refuse. Almost every type of rubbish and swill with the exception of rags and tins is finely ground, then rinsed down the drain. It is the most modern and hygienic method of waste disposal. Care should be taken by handlers not to push waste into the machine with a metal object as this can cause damage.

SMALL EQUIPMENT AND UTENSILS

Small equipment and utensils are made from a variety of metals such as iron, steel, copper, aluminium, wood, etc.

IRON

Items of equipment used for frying, such as fritures and frying-pans of all types, are usually made of heavy, black wrought iron.

Fritures should be washed in a strong grease solvent solution, then thoroughly rinsed and dried, or they can be thoroughly cleaned with clean cloth or sacking.

Frying-pans (*poêles*) should not be washed. When new they should be 'proved' or 'seasoned'; they are spread with a thick layer of salt and placed on a hot stove or hot oven for 15–20 minutes, then wiped firmly with a wad of clean sacking. The salt is removed and a little fat or oil is added and they are wiped with a clean cloth. If an abrasive is necessary to clean the pan, salt may be used, if not, a good firm rub with dry sacking and a final light greasing are sufficient.

Frying-pans are available in several shapes and many sizes; for example:

Omelette-pans
Frying-pans
Oval fish frying-pans
Pancake-pans

Baking sheets are made in various sizes of black wrought steel. The less they are washed the less they are likely to cause food to stick. New baking sheets should be well heated in a hot oven, thoroughly wiped with a piece of clean sacking and then lightly oiled. Before being used baking trays should be lightly greased with a pure fat or oil. Immediately after use and while still warm they should be cleaned by scraping and dry-wiping. If washing is necessary hot soda or detergent water should be used.

Tartlet and barquette moulds and cake tins should be cared for in the same way as for baking sheets.

TINNED STEEL

A number of items are made from this metal; for example:

Conical strainer (*chinois*), used for passing sauces and gravies.

Fine conical strainer (*chinois fin*), used for passing sauces and gravies.

Colander.

Vegetable reheating container (*passoir*), used for reheating vegetables.

Soup machine and mouli strainer, used for passing thick soups, sauces and potatoes for mash.

Sieves (*tammis*).

All the above items should be thoroughly washed immediately after each use and dried; if this is done, washing is simple and quick. If the food or liquid clogs and dries in the mesh it is difficult to clean; the easiest way to wash a sieve is to hold it upside down under running water and tap vigorously with the bristles of a stiff scrubbing brush. If the sieve is moved up and down quickly in water, clogged food will be loosened.

Care should be taken when using sieves; they should be the right way up when food is passed through, the food should be stroked through with a wooden mushroom, not banged, as this can damage the mesh. Only foodstuffs such as flour should be passed through the sieve upside down.

COPPER

Pans of copper, lined with tin, are made in various shapes, sizes and capacities used to cook practically every kind of food.

Shallow saucepan with sloping sides	*sauteuse*
Shallow flat round pan with vertical sides	*plat à sauter*
Saucepan	*russe*
Stockpot	*marmite*
Large round deep pan	*rondeau*
Rectangular braising-pan	*braisière*
Roasting tray	*plaque à rôtir*
Turbot kettle	*turbotière*
Salmon kettle	*saumonière*
Gravy, soup, sauce storage pans	*bain-marie*
Moulds of various sizes and shapes	*dariole, charlotte, savarin, bombe, timbale*

Copper equipment is expensive, but it is first-class for cooking. This is because copper is a good conductor of heat; also, food burns less easily in copper pans than in pans of many other metals.

The disadvantages of copper are that it tarnishes easily and looks dirty. The tin lining of copper pans can be damaged by misuse—excessive dry heat can soften the tin and spoil the lining. Putting a pan on a fierce fire without liquid or fat is bad practice that can damage the tin lining.

Copper equipment should be inspected periodically to see if the tin is being worn away; if so, it should be collected by a tinsmith and retinned.

Certain items of copper equipment are not lined with tin, but are made of copper; for example: large vegetable boiler; sugar boiler; mixing bowl; egg white bowl.

The Cleaning of Copper Equipment

To keep large quantities of copper equipment clean the following points should be observed:

1. Two large sinks into which the pots may be completely immersed should be available. The water in one sink should be capable of being raised to boiling point.
2. All dirty pans should be well soaked for a few minutes in boiling water to which a little soda has been added.
3. They should be well scoured, using either a brush or wire wool or similar agent with a scouring powder.
4. The pans are then rinsed in clean hot water and placed upside down to dry.
5. The copper surfaces, if tarnished, may be cleaned with a paste made from $\frac{1}{3}$ silver sand, $\frac{1}{3}$ salt and $\frac{1}{3}$ flour mixed with vinegar; the pans are then thoroughly rinsed and dried.

CAST ALUMINIUM

Saucepans, stock pots, sauteuses, sauté pans, braising pans, fish kettles and large round deep pans and dishes of all sizes are made in cast aluminium. They are expensive, but one advantage is that the pans do not tarnish; also, because of their strong heavy construction, they are suitable for many cooking processes.

A disadvantage is that in the making of aluminium pans other metals are used to make then stronger and as a result certain foods can become discoloured when prepared in aluminium pans; for example, care should be taken when making white sauces and white soups. A wooden spoon should be used for mixing, then there should be no discoloration. The use of metal whisks or spoons should be avoided.

Water boiled in aluminium pans is unsuitable for tea-making as it gives the tea an unpleasant colour.

Cleaning of Cast Aluminium Pans

1. All pans should be well soaked in hot detergent water, soda should not be used.
2. After a good soaking, pans should be scoured with a hard bristle brush or rough cloth with an abrasive powder if necessary. Harsh abrasives should be avoided if possible.
3. After scouring, the pans are rinsed in clean hot water and thoroughly dried.

STAINLESS STEEL

Stainless steel is a relatively poor conductor of heat which together with the high price makes it a questionable metal for kitchen pans. To overcome the first point manufacturers add a thick layer of copper to the base of pans. This overcomes the problem of poor heat conduction, but also makes the pan still more expensive. Stockpots and pans of various shapes and sizes are available with or without copper bases.

Stainless steel is used for many small items of equipment.

WOOD

Chopping Boards are an important item of kitchen equipment which should be kept in use on all table surfaces to protect the table and the edges of cutting knives.

Chopping boards will warp or splinter if the following points are not observed:

1. A strong, well-constructed board should be used.
2. After use, boards should be scrubbed with a bristle brush, using hot detergent water, rinsed with clean water and dried as much as possible.
3. The boards should not be put over a stove or in a hot-cupboard. Excess heat and water cause wood to warp.
4. Heavy chopping should not occur on boards as this causes splintering. The place for heavy chopping is on the chopping block.

Rolling-pins, Wooden Spoons and Spatulas

These items should be scrubbed in hot detergent water, rinsed in clean water and dried.

Rolling-pins should not be scraped with a knife; this can cause the wood to splinter. Adhering paste can be removed with a cloth.

Wooden Sieves and Mandolins

When cleaning, care of the wooden frame should be considered in the light of the previous remarks. The blades of the mandolin should be kept lightly greased to prevent rust (stainless-steel mandolins are available).

RUBBER

Chopping boards are also made of hard rubber. These are hygienic because they are solid, in one piece and do not warp, crack or absorb flavours. They are cleaned by scrubbing with hot water and drying.

MATERIALS

Muslin (*Mouseline*)

The Tammy cloth (*étamine*) which is made from calico. Both muslin and tammy cloth are used for straining soups and sauces.

The Jelly Bag made from thick flannel or nylon for straining jellies.

Piping Bags (*poche*) are made from linen, nylon or plastic and are used for piping preparations of all kinds.

All materials should be washed immediately after use in hot detergent water, rinsed in hot clean water and then dried. Tammy-cloths, muslins and linen piping bags must be boiled periodically in detergent water.

MICROWAVE COOKING

Microwave is a method of cooking and heating food by using high-frequency power. The energy used is the same as that which carries television from the transmitter to the receiver but is at a higher frequency.

The waves disturb the molecules or particles of food and agitate them, thus causing friction which has the effect of cooking the whole of the food from the inside, whereas in the conventional method of cooking heat penetrates the food only by conduction from the outside. Food being cooked by microwave needs no fat or water and is placed in a glass, earthenware, plastic or paper container before being put in the oven. Metal is not used as the microwaves are reflected by it.

The advantage of microwave cooking is its speed; for instance a 1·5 kg chicken takes only seven minutes' cooking time.

RECOMMENDED BOOKS

Fuller, *Chef's Manual of Kitchen Management* (Batsford), and *Catering Management in a Technological Age* (Barrie & Rockliff, ch. 6). *Microwave Cookery Book* (Dysona).

Napleton, *Microwave Cookery* (Northwood Publications).

7. Elementary Nutrition

A food is any substance, liquid or solid, which provides the body with materials—

(*a*) for heat and energy;
(*b*) for growth and repair;
(*c*) to regulate the body processes.

These materials are known as *nutrients*. They are

protein
fats
carbohydrates
vitamins
mineral salts
water

The study of these nutrients is termed nutrition. Only those substances containing nutrients are foods. Most foods contain several nutrients, a few foods contain only one nutrient, for example sugar.

For the body to obtain the maximum benefit from food it is essential that everyone concerned with the buying, storage, cooking and serving of food and the compiling of menus should have some knowledge of nutrition.

DIGESTION

This is the breaking down of the food and takes place

(*a*) in the mouth, where food is mixed with saliva;

(*b*) in the stomach, where the food is mixed and gastric juices are added;

(*c*) in the small intestine, where the nutrients are broken down further and additional juices are added.

ABSORPTION

To enable the body to benefit from food it must be absorbed into the blood-stream; this absorption occurs after the food has been broken down; the product then passes through the walls of the digestive tract into the blood-stream.

This occurs in:

(*a*) the stomach where simple substances are formed as a result of digestion and pass through the stomach lining into the blood-stream;

(*b*) in the small intestine where more of the absorption of the nutrients takes place due to a further breakdown of the food;

(*c*) in the large intestine, where very little is absorbed.

For the body to obtain the full benefit from foods it should be remembered that to stimulate the flow of saliva and gastric juices food must smell, look and taste attractive. Furthermore, food which is hurried through the body does not allow full absorption to take place.

When the full benefit is not obtained or there is a lack of one or more nutrient then this leads to a state of malnutrition.

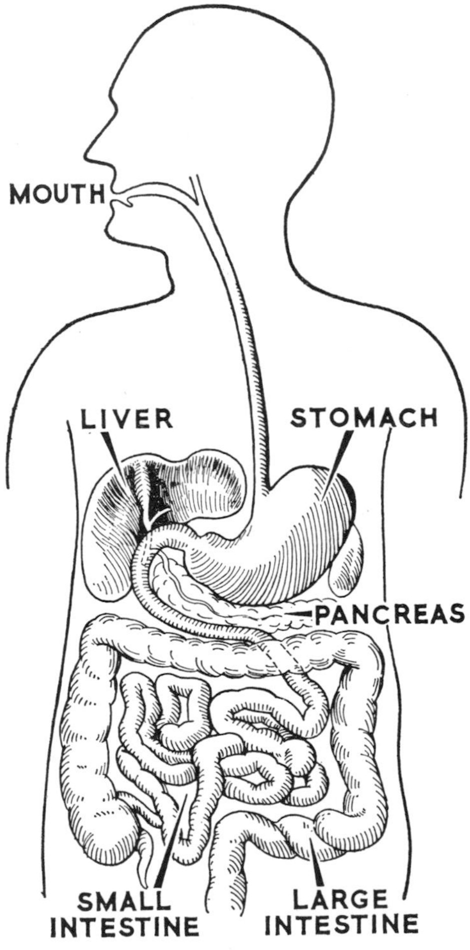

The digestive tract.

THE MAIN FUNCTION OF NUTRIENTS

Energy	*Growth and repair*	*Regulation of body processes*
Carbohydrates	Proteins	Vitamins
Fats	Minerals	Minerals
Proteins	Water	Water

PROTEIN

Protein is an essential part of all living matter; it is therefore needed for the growth of the body and for the repair of body tissues.

There are two kinds of protein:

(*a*) Animal protein found in meat, game, poultry, fish, eggs, milk, cheese;

(*b*) Vegetable protein found mainly in the seeds of vegetables. The proportion of protein in green and root vegetables is small. Peas, beans and nuts contain most protein and the grain of cereals, such as wheat, have a useful amount because of the large quantity eaten.

PROPORTION OF PROTEIN IN SOME FOODS

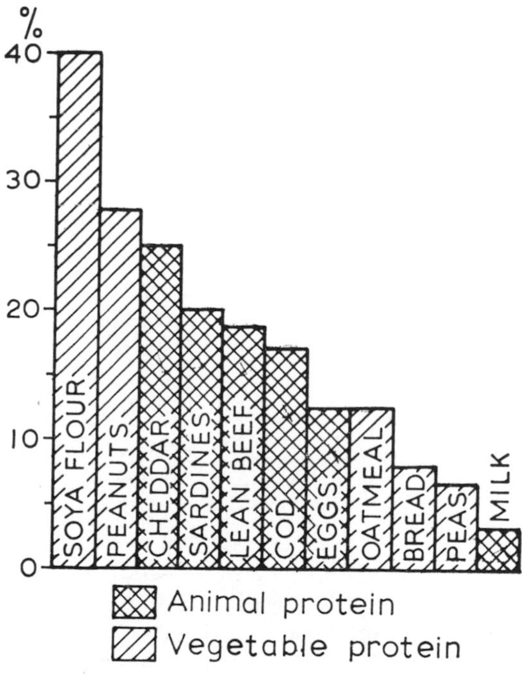

Proportion of protein in some foods.

It follows that as protein is needed for growth, growing children and expectant and nursing mothers will need more protein than other adults whose requirements are mainly for repair. Any spare protein is used for producing heat and energy.

FOODS WITH PROTEIN

Main supply of protein in the average diet.

WHAT PROTEIN IS

Protein is composed of amino-acids, and the protein of cheese is different from the protein of meat because the number and arrangement of the acids are not the same. A certain number of these amino-acids are essential to the body and have to be provided by food. Proteins containing all the essential amino-acids in the correct proportion are said to be of high biological value. The human body is capable of changing the other kinds of amino-acids to suit its needs.

It is preferable that the body has both animal and vegetable protein, so that a complete variety of the necessary amino-acids is available. During digestion protein is split into amino-acids; these are absorbed into the blood-stream and used for building body tissues and to provide some heat and energy.

COOKING EFFECTS ON PROTEIN

On being heated, the different proteins in foods set at different temperatures; above these temperatures shrinkage occurs, this is particularly noticeable in grilling or roasting meat. Moderately cooked protein is the most easy to digest—for example, a lightly cooked egg is more easily digested than a raw egg or a hard-boiled egg.

FATS

There are two main groups of fats, animal and vegetable. The function of fat is to protect vital organs of the body, to provide heat and energy, and certain fats also provide vitamins.

Fats can be divided into:

(*a*) solid fat;
(*b*) oils (fat which is liquid at room temperature).

Fats are obtained from the following foods:

animal origin: dripping, butter, suet, lard, cheese, cream, bacon, meat fat, oily fish;
vegetable origin: margarine, cooking fat, nuts, soya-bean.

Oils are obtained from the following foods:

animal origin: halibut and cod-liver oil;
vegetable origin: from seeds or nuts.

Main supply of fat in the average diet.

Fats differ because of the fatty acids from which they are derived. These may be, for example, butyric acid in butter, stearic acid in solid fat, such as beef suet, oleic acid in most oils. These fatty acids affect the texture and flavour of the fat.

To be useful to the body, fats have to be broken down into fatty acids so that they can be absorbed, they can then provide heat and energy.

The food value of the various kinds of fat is similar, although some animal fats contain vitamins A and D.

Fats should be eaten with other foods such as bread, potatoes, etc., as they can then be more easily digested and utilised in the body.

Certain fish, such as herrings, mackerel, salmon, sardines, contain oil (fat) in the flesh. Other fish such as cod and halibut contain the oil in the liver.

Vegetables and fruit contain very little fat, but nuts have a considerable amount.

PROPORTION OF FAT IN SOME FOODS

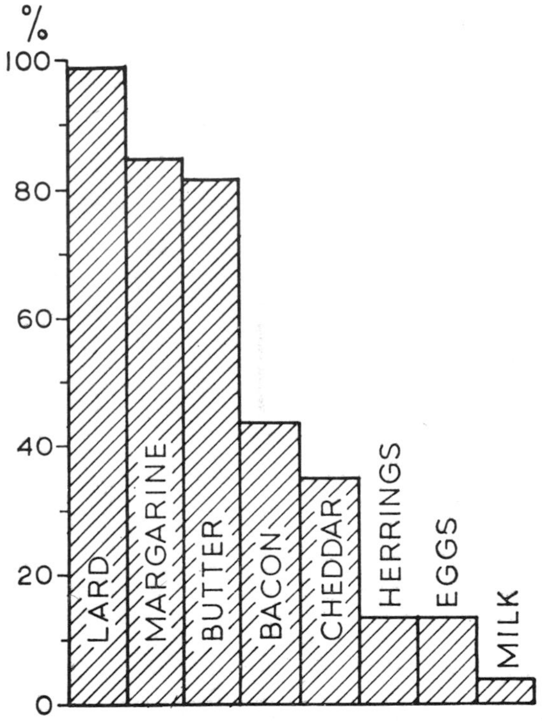

Proportion of fat in some foods.

COOKING EFFECTS ON FAT

Cooking has little effect on fat except to make it more digestible.

CARBOHYDRATES

There are three main groups of carbohydrates:

(*a*) sugar
(*b*) starch
(*c*) cellulose

Plate 1. Shell-fish (Molluscs). 1. Scallops. 2. Oysters. 3. Mussels.

Plate 2. Shell-fish (Crustaceans). 1. Crab. 2. Scampi. 3. Dublin Bay Prawn. 4. Lobster. 5. Crawfish. 6. Prawn.

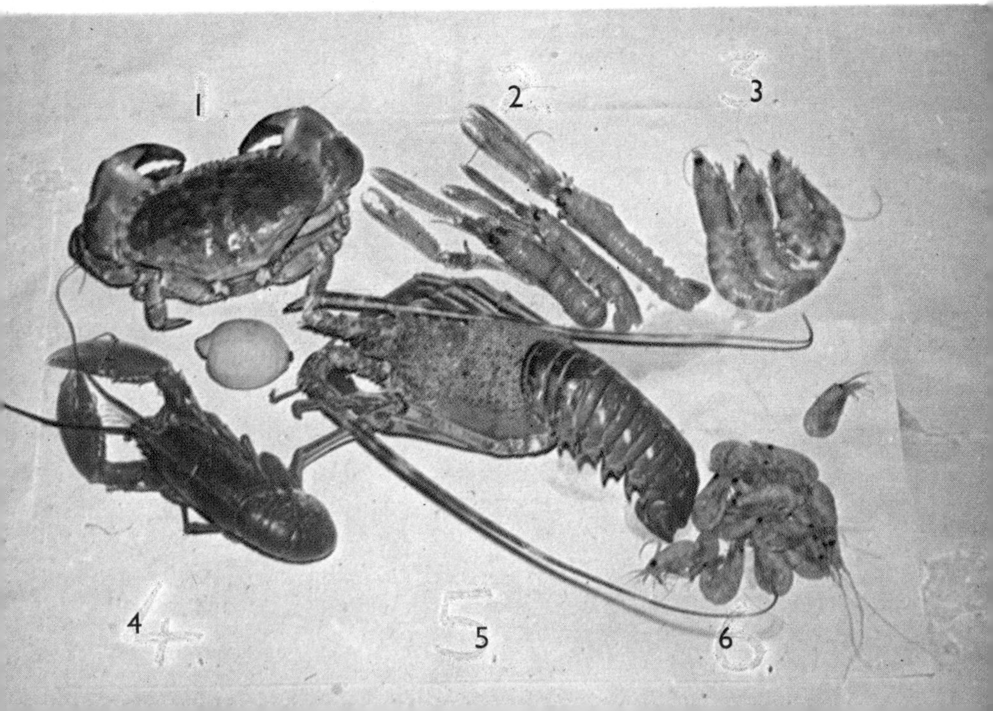

The function of carbohydrates is to provide the body with most of its energy. Starch is composed of a number of glucose molecules (particles), and during digestion starch is broken down into glucose.

(*A*) SUGAR

There are several kinds of sugar:

Glucose: found in the blood of animals and in fruit and honey.
Fructose: found in fruit, honey and cane sugar.
Sucrose: found in beet and cane sugar.
Lactose: found in milk.
Maltose: produced naturally during the germination of grain.

Sugars are the simplest form of carbohydrate and the end-products of the digestion of carbohydrates. They are absorbed in the form of glucose and used to provide heat and energy.

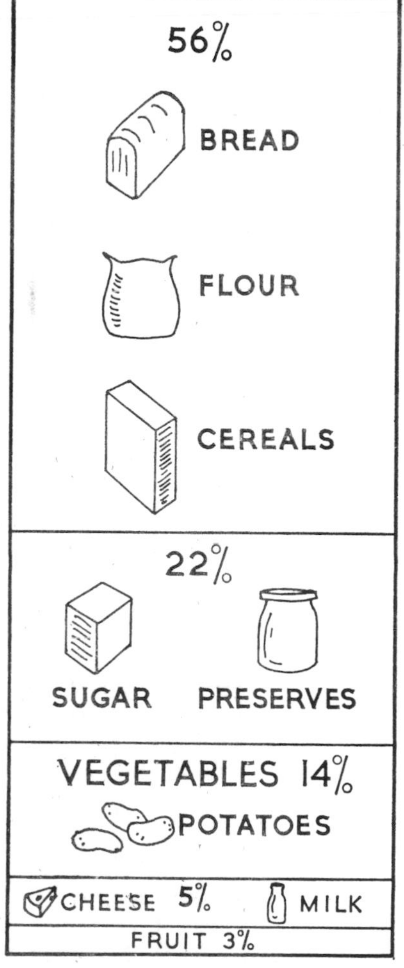

Main supply of carbohydrate in the average diet.

(*B*) STARCH

This is contributed to the diet by the following foods:

Whole grains: rice, oats, barley, tapioca.
Powdered grains: flour, cornflour, ground rice, arrowroot.
Vegetables: potatoes, parsnips, peas, beans.
Unripe fruit: bananas, apples, cooking pears.
Cereals: cornflakes, shredded wheat, etc.
Cooked starch: cakes, biscuits.
Pastes: macaroni, spaghetti, vermicelli.

Foods containing starch have cells with starch granules, covered with a cellulose wall which breaks down when heated or made moist. When browned, as with the crust of bread, toast, roast potatoes, skin on rice pudding, etc., the starch forms dextrins and these taste sweeter.

CELLULOSE

This is the coarser structure of vegetables and cereals which is not digested but is used as roughage in the intestine.

PROPORTION OF CARBOHYDRATE IN SOME FOODS

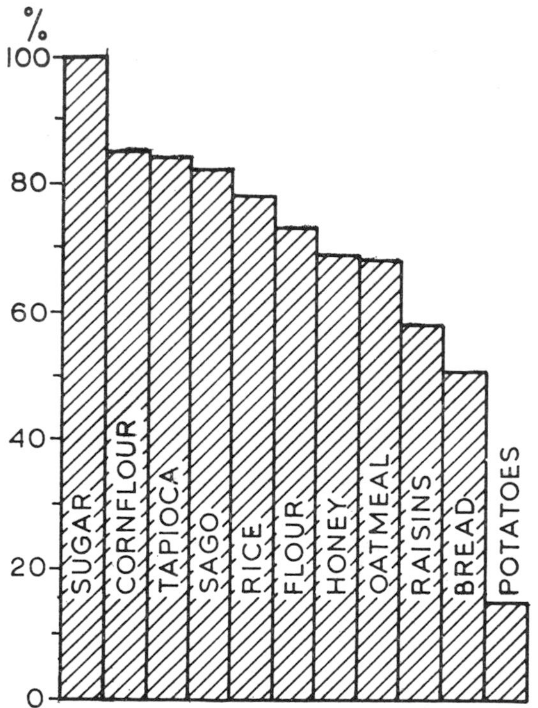

Proportion of carbohydrate in some foods.

COOKING EFFECTS ON CARBOHYDRATE

Thorough cooking is essential if starch is to be absorbed; uncooked starch granules are not digestible.

VITAMINS

Vitamins are chemical substances which are vital for life, and if the diet is deficient in any vitamin, ill-health results. As they are chemical substances they can be produced synthetically.

GENERAL FUNCTION OF VITAMINS

To assist the regulation of the body processes, e.g.:

1. To help the growth of children.
2. To protect against disease.

VITAMIN A

Function

1. Assists in the growth of children.
2. Helps to resist infection.
3. Enables people to see better in the dark.

Vitamin A is fat soluble, therefore it is to be found in fatty foods. It can be made in the body from carotene, the yellow substance found in many fruits and vegetables.

Dark green vegetables are a good source of vitamin A, the green colour masking the yellow of the carotene.

Foods in which it is found

Halibut liver oil	Margarine (to which vitamin A is added)	Carrots
Cod-liver oil	Cheese	Spinach
Kidney	Eggs	Watercress
Liver	Milk	Tomatoes
Butter	Herrings	Apricots

Fish-liver oils have the most vitamin A. The amount of vitamin A in dairy produce varies. Because cattle eat fresh grass in summer and stored feeding-stuffs in winter, the dairy produce contains the highest amount of vitamin A in the summer.

Kidney and liver are also useful sources of vitamin A.

VITAMIN D

Function

This vitamin controls the use the body makes of calcium. It is therefore necessary for healthy bones and teeth.

Like vitamin A it is fat soluble.

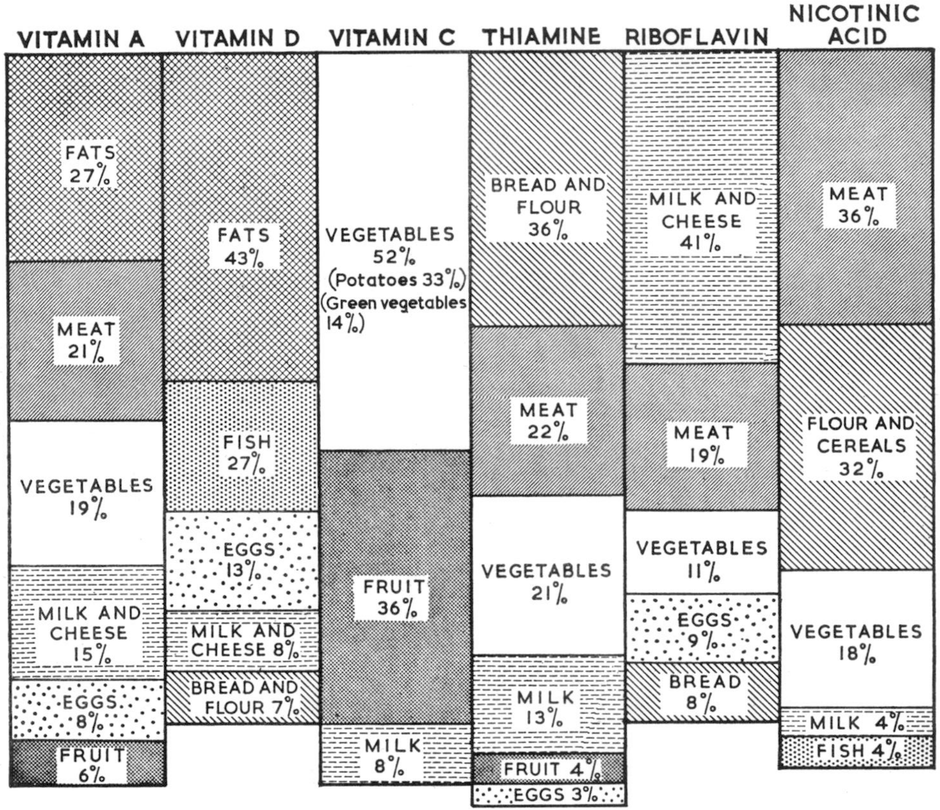

Main supply of vitamins in the average diet.

Sources of Vitamin D

An important source of vitamin D is from the action of sunlight on the deeper layers of the skin.

Fish-liver oils	Margarine (to which vitamin D is added)
Oily fish	Dairy produce
	Egg yolk

Compared with vitamin A there are fewer sources of vitamin D, the fish-liver oils being the most important.

VITAMIN B

When first discovered vitamin B was thought to be one substance only; it is now known to consist of at least eleven substances, the three main ones are:

Thiamine (B 1)
Riboflavin (B 2)
Nicotinic acid, or Niacin

Function

Vitamin B is required to:

1. Keep the nervous system in good condition.
2. Enable the body to utilise the carbohydrates.
3. Encourage the growth of the body.

Vitamin B is water soluble and can be lost in cooking water.

Some foods in which it is found

Thiamine (B 1)	*Riboflavin (B 2)*	*Nicotinic acid*
Yeast	Yeast	Meat extract
Bacon	Liver	Brewers' Yeast
Oatmeal	Meat extract	Liver
Peas	Cheese	Kidney
Wholemeal bread	Egg	Beef
		Bacon

VITAMIN C (ASCORBIC ACID)

Function

1. Vitamin C is necessary for the growth of children.
2. Assists in the healing of cuts and the uniting of bones.
3. Prevents gum and mouth infection.

Vitamin C is water soluble and can be lost during cooking or soaking in water. It is also lost by bad storage (keeping foods for too long, bruising, or storing in a badly ventilated place) and by cutting vegetables into small pieces.

Some Foods in which Vitamin C is found

Blackcurrants	Watercress	Sprouts and other greens
Strawberries	Lemons	Oranges
Grapefruit	Tomatoes	

MINERAL ELEMENTS

There are nineteen mineral elements, most of which are required by the body in very small quantities. The body has at certain times a greater demand for certain mineral elements and there is a danger then of a deficiency in the diet. Calcium, iron and iodine are those most likely to be deficient.

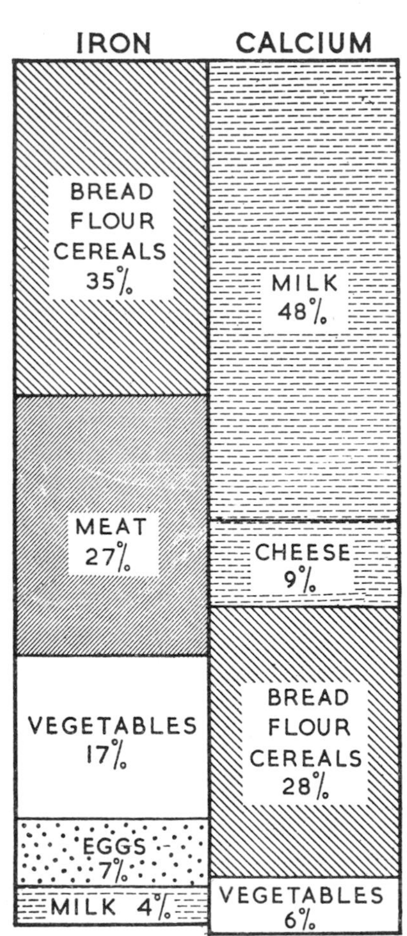

Main supply of iron and calcium in the average diet.

CALCIUM—this is required for:

1. Building bone and teeth.
2. Clotting of the blood.
3. The working of the muscles.

The use the body makes of calcium is dependent on the presence of Vitamin D.

Sources of Calcium

Milk and milk products.
The bones of tinned oily fish.
Wholemeal bread and white bread (to which calcium is added).
Vegetables (greens).
It may also be present in drinking water.

Although calcium is present in certain foods (spinach, cereals) the body is unable to make use of it as it is not in a soluble form and therefore cannot be absorbed.

Owing to extra growth of bones and teeth, infants, adolescents, expectant and nursing mothers have a greater demand for calcium.

PHOSPHORUS—is required for:

1. Building the bone and teeth (in conjunction with calcium and vitamin D).
2. The control of the structure of the brain cells.

Sources of Phosphorus

Liver, kidney.
Eggs, cheese.
Bread, fish.

IRON—is required for building the haemoglobin in blood and is therefore necessary for transporting oxygen and carbon-dioxide round the body.

Sources of Iron

Lean meat, offal.
Egg yolk.
Wholemeal flour.
Green vegetables.
Fish.

It may also be present in drinking water and obtained from iron utensils in which food is prepared.

As the haemoglobin in the blood should be maintained at a constant level, the body requires more iron at certain times than others, after loss of blood, etc.

SODIUM—is required in all body fluids, and is found as salt (sodium chloride). Salt is continually lost from the body in the urine and in sweat.

Sources of Sodium

Many foods are cooked with salt or have salt added (bacon and cheese) or contain salt (meat, eggs, fish).

IODINE—is required for:

The functioning of the thyroid gland which regulates basal metabolism (see page 120).

Sources of Iodine

Sea foods.
Vegetables grown near the sea.
Drinking water obtained near the sea.

Potassium, magnesium, sulphur and copper are some of the other minerals required by the body.

WATER

Water is required for:

1. All body fluids.
2. Digestion.
3. Absorption.
4. Metabolism.
5. Excretion.
6. Secretion.
7. Playing a part in regulation of body temperatures by evaporation of perspiration.

Sources of Water

(*a*) Drinks—beverages.

(*b*) Foods—lettuce; cabbage; apples; potatoes; eggs; beef; bread; cheese; margarine.

(*c*) Combustion or oxidation—when fats, carbohydrates and protein are used for energy a certain amount of water is produced within the body.

THE COOKING OF NUTRIENTS

Protein

When protein is heated it coagulates and shrinks. Too much cooking reduces the nutritive value of the food—for example, scrambled eggs.

Carbohydrate

Unless starch is thoroughly cooked it cannot be digested properly. (For example, insufficiently cooked pastry or bread.) When cooked, the starch granules swell, burst and then the starch can be digested.

Fat

The nutritive value of fat is not affected by cooking. During cooking processes a certain amount of fat may be lost from food as with the grilling of meat, for example.

Mineral Elements

There is a possibility of some minerals being lost in the cooking liquor so diminishing the amount available in the food.

Iron

Iron may be acquired from foods cooked in iron utensils. The ron in foods is not affected by the cooking.

Calcium

Cooking foods in hard water may increase the amount of calcium in food.

Vitamins

Vitamins A and D withstand cooking temperatures, and they are not lost in the cooking.

Vitamin B (Thiamine) can be destroyed by high temperatures and by the use of bicarbonate of soda. It is soluble in water and can be lost in the cooking.

Vitamin C is lost by cooking and by keeping food warm in a hot place. It is also soluble in water (the soaking of foods for a long time and bruising are the causes of losing vitamin C).

FOOD REQUIREMENTS

Energy is required to enable the heart to beat, for the blood to circulate, the lungs and other organs of the body to function, for every activity such as talking, eating, standing, sitting and for strenuous exercise and muscular activity.

Young and active people require a different amount of food from elderly, inactive people because they expend more energy, and this energy is obtained from food during chemical changes taking place in the body.

The energy value of a food is measured by a term called a Calorie (this term is written with a capital C). This is the amount of heat required to raise the temperature of 1000 grammes of water from 15° to 16°C.

Foods contain certain amounts of the various nutrients which are measured in grammes.

The energy value of nutrients is

1 gramme carbohydrates produces 4 calories.
1 gramme protein produces 4 calories.
1 gramme fat produces 9 calories.

The energy or calorific value of a food, diet or menu is calculated from the nutrients it contains; for example, 28 grammes of food containing

10 grammes carbohydrate	will produce	$10 \times 4 = 40$	Calories
2 grammes protein	will produce	$2 \times 4 = 8$	Calories
5 grammes fat	will produce	$5 \times 9 = 45$	Calories
		Total 93	Calories

Foods having a high fat content will have a high Calorie value; those containing a lot of water, a low Calorie value. All fats, cheese, bacon and sugar have a high Calorie value.

Men require more Calories than women, big men and women require more than small men and women, and people engaged on energetic work require more Calories than those with sedentary occupations.

BASAL METABOLISM

Basal metabolism is the term given to the amount of energy required to maintain the functions of the body and to keep the body warm when it is still and without food. The number of Calories required for basal metabolism is affected by the size, sex and general condition of the body. The number of Calories required for basic metabolism is approximately 1700 Calories per day.

In addition to the energy required for basal metabolism, energy is also required for everyday activities, such as getting up, dressing, walking, etc., and the amount required will be closely related to a person's occupation.

The approximate Calorie requirements per day for the following examples are:

Clerk	2000 Calories
Carpenter	3000 Calories
Blacksmith	4000 Calories

The table below indicates the recommended daily allowance of Calories to provide a healthy diet for the categories of people shown.

Age and sex	*Calories*
Boys and Girls:	
0–1 year	1000
2–6 years	1500
7–10 years	2000
Boys:	
11–14 years	2750
15–19 years	3500

Men:	
20 + years (for average activity)	3000
Girls:	
11–14 years	2750
15–19 years	2500
Women:	
20 + years (for average activity)	2500

VALUE OF FOODS IN THE DIET

MILK

Cows' milk is almost the perfect food for human beings; it contains protein, carbohydrate, fat, minerals, vitamins and water.

When milk is taken into the body it coagulates in the same way as in the making of junket. This occurs in the stomach when digestive juices (rennin) are added. Souring of milk is due to the lactic acid in milk which brings about curdling.

Composition of Milk

Approximately	87%	water
	3–4%	protein
	3–4%	fat
	4–5%	sugar
	·7%	minerals (particularly calcium)
	Vitamins A, B and D	

(There are legal minimum requirements for the various grades of milk.)

Milk, therefore, is a body-building food because of its protein, an energy food because of the fat and sugar, and a protective food as it contains vitamins and minerals. Owing to the large amount of water, whilst it is a suitable food for babies, it is too bulky to be the main source of protein and other nutrients, after the first few months of life. It is also deficient in iron and vitamin C.

However, it should be included in everyone's diet as a drink and it may be used in a variety of ways.

CREAM

This is the fat of milk and the minimum fat content of single cream is approximately 18%, for double cream 48% and clotted cream 60%.

It is therefore an energy-producing food which also supplies vitamins A and D. It is easily digested because of the small globules of fat.

BUTTER

Butter is made from the fat of milk and contains vitamins A and D, the amount depending on the season. Like cream it is easily digested.

Composition of Butter

Approximately 85% fat
13% water
1% salt
Vitamins A and D

Butter is also an energy-producing food and a protective food in so far as it provides vitamins A and D.

MARGARINE

Margarine which is made from vegetable and animal oils has vitamins A and D added to it. The composition and food value of margarine are similar to butter.

CHEESE

Cheese is made from milk, the composition varying according to whether the cheese has been made from whole milk, skimmed milk or milk to which extra cream has been added.

The food value of cheese is exceptional because of the concentration of the various nutrients it contains. The minerals in cheese are useful, particularly the calcium and phosphorus. Cheese is also a source of vitamins A and D.

It is a body-building, energy-producing and protective food because of its protein, fat and mineral elements and vitamin content.

Cheese is easily digested, provided it is eaten with starchy foods and eaten in small pieces as when grated. The composition of Cheddar cheese is: 25% protein; 35% fat; 30% water; also calcium and iron.

MEAT, POULTRY AND GAME

Meat consists of fibres which may be short, as in a fillet of beef, or long as in the silverside of beef. The shorter the fibre the more tender and easily digested the meat. Meat is carved across the grain to assist mastication and digestion of the fibres.

Hanging of meat helps to make the flesh of meat more tender; this is because acids develop and soften the muscle fibres. Marinading in wine or vinegar prior to cooking also helps to tenderise meat so that it is more digestible.

Expensive cuts of meat are not necessarily more nourishing than the cheaper cuts.

Meat contains protein, variable amounts of fat, water, also calcium, iron, vitamin A and thiamine. It is therefore an important body building food. (Bacon is particularly valuable because of its thiamine.)

Liver and kidney are also protein foods. They contain less fat than most meats, but are a good source of iron and vitamin A.

Sweetbreads are protein foods, particularly valuable to invalids because they are easily digested.

Tripe in addition to its protein is a good source of calcium as it is treated with lime during its preparation. It is also easily digested.

FISH

Fish is as useful a source of animal protein as meat.

The amount of fat in different fish varies: oily fish contain 5–18%, white fish less than 2%.

When the bones are eaten calcium is obtained from fish (tinned sardines or salmon).

Oily fish is not so easily digested as white fish because of the fat, shellfish is not easily digested because of the coarseness of the fibres.

Fish is important for body building, and certain types (oily fish) are energy producing and protective because of the fat and vitamins A and D.

EGGS

Egg white contains protein known as egg albumin and the amount of white is approximately twice the amount of the yolk.

The yolk is more complex; it contains more protein than the white, also fat, vitamins A and D, thiamine, riboflavin, calcium, iron, sulphur and phosphorus.

Composition of Eggs (approximate)

	Whole egg	*White*	*Yolk*
Water	73%	87%	47%
Protein	12%	10%	15%
Fat	11%		33%
Minerals	1%	·5%	2%
Vitamins			

Because of the protein, vitamins, mineral elements and fat, eggs are body-building, protective and energy-producing food.

FRUIT

The composition of different fruit varies considerably; for example, avocado pears contain a large amount of fat, whereas most other fruits contain none. In unripe fruit the carbohydrate is in the form of starch which changes to sugar as the fruit ripens.

The cellulose in fruits acts as roughage.

Fruit is valuable because of the vitamins and minerals it contains. Vitamin C is present in certain fruits, particularly citrus varieties (oranges, grapefruit) and blackcurrants and other summer fruits. Dried fruits such as raisins and sultanas are a useful source of energy because of their sugar content.

Composition of Fruit

Approximately:	Water	85%
	Carbohydrate	5–10%
	Cellulose	2–5%
	Minerals	·5%
	Vitamin C	

Very small amounts of fat and protein are found in most fruits.

Fruit is a protective food because of its minerals and vitamins.

NUTS

Nuts are highly nutritious because of their protein, fat and minerals. Vegetarians rely on nuts to provide the protein in their diet.

Nuts are not easily digested because of their fat content and cellulose.

VEGETABLES

Green Vegetables

Green vegetables are particularly valuable because of their vitamins and minerals; they are therefore protective foods. The most important minerals they contain are iron and calcium. Green vegetables are rich in carotene which is made into vitamin A in the body.

The greener the vegetable the greater its nutritional value. Vegetables which are stored for long periods or are damaged or bruised, quickly lose their value, therefore they should be used as quickly as possible.

Green vegetables also act as roughage in the intestines.

Root Vegetables

Compared with green vegetables most root vegetables contain starch and sugar; they are therefore a source of energy. Swedes and turnips contain a little vitamin C and carrots, and other yellow-coloured vegetables contain carotene which is changed into vitamin A in the body.

Potatoes

Potatoes contain a large amount of starch and a small amount of protein just under the skin. Because of the large quantities eaten, the small amount of vitamin C they contain is of value in the diet.

Onions

The onion is used extensively and contains some sugar, but its main value is to provide flavour.

Peas and Broad Beans

These vegetables contain carbohydrate, protein and carotene.

CEREALS

Cereals contain from 60 to 80% carbohydrate in the form of starch and are therefore energy foods. They also contain 7–13% protein, depending on the type of cereal, and 1–8% fat.

The vitamin B content is considerable in stone ground and whole meal flour.

Oats are the most useful of the cereals as they have the highest food value because of their fat and protein.

SUGAR

There are several kinds of sugar, such as those found in fruit (glucose), milk (lactose), cane and beet sugar (sucrose).

Sugar, with fat, provides the most important part of the body's energy requirements.

Saccharine although sweet is chemically produced and has no food value.

LIQUIDS

Water

Certain waters contain mineral salts; for example, hard waters contain soluble salts of calcium. Some spas are known for the mineral salts contained in the local water.

Artificial Mineral Waters

These consist of sweetened water flavoured with acid.

Tea and Coffee

These drinks have no food value, but they do act on the nervous system as a stimulant.

Cocoa

Cocoa contains some fat, starch and protein, also some vitamin B and mineral elements.

Because tea, coffee and cocoa are usually served with milk and sugar they do have some food value.

BALANCED DIET

A balanced diet provides adequate amounts of the various nutrients for energy, growth, repair and regulation of body processes.

As a guide to a nutritionally satisfactory diet these points should be observed:

Milk—½ litre (one pint) daily (more for children).
Meat, fish, poultry—once a day.
Eggs, cheese, pulses—daily.
Fruit—once a day (preferably citrus fruit).
Vegetables—daily, as well as potatoes.
Fats (butter or margarine)—daily.
Cereals (wholemeal bread or oatmeal)—daily.
Sugar—daily.
Water—1½ litres liquid daily, some in the form of water.

In the compiling of a balanced diet the *protective foods* are considered first:

1. *Dairy produce* (including eggs) to provide calcium, vitamins and iron (from eggs), amongst other things.
2. *Fresh fruit and vegetables* for calcium, iron, vitamin C and some vitamin A.
3. *Whole grain cereals* for vitamin B.
4. *Oily fish and liver* for vitamins A and D and iodine.

Next, the *body-building foods* are considered:
Meat (including bacon, fish, poultry, game and pulses).

Finally, the *energy-producing foods* are added:

Fats, sugar and starchy foods.

Provided the protective and body-building foods are well represented in the diet the appetite can normally be left to determined the energy-producing food requirements.

RECOMMENDED BOOKS

Mottram, *Human Nutrition* (Arnold).
Manual of Nutrition (H.M. Stationery Office).
Hildreth, *Elementary Science of Food* (Allman).
Kilgour, *Science for Catering Students* (Heinemann).

FOODS CONTAINING THE VARIOUS NUTRIENTS AND THEIR USE IN THE BODY

Name	*Food in which it is found*	*Use in body*
Protein	Meat, fish, poultry, game, milk, cheese, eggs, pulses, cereals	For building and repairing body tissues. Some heat and energy
Fat	Butter, margarine, cooking-fat, oils, cheese, fat meat, oily fish	Provides heat and energy
Carbohydrate	Flour, flour products and cereals, sugar, syrup, jam, honey, fruit, vegetables	Provides heat and energy
Vitamin A	Oily fish, fish-liver oil, dairy foods, carrots, tomatoes, greens	Helps growth. Resistance to disease
Vitamin B—Thiamine	Yeast, pulses, liver, whole grain cereals, meat and yeast extracts	Helps growth. Strengthens nervous system
Vitamin B_2—Riboflavin	Yeast, liver, meat, meat extracts, whole grain cereals	Helps growth, and helps in the production of energy
—Nicotinic acid (Niacin)	Yeast, meat, liver, meat extracts, whole grain cereals	Helps growth
Vitamin C—Ascorbic acid	Fruits such as strawberries, citrus fruits, green vegetables, root vegetables, salad vegetables, potatoes	Helps growth, promotes health

FOODS CONTAINING THE VARIOUS NUTRIENTS AND THEIR USE IN THE BODY—*continued*

Name	*Food in which it is found*	*Use in body*
Vitamin D—Sunshine vitamin	Fish-liver oils, oily fish, dairy foods	Helps growth. Builds bones and teeth
Iron	Lean meat, offal, egg yolk, wholemeal flour, green vegetables, fish	Building up of the blood
Calcium (lime)	Milk and milk products, bones of fish, wholemeal bread	Building bones and teeth, clotting the blood, the working of the muscles
Phosphorus	Liver and kidney, eggs, cheese, bread	Building bones and teeth, regulating body processes
Sodium (salt)	Meat, eggs, fish, bacon, cheese	Prevention of muscular cramp

8. Commodities

	PAGE		PAGE
1. Meat	129	15. Yeast	212
2. Offal	140	16. Sugar	214
3. Poultry	145	17. Cocoa	215
4. Game	149	18. Coffee	216
5. Fish	153	19. Tea	218
6. Vegetables	168	20. Pulses	219
7. Fruits	177	21. Herbs	220
8. Nuts	185	22. Spices	222
9. Eggs	187	23. Condiments	225
10. Milk	191	24. Colours	228
11. Fats and Oils	194	25. Essences	229
12. Cheese	198	26. Grocery and Delicatessen Goods	229
13. Cereals	204	27. Confectionery Goods	235
14. Baking Powder	211		

Owing to price fluctuations, and lack of information on metric purchasing units, we have left vacant spaces for commodity prices and sizes. It is hoped that the completion of these spaces will be a useful exercise for students.

MEAT

Cattle, sheep and pigs are reared for fresh meat and certain pigs are specifically produced for bacon. The animals are humanely killed and prepared in hygienic conditions, the skins or hides are removed, the innards are taken out of the carcass and the offal is put aside. The carcasses of beef are split into two sides and those of lambs, sheep, pigs and calves are left whole: they are then chilled in a cold room before being sent to market.

Butchers' meat *La Viande*

	French	*Purchasing unit*	*Wholesale cost Home-killed*	*Imported*	*Season Home-killed*
Lamb	l'Agneau	Carcass or joint			April–May
Mutton	le Mouton	Carcass or joint			All year round
Veal	le Veau	Carcass, side or joint			Summer
Beef	le Bœuf	Side, quarter or joint			All year round
Pork	le Porc	Carcass, side or joint			September–April

Main sources of supply

Lamb and mutton: England, Scotland, New Zealand, Australia and Argentine.

Beef: England, Scotland and Argentine.

Veal: England, Scotland and Holland.

Bacon: England and Denmark.

STORAGE

FRESH MEAT

1. Fresh meat must be hung to allow it to become tender.
2. The time for hanging depends on the temperature of the cold store. The lower the temperature, the longer it can be hung.
3. The time for hanging at 1°C would be up to fourteen days.
4. Meat should be suspended on hooks.

BACON

1. This is kept in a well-ventilated cold room.
2. Joints of bacon should be wrapped in muslin and hung, preferably in a cold room.
3. Sides of bacon are also hung on hooks.
4. Cut bacon is kept on trays in the refrigerator or cold room.

QUALITY

BEEF

1. Lean meat should be bright red, with small flecks of white fat (marbled).
2. The fat should be firm, brittle in texture, creamy white in colour and odourless.
3. Home killed beef is best.
4. Argentine beef is very good.

VEAL

1. The flesh should be pale pink, firm, not soft or flabby.
2. Cut surfaces must not be dry, but moist.
3. Bones in young animals should be pinkish white, porous and with a small amount of blood in their structure.
4. The fat should be firm and pinkish white.
5. The kidney ought to be firm and well covered with fat.

LAMB AND MUTTON

1. Lamb is under one year old—after one year it is termed mutton.
2. The carcass should be compact and evenly fleshed.
3. The lean flesh ought to be firm and of a pleasing dull red colour and of a fine texture or grain.

4. The fat should be evenly distributed, hard, brittle, flaky and clear white in colour.
5. The bones should be porous in young animals.

PORK

1. Lean flesh should be pale pink.
2. The fat should be white, firm, smooth and not excessive.
3. Bones must be small, fine and pinkish.
4. The skin, or rind, ought to be smooth.

BACON

1. There should be no sign of stickiness.
2. There must be no unpleasant smell.
3. The rind should be thin, smooth and free from wrinkles.
4. The fat ought to be white, smooth and not excessive in proportion to the lean.
5. The lean should be deep pink in colour and firm.

FOOD VALUE

Meat, having a high protein content, is valuable for the growth and repair of the body and as a source of energy.

PRESERVATION

SALTING

Meat can be pickled in brine; this method of preserving meat may be applied to silverside, brisket and ox-tongues. Salting is also used in the production of bacon, before the sides of pork are smoked. This also applies to hams.

CHILLING

Meat imported from the Argentine is chilled. This means that it is kept at a temperature just above freezing-point in a controlled atmosphere. Chilled meat cannot be kept in the usual type of cold room for more than a few days, and this is sufficient time for the meat to hang to enable the meat to become tender.

FREEZING

Small carcasses, that is lamb and mutton, can be frozen and the quality is not affected by freezing. They can be kept frozen until required and then thawed out before being used.

Some beef is frozen, but it is inferior in quality to chilled beef.

CANNING

Large quantities of meat are canned and corned beef is of importance since it has a very high protein content. Pork is used for tinned luncheon meat.

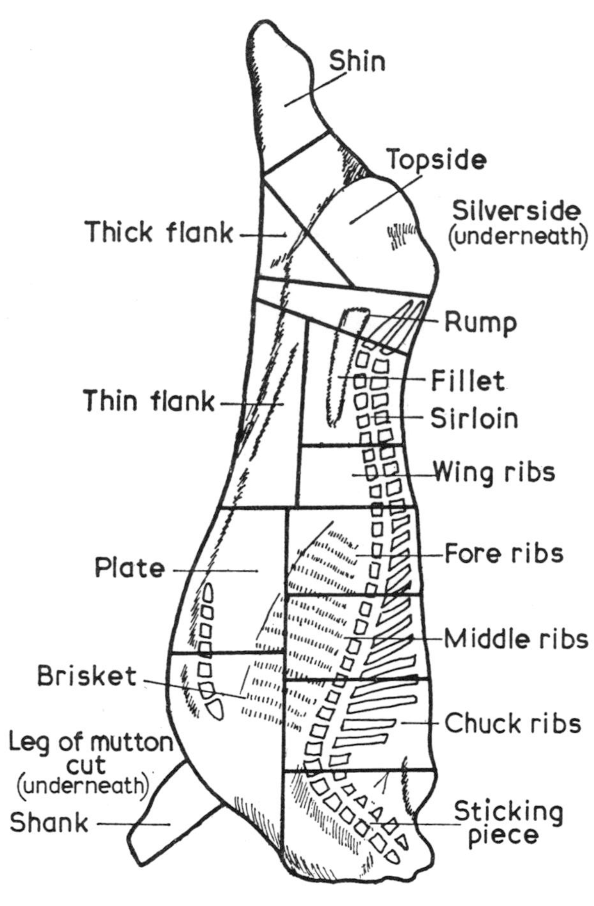
Shin
Topside
Silverside
(underneath)
Thick flank
Rump
Fillet
Thin flank
Sirloin
Wing ribs
Fore ribs
Plate
Middle ribs
Brisket
Chuck ribs
Leg of mutton
cut
(underneath)
Shank
Sticking
piece

Side of beef.

Beef *Bœuf*

Joint	*French*	*Use*	*Menu example*
Hindquarter:			
Shin	la Jambe	Consommé, beef tea, stewing	Consommé Royale
Topside	la Tranche tendre	Braising, stewing, second-class roasting	Bœuf Braisé aux Nouilles
Silverside	la Gite à la noix	Pickled and boiled	Boiled Silverside, Carrots and Dumplings
Thickflank	la Tranche grasse	Braising and stewing	Ragoût de Bœuf aux Légumes
Rump	la Culotte de Bœuf	Grilling and frying as steaks	Grilled Rump Steak
Sirloin	l'Aloyau de Bœuf	Roasting, grilling and frying as steaks	Contrefilet de Bœuf Rôti: Entrecôte Grillé
Wing ribs	la Côte de Bœuf	Roasting, grilling and frying as steaks	Côte de Bœuf Rôti à l'Anglaise
Thin flank	la Bavette	Stewing, boiling, sausages	Bœuf Bouilli à la Française
Fillet	le Filet de bœuf	Roasting, grilling, frying	Tournedos Chasseur, Filet de Bœuf Bouquetière
Forequarter:			
Fore-ribs Middle ribs }	les Côtes	Roasting, braising	Côte de Bœuf Rôti
Chuck ribs	les Côtes du Collier	Stewing, braising	Beef Steak Pie
Sticking piece	la Collier	Stewing, sausages	Sausage Toad in the Hole
Plate and Brisket	la Poitrine	Pickled and boiled	Pressed Beef
Leg of mutton cut	la Tallon du Collier	Braising and stewing	Hachis de Bœuf Duchesse
Shank	la Jambe	Consommé, beef tea	Consommé aux Profiterolles

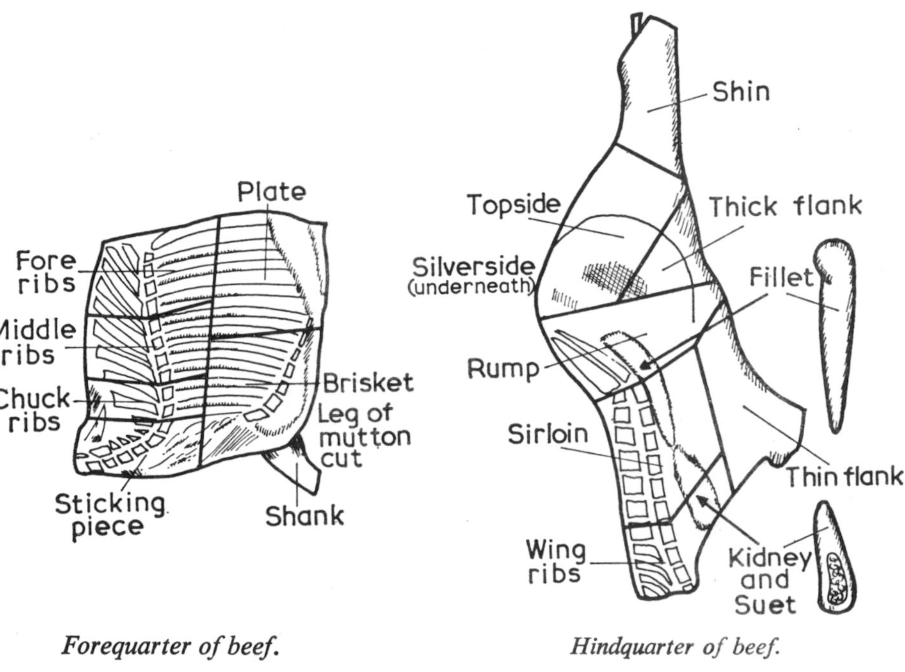

Forequarter of beef.

Hindquarter of beef.

Veal

Joint	*French*	*Use*	*Menu example*
Leg	le Cuissot de Veau	See below*	Cuissot de Veau Rôti
Loin	la Longe de Veau	Roasting, frying, grilling	Côte de Veau Napolitaine
Best-end	le Carré de Veau	Roasting, frying, grilling	Côte de Veau Milanaise
Shoulder	l'Épaule de Veau	Braising, stewing	Goulash de Veau à l'Hongroise
Neck-end	le Cou de Veau	Stewing	Fricassée de Veau à l'Ancienne
Scrag	le Cou de Veau	Stock, stewing	Stock
Breast	la Poitrine de Veau	Stewing, roasting	Blanquette de Veau aux Nouilles
*Leg of Veal:**			
Knuckle	le Jarret de Veau	Stewing	Osso Buco
Cushion	la Noix de Veau	Escalopes, roasting, sauté, braising	Noix de Veau Braisé Belle Hélène
Under cushion	la Sous noix	Escalopes, roasting, sauté, braising	Escalope de Veau Viennoise
Thick flank	le Quasi	Escalopes, roasting, sauté, braising	Sauté de Veau Marengo

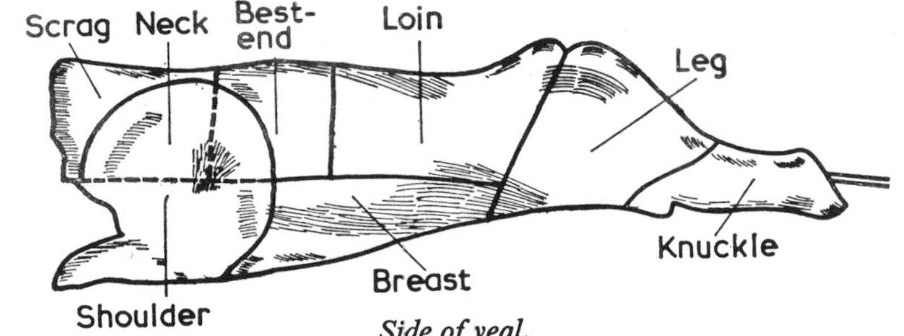

Side of veal.

Lamb and Mutton

L'Agneau et Mouton

Joint	*French*	*Use*	*Menu example*
Shoulder	l'Épaule d'Agneau ou de Mouton	Roasting, stewing	Épaule d'Agneau Boulangère
Leg	le Gigot d'Agneau	Roasting. (Mutton—boiled)	Gigot d'Agneau Rôti; Sauce Menthe. Gigot de Mouton Bouilli. Sauce aux Câpres
Breast	la Poitrine	Stewing, roasting	Irish Stew
Middle neck	le Cou	Stewing	Navarin d'Agneau Printanier
Scrag end	le Cou	Broth	Mutton Broth
Best end	le Carré d'Agneau	Roasting, grilling, frying	Carré d'Agneau Persillé
Saddle	la Selle d'Agneau	Roasting, grilling, frying	Selle d'Agneau Niçoise
Loin	la Longe d'Agneau	Roasting, grilling, frying	Longe d'Agneau Farci
Chop	Chop d'Agneau	Grilling, frying	Grilled Loin Chop
Cutlet	la Côtelette d'Agneau	Grilling, frying	Côtelette d'Agneau Réforme
Fillet	le Filet mignon	Grilling, frying	Filet Mignon Fleuriste

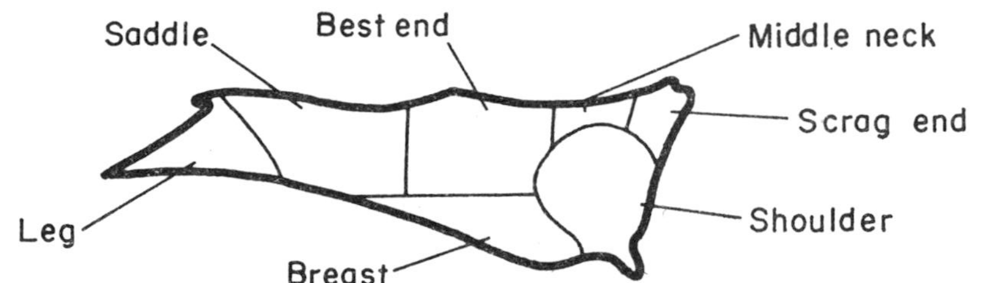

Pork *le porc*

Joint	*French*	*Use*	*Menu example*
Leg	le Cuissot de Porc	Roasting, boiling	Cuissot de Porc Rôti, Sauce Pommes
Loin	la Longe de Porc	Roasting, frying, grilling	Longe de Porc Rôti; Côte de Porc à la Flamande
Spare rib	la Basse Côte	Roasting, pies	Pork Pie
Belly	la Poitrine	Pickling, boiling	Boiled Belly of Pork and Pease Pudding
Shoulder	l'Épaule de Porc	Roasting, sausages, pies	Saucisse de Porc Grillé, Sauce Charcutière

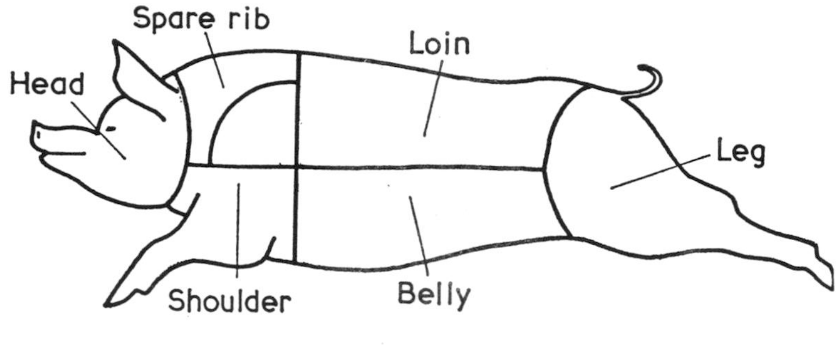

Side of pork.

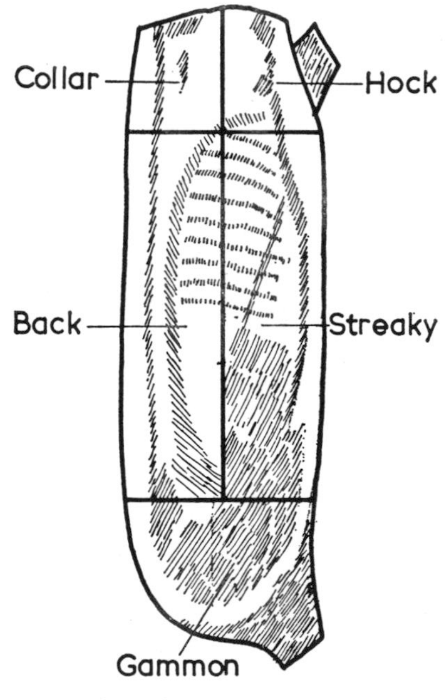

Side of bacon.

Bacon

Lard

Joint	*Use*	*Menu example*
Collar	Boiling, grilling	Boiled Bacon, Pease Pudding and Parsley Sauce
Hock	Boiling, grilling	
Back	Grilling, frying	Œuf au Lard
Streaky	Grilling, frying	Canapé Diane
Gammon	Boiling, grilling, frying	Jambon Braisé au Madère Jambon Grillé, Sauce Diable

Further information can be obtained from The Bacon Information Council, Williams House, Eastbourne Terrace, London, W.2.

OFFAL

and other edible parts of the Carcass

Offal is the name given to the edible parts taken from the inside of the carcass: liver, kidney, heart, sweetbread.

Tripe, brains, oxtail, tongue and head are sometimes included under this term.

Liver *Le Foie*

English	*French*	*Purchasing unit*	*Cost Wholesale*	*Retail*	*Use*	*Menu example*
Calf's liver	le Foie de Veau				Frying	Foie de Veau au Lard
Lamb's liver	le Foie d'Agneau				Frying	Brochette de Foie d'ag-neau
Pig's liver	le Foie de Porc				Frying, pâté	Pâté de Foie
Ox liver	le Foie de Bœuf				Braising, frying	Foie de Bœuf Lyonnaise

Quality

1. Liver should appear fresh and have an attractive colour.
2. It must not be dry or contain tubers in the flesh.
3. It should be smooth in texture.
4. The smell must be pleasant.

Food Value

Liver is valuable as a protective food; it consists chiefly of protein and contains useful amounts of vitamin A and iron.

Kidney

Le Rognon

English	*French*	*Purchasing unit*	*Cost*		*Use*	*Menu example*
			Wholesale	*Retail*		
Calf's kidney	le Rognon de Veau				Stewing (pies, puddings)	Steak and Kidney Pudding
Lamb's kidney	le Rognon d'Agneau				Grilling, sauté	Rognons Sautés Turbigo
Pig's kidney	le Rognon de Porc				Grilling, sauté	Rognon de Porc Grillé
Ox kidney	le Rognon de Bœuf				Stewing, soup	Soupe aux Rognons

Quality

Ox Kidney:

1. Ox kidney should be fresh.
2. The suet is left on the kidney until it is to be prepared for cooking.
3. If the suet is removed the kidney does not remain moist.
4. The colour should be deep red.

Lamb's Kidney:

1. Lamb's kidney should be covered in fat, which is removed just before use.
2. The fat should be crisp and the kidney moist.
3. Both the fat and kidney must have a pleasant smell.

Food Value

The food value of kidney is similar to liver: it is a protective food containing vitamin A and iron.

Hearts *Le cœur*

English	*French*	*Purchasing unit*	*Cost Wholesale*	*Cost Retail*	*Use*	*Menu example*
Sheep's heart	le Cœur d'Agneau				Braising	Cœur d'Agneau Farci
Ox heart	le Cœur de Bœuf				Braising	Cœur de Bœuf Braisé

Quality

Hearts should not have an excessive amount of fat or tubes. When cut they should be moist.

Food Value

They have a high protein content and are therefore valuable for growth and repair of the body.

Tongues *La Langue*

English	*French*	*Purchasing unit*	*Cost Wholesale*	*Cost Retail*	*Use*	*Menu example*
Lamb's tongue	la Langue d'Agneau				Boiling, braising	Langue d'Agneau Poulette
Ox-tongue	la Langue de Bœuf				Boiling, braising	Langue de Bœuf Braisée au Madère

Quality

1. Tongues must be fresh.
2. They should not have an excessive amount of waste at the root-end.
3. They must smell pleasant.
4. Ox-tongues may be used fresh or salted.
5. Sheep's tongues are used unsalted.

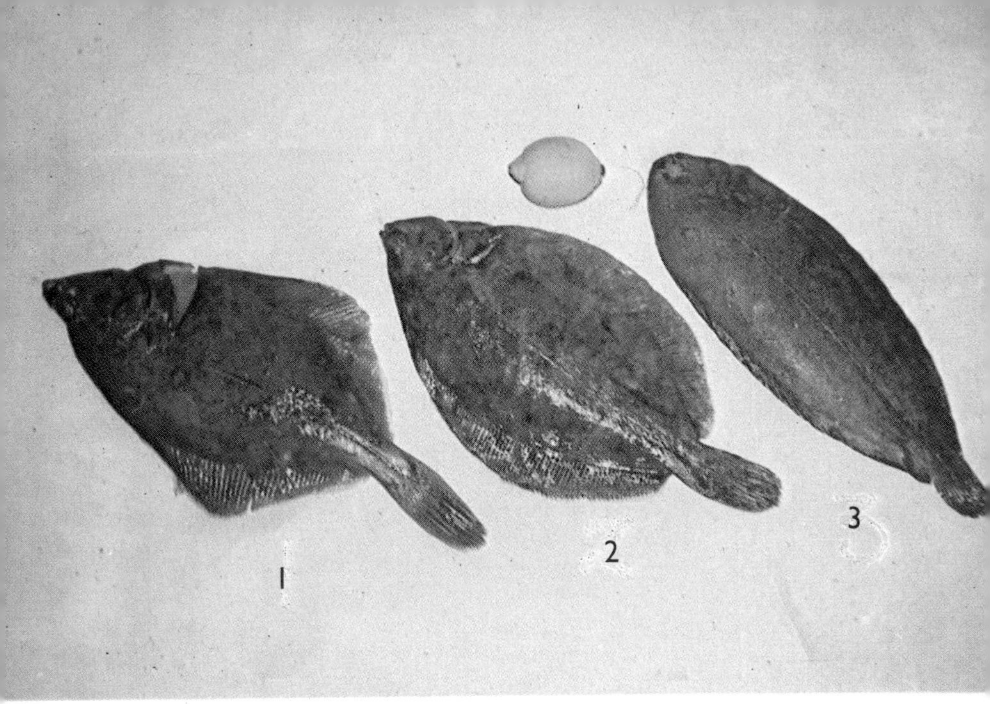

Plate 3. Flat Fish. 1. Plaice 2. Lemon Sole. 3. Dover Sole.

Plate 4. Flat Fish. 1. Halibut. 2. Turbot. 3. Brill.

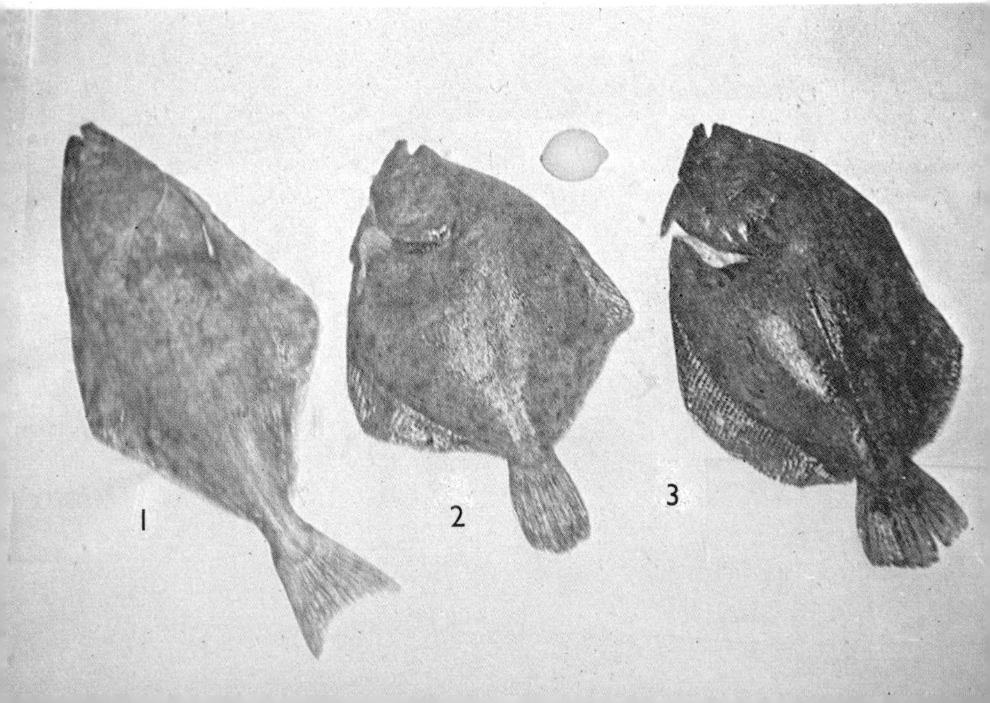

Sweetbreads

Le Ris

English	*French*	*Purchasing unit*	*Cost Wholesale*	*Cost Retail*	*Use*	*Menu example*
Lamb's sweetbread	le Ris d'Agneau				Braising, frying	Ris d'Agneau Braisé Clamart
Calf's sweetbread	le Ris de Veau				Braising, frying	Ris de Veau Bonne-Maman

Quality

1. The thymus (throat) and the pancreas (stomach) sweetbreads should be fleshy and large.
2. They ought to be creamy white in colour.
3. They must have a pleasant smell.
4. The pancreas (heart-shaped) sweetbreads are superior in quality to the thymus sweetbreads.

Food Value

Both throat and stomach sweetbreads are valuable as foods, particularly for hospital diets. They are very easily digested and useful for building and repairing body tissues.

Tripe *La Tripe*

Tripe is the stomach lining of the ox which is cleaned thoroughly. It may be boiled or braised.

Menu example: Tripe and Onions

Oxtail *La Queue de Bœuf*

Oxtails should be of good size and lean with no signs of stickiness. They are usually braised or used for soup.

Menu examples: Queue de Bœuf Braisée au Primeurs
Queue de Bœuf Liée

Head *La Tête*

Sheeps' heads can be used for stock, and pigs' heads for brawn. The calfs' head is used for soup and certain dishes such as Tête de Veau Vinaigrette.

Heads should not be sticky; they should be well fleshed and odourless.

Suet *La Graisse de Rognon*

Beef suet should be creamy white, brittle and dry. It is used for suet paste. Other fat should be fresh and not sticky. Suet and fat may be rendered down for dripping.

Marrow *La Moëlle*

Beef marrow is obtained from the bones of the leg of beef. It should be of good size, firm, creamy white and odourless. It is used as a garnish as with Entrecôte Bordelaise and for savouries.

Menu example: Croûte Baron

Brains *La Cervelle*

Calfs' brains are those usually used; they must be fresh.

Menu example: Cervelle au Beurre Noir

Bones *Les Os*

These must be fresh, not sticky, and they are used for stock.

POULTRY *LA VOLAILLE*

Poultry is the name given to domestic birds specially bred to be eaten.

TYPES OF POULTRY

English	*French*	*Undrawn weight (approx.)*	*Number of portions (approx.)*	*Cost* *Wholesale*	*Cost* *Retail*	*Season*	*At best*
Single baby chicken (Spring chicken)	le Poussin	360 g – $\frac{1}{2}$ kg	1			Spring	
Double baby chicken	le Poussin Double	$\frac{1}{2}$ kg– $\frac{3}{4}$ kg	2			Spring	
Small roasting chicken	le Poulet de Grain	$\frac{3}{4}$ kg– 1 kg	3–4			Spring and early summer	
Medium roasting chicken	le Poulet Reine	1 kg– 2 kg	4–6			Spring, summer	
Large roasting or boiling chicken	la Poularde	2 kg– 3 kg	6–8			All year round	Autumn
Capon	le Chapon	3 kg–4$\frac{1}{2}$ kg	8–12			All year round	Autumn
Boiling fowl	la Poule	2$\frac{1}{2}$ kg– 4 kg	8–10			All year round	
Young turkey	le Dindonneau	3$\frac{1}{2}$ kg	* *			September	
Turkey	la Dinde	3–$\frac{1}{2}$ kg–20 kg	* *			Sept.–Mar.	Winter
Duckling	le Caneton	1 kg–1$\frac{1}{2}$ kg	3–4			Mar.–Sept.	Summer
Duck	le Canard	1$\frac{1}{2}$ kg–2$\frac{1}{2}$ kg	4–6			Aug.–Feb.	Autumn
Gosling	l'Oison	2 kg–3$\frac{1}{2}$ kg	* *			Aug.–Oct.	Summer
Goose	l'Oie	3$\frac{1}{2}$ kg– 7 kg	* *			Sept.–Feb.	Autumn
Guinea fowl	la Pintarde	1–1$\frac{1}{2}$ kg	3–4			All year round	Summer
Pigeon	le Pigeon		1–2			All year round	Spring

Drawn poultry loses approximately 25% of its original weight.
All poultry is bought by number and weight.
* * For turkey and goose allow $\frac{1}{4}$ kg undrawn weight per portion.

SEASON

Owing to present-day methods of poultry production by the battery method, and to deep freezing, poultry is available all the year round.

FOOD VALUE

The flesh of poultry is more easily digested than that of butchers' meat. It contains protein and is therefore useful for building and repairing body tissues and providing heat and energy.

STORAGE

Fresh poultry must be hung by the legs in a well-ventilated room for at least 24 hours, otherwise it will not be tender.

The innards are not removed until the bird is required.

Frozen birds must be kept in a deep-freeze cabinet until required; they are then allowed to thaw out before cooking.

QUALITY

1. The breast of the bird should be plump.
2. The vent-end of the breast-bone must be pliable.
3. The flesh should be firm.
4. The skin to be white, unbroken and with a faint bluish tinge.
5. The legs should be smooth, with small scales and small spurs.
6. Old birds have large scales and large spurs on the legs.

USE

Baby Chicken (Spring Chicken) *Le Poussin*

Spring chickens are from 4–6 weeks old; they may be roasted, pot-roasted or grilled.

Menu examples: Poussin Polonaise
Poussin Grillé au Lard

Small Roasting Chicken *Le Poulet de Grain*

These 3–4-month-old birds are roasted, pot-roasted or grilled.

Menu examples: Poulet Rôti à l'Anglaise
Poulet de Grain Grillé à l'Américaine

Medium Roasting Chicken (Broiler) *Le Poulet Reine*

These are prime tender chickens, they are used for sautés, pies, suprêmes, roasting, grilling and pot-roasting. They are also referred to as broilers which is an American term. To broil means to grill.

Menu examples: Chicken Pie
Poulet Sauté Parmentier
Suprême de Volaille Princesse
Poulet en Casserole Bonne-Femme

Large Roasting or Boiling Bird *La Poularde*

These are the fully grown birds which are roasted, pot-roasted and boiled. They are also used for sandwiches, salads and bouchées.

Menu examples: Galantine de Volaille
Vol-au-Vent de Volaille
Poularde Pochée au Riz, Sauce Suprême
Poularde Poêlé aux Champignons
Poularde en Chaud-froid

Capon *Le Chapon*

A capon is a castrated or caponised bird specially fattened for roasting.

Menu example: Roast Surrey Capon

Boiling Fowl *La Poule*

This is an old hen suitable for stocks, and soups.

Menu examples: Crème Reine
Sauce Suprême
Consommé de Volaille
Cockie-leekie

Duckling *Le Caneton*
Duck *Le Canard*
Gosling *L'Oison*
Goose *L'Oie*

QUALITY

1. The feet and bills should be bright yellow.
2. The upper bill should break easily.
3. The web feet must be easy to tear.

USE

Ducks and geese may be roasted or braised.

Menu examples: Roast Aylesbury Duckling
Caneton à l'Orange
Canard Braisé aux Petits Pois
Roast Goose, Sage and Onion Stuffing
Oison Braisé aux Navets

Turkey[1] *Le Dindonneau*
La Dinde

QUALITY

1. The breast should be large, the skin undamaged and with no signs of stickiness.

USE

These birds are usually roasted.

Menu examples: Roast Norfolk Turkey and Chestnut Stuffing
Dindonneau Rôti, Sauce Airelles
Emincé de Dinde à la King
Turkey Sandwich

Guinea Fowl *Le Pintarde*

When plucked these grey-and-white feathered birds resemble a chicken with darker flesh.

The points relating to chicken apply to guinea fowl.

Menu examples: Pintarde en Cocotte Grande-Mère
Pintarde Rôti

Pigeon *Le Pigeon*

Pigeon should be plump, the flesh mauve-red in colour and the claws pinkish. Tame pigeons are smaller than woodpigeons.

Menu examples: Pigeon Pie
Pigeon Braisé aux Olives

[1] Further information: British Turkey Federation, The Bury, Church Street, Chesham, Bucks.

GAME *LE GIBIER*

Game is the name given to certain wild birds and animals which are eaten; they are usually termed feathered game and furred game.

GAME

English	*French*	*Weight (approx.)*	*Number of portions (approx.)*	*Cost* *Wholesale*	*Cost* *Retail*	*Season*	*At best*
Furred:							
Venison	la Venaison	15 kg	15–20			July–Feb.	Autumn
Hare	le Lièvre	$2\frac{1}{2}$–$3\frac{1}{2}$ kg	6–8			Aug.–Feb.	Winter
Rabbit	le Lapin	1 kg	4			Sept.–April	Winter
Feathered:							
Pheasant	le Faisan	$1\frac{1}{2}$–2 kg	4			Oct. 1–Feb. 11	Winter
Partridge	le Perdreau	$\frac{1}{4}$– $\frac{1}{2}$ kg	1–2			Sept. 1–Feb. 11	Autumn
Grouse	la Grouse	360 grammes	1–2			Aug. 12–Dec. 20	Sept.
Woodcock	la Bécasse	$\frac{1}{4}$ kg–360 grammes	1			Oct.–Nov.	Autumn
Snipe	la Bécassine	120 grammes	1			Oct.–Nov.	Autumn
Plover	le Pluvier	$\frac{1}{4}$ kg	1			Oct.–Dec.	Winter
Quail	la Caille	150 grammes	1			All year round	Autumn
Wild duck	le Canard-sauvage	1 –$1\frac{1}{2}$ kg	2–4			Sept.–Mar.	Winter
Teal	la Sarcelle	$\frac{1}{2}$– $\frac{3}{4}$ kg	1–2			Oct.–Jan.	Winter
Wood pigeon	le Pigeon	360 grammes	1			Mar.–Oct.	Autumn

FOOD VALUE

As game is less fat than poultry or meat it is easily digested. Water fowl are not so easily digested, owing to their oily flesh. Game is useful for building and repairing body tissues and for energy.

STORAGE

1. Game must be hung to enable it to become tender and to develop flavour.
2. The hanging time is determined by the type, condition and age of the game and the storage temperature.
3. Old birds need to hang for a longer time than young birds.
4. Game birds are not plucked or drawn before hanging.
5. Venison and hare are hung with their skins on.
6. Game must be hung in a well-ventilated, dry, cold storeroom; this need not be refrigerated.

QUALITY

Venison

The joints should be well fleshed and a dark brownish-red colour.

Hares and Rabbits

The ears should tear easily. With old hares the hare lip is more pronounced than in young animals.

Birds

1. The beak should break easily.
2. The breast plumage is soft.
3. The breast should be plump.
4. Quill feathers should be pointed, not rounded.
5. The legs should be smooth.

USE

Venison *La Venaison*

This is the flesh of deer. The roebuck (Fr. *chevreuil*) is the deer which is frequently used.

Venison is usually roasted or braised in joints. Small cuts may be fried. Before cooking it is always marinaded to counteract the toughness and dryness of the meat.

Menu examples: Roast Haunch of Venison: Cumberland Sauce
Selle de Chevreuil: Sauce Poivrade

Hare *La Lièvre*

Hare is cooked as a stew called jugged hare (*civet de lièvre*) and the saddle (*rable de lièvre*) is roasted.

Menu examples: Civet de Lièvre Bourguignonne
Rable de Lièvre, Sauce Grand Veneur

Rabbits *Le Lapin*

Tame and wild rabbits are roasted, stewed and used in pies.

Menu examples: Currie de Lapin
Rabbit Pie

Pheasant *Le Faisan*

These birds are hung for 5–8 days. They may be roasted, braised or pot-roasted.

Menu examples: Salmis de Faisan
Faisan Poêlé au Céleri

Partridge *Le Perdreau*

Partridge are usually hung for 3–5 days and then roasted or braised. Red-legged partridge are more suitable for braising.

Menu examples: Perdreau aux Choux
Perdreau Rôti

Grouse *La Grouse*

This popular game bird is served roasted, either hot or cold.

Menu example: Roast Grouse

Woodcock *La Bécasse*
Snipe *La Bécassine*

These are hung for 3–4 days and may be cooked undrawn. They are usually roasted. The head is cleaned and the beak is left on the head and used for trussing.

Menu example: Bécasse Rôtie

Plover *Le Pluvier*

Plovers are cooked undrawn and usually roasted.

Menu example: Pluvier Rôti

Quail *La Caille*

Quail are not hung. They are roasted or braised.

Menu examples: Caille Rôtie
Caille en Aspic

Wild Duck *Canard-Sauvage*

Wild duck are usually roasted or braised.

Menu example: Canard Sauvage Bigarade

Teal *La Sarcelle*

Teal and wild duck must be eaten in season otherwise the flesh is coarse and has a fishy flavour. Teal is a small species of wild duck which is roasted or braised.

Menu example: Sarcelle Rôtie à l'Orange

FISH *LES POISSONS*

TYPES OR VARIETIES

(1) *White Fish*

(*a*) Round (e.g. cod, whiting, hake)
(*b*) Flat (e.g. plaice, sole, turbot)

(2) *Oily Fish*

These are all round in shape (e.g. herring, mackerel, salmon)

(3) *Shellfish*

(*a*) Crustacea (e.g. lobsters, crabs)
(*b*) Mollusca (e.g. oysters, mussels)

Fish	*French*	*Season*	*Purchasing unit*	*Cost per kg*
OILY FISH:				
Anchovy	l'Anchois		60 grammes, 390 gramme tins	
Conger Eel	le Congre	All year round; best, summer	By the kilogramme	
Eel	l'Anguille	All year round	By the kilogramme	
Herring	le Hareng	Oct.–Dec.* May–Aug.	Number and weight	
Mackerel	le Maquereau	Winter, spring and summer	Number and weight	
Salmon	le Saumon	Feb.–Aug.	Number and weight	
Salmon trout	la Truite Saumonée	Mar.–Aug.	Number and weight	
Sprat	le Sprat	Nov.–Mar.	By the kilogramme	
Trout	la Truite	Feb.–Sept.	Number and weight	
Tunny	le Thon		127 grammes, 240 grammes tins	
Sardine	la Sardine		135 grammes, 345 grammes, 795 gramme tins	
Whitebait	la Blanchaille	Feb.–Aug.	By the kilogrammes	
WHITE FISH:				
Flat Fish:				
Brill	la Barbue	All year round	Whole fish by number and weight	
Halibut	le Flétan	July–March	Whole fish by number and weight	

* Season given is for home-fished herring. Norwegian herring available January and February.

Fish	French	Season	Purchasing unit	Cost per kg.
Flat Fish (contd.)				
Plaice	la Plie	All year round; best, May–Jan.	Fillets or number and weight	
Skate	la Raie	Summer, winter and autumn	By the kilogramme	
Sole	la Sole	All year round	Fillets, number and weight	
Turbot	le Turbot	All year round	Number and weight	
Round Fish:				
Bream	la Bréme	All year round	Fillets or whole fish by number and weight	
Cod	le Cabillaud	All year round; Sept.–Mar.	Fillets or whole fish or weight	
Haddock	l'Aigrefin	All year round	Fillets or whole fish, by number or weight	
Hake	le Colin	All year round; best, June to Jan.	Whole fish or by the pound	
Red mullet	le Rouget	July–Oct.	Number and weight	
Smelt	l'Éperlan	Oct.–May	Boxes, or by the kilogramme	
Whiting	le Merlan	All year round; best, May–Jan.	Number and weight	

SEASONS

Supplies of fish are subject to weather conditions and to the fact that shoals of certain fish vary their positions at different times of the year. Therefore the fish which are in season all the year round may not be available everywhere. To remember the fish in season—that is to say, when they are at their best, the following table will be useful.

AVAILABLE ALL THE YEAR ROUND

Bream, cod, plaice, halibut, whiting, brill, haddock, turbot, sole.

SPRING

Eel, mackerel, whitebait, conger eel, salmon.

SUMMER

Eel, herring, salmon, skate, conger eel, mullet, salmon-trout, whitebait.

AUTUMN

Skate.

WINTER

Mackerel, skate, smelt.

PURCHASING UNIT

Fresh fish is bought by the kilogramme or by the number of fillets or whole fish of the weight that is required. For example 30 kg of salmon could be ordered as 2 × 15 kg, 3 × 10 kg or 6 × 5 kg. Frozen fish can be purchased in 15 kg blocks.

SOURCE

As we live on an island, fish is plentiful. Most catches are made off Iceland, Scotland, the North Sea, Irish Sea and the English Channel. Salmon are caught in certain English and Scottish rivers. Frozen fish is imported from Scandinavia, Canada and Japan; the last two countries send frozen salmon to Britain.

STORAGE

1. Fresh fish are stored in a fish-box containing ice, in a separate refrigerator or part of a refrigerator used only for fish.
2. The temperature must be maintained just above freezing-point.
3. Frozen fish must be stored in a deep-freeze cabinet or compartment.
4. Smoked fish should be kept in a refrigerator.

QUALITY POINTS FOR BUYING

When buying fish the following points should be looked for to ensure freshness:

1. Eyes: bright, full and not sunken.
2. Gills: bright red in colour.
3. Flesh: firm and resilient so that when pressed the impression goes quickly. The fish must not be limp.
4. Scales: these should lie flat, be moist and plentiful.
5. Skin: this should be covered with a fresh sea slime.
6. Smell: the smell must be pleasant.

BUYING POINTS

1. Fish should be purchased daily.
2. If possible, it ought to be purchased direct from the market or supplier.

3. The fish should be well iced so that it arrives in good condition.
4. The flesh of the fish should not be damaged.
5. Fish may be bought on the bone or filleted. (The approximate loss from boning and waste is 50% for flat fish, 60% for round fish.)
6. Fillets of plaice and sole can be purchased according to weight. They are graded from 45 g–180 g per fillet and go up in weight by 15 g.
7. Medium-sized fish are usually better than large fish which may be coarse; small fish often lack flavour.

FOOD VALUE

Fish is as useful a source of animal protein as meat. The oily fish such as sardines, mackerel, herrings and salmon contain vitamins A and D in their flesh, but in white fish, such as halibut and cod, these vitamins are present in the liver.

The bones, when eaten, of sardines, whitebait and tinned salmon, provide the body with calcium and phosphorus.

Since all fish contain protein it is a good body-building food and the oily fish is useful for energy and as a protective food because of its vitamins.

Owing to its fat content oily fish is not so digestible as white fish and is not so suitable for invalid cookery.

PRESERVATION

FREEZING

Fish is either frozen at sea or as soon as possible after reaching port. It should be thawed out before being cooked. Plaice, halibut, turbot, haddock, sole, cod, trout, salmon, herring, whiting, scampi, smoked haddock and kippers are frozen.

CANNING

The oily fish are usually used for canning. Sardines, salmon, anchovies, pilchards, herring and herring roe are canned in their own juice, as with salmon, or in oil or tomato sauce.

SALTING

In this country salting is usually accompanied by smoking.

Kippers

The herring is split, gutted, washed and placed in a brine solution for 15–30 minutes. The fish are then impaled on tenterhooks and smoked in a kiln for up to 6 hours. The smoke is produced by very slowly burning wood-shavings and sawdust.

Bloaters

These are salted and lightly smoked whole herring.

Cured Herrings

These are packed in salt and red herrings are salted and then smoked.

Caviar

This is the slightly salted roe of the sturgeon which is sieved, tinned and refrigerated. Imitation caviar is also obtainable.

SMOKING

Haddocks

These are slit open, salted slightly and then smoked.

Salmon

These are filleted and smoked.

Cod Roes, Eel, Sprats, Trout

These are also smoked.

Buckling

These are whole smoked herring.

PICKLING

Herrings

These are pickled in vinegar, either filleted or as rollmops, when they are filleted, rolled and skewered.

USE

Fish is cooked by boiling, poaching, grilling, shallow and deep frying. It may also be baked. Certain fish are not cooked, apart from the smoking or curing process. This applies for example to smoked salmon, smoked eel, smoked trout, and buckling.

OILY FISH

Anchovies *Les Anchois*

Anchovies are small round fish used tinned in this country; they are supplied in 60 g and 390 g tins. They are filleted and packed in oil.

They are used for making anchovy butter and anchovy sauce, for garnishing dishes such as Scotch Woodcock and Escalope de Veau

Viennoise. They may be used as a dish in a selection of hors d'œuvre, as a savoury, and they can be used in puff pastry and served at cocktail parties.

Conger Eel *Le Congre*

This is a dark grey sea-fish with white flesh which grows up to 3 metres in length. It may be used in the same way as eels, or it may be smoked.

Menu example: Anguille Fumée; Sauce Raifort

Eel *L'Anguille*

Eels live in fresh water and grow up to 1 metre in length. They must be kept alive until the last minute before cooking and they are generally used in fish stews.

Menu example: Bouillebaisse; Jellied Eels

Herring *Le Hareng*

Fresh herrings are used for breakfast and lunch menus; they may be grilled, fried or soused. Kippers are served mainly for breakfast and also for a savoury. Average weight, $\frac{1}{4}$ kg.

Menu example: Hareng Grillé, Sauce Moutarde.

Mackerel *Le Maquereau*

Mackerel are grilled, shallow fried or soused, and may be used on breakfast and lunch menus. They must be used fresh. Average weight, 360 grammes.

Menu example: Maquereau Grillé; Beurre d'Anchois

Salmon *Le Saumon*

Scotch salmon is considered to be the best. Salmon is also caught in England, Norway, Canada and Japan. Apart from using it fresh, salmon is tinned or smoked. When fresh, it is usually boiled or grilled. When boiled it is cooked in a court-bouillon. Frequently, whole salmon are cooked and when cold decorated and served on buffets. Weight varies from $3\frac{1}{2}$–15 kg. Salmon under $3\frac{1}{2}$ kg are known as grilse.

Menu examples: Darne de Saumon Pochée; Sauce Hollandaise
Darne de Saumon Grillée; Sauce Verte
Mayonnaise de Saumon

Salmon Trout *La Truite Saumonée*

These are like salmon, but smaller, and they are used in a similar way. Average weight, 1½–2 kg.

Menu example: Truite Saumonée Froide; Sauce Mayonnaise

Sardines *Les Sardines*

These small fish are tinned and used for hors d'œuvre, sandwiches and as a savoury.

Sprats *Le Sprat*

These small fish are fried whole and are also smoked and served as an hors d'œuvre.

Trout *La Truite*

Trout live in rivers and lakes and in this country they are cultivated on trout farms. When served *au bleu*, they must be alive just before cooking; they are then killed, cleaned, sprinkled with vinegar and cooked in a court-bouillon. Trout are also served grilled or shallow fried, and may also be smoked and served as an hors d'œuvre. Average weight, 180–230 grammes.

Menu examples: Truite fumée
Truite de Rivière Grenobloise

Tunny *Le Thon*

This very large fish is cut into sections, tinned in oil and is used mainly in hors d'œuvre and salads.

Whitebait *La Blanchaille*

These are the fry or young of herring, 2 cm–4 cm long, and they are deep fried.

Menu example: Blanchailles Diablées

WHITE FISH

FLAT FISH

Brill *La Barbue*

This is a large flat fish which should not be confused with turbot. Brill is oval in shape; the mottled brown skin is smooth with small scales. It can be distinguished from turbot by lesser breadth in proportion to length. Average weight, 3–4 kg.

It is usually served in the same way as turbot.

Menu examples: Tronçon de Barbue Grillé; Sauce Anchois
Suprême de Barbue Mornay

Halibut *Le Flétan*

This fish can be 3 metres long and weigh 150 kg. Halibut is served on good-class menus as it is valued very highly for its flavour. It is poached, boiled, grilled or shallow fried.

Menu example: Suprême de Flétan Belle Meunière

Plaice *La Plie*

Plaice are used on all types of menus; they are usually deep fried or grilled. Average weight, 360–450 grammes.

Menu example: Plie Grillé; Beurre Maître d'Hôtel

Larger plaice known in French as 'carrelet' are also used for poached, fried and grilled dishes.

Menu example: Filet de Carrelet Dugléré

Skate *La Raie*

Skate is a very large fish and only the wings are used. It is always served on the bone and either shallow or deep fried or cooked in a court-bouillon and served with black butter.

Menu example: Raie au Beurre Noir

Sole *La Sole*

This is considered to be the best of the flat fish. The quality of the Dover sole is well known for its excellence. Other varieties such as lemon sole and the witch are inferior to it.

Soles are cooked by poaching, grilling or frying both shallow and deep. They are served whole or filleted and garnished in a great many ways.

The usual size for soles is 180 g–$\frac{3}{4}$ kg; fillets are taken from sole of 1$\frac{1}{2}$ kg and over. A 180 g–$\frac{1}{4}$ kg sole is referred to as a slip sole. When serving a whole fish a $\frac{1}{4}$ kg, 300 g, 360 g or $\frac{1}{2}$ kg sole may be used, the size depending on the type of establishment and the meal for which it is required.

Menu examples: Sole Colbert
Sole Dieppoise
Filet de Sole Waleska
Paupiette de Sole Newburg

Turbot *Le Turbot*

Turbot has no scales and is roughly diamond in shape; it has knobs known as tubercules on the dark skin. In proportion to its length it is wider than brill. 3$\frac{1}{2}$–4 kg average weight.

It may be cooked whole, filleted or cut into portions on the bone. It may be boiled, poached, grilled or shallow fried.

Menu examples: Turbot Poché; Sauce Hollandaise
Suprême de Turbot Florentine
Tronçon de Turbot Grillé; Beurre Maître d'Hôtel

ROUND FISH

Bream *La Brème*

Sea bream is used on many menus of less expensive price, it is usually filleted and deep fried but other methods of cooking are employed. Average weight, $\frac{1}{2}$–1 kg.

Menu examples: Filet de Brème Frit; Sauce Tartare
Filet de Brème Meunière

Cod *Le Cabillaud*

Cod is mainly used on cheaper menus; it is cut into steaks or it is filleted and then cut into portions, and it can be deep or shallow, fried or boiled. Small cod are known as codling. Average weight of Cod, $2\frac{1}{2}$–$3\frac{1}{2}$ kg.

Menu examples: Darne de Cabillaud Pochée; Sauce Persil
Grilled Cod Steak

Gudgeon *Le Goujon*

These are small fish found in continental lakes and rivers. They may be deep fried whole. On menus in this country the French term '*en goujon*' refers to other fish such as sole or turbot, cut into pieces the size of gudgeon.

Menu example: Filets de Sole en Goujons; Sauce Tartare

Haddock *L'Aigrefin*

Haddock is distinguished from cod by the thumb mark on the side and by the lighter colour. Every method of cooking fish may be applied to haddock, and it appears on all kinds of menus. Apart from fresh haddock, smoked haddock is used a great deal for breakfast: it may also be served for lunch and as a savoury. Average weight, $\frac{1}{2}$–2 kg.

Menu examples: Filet d'aigrefin à l'Orly
Haddock Monté Carlo
Canapé Ivanhoe

Hake *Le Colin*

Owing to overfishing hake is not plentiful. It is easy to digest. The flesh is very white and of a delicate flavour. It is usually boiled.

Menu example: Boiled Hake and Egg Sauce

Red Mullet *Le Rouget*

Red mullet is on occasion cooked with the innards left in, as it is considered that they help to impart a better flavour to the fish. Mullet are usually cooked whole. Average weight, 360 grammes–¾ kg.

Menu examples: Rouget Grenobloise
Rouget en Papillote

Smelt *L'Eperlan*

These small fish are imported from Holland; they are usually deep fried or grilled. When grilled they are split open. 60–90 grammes each in weight.

Menu example: Eperlan Frit à l'Anglaise

Whiting *Le Merlan*

Whiting are very easy to digest and they are therefore suitable for invalid cookery. They may be poached, grilled or deep fried and used in the making of fish stuffing (farce de poisson). Average weight, 360 grammes.

Menu example: Merlan en Colère

SHELLFISH

	French	*Season*	*Purchasing unit*	*Cost per unit*
Shrimp	la Crevette Grise	All year round		
Prawn	la Crevette Rose	All year round		
Dublin Bay Prawn or Scampi	la Langoustine	All year round	Number	
Crayfish	l'Ecrevisse (f.)			
Lobster	le Homard	All year round; best, summer	Number and weight	
Crawfish	la Langouste	Summer	Number and weight	
Crab	le Crabe	All year round; best, summer	Number and weight	
Oysters	les Huîtres	Sept.–April	Dozen	
Mussels	les Moules	Sept.–March		
Scallop	la Coquille St. Jacque	Nov.–March	Number	

SEASONS

AVAILABLE ALL YEAR ROUND

Shrimps, prawns, lobsters, crabs.

SPRING

Oysters, mussels, scallops.

SUMMER

Lobster, crawfish, crab.

AUTUMN

Crab.

WINTER

Crab, oysters, mussels, scallops.

FOOD VALUE

Shellfish is a good body building food. As the flesh is coarse and therefore indigestible a little vinegar is used in the cooking to soften the fibres.

STORAGE

1. With the exception of shrimps and prawns all shellfish, if possible, should be purchased alive, so as to ensure freshness.
2. They should be stored in a cold room.
3. Shellfish are kept in boxes and covered with damp sacks.
4. Shellfish should be cooked as soon as possible after purchasing.

QUALITY, PURCHASING POINTS AND USE

SHRIMPS AND PRAWNS

These are usually bought cooked and may be obtained with the shell on or peeled. They should be freshly boiled, of an even size and not too small. Frozen shrimps and prawns are obtainable in packs ready for use.

Shrimps

Shrimps are used for garnishes, decorating fish dishes, cocktails, sauces, salads, hors d'œuvre, potted shrimps, omelettes and savouries.

Menu examples: Cocktail de Crevettes
Omelette aux Crevettes

Prawns *La Crevette Rose*

These are larger than shrimps, they may be used for garnishing and decorating fish dishes, for cocktails, canapé moscovite, salad, hors d'œuvre and for such hot dishes as curried prawns.

Menu examples: Crevettes Roses
Curried Prawns

Scampi, Dublin Bay Prawn *La Langoustine*

Scampi are found in the Mediterranean and the Dublin Bay Prawn which is the same family are caught around the Scottish coast. These shellfish resemble small lobster about 16 cm long and only the tail part is used.

Crayfish *L'Ecrevisse*

These are a type of small fresh water lobster.

Lobster *Le Homard*

QUALITY AND PURCHASING POINTS

1. Live lobsters are bluish-black in colour and when cooked they turn bright red.
2. They should be alive when bought.
3. Lobsters should have both claws attached.
4. They ought to be fairly heavy in proportion to their size.
5. Price varies considerably with size. For example, small ½ kg lobsters are more expensive per kilogramme than are large lobsters.
6. Lobster prices fluctuate considerably during the season.
7. Hen lobsters are distinguished from the cock lobsters by a broader tail.
8. There is usually more flesh on the hen, but it is considered inferior to that of the cock.
9. The coral of the hen lobster is necessary to give the required colour for certain soups, sauces and lobster dishes. For these, 1 kg hen lobsters should be ordered.
10. When required for cold individual portions, cock lobsters of ¼–½ kg are used to give two portions.

USE

Lobsters are served cold in cocktails, hors d'œuvre, salads, sandwiches and on buffets. When hot they are used for soup, grilled and served in numerous dishes with various sauces. They are also used as a garnish to fish dishes.

Menu examples: Mayonnaise de Homard
Homard Mornay
Bisque de Homard (Lobster Soup)

Crawfish *La Langouste*

Crawfish are like large lobsters without claws, but with long antennae. They are brick red in colour when cooked. Owing to their size and appearance they are used mostly on cold buffets but they can be served hot.

Menu example: Langouste Parisienne

Crab *Le Crabe*

QUALITY AND PURCHASING POINTS

1. They should be alive when bought and both claws attached to the body.
2. The claws should be large and fairly heavy.
3. The hen crab has a broader tail which is pink. The tail of the cock is narrow and whiter.
4. There is usually more flesh on the hen crab, but it is considered to be of inferior quality to that of the cock.

USE

Crabs are used for hors d'œuvre, cocktails, salads, dressed crab, sandwiches and bouchées.

Oysters *Les Huîtres*

Whitstable, Colchester and Helford are the chief British centres of oyster cultivation. Since the majority of oysters are eaten raw it is essential that they are thoroughly cleansed before the hotels and restaurants receive them.

QUALITY AND PURCHASING POINTS

1. Oysters must be alive; this is indicated by the firmly closed shells.
2. They are graded in sizes and the price varies accordingly.
3. Oysters should smell fresh.
4. They should be purchased daily.
5. They are in season from September to April (when there is an R in the month).

STORAGE

Oysters are stored in barrels or boxes, covered with damp sacks and kept in a cold room.

USE

The popular way of eating oysters is in the raw state. They may also be served in soups, hot cocktail savouries, fish garnishes, as a fish dish, in meat puddings and savouries.

Menu examples: Whitstable Natives
Huîtres Frits; Sauce Tartare
Anges à Cheval
Steak, Kidney and Oyster Pudding

Mussels *Les Moules*

BUYING AND QUALITY POINTS

1. The shells must be tightly closed.
2. The mussels should be large.
3. There should not be an excessive number of barnacles attached to the mussels.
4. Mussels should smell fresh.

STORAGE

Mussels are kept in boxes, covered with a damp sack and stored in a cold room.

USE

They may be served hot or cold or as a garnish.

Menu examples: Moules Marinières
Moules Vinaigrette

Scallops *La Coquille St. Jacque*

BUYING AND QUALITY POINTS

1. As these are dirty to prepare it is advisable to purchase them cleaned.
2. If scallops are not bought cleaned the shells should be tightly closed.
3. The orange part should be bright in colour and moist.
4. If they have to be kept, they should be stored in an ice-box or refrigerator.

USE

Scallops are usually poached or fried.

Menu example: Coquille St. Jacque Bonne Femme.

FISH OFFAL

Liver

An oil rich in vitamins A and D is obtained from the liver of cod and halibut. This is used medicinally.

Roe

Those used are the soft and hard roes of herring, cod, sturgeon and the coral from lobster.

Soft herring roes are used to garnish fish dishes and as a savoury. Cod's roe is smoked and served as hors d'œuvre. The roe of the sturgeon is salted and served raw as caviar and the coral of lobster is used for colouring lobster butter and lobster dishes and also as a decoration to fish dishes.

Further information can be obtained from: Fishmongers' Company, Fishmongers Hall, London Bridge, E.C.4, and the White Fish Authority.

VEGETABLES *LES LÉGUMES*

TYPE OR VARIETIES

1. *Roots*
   (*a*) Roots: carrots, parsnips, beetroots, swedes, turnips, radishes.
   (*b*) Tubers: potatoes, jerusalem artichokes.
   (*c*) Bulbs: onions, shallots, leeks, garlic.

2. *Green Vegetables*
   (*a*) Leaves: cabbage, lettuce, sprouts, spinach.
   (*b*) Flowers: cauliflower, broccoli, globe artichoke.
   (*c*) Fruits: tomatoes, marrow, cucumber.
   (*d*) Legumes: peas, beans.
   (*e*) Blanched stems: asparagus, sea-kale, celery, chicory.

Vegetable	French name	*Purchasing unit*				Season
		Wholesale	*Cost*	*Retail*	*Cost*	
Artichoke, Globe	l'Artichaut	Dozen		Single		June–Sept.
Artichoke, Jerusalem	le Topinambour	Box				Oct.–April
Asparagus	l'Asperge	Bundle		Bundle		April–June
Aubergine	l'Aubergine	Crate		Single		June–Oct.
Beans, Broad	les Fèves	Bag				June–August
Beans, Runner		Box				August–Sept.
Bean, French	les Haricots Verts	'Chip'				June–Sept.
Beetroot	la Bétterave	Half-bag				All the year
Broccoli, White	le Brocoli	Crate (12 heads)		or head		Jan.–March
Broccoli, Purple	le Brocoli	Crate				Feb.–March
Brussels Sprouts	les Choux de Bruxelles	Net				Oct.–March
Cabbage	le Chou Vert	Half-bag				All the year
Cabbage, Red	le Chou Rouge	Box				Sept.–Jan.
Cabbage, Savoy		Bags				Oct.–March
Carrots	la Carotte	Half-bag				*New:* May–June *Old:* Rest of year
Cauliflower	le Chou-fleur	Crate (12 heads approx.)		Head		March–Dec.
Celeriac	le Céleri Rave					Oct.–Feb.
Celery	le Céleri	'Fan' (12 heads)		Head		Sept.–March
Chicory	l'Endive (f.)	Box				Nov.–March
Cucumber	le Concombre	Tray (12)		Single		All the year; at best, May–Sept.
Kale, Curly	le Chou Frisé	Crate				Jan.–March
Leek	le Poireau	Crate				All the year
Lettuce, Cos	la Laitue Romaine	Crate (24)		Single		June–Sept.

Vegetable	*French name*	*Purchasing unit*				*Season*
		Wholesale	*Cost*	*Retail*	*Cost*	
Lettuce, Round	la Laitue	Crate (24)		Single		All the year. *English:* April–Sept. *Dutch:* *French:* Oct.–March *Hot-house:*
Marrow	la Courge	Box (6 pieces)		Piece		July–Sept.
Mushroom, field	le Champignon	'Chip'				Sept.–Oct.
Mushroom, cultivated	le Champignon	'Chip'				All the year
Onion	l'Oignon	Bag				All the year
Parsnip	le Panais	Crate				Oct.–April
Peas	les Petits Pois	Bag				June–August
Peppers	le Piment			Single		Sept.–Nov.
Potatoes, old	la Pomme de Terre					All the year
Potatoes, new	la Pomme Nouvelle	Bag				March–Sept.
Radishes	le Radis	Crate (12/18 bunches)		Bunch		March–August
Salsify	le Salsifi					Oct.–March
Sea-kale	le Chou de Mer					*Indoor:* Dec.–April *Outdoor:* April–June
Shallot	l'Échalote (f.)	Bag				Sept.–Oct.
Spinach	l'Épinard (m.)	Crate				All the year
Spring Greens	le Chou de Printemps	Bag				March–May
Swedes	le Rutabaga	Bag				Oct.–March
Sweetcorn or Corn on the Cob	le Maïs	Dozen				July–Sept.
Tomatoes	la Tomate	Trays				All the year
Truffles	la Truffe					Oct.–March
Turnips	le Navet	Box				*New:* May–July *Old:* August–March
Watercress	le Cresson	'Chip'		Bunch		All the year

SEASONS

It is extremely difficult to memorise a list of the months. The student is advised to think in terms of seasons of the year.

Spring

Asparagus	Greens	Broccoli—White and Purple
Artichokes, Jerusalem	Cauliflower	New Potatoes
New Carrots	New Turnips	

Summer

Artichokes, Globe	Turnips	Asparagus
Cauliflower	Aubergine	Cos Lettuce
Beans, Broad	Peas	Radishes
Beans, French	Carrots	Sea-kale
Sweetcorn		

Autumn

Artichokes, Globe	Parsnips	Field Mushrooms
Artichokes, Jerusalem	Aubergine	Peppers
Beans, Runner	Cauliflower	Red Cabbage
Salsify	Celery	Shallots
Celeriac	Swedes	Marrow
Turnips		

Winter

Brussels sprouts	Chicory	Cabbage
Kale	Celery	Parsnips
Cauliflower	Broccoli	Red Cabbage
Savoy Cabbage	Celeriac	Swedes
Turnips		

All the year round

Although the following vegetables are available all the year round, nevertheless at certain times, owing to bad weather, a heavy demand or other circumstances, supplies may be temporarily curtailed.

Beetroot	Leeks	Cabbage
Mushrooms	Carrots	Onions
Cucumber	Spinach	Lettuce
Tomatoes	Watercress	Potatoes

FOOD VALUE

ROOT VEGETABLES

Root vegetables are useful in the diet because they contain starch or sugar for energy, a small but valuable amount of protein, some mineral salts and vitamins. They are also useful sources of cellulose and water.

GREEN VEGETABLES

The food value is not the same as for root vegetables because no food is stored in the leaves, it is only produced there; therefore little protein or carbohydrate is found in green vegetables. They are rich in mineral salts and vitamins, particularly vitamin C and carotene. The greener the leaf the larger the quantity of vitamin present.

The chief mineral salts are calcium and iron.

QUALITY AND PURCHASING POINTS

ROOT VEGETABLES

1. Must be clean and free from soil (earth increases weight and consequently the price).
2. They must be firm, sound and free from spade marks.

GREEN VEGETABLES

1. They must be absolutely fresh.
2. The leaves must be bright in colour, crisp and not wilted.
3. Cabbage and brussels sprouts should have tightly growing leaves and be compact.
4. Cauliflowers should have closely grown flower and firm, white head; not too much stalk or outer leaves.
5. Peas and beans should be crisp and of medium size. Pea-pods should be full, beans not stringy.
6. Blanched stems must be firm, white, crisp and free from soil.

STORAGE

1. Root vegetables should be emptied from sacks and stored in bins or racks.
2. Green vegetables should be stored on well-ventilated racks.
3. Salad vegetables can be left in their containers and stored in a cool place.

PRESERVATION

CANNING

Certain vegetables are preserved in tins: artichokes, asparagus, carrots, celery, beans, peas (fins, garden, processed), tomatoes (whole, purée), mushrooms, truffles.

DEHYDRATION

Onions, carrots, potatoes and cabbage are shredded and quickly dried until they contain only 5% water.

DRYING

The seeds of legumes (peas and beans) have the moisture content reduced to 10%.

PICKLING

Onions and red cabbage are examples of vegetables preserved in spiced vinegar.

SALTING

French and runner beans may be sliced and preserved in dry salt.

FREEZING

Many vegetables such as peas, beans, sprouts, spinach and cauliflower are deep frozen.

USE

Vegetable	*Uses*	*Menu example*
Artichoke, Globe	Hot vegetable	Artichaut en Branche; Sauce Hollandaise
	Cold vegetable	Artichaut en Branche; Sauce Vinaigrette
	Garnish (trimmed into fonds)	Used in garnish Clamart
	Cold quartered for hors d'œuvre	Artichauts à la Grecque
Artichoke, Jerusalem	Soup	Crème Palestine
	Hot vegetable	Topinambours à la Crème
Asparagus	Hot vegetable	Asperges, Beurre Fondu
	Cold vegetable	Asperges, Sauce Mayonnaise
	Soup	Crème d'Asperges
Asparagus points	Garnish for egg, fish, meat, poultry and cold dishes	Omelette aux Pointes d'Asperges Suprême de Volaille Princesse
Aubergine	Hot vegetable	Aubergine Frite
	Hot hors d'œuvre	Aubergine Provençale
	Hot stuffed vegetable	Aubergine Farcie
	Garnish for fish and meat dishes	Sole Meunière aux Aubergines
Beans, Broad	Hot vegetable	Fèves au Beurre
Beans, Runner	Hot vegetable	
Beans, French	Hot vegetable	Haricots Verts Sautés au Beurre
Beans, French	Salad	Salade Niçoise
Beans, French	Hors d'œuvre	

Vegetable	*Uses*	*Menu example*
Beetroot	Soup	Bortch
	Hors d'œuvre	
	Salads	Salade de Betterave
Broccoli, White	Hot vegetable	Brocolis Polonaise
	Hors d'œuvre	Brocolis à la Grecque
Broccoli, Purple	Hot vegetable	Brocolis au Beurre
Brussels sprouts	Hot vegetable	Choux de Bruxelles Nature
Cabbage	Hot vegetable	Choux Verts
Cabbage, Red	Pickled	
	Hot vegetable	Choux rouge à la Flamande
Cabbage, Savoy	Hors d'œuvre	Cole Slaw
	Hot vegetable	
Carrots	Hot vegetable	Carottes Vichy
	Soup	Purée Crécy
	Hors d'œuvre and Garnishes	
Cauliflower	Hot vegetable	Chou-fleur Sauce Crème
	Soup	Crème Dubarry
	Hors d'œuvre	Chou-fleur Provençale
Celeriac	Soup	
	Hors d'œuvre	
	Salad	Salade Waldorf
Celery	Soup	Crème de Céleri
	Hors d'œuvre	Céleri à la Grecque
	Hot vegetable	Céleri Braisé
	Salad	
	Garnish	
Chicory	Salad	
	Hot vegetable	Endive au Jus
Cucumber	Hors d'œuvre	
	Salad	
	Garnish	Filet de Sole Doria
Kale, Curly	Hot vegetable	Chou-frisé Nature
Leeks	Soup	Cockie-leekie
	Hors d'œuvre	Poireaux; Sauce Vinaigrette
	Hot vegetable	Poireaux Braisés
Lettuce, Cos	Salads	Laitue Romaine
Lettuce, Round or Cabbage	Salads	
	Hot vegetable	Laitue Braisée
	Garnish to meat dishes	
Marrow	Hot vegetable	Courge Provençale
	Hot vegetable	Courge Persillées
Marrow, small	Hot vegetable	Courgette Farci
Mushrooms	Soup	Crème de Champignons
	Sauces	Sauce Chasseur
	Hot vegetables	Champignons Grillés
	Garnish	

Vegetable	*Uses*	*Menu example*
Mushrooms	Savouries	
	Hot hors d'œuvre	Champignons à la Crème
Onion	Soup	Soupe à l'Oignon
	Sauces	Sauce Soubise
	Hors d'œuvre	
	Salads	
	Hot vegetables	Oignons Frits à la Française
	Egg dishes	Omelette Lyonnaise
Parsnips	Hot vegetable	Panais au Beurre
Peas	Soup	Purée St. Germain
	Hors d'œuvre	
	Hot vegetable	Petits Pois à la Flamande
	Salads	
	Garnishes	Clamart
Peppers	Hors d'œuvre	
(Pimentos)	Salad	
	Hot vegetable	Piment Farci
Potatoes	Soup	Purée Parmentier
	Hors d'œuvre	Salade de Pomme de Terre
	Hot vegetable	
	Garnishes	Parmentier
	Salads	
Radishes	Hors d'œuvre	
	Salads	
	Decorating aspic work	
Salsify	Hot vegetable	Salsifis au Gratin
		Salsifis Sautés
Sea-kale	Hot vegetable	Chou de Mer Mornay
	Cold vegetable	Chou de Mer; Sauce Mayonnaise
Shallots	Hors d'œuvre	
	Sauces	
Spinach	Soup	
	Hot vegetable	Épinard en Branche
	Garnish	Florentine
	Soufflé	Soufflé aux Epinards
Spring greens	Hot vegetable	Choux de Printemps
Swedes	Hot vegetable	Purée de Rutabaga
Sweetcorn	Hors d'œuvre	
	Vegetable	Mais, Beurre Fondu
	Garnish	Suprême de Volaille Maryland
		Oeuf Poché Washington
Tomatoes	Soups	Crème Portugaise
	Sauces	Sauce Tomate
	Hors d'œuvre	
	Salads	Salade de Tomates
	Hot vegetable	Tomates Farcies
	Garnish	

Vegetable	*Use*	*Menu example*
Truffles	Hot vegetable	
	Garnishes	Périgord
	Decorating aspic dishes	
Turnips	Hors d'œuvre	
	Hot vegetable	Navets au Beurre
	Garnishes	
Watercress	Soup	Purée Cressonnière
	Salads	
	Garnishes	

FRUITS *LES FRUITS*

For culinary purposes fruit may be divided into the following groups:

Soft fruits: Raspberries, strawberries, loganberries, gooseberries, blackberries, red and black currants.

Hard fruits: Apples and pears.

Stone fruits: Cherries, damsons, plums, apricots, greengages, peaches, nectarines.

Citrus fruits: Oranges, lemons, grapefruit, mandarines, clementines, tangerines.

Tropical and other fruits: Bananas, pineapples, dates, figs, grapes, melons, rhubarb, cranberries.

SEASONS

The chief citrus fruits (oranges, lemons and grapefruit) are available all the year. Mandarines, clementines and tangerines are available in the winter.

Rhubarb is in season in the spring and the soft and stone fruits then become available from June in the following order: gooseberries, strawberries, raspberries, cherries, currants, damsons, plums.

Imported apples and pears are available all the year round; home-grown mainly from August to April.

English	French	Wholesale		Retail		Season
		Unit	Cost	Unit	Cost	
Apple	la Pomme					All year round; cheapest, Oct.–Dec.
Apricot	l'Abricot (m.)					May–Sept.
Banana	la Banane	'Coffin'		By number and weight		All year round
Blackberry	la Mur de Ronce	'Chip'				Sept.–Oct.
Blackcurrants	le Cassis	'Chip'				July–Sept.
Red Currants	les Groseilles Rouges	'Chip'				July–Sept.
Cherry	la Cerise	'Chip'				June–August
Clementine		Box				
Cranberries	les Airelles					Nov.–Jan.
Damson	la Prune de Damas					Sept.–Oct.
Date	la Datte			Box or pkt.		
Fig	la Figue			Pkt.		July–Sept.
Gooseberry	la Groseille à Macquereau	'Chip'				July–Sept.
Grapefruit	la Pamplemousse	Case (approx. 60)		Number		All year round
Grapes	les Raisins					All year round; best in autumn

English	French	Wholesale Unit	Wholesale Cost	Retail Unit	Retail Cost	Season
Greengage	la Reine-Claude					August
Lemon	le Citron	Case (approx. 300)		Number		All year round
Mandarine						Nov.–June
Melon	le Melon	Box (number varies according to size)		Number		*See* page 194
Orange	l'Orange (f.)	Case (approx. 210)		Number		All year round
Peach	la Pêche	Box		Number		Sept.
Pear	la Poire					Sept.–March
Pear, Avocado				Number		
Pineapple	l'Ananas (m.)	Box		Number		All year round; best in summer
Plum	la Prune	'Chip'		Number		July–Oct.
Raspberry	la Framboise	Punnet		Punnet		June–August
Rhubarb	la Rhubarbe	Box				Dec.–June
Strawberry	la Fraise	'Chip' Punnet		Punnet		June–August
Tangerine		Box				

FOOD VALUE

The nutritive value of fruit depends on its vitamin content, especially vitamin C; it is therefore valuable as a protective food.

The cellulose of fruit is useful as roughage.

STORAGE

Hard fruits, such as apples, are left in boxes and kept in a cool store.

Soft fruits, such as raspberries and strawberries, should be left in their punnets or baskets in a cold room.

Stone fruits are best placed in trays so that any damaged fruit can be seen and discarded.

Peaches are left in their delivery trays or boxes.

Citrus fruits remain in the delivery trays or boxes.

Bananas should not be stored in too cold a place because the skins turn black.

QUALITY AND PURCHASING POINTS

1. Soft fruits deteriorate quickly, especially if not sound. Care must be taken to see that they are not damaged or too ripe when bought.
2. The fruit should appear fresh; there should be no shrinking, wilting or signs of mould.
3. The colour of certain soft fruits is an indication of ripeness (strawberries, gooseberries).
4. Hard fruit should not be bruised. Pears should not be over-ripe

PRESERVATION

DRYING

Apples, pears, apricots, peaches and figs are dried. Plums when dried are called prunes, and currants, sultanas and raisins are produced by drying grapes.

CANNING

Almost all fruits may be canned. Apples are packed in water and known as solid packed apples; other fruits are canned in syrup.

BOTTLING

Bottling is used domestically, but very little fruit is commercially preserved in this way. Cherries are bottled in maraschino.

CANDIED

Orange and lemon peel are candied; other fruits with a strong flavour, such as pineapple, are preserved in this way.

The fruit is covered in hot syrup which is increased in sugar content from day to day until the fruit is saturated in a very heavy syrup. It is then allowed to dry slowly until it is no longer sticky.

GLACÉ

The fruit is first candied and then dipped in fresh syrup to give a clear finish. This method is applied to cherries.

CRYSTALLISED

After the fruit has been candied it is left in fresh syrup for 24 hours and then allowed to dry very slowly until crystals form on the surface of the fruit.

Most of the candied, glacé and crystallised fruits are imported from France.

JAM

Fruit which is edible but slightly imperfect is used in the manufacture of jam.

JELLY

Jellies are produced from fruit juice.

QUICK FREEZING

Strawberries, raspberries, loganberries, apples, blackberries, gooseberries, grapefruit and plums are frozen and they must be kept below zero.

COLD STORAGE

Apples are stored at temperatures between 1°C–4°C, depending on the variety of apple.

GAS STORAGE

Fruit can be kept in a sealed store room where the atmosphere is controlled. The amount of air is limited, the oxygen content of the air is decreased and the carbon dioxide increased.

FRUIT JUICES, SYRUPS AND DRINKS

Fruit juices such as orange, lemon, blackcurrant are canned.

Syrups such as rose hip and orange are bottled.

Fruit drinks are also bottled; they include orange, lime and lemon.

USES

GENERAL USE

With the exception of certain fruits (lemon, rhubarb, cranberries) fruit can be eaten as a dessert or in its raw state. Some fruits have dessert and cooking varieties—e.g. apples, pears, cherries and gooseberries.

STONE FRUITS

These are used as a dessert, stewed (compôte) for jam, pies puddings and in various sweet dishes. Peaches are also used to garnish certain meat dishes.

Menu examples: Damson Pie | Compôte de Reine-Claude
Condé d'Abricot | Pêche Melba
Flan aux Prunes | Nectarine au Kirsch
Cerises Jubilée | Jambon Braisé aux Pêches
Caneton aux Cerises

HARD FRUITS

APPLES

The popular English dessert varieties include Beauty of Bath, Worcester Pearmain, Cox's Orange Pippin, Blenheim Orange, Laxton's Superb and James Grieve. Imported apples include Jonathans, Granny Smith and Sturmers. The Bramley is the most popular cooking apple.

PEARS

The William and Doyenne du Comice are among the best-known pears.

Apples and pears are used in many pastry dishes. Apples are also used for garnishing meat dishes and for sauce which is served with roast pork and duck.

Menu examples: Apple Pie | Apple Pudding and Custard
Charlotte aux Pommes | Apfelstrudel
Beignet de Pomme | Poire Belle Hélène
Flan aux Poires

The avocado pear is used as a first course. This is a tropical, pear-shaped fruit usually served with vinaigrette and lettuce, or a variety of fillings, e.g. crab, shrimp.

SOFT FRUIT

Raspberries, strawberries, loganberries and gooseberries are used as a dessert. Gooseberries, black and red currants, and blackberries are stewed, used in pies and puddings. They are used for jam and flavourings.

Menu examples: Gooseberry fool
Stewed red currants and raspberries
Blackcurrant tart
Glace aux Fraises
Barquette de Fraises
Pêches et Framboises Rafraîchies au Kirsch

CITRUS FRUITS

Oranges, lemons and grapefruit are not usually cooked, except for marmalade. Lemons are used for flavouring and garnishing, particularly fish dishes. Oranges are used mainly for flavouring, and in fruit salads also to garnish certain poultry dishes. Grapefruit are served for breakfasts and as a first course generally for luncheon.

Menu examples: Soufflé au Citron
Crêpe au Citron
Glace au Citron
Bavarois à l'Orange
Florida Cocktail
Filet de Sole Frit au Citron
Caneton Bigarade
Salade d'Orange

TROPICAL AND OTHER FRUIT

BANANA

As well as being used as a dessert bananas are grilled for a fish garnish, fried as fritters and served as a garnish to poultry (Maryland). They are used in fruit salad and other sweet dishes.

Menu examples: Beignets de Banane
Flan au Banane
Filet de Sole Caprice
Poulet Maryland

PINEAPPLE

This fruit is served as a dessert; it is used in many sweet dishes and as a garnish to certain meat dishes. It is fried as a fritter.

Menu examples: Ananas Créole
Ananas en Surprise
Grilled Gammon and Pineapple

GRAPES

Black and white grapes are used as a dessert, in fruit salad, as a petits fours and also as a fish garnish (véronique).

MELON

There are several types of melon. Those most used are as follows:

Honeydew

These are long, oval-shaped melons with dark green skins. The flesh is white with a greenish tinge. Imported from North Africa and Spain. Season—late summer, autumn, winter.

Charentais

Charentais melon are small and round with a mottled green and yellow skin. The flesh is orange coloured. They are imported from France. Season—late summer.

Cantaloup

These are large round melons with regular indentations. The rough skin is mottled orange and yellow and the flesh is light orange in colour. They are imported mainly from France and Holland. Season—late summer.

Care must be taken when buying. Melons should not be over- or under-ripe. This can be assessed by carefully pressing the top or bottom of the fruit. There should be a slight degree of softness to the cantaloup and charentais melons.

The stalk should be attached, otherwise the melon deteriorates quickly.

USES

Melon is mainly used as a dessert and for hors d'œuvre and sweet dishes.

Menu examples: Melon Frappé
Melon en Surprise

CRANBERRIES

These hard red berries are used for cranberry sauce, which is served with roast turkey.

RHUBARB

Forced or early rhubarb is obtainable from January. The natural rhubarb from April–June.

Used for pies, puddings, fool and compôte.

FIGS

Fresh figs may be served as a first course or dessert. Dried figs are used for fig puddings.

DATES

Whole dates are served as a dessert; stoned dates are used in various sweet dishes and petits fours.

Menu examples: Date Pudding, Almond Sauce
Date and Apple Slice

NUTS *LES NOIX (f.)*

		Wholesale		*Retail*	
		Unit	*Cost*	*Unit*	*Cost*
Almond	l'Amande (f.)				
Brazil	la Noix de Bresil				
Chestnut	le Marron				
Coconut	la Noix de Coco				
Filbert					
Hazel	la Noisette				
Pistachio	la Pistache				
Walnut	la Noix				

SEASON

Dessert nuts are in season during the autumn and winter.

FOOD VALUE

Nuts are highly nutritious because of their protein, fat and mineral salts. They are of considerable importance to vegetarians who use nuts in place of meat, it is therefore a food which builds, repairs and provides energy. Nuts are difficult to digest.

STORAGE

Dessert nuts, those with the shell on, are kept in a dry, ventilated store. Nuts without shells, whether ground, nibbed, flaked or whole, are kept in air-tight containers.

QUALITY AND PURCHASING POINTS

1. Nuts should be of good size.
2. They should be heavy for their size.
3. There must be no sign of mildew.

USE

Nuts are used as a dessert, as a main ingredient to vegetarian dishes, also for decorating and flavouring.

They are used whole, or halved, and almonds are used ground, nibbed and flaked.

ALMONDS

Salted almonds for cocktail parties and bars.

Ground, flaked, nibbed, for use in sweet dishes and for decorating cakes.

For cake mixtures, large and small, such as Dundee cake, Congress tarts, macaroons; for petit fours and large cakes.

Marzipan and frangipan for Bakewell tarts.

Praliné for ice cream and gâteaux.

Coating for Pomme Berny.

BRAZILS

Dessert.

CHESTNUTS

Stuffing for turkeys.

Chestnut flour for soup.

Chestnut purée for large and small cakes.

Garnish for ice cream.

As a sweet dish (Mont Blanc aux Marrons).

Petits fours.

Marron glacé.

COCONUT

This is used in desiccated form for curry preparations, in cakes and for decorating cakes, such as madeleines.

FILBERTS AND HAZELS

These nuts are used as a dessert and for praliné.

PISTACHIO

These small green nuts are used for decorating galantines, small and large cakes and petits fours. They are also used for ice cream.

WALNUTS

Walnuts are used as a dessert, in salads and for decorating cakes and sweet dishes. They are also pickled.

PEANUTS AND CASHEW

These are salted and used in cocktail bars.

EGGS *LES ŒUFS*

The term eggs not only applies to those of the hen, but also to the edible eggs of other birds, such as turkeys, geese, ducks, guinea fowls, plovers and gulls.

HENS' EGGS

PURCHASING UNIT

Wholesale unit	crate 360 eggs
Retail unit	dozen

QUALITY POINTS FOR BUYING

1. The shell should be clean, well shaped, strong and slightly rough.
2. When broken there ought to be a high proportion of thick white to thin white.
3. The yolk should be firm, round and of a good even colour.

If an egg is kept, the thick white gradually changes into thin white and water passes from the white into the yolk. The yolk loses strength and begins to flatten, water evaporates from the egg and is replaced by air and as water is heavier than air fresh eggs are heavier than stale ones.

The professional method of testing eggs for quality is by a process known as 'candling' in which a candling lamp is used; this produces a beam of light strong enough to penetrate the shell of an egg to illuminate the contents and to show up any defects.

It is also possible to determine the freshness of an egg by placing it in a 10% solution of salt (60 grammes salt to ½ litre water). A two-day-old egg will float near the bottom of the solution with its broad end upward. As the egg ages it becomes lighter and floats closer to the surface of the solution.

STORAGE

1. Eggs must be stored in a cool but not too dry place; a refrigerator of 0–5°. is ideal.
2. No strongly smelling foods such as cheese, onions and fish should be stored near the eggs because the egg-shells are porous and the egg will absorb strong odours.

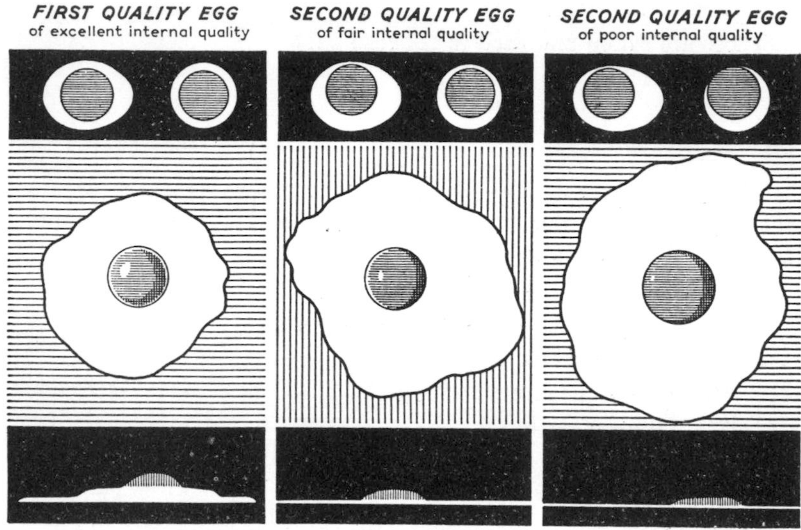

Quality of eggs.

3. They should not be washed before being stored as washing would remove the natural protective coating.
4. Eggs are stored point end down.

FOOD VALUE

Eggs contain most nutrients; they are a protective food and provide energy and material for growth and repair of the body.

PRODUCTION

Hens' eggs are graded in four sizes:

Small
Medium
Standard
Large

Small eggs are usually more plentiful in late summer and autumn. The size of an egg does not affect the quality but does affect the price. Eggs are collected from the farmers at least once a week by the Egg Packing Station. The eggs are tested for quality by candling, then weighed and stamped with the grade, the packing station number and the British Egg Marketing Board's lion mark. They are then packed into boxes containing 30 dozen, 360 (3 long hundreds).

The wholesale price of eggs is quoted per long hundred (120).

All egg-boxes leaving the packing station are dated.

PRESERVATION

COLD STORAGE

Eggs are kept a little above freezing-point. The humidity of the air and the amount of carbon dioxide in the air are controlled. They will keep about nine months under these conditions.

FROZEN EGGS

These are used mainly by bakers and confectioners; they are sold in 14, 16, 28 and 42 lb. tins. The eggs are broken, thoroughly mixed and then frozen.

DRIED EGGS

The eggs are broken, well mixed and then spray dried at a temperature of approx. 71°C. These are also used mainly by bakers and confectioners.

GREASE METHOD

A pure grease free from salt, water and other impurities must be used, such as Oteg, paraffin wax or lard. The eggs are dipped into the liquid grease and then allowed to dry. The grease fills up the porous shell, forms a skin and so excludes air. They may then be stored in the same way as fresh eggs.

WATERGLASS—SODIUM SILICATE

A solution is made up with sodium silicate and boiling water. When used it must be quite cold; the new-laid eggs are packed point downwards in an earthenware bowl or galvanised pail and covered with the solution. A lid is placed on the container to prevent evaporation.

USES OF EGGS

HORS D'ŒUVRE

Chiefly hard boiled for egg mayonnaise and for many composed salads such as fish salad.

SOUPS

In the preparation of royales for garnishing consommé, for thickening certain soups, e.g. Germiny and Veloutés.

EGG DISHES

These dishes are very popular on breakfast and luncheon menus and include scrambled, poached, soft-boiled, hard-boiled, en cocotte, sur le plat and omelets.

FARINACEOUS

Eggs are used in the making of pastes for ravioli, canneloni and noodles.

FISH

In the preparation of frying batters and for coating fish prior to crumbing.

SAUCES

Mayonnaise, hollandaise, béarnaise, sabayon are some of the sauces made with eggs.

MEAT AND POULTRY

For binding mixtures such as Vienna Steaks and chicken cutlets, and for coating cuts of meat and poultry prior to cooking.

SALADS

Usually hard-boiled and included in many composed salads.

SWEETS AND PASTRIES

Eggs are used in many ways for these dishes.

SAVOURIES

Scotch woodcock, cheese soufflé, savoury flans are some of the dishes in which eggs are used.

OTHER EGGS

Turkeys' and guinea fowls' eggs may be used in place of hens' eggs.

The eggs of the goose or duck may be used only if they are throughly cooked.

Plovers' and gulls' eggs are hard boiled and served as an hors d'œuvre.

Further information may be had from: British Egg Council, 52 High Holborn, London, W.C.1.

MILK *LE LAIT*

The milk most used in this country is that obtained from cows. Goats' milk and ewes' milk can also be used.

	Wholesale		*Retail*	
Milk	*Unit*	*Cost*	*Unit*	*Cost*
Pasteurised				
T.T.				
Channel Island				
T.T. pasteurised				
Homogenised				
Dried milk	Bags, tins			
Evaporated	Case		Tin	
Condensed	Case		Tin	
Cream				
Double				
Single				
Devon				
Imitation				

FOOD VALUE

Milk is almost a perfect food as it contains all the nutrients required for growth, repair, energy, protection and regulation of the body.

STORAGE

Milk keeps less well than almost any other food; it readily becomes dirty and unsafe, therefore it must be stored with care.

Milk is an excellent food for human beings; it is also, unfortunately, an excellent food for bacteria. Cows are subject to tuberculosis and other infections, precautions therefore are taken and herds are tested for T.B.

As milk is so easily contaminated it can be dangerous. Contamination can occur before milking—cows may be diseased; during milking—by unclean cows, premises, utensils or milker; after milking—at the dairy, in transit or in the kitchen.

STORAGE POINTS

1. Fresh milk should be kept in the container in which it is delivered.
2. It must be stored in the refrigerator.

3. Milk should be kept covered as it absorbs strong smells such as onion or fish.
4. Fresh milk and cream should be purchased daily.
5. Tinned milk is stored in a cool, dry ventilated room.
6. Dried milk is stored in air tight tins and kept in a dry store.
7. Imitation cream is kept in the refrigerator.

PRODUCTION

PASTEURISED

Milk which has been subjected to 15 seconds at 72°C to kill harmful bacteria.

UHT

Milk which has been subjected to ultra heat treatment that is 132°C for one second. Under sterile conditions it will keep for 2–3 weeks.

HOMOGENISED

Milk which is homogenised is treated so that the cream is dispersed throughout the milk. The milk and cream do not separate when left to stand.

T.T. (TUBERCULIN TESTED)

This milk is obtained from herds that have been tested every six months for T.B.

CHANNEL ISLAND MILK

This is produced by Jersey and Guernsey herds in this country. It has a high (4%) fat content.

STERILISED MILK

This is homogenised milk which is heated to 104°C–110°C for 30–40 minutes. It keeps for two–three months in the unopened bottle, but has a different taste from fresh milk.

PRESERVATION

EVAPORATED MILK

Has had 60% of the water removed by evaporation before canning.

CONDENSED MILK

Is richer than evaporated because more water has been removed. It can be sweetened or unsweetened.

DRIED MILK

Is either spray or roller processed.

CREAM

This is the concentrated milk fat which is skimmed off the top of the milk.

SINGLE CREAM

Does not whip, but it can be used in its liquid state with sweet dishes and for finishing soups, fish, meat and poultry sauces and stews (Blanquette, Fricassée).

DOUBLE CREAM

Owing to its higher fat content, whips and is used for decorating and filling pastries, gâteaux and with sweet dishes.

DEVON OR CLOTTED CREAM

Is made by allowing milk to stand for 12 hours, then scalding it and allowing it to stand again before separating. It is served with Devon Teas and fresh fruit; also fruit compôtes and pies.

IMITATION CREAMS

There are several types and qualities available. They are produced from an emulsion of oil, margarine or butter with milk powder and water. Imitation cream is used for filling and decorating small and large cakes and making and finishing sweet dishes.

USE OF CREAM

1. Fresh cream must be cold when required for whipping.
2. For preference it should be whipped in china or stainless steel bowls. If any other metal is used, the cream should be transferred to china bowls as soon as possible.
3. If fresh cream is whipped too much it turns to butter. This is more likely to happen in hot conditions. To prevent this, stand the bowl of cream in a bowl of ice whilst whisking.
4. When adding cream to hot liquids dilute the cream with some of the liquid before adding to the main bulk. This helps to prevent the cream from separating.

Further information from National Dairy Council, National Dairy Centre, John Princes Street, London, W.1.

FATS AND OILS

FATS

	Wholesale		*Retail*	
	Unit	*Cost*	*Unit*	*Cost*
Butter Margarine	Boxes or packets			
Lard Suet Cooking fat	Cartons			

STORAGE OF ALL FATS

Fats should be kept in a cold store and in warm weather in a refrigerator.

BUTTER

Must be kept away from strong-smelling foods. Butter is produced by churning the cream of milk. One litre of cream yields approximately one ½ kilo butter.

FOOD VALUE

Butter is an energy food as it has a very high fat content.

QUALITY

1. The taste should be creamy and pleasant.
2. The texture soft and smooth.
3. It must smell fresh.
4. The colour of pure butter is almost white or very pale yellow.
5. Fresh butter should be used fairly quickly, otherwise it goes rancid (acquires an unpleasant taste and smell).

PRODUCTION

Butter consumed in this country is produced in England, New Zealand, Australia, France, Holland and Denmark. Butter is often blended and can be salted or unsalted; the salt does act as a preservative. Butter is also mixed with margarine and sold as a special blend.

USE

Butter is used for most kitchen purposes where expense does not have to be considered.

It can be used for: making roux for soups and sauces; finishing sauces such as sauce vin blanc for fish, sauce madère for meat; hard butter sauces (maître d'hôtel) and butter sauces (hollandaise); pot-roasting meat, poultry and game; finishing vegetables (petits pois au beurre); making of all pastes except suet, hot water and nouille paste; decorating cold dishes and cocktail savouries; making cakes and butter creams.

It can be clarified and used for shallow frying of all kinds of food.

MARGARINE

This is produced from whole cream, milk and a vegetable oil (groundnut, palm, coconut, cotton seed or soya bean).

FOOD VALUE

Margarine is an energy and protective food. With the exception of palm oil, the oils used in the manufacture of margarine do not contain vitamins A and D; these are added during production. Margarine is not inferior to butter from the nutritional point of view.

QUALITY

There are several grades of margarine and some are blended with butter. Taste is the best guide to quality.

PRODUCTION

The vegetable oils are obtained from Commonwealth countries, West Africa and South-East Asia. Margarine is made by first extracting the oils and fats from the raw materials. These are refined, blended, flavoured and coloured, then mixed with fat-free pasteurised milk. The emulsion is then churned, cooled and packed. Cake and pastry margarines are blended in a different manner to table margarine to produce the required texture suitable for mixing.

USE

Margarine can be used in place of butter. The difference being: the smell is not so pleasant; nut brown (beurre noisette) or black butter (beurre noir) cannot satisfactorily be produced from it; the flavour when used in the kitchen is inferior to butter—it is therefore not so suitable for finishing sauces and dishes.

It should be remembered that it is equally nutritious and considerably cheaper than butter.

ANIMAL FATS

LARD

This is the rendered fat from the pig. Lard has almost 100% fat content. Wholesale unit 28 lbs in ½ lbs. It may be used in hot water paste and with margarine to make short paste. It can also be used for deep or shallow frying.

SUET

This is the hard solid fat deposits in the kidney region of animals. Beef suet is the best and it is used for suet paste stuffing and mincemeat. Packet suet is obtainable in 4 × 7 lb. cartons and ½-lb. and 1-lb. packets.

DRIPPING

This is obtained from clarified animal fats and it is used for frying. Wholesale unit is 28 lb.

Further information from: Butter Information Council, Salisbury House, London Wall, E.C.2 and Unilever Ltd., Unilever House, Blackfriars, London, E.C.4, and Van Den Bergs and Jurgens, Bromborough, Cheshire.

OIL

Oils are fats which are liquid at room temperature.

	Wholesale		*Retail*	
	Unit	*Cost*	*Unit*	*Cost*
Olive	Cans			
Maize	Cans			
Groundnut	Cans or drums			

Other varieties are sunflower seed oil, soya bean, tea seed and walnut oil.

FOOD VALUE

As oil has a very high fat content it is useful as an energy food.

STORAGE

1. Oil should be kept in a cool place.
2. If refrigerated some oils congeal; they return to a fluid state in a warm temperature.

3. Oils keep for a fairly long time, but they do go rancid if not kept cool.

QUALITY

Olive oil is the best, owing to its flavour. Better grade oils are almost without flavour, odour and colour.

PRODUCTION

Olive oil is extracted from olives grown in Mediterranean countries particularly Spain, Italy, Greece and France.

Groundnut oil is obtained from groundnuts grown in West Africa.

Maize oil is obtained from maize grown in Europe and the U.S.A.

The oil is extracted from the raw material, refined and stored in drums.

USE

Olive oil is used for making vinaigrette and mayonnaise and in the preparation of hors d'œuvre dishes. It is also used in making farinaceous pastes and for shallow frying.

Other oils are used for deep frying. Oil is used for lubricating utensils, trays and also marble slabs to prevent cooked sugar from sticking.

It may also be used to preserve foods by excluding air.

POINTS ON THE USE OF ALL FATS AND OILS

For frying purposes a fat or oil must, when heated, reach a high temperature without smoking. The food being fried will absorb the fat if the fat smokes at a low temperature.

Fats and oils should be free from moisture, otherwise they splutter.

As they are combustible, fats and oils can catch fire. In some fats the margin between smoking and flash point may be narrow.

A good frying temperature is 175–180°C.

Type	*Approx. flash-point* (°C)	*Smoke point* 175°–180°C (°C)	*Recommended frying temp.* (°C)
Finest quality vegetable oils	324	220	180
Finest vegetable fat	321	220	180
High-class vegetable oil	324	204	180
Pure vegetable fat	318	215	170–182
Pure vegetable oil	330	220	
Finest quality maize oil	224	215	180
Finest fat	321	202	180
Finest quality dripping	300	165	170–180
Finest natural olive oil	270–273	148–165	175

CHEESE *LES FROMAGES*

Cheese is made from milk and it takes approximately 5 litres of milk to produce ½ kilo of cheese.

There are many hundreds of varieties; most countries manufacture their own special cheeses.

TYPES

There are four main types of cheese with numerous varieties of each:

1. Hard cheese
2. Semi-hard cheese
3. Soft or cream cheese.
4. Blue-vein cheese.

Varieties	*Country*	*Wholesale purchasing unit (whole cheese)*	*Approx. price per unit*	*Retail purchasing unit*	*Approx. price per unit*
Hard cheeses:					
Cheddar	England				
Cheshire	England				
Double Gloucester	England				
Caerphilly	England				
Derby	England				
Lancashire	England				
Leicester	England				
White Stilton	England				
White Wensleydale	England				
Emmental	Switzerland				
Gruyère	Switzerland				
Edam	Holland				
Gouda	Holland				
Parmesan	Italy				
Semi-hard cheeses:					
St.–Paulin	France				
Pont l'Éveque	France				
		Square chip boxes		Square chip boxes	
Bel Paese	Italy				
Soft cheeses:					
Camembert	France	Case of 24 cheeses		1 round cheese in chip box	
Camembert	France	Case of 48 × ½ cheeses		1 or half round cheese in chip box	

Varieties	*Country*	*Wholesale purchasing unit (whole cheese)*	*Approx. price per unit*	*Retail purchasing unit*	*Approx. price per unit*
Soft cheeses—cont.					
Brie	France			Large wedge: in chip box	
Brie	France			Small wedge: in chip box	
Carré de l'Est	France	Case of 24 cheeses each		1 square cheese in chip box	
Pommel Demi-Sel	France	Boxes of 6 cheeses		Individual cheeses	
Pommel Demi-Suisse	France	Boxes of 3 cheeses		Individual cheeses	
Blue-vein cheeses:					
Stilton	England				
Wensleydale	England				
Cheshire	England				
Roquefort	France				
Gorgonzola	Italy				
Danish Blue	Denmark				

QUALITY

1. The skin or rind of cheese should not show spots of mildew, as this is a sign of damp storage.
2. Cheese when cut should not give off an over-strong smell or any indication of ammonia.
3. Hard, semi-hard and blue-vein cheese when cut should not appear dry.
4. Soft cheese when cut should not appear runny, but should have a delicate creamy consistency.

PRODUCTION

Cheese is produced by almost every country in the world, and is usually made from cows' milk, but some cheese is made from goats' milk, e.g. certain types of Parmesan; and some from ewes' milk, e.g. Roquefort.

Rennet is the chief fermenting agent used in cheese-making and is a chemical substance found in the gastric juice of a calf or lamb.

A typical cheese-making process, briefly, is as follows:

1. One gallon of milk makes approximately one pound of cheese.

2. The milk is tested for acidity and then made sour by using a starter (bacteria which produce lactic acid).
3. Rennet is added which causes the milk to curdle.
4. The curds are stirred, warmed and then allowed to settle.
5. The liquid (whey) is run off.
6. The curds are ground, salted and put into moulds. If a hard cheese is being made, then pressure is applied in order to squeeze out more of the whey.
7. The curds are now put into the special mould and a skin or rind is allowed to form.
8. When set, the cheese is removed from the mould and is then kept in special storage in order to mature and develop flavour.

STORAGE

All cheese should be kept in a cool, dry, well-ventilated store and whole cheeses should be turned occasionally if being kept for any length of time. Cheese should be kept away from other foods which may be spoilt by the smell.

FOOD VALUE

Cheese is a highly concentrated form of food. Fat, protein, mineral salts and vitamins are all present. Therefore it is an excellent body-building, energy-producing, protective food.

PRESERVATION

Certain cheeses may be further preserved by processing. A hard cheese is usually employed, ground to a fine powder, melted, mixed with pasteurised milk, poured into moulds then wrapped in lacquered tin-foil. E.g. processed Gruyère, Kraft, Primula.

USES

Cheese has many uses in cookery:

SOUPS

Grated Parmesan cheese is served as an accompaniment to many soups: e.g. Minestrone.

It is also used to form a crust on top of brown onion soup: e.g. Soupe à l'oignon.

FARINACEOUS

A grated hard cheese, usually Parmesan is mixed in with or is also served as an accompaniment to most farinaceous dishes: e.g. Spaghetti Italienne; Ravioli.

EGG DISHES

Omelette au Fromage
Oeuf dur Chimay

FISH DISHES

Coquille Saint-Jacques Mornay
Filets de Sole Florentine

VEGETABLES

Chou-fleur au Gratin
Chou de Mer Mornay

SAVOURIES

Welsh Rarebit
Beignets de Fromage
Quiche Lorraine
Canapé Ritchie
Soufflé au Fromage

A well-ordered restaurant should always be able to offer a good selection of assorted cheeses on a 'cheese board', and this should be available after lunch and dinner. At least six varieties should be presented. E.g.:

Cheddar	Gorgonzola
Gruyère	Edam
Camembert	Caerphilly

BRIEF DESCRIPTION OF SOME OF THE POPULAR CHEESES

HARD CHEESES

CHEDDAR

One of the oldest English cheeses, originally made in the Cheddar district of Somerset. It is now made in Scotland, Canada, Australia, New Zealand and South Africa all using the original 'cheddaring process'. There are two main types: (*a*) Factory Cheddar which is made whenever and wherever milk is plentiful, therefore it is made in large quantities and the price is economical. (*b*) Farmhouse Cheddar is made from May to October when the cows are out to grass on fresh feed. The flavour of the resulting cheese is buttery, mellow and nutty.

CHESHIRE

Is the oldest English cheese. As with Cheddar it is produced by 'factory' and 'farmhouse' methods. It is made in two colours, red and white, and is loose, flaky cheese with a mild flavour.

DOUBLE GLOUCESTER

A close, crumbly cheese, similar to Cheshire, which ripens slowly and takes six months to mature.

CAERPHILLY

Originally made in Wales, now produced in the south-west of England. A white, fairly firm cheese, delicate and mild in flavour, and it will keep for about three weeks only.

LANCASHIRE

A hard cheese, excellent for toasting. It has a rich mellow flavour and is at its best at about three months old.

GRUYÈRE AND EMMENTAL (SWISS)

A cooked, hard cheese, pale yellow in colour, honeycombed with holes caused by rapid fermentation during manufacture. About ten months is needed for this cheese to ripen.

PARMESAN (ITALIAN)

This is the hardest cheese of all; when ripe the crust is black, the cheese pale yellow. It is always used for cooking or grated as an accompaniment, never on a cheese board.

SEMI-HARD CHEESES

ST.-PAULIN (FRENCH)

Originally known as Port-Salut. A spongy cheese, round in shape, 14–20 cm diameter and 3–6 cm thick.

PONT L'ÉVEQUE (FRENCH)

Made in 8 cm squares, 3 cm thick. It has a rough, thick rind and elastic spongy texture and a slightly sour flavour.

BEL PAESE (ITALIAN)

Similar to St.-Paulin.

SOFT CHEESES

CAMEMBERT (FRENCH)

One of the most famous of the French soft cheeses. It is made round, 9 cm in diameter, 1½ cm thick, during the summer when the cows' milk is at its creamiest. To serve this cheese at its best it must be ripe—that is, of a soft creamy consistency. When under-ripe it has a white, chalky appearance and when over-ripe it turns a dark, unpleasant colour and gives off an unpleasant smell.

BRIE (FRENCH)

Another very famous cheese which is 36–48 cm in diameter. It is traditionally served on a mat of straw. Made during the autumn and usually obtainable November–May. It should be served ripe like Camembert.

CARRÉ DE L'EST (FRENCH)

A square-shaped cream cheese similar to the Camembert.

POMMEL DEMI-SUISSE (SWISS)

Sometimes referred to as Petit Suisse, are white and creamy croquette shaped, 3 cm diameter and 5 cm high.

BLUE-VEIN CHEESES

STILTON

Originally made in a village of the same name in Huntingdonshire. It is a rich double cream cheese with blue veins radiating from the centre. The blue veins are caused by inoculating the cheese with a mould. The rind should be slightly wrinkled, moist and of a drab colour. Must be eaten ripe. It takes about 6–9 months to mature.

WENSLEYDALE

Made in Yorkshire; blue-veined; similar to Stilton, but smaller.

ROQUEFORT (FRENCH)

Made from ewes' milk in the South of France during the lambing season and matured in limestone caves. The rennet used is taken from the lambs. Blue-veining is made by placing layers of mouldy breadcrumbs between the curds during manufacture.

GORGONZOLA (ITALIAN)

Originally made in a village of the same name near Milan in North Italy. It is a very rich, fully flavoured, blue-vein cheese.

DANISH BLUE (DANISH)

An imitation of Roquefort cheese.

Further information from: The Cheese Bureau, 40 Berkeley Square, London, W.1, and The English Country Cheese Council, 148 Charing Cross Road, London, W.C.2. and Comité National de Propagande des Produits Laitiers Français, 7 Rue Scribe, Paris IX, and Crowsons & Sons Ltd., 17–23 Farringdon Road, London, E.C.1.

CEREALS

Cereals are cultivated grasses, but the term is broadened to include sago, rice and arrowroot. All cereal products contain starch. The following are the important cereals used in catering: wheat, oats, barley, maize, rice, tapioca, sago, arrowroot.

WHEAT

Products	*Wholesale purchasing unit*	*Cost per unit*	*Retail purchasing unit*	*Cost per unit*
Flour (soft)	Bags			
Flour (strong)	Bags			
Flour (wholemeal)	Bags			
Semolina	Bags			
Macaroni	Boxes			
Spaghetti	Boxes			
Vermicelli				
Noodles				
Alphabets				

SOURCE

Wheat is grown in most temperate regions. Large quantities are home-grown and a great deal, particularly in the form of strong flour, is imported from Canada.

FOOD VALUE

Cereals are one of the best energy foods. Whole grain cereals provide vitamin B and are therefore protective foods.

STORAGE

1. The store room must be dry and well ventilated.
2. Flour should be removed from the sacks and kept in wheeled bins with lids.
3. Flour bins should be of a type that can be easily cleaned.

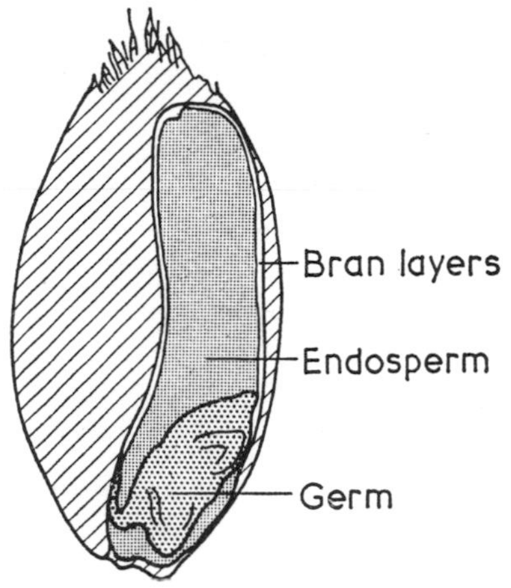

A grain of wheat.

PRODUCTION OF FLOUR

The endosperm contains all the material used by the baker. It consists of numerous large cells of net-like form in which starch grains are tightly packed. In addition, the cells contain an insoluble protein called gluten. When flour is mixed with water it is converted into a sticky dough. This characteristic is due to the gluten which becomes sticky when moistened. The relative proportion of starch and gluten varies in different wheats, and those with a low percentage of gluten are not suitable for bread-making, i.e. soft flour. For this reason, wheat is blended.

In milling, the whole grain is broken up, the parts separated, sifted, blended and ground into flour. Some of the outer coating of bran is removed as is also the wheat germ which contains oil and is therefore likely to become rancid and so spoil the flour. For this reason wholemeal flour should not be stored for more than 14 days.

White flour contains 70–72% of the whole grain.

Wholemeal flour contains 100% of the whole grain.

USES OF WHEAT PRODUCTS

SOFT FLOUR

Large and small cakes, biscuits and all pastes except puff pastry.

STRONG FLOUR

Bread, puff pastry, Italian pastes (spaghetti, macaroni), thickening soups and sauces, batters, coating various foods.

WHOLEMEAL

Wholemeal bread and rolls.

SEMOLINA

Gnocchi, milk puddings, moulds and as a dusting for certain pastes such as noodle and ravioli.

Menu example: Gnocchi romaine

MACARONI AND SPAGHETTI

Soups, farinaceous dishes, garnishes.

Menu examples: Minestrone
Macaroni au Gratin
Escalope de Veau Napolitaine

VERMICELLI

Garnishing soups, milk pudding.

Menu example: Purée Longchamps

NOODLES

Garnishing soups, farinaceous dishes, meat dishes.

Menu examples: Nouilles au beurre
Bœuf braisé aux nouilles

ALPHABETS

Garnishing soups.

Menu example: Consommé Alphabétique

OATS

These are either rolled into flakes or ground into three grades of oatmeal, coarse, medium and fine.

	Wholesale purchasing unit	*Cost per unit*	*Retail purchasing unit*	*Cost per unit*
Rolled oats				
Oatmeal (coarse)				
Oatmeal (medium)				
Oatmeal (fine)				

SOURCE

Oats are one of the hardiest cereals, and are grown in large quantities in Scotland and the north of England.

Plate 5. Round Oily Fish. 1. Herring. 2. Mackerel. 3. Trout. 4. Salmon Trout. 5. Salmon.

Plate 6. Round White Fish. 1. Whiting. 2. Haddock. 3. Cod. 4. Hake.

FOOD VALUE

Oats have the highest food value of any of the cereals. They contain a good proportion of protein and fat.

STORAGE

Because of the fat content, the keeping quality of oat products needs extra care. They should be kept in containers with tight-fitting lids, and stored in a cool, well-ventilated store room.

USES

ROLLED OATS

Porridge.

OATMEAL

Porridge, thickening soups, coating foods, cakes and biscuits, haggis.

BARLEY

This is made into pearl barley when the grains are husked, steamed, rounded and polished. Pearl barley is also ground into a fine flour (crème d'orge). These products are used for making barley water for thickening soups and certain stews.

Barley, when roasted, is changed into malt and as such is used extensively in the brewing and distilling of vinegar.

Barley needs the same care in storage as oats.

	Wholesale purchasing unit	*Cost per unit*	*Retail purchasing unit*	*Cost per unit*
Pearl barley				
Crème d'orge				

MAIZE

Is also known as corn, sweetcorn or corn-on-the-cob, and besides being served as a vegetable it is processed into corn-flakes and cornflour. Maize yields a good oil suitable for cooking.

CORNFLOUR

Is the crushed endosperm of the grain which has the fat and protein washed out so that it is practically pure starch.

Cornflour is used for making custard and blanc-mange powders, because it thickens very easily with a liquid, and sets when cold into a smooth paste that cannot be made from other starches.

Custard powder consists of cornflour, colouring and flavouring.

Cornflour is used for thickening soups, sauces, custards and also in the making of certain small and large cakes.

	Wholesale purchasing unit	*Cost per unit*	*Retail purchasing unit*	*Cost per unit*
Cornflour				
Custard powder				

RICE

Needs a hot, wet atmosphere and is grown chiefly in India, the Far East, South America and Italy.

There are two types used in this country:

(*a*) *Patna type:* a narrow, pointed grain, best suited for savoury dishes and plain boiled rice because of its firm structure, which helps to keep the rice grains separate.

Menu examples: Pilaff aux Foies de Volailles
Curried Beef and Rice
Kedgeree
Oeuf Poché Bombay

(*b*) *Carolina type:* a short, rounded grain, best suited for milk puddings and sweet dishes because of its soft structure.

Menu examples: Baked Rice Pudding
Riz à l'Impératrice
Poire Condé

GROUND RICE

Is used for milk puddings.

Menu example: Ground Rice Pudding

RICE FLOUR *Crème de riz*

Is used for thickening certain soups, e.g. cream soups.

RICE PAPER

This is a thin edible paper produced from rice, used in the making of macaroons and nougat.

STORAGE

Rice should be kept in tight-fitting containers in a cool, well-ventilated store.

	Wholesale purchasing unit	Cost per unit	Retail purchasing unit	Cost per unit
Patna type				
Carolina type				
Ground rice				
Crème de riz				

A ready prepared, cooked, sweetened rice is obtainable in tins.

TAPIOCA

Is obtained from the roots of a tropical plant called Cassava.

TYPES

Flake (rough); seed (fine).

USES

Garnishing soups, milk puddings.

Menu examples: Purée Lamballe
Tapioca Pudding

	Wholesale purchasing unit	Cost per unit	Retail purchasing unit	Cost per unit
Flake tapioca				
Seed tapioca				

STORAGE

Tapioca should be stored as for rice.

SAGO

Is produced from the pith of the sago palm. It is used for garnishing soups and for making milk puddings.

Menu example: Consommé au Sagou

	Wholesale purchasing unit	Cost per unit	Retail purchasing unit	Cost per unit
Sago				

STORAGE

Sago should be stored as for rice.

ARROWROOT

Is obtained from the roots of a West Indian plant called Maranta.

It is used for thickening sauces and is particularly suitable when a clear sauce is required as it becomes transparent when boiled. Arrowroot is also used in certain cakes and puddings, and is particularly useful for invalids as it is easily digested.

STORAGE

Arrowroot is easily contaminated by strong-smelling foods therefore it must be stored in air-tight tins.

	Wholesale purchasing unit	*Cost per unit*	*Retail purchasing unit*	*Cost per unit*
Arrowroot				

POTATO FLOUR *Fécule de Pomme de Terre*

Is a preparation from potatoes, suitable for thickening certain soups and sauces.

	Wholesale purchasing unit	*Cost per unit*	*Retail purchasing unit*	*Cost per unit*
Fecule				

BREAKFAST CEREAL FOODS

Cereals	*Wholesale purchasing unit*	*Wholesale cost*		*Retail cost per packet*
Barley Kernels	Packets		Doz.	
Breakfast Flakes	Packets		Case	
Force Wheat	Packets		Case	
Sunnybrisk	Packets		Case	
Grapenuts	Packets		Case	
Grape Flakes	Packets		Case	
All Bran	Packets		Case	
Bran Flakes	Packets		Case	
Corn Flakes	Packets		Case	
Corn Flakes	Packets		Case	
Rice Krispies	Packets		Case	
Rice Krispies	Packets		Case	
Sugar Frosted Corn Flakes	Packets		Case	
Sugar Ricicles	Packets		Case	
Post Toasties	Packets		Case	
Post Toasties	Cartons			

Cereals	*Wholesale purchasing unit*	*Wholesale cost*	*Retail cost per packet*
Puffed Wheat	Packets	Case	
Sugar Puffs	Packets	Case	
Sugar Puffs	Packets	Case	
Rice Toasties	Packets	Case	
Rice Toasties	Cartons		
Shredded Wheat	Packets	Case	
Shredded Wheat	Packets	Case	
Cubs	Packets	Case	
Shreddies	Packets	Case	
Weetabix	Packets	Case	
Weetabix	Packets	Case	
Weetabix	Packets	Case	
Weetabix	Hotel pack		
Weetabix	Caterers' pack		

RAISING AGENTS

The method of making mixtures light or aerated may be effected in several ways:

1. Whisking or beating (with a commodity).
2. Using baking powder.
3. Using yeast.

1. WHISKING OR BEATING with

(*a*) eggs—for sponges, genoise, swiss rolls
(*b*) egg whites for meringue
(*c*) butter or margarine for puff or rough puff pastry
(*d*) sugar and fat for creaming method of sponge puddings and rich cakes.

In all cases the whisking, beating or rolling (as with puff pastry), encloses air in the mixture.

2. BAKING POWDER

Wholesale		*Retail*	
Unit	*Cost*	*Unit*	*Cost*
Tin			

Baking powder is made from 1 part sodium-bicarbonate to 2 parts of cream of tartar.

When used under the right conditions it produces carbon dioxide gas; to produce gas a liquid and heat are needed. As the acid has a delayed action, only a small amount being given off when the liquid is added, the majority of the gas is released when the mixture is heated. Therefore cakes and puddings when mixed do not lose their property of the baking powder if they are not cooked right away.

HINTS ON USING BAKING POWDER

1. Mix the baking powder thoroughly with the flour.
2. Replace the lid tightly on the tin.
3. Measure accurately.
4. Do not slam oven doors in early stages of cooking.
5. Excess baking powder causes a cake to collapse in the middle and dumplings to break up.
6. Insufficient baking powder results in a close, heavy texture.

USE

It is used in sponge puddings, cakes and scones and in suet puddings and dumplings.

Further information from: The Baking Powder Information Bureau, Orchard House, Orchard Street, London, W.1.

3. YEAST

Yeast is a form of plant life.

	Wholesale		*Retail*	
	Unit	*Cost*	*Unit*	*Cost*
Fresh yeast				
Dried yeast				

STORAGE AND QUALITY POINTS

1. Yeast should be wrapped and stored in a cold place.
2. It is ordered only as required.
3. It must be perfectly fresh and moist.
4. It should have a pleasant smell.
5. Yeast should crumble easily.
6. It is pale grey in colour.

FOOD VALUE

Yeast is rich in protein and vitamin B. It is therefore a help towards building and repairing the body and provides protection.

PRODUCTION

Yeast is a form of plant life consisting of minute cells; these grow and multiply at blood heat provided they are fed with sugar and liquid. The sugar causes fermentation—this is the production of gas (carbon dioxide) in the form of small bubbles in the mixture or dough. When heat is applied to the mixture or dough it causes it to rise.

Dried yeast has been dehydrated and requires creaming with a little water before use. Its main advantage is that it will keep for several months in its dry state.

USE

To use yeast these points should be remembered:

1. The yeast should be removed from the refrigerator and used at room temperature.
2. Salt retards the working of yeast.
3. The more salt used the slower the action of yeast.
4. Best temperature for yeast action is 21–27°C.
5. The liquid for mixing the dough should be 36°–37°C.
6. Temperatures over 52°C destroy yeast.
7. Yeast can withstand low temperatures without damage.

HINTS ON THE USE OF YEAST

1. *Warmth*—the flour, bowl and liquid should be warm.
2. *Kneading*—yeast doughs must be kneaded (worked) to make an elastic dough and to evenly distribute the yeast. An elastic dough is required to allow the gases to expand.
3. *Proving*—this term means that the dough is allowed to double its size. This should occur in a warm place, free from draughts. The dough must be covered. The quality of the dough is improved by 'knocking back'. This means the dough is pressed down to its original size and allowed to prove again. The dough is lightly kneaded, moulded and proved again before baking.

OVERPROVING

The dough should not overprove, either in the bowl or in the moulded state. Excess or uneven heat or too long a proving time can cause overproving.

USE

Bread doughs: rolls, white, brown, wholemeal loaves, etc.
Bun doughs: currant, Chelsea, Swiss, Bath, doughnuts.
Baba, Savarin and Marignans.
Croissants and Brioche.
Danish pastry.
Frying batter.

SUGAR *LE SUCRE*

	Wholesale		*Retail*	
	Unit	*Cost*	*Unit*	*Cost*
Granulated				
Castor				
Cube				
Coffee crystals				
Icing				
Demerara				
Barbados				
Syrup				
Treacle				

Sugar is produced from sugar cane from the West Indies and Australia and from sugar beet which is grown in Great Britain and Canada.

FOOD VALUE

As sugar contains 99·9% pure sugar, it is invaluable for producing energy.

STORAGE

Sugar should be stored in a dry, cool place. When purchased by the sack, the sugar is stored in covered bins.

PRODUCTION

The sugar is extracted from the cane or beet, crystallised, refined and then sieved. The largest holed sieve produces granulated, the next size castor and fine linen sieves are used for icing sugar. Loaf or cube sugar is obtained by pressing the crystals while slightly wet, drying them in blocks and then cutting the blocks into squares.

Demerara sugar or brown sugar is unrefined.

Syrup is produced during the production of sugar. It is filtered and evaporated to become the required colour and thickness.

USE

Sugar is chiefly used for pastry, confectionery and bakery work.

Pastry uses: for pies, puddings, sweet dishes, ice creams and pastries.

Confectionery uses: decorating gateaux and celebration cakes (birthday, christening, wedding), sweets and petits fours. Sugar work (pulled, blown and spun).

Bakery uses: yeast doughs, large and small cakes.

In the kitchen it is used in certain sauces, such as mint and Robert. Sugar may be added to peas and carrots. It is used in some meat dishes e.g., Carbonnade de Bœuf, Baked Sugar Ham. Sugar is also added to the brine solution.

As well as being used to sweeten foods it is also used to give colour, e.g. Crème Caramel and the production of blackjack.

Further information from: Tate & Lyle Ltd., 21 Mincing Lane, London, E.C.3.

COCOA

Cocoa is a powder produced from the beans of the cacao tree. It is imported mainly from West Africa.

PURCHASING UNITS

Wholesale		*Retail*	
Unit	*Cost*	*Unit*	*Cost*
Bags			
Bags			
Cask			

FOOD VALUE

As cocoa contains some protein and a large proportion of starch it helps to provide the body with energy. Iron is also present.

STORAGE

Cocoa should be kept in air-tight containers in a well-ventilated store.

PRODUCTION

The cocoa beans grow in the pods of the cacao tree. The beans are dried, fermented, re-dried and roasted. The shells are cracked and removed, the nibs which are left are ground to a thick brown liquid called cocoa mass. The mass is compressed, then crushed, ground and sifted, making cocoa. The cocoa butter has been removed, because it would make the drink greasy.

USES

For hot drinks cocoa is mixed with milk, milk and water, or water. Hot liquid is needed to cook the starch and make it more digestible.

It can be used to flavour puddings, cakes, sauces, icings and ice cream.

CHOCOLATE

This is produced from cocoa mass mixed with fine sugar and cocoa butter. They are all ground well together and extra flavourings are sometimes added.

PURCHASING UNITS

	Wholesale	
	Unit	*Cost*
Couverture (sweetened)	Blocks	
Couverture (unsweetened)	Blocks	

USES

Chocolate or couverture is used for icings, butter creams and sauces.

DRINKING CHOCOLATE

This is ground cocoa from which less fat has been extracted and to which sugar has been added. It can be obtained in flake or powder form.

Further information from: The Ghana Cocoa Marketing Board, P.O. Box 933, Accra, Ghana, or Cadbury Bros. Ltd., Bournville.

COFFEE *LE CAFÉ*

Coffee is produced from the beans of the coffee tree.

VARIETIES

Coffee is grown in South America, Central America, Mexico, West Indies, East and Central Africa, Madagascar, India and Indonesia and the varieties of coffee are named after the areas where they are grown: e.g. Mysore; Kenya; Brazil; Mocha; Java; Jamaican (Blue Mountain).

PURCHASING UNIT

Coffee beans (*a*) unroasted; (*b*) roasted; (*c*) ground, are sold by the pound and in 7-lb., 14-lb. or 28-lb. parcels or tins.

Coffee essence is obtained in 5½-oz., 10-oz., 25-oz. and 1-gallon bottles.

QUALITY POINTS FOR BUYING

1. A good quality coffee bean should be bought.
2. The beans should be freshly ground.
3. As water varies in different areas, sample brews with several kinds of coffee should be made to select the best result.

STORAGE

Coffee should be kept in air-tight containers in a well-ventilated store. The beans should be roasted and ground as they are required.

FOOD VALUE

It is the milk and sugar served with coffee that have food value. Coffee has no value as a food by itself.

PRODUCTION

The coffee tree or bush produces fruit called a cherry which contains seeds. The outer-side pulp is removed and the seeds or beans are cleaned, graded and packed into sacks. When required, the beans are blended and roasted to bring out the flavour and aroma.

French coffee usually contains chicory; the root is washed, dried, roasted and ground. The addition of chicory gives a particular flavour and appearance to the coffee.

Coffee essence is a concentrated form of liquid coffee which may contain chicory.

Instant coffee is liquid coffee which has been dried into powder form.

USES

Mainly used as a beverage which may be served with milk, or as a flavouring for cakes, icings, bavarois and ice cream.

There are several methods for making coffee:

1. Still set
2. Jug method
3. Drip or filter method
4. Saucepan method
5. Cona
6. Espresso

For details of these methods see the chapter on beverages.

POINTS TO NOTE WHEN MAKING COFFEE

1. Use a good quality coffee.
2. Measure the quantity of coffee to be used—300–360 grammes per 5 litres.
3. Strain soon after being made so as to avoid a bitter flavour.
4. Serve milk which is hot, but has not been allowed to boil.

Further information from: Coffee Publicity Association Ltd., 10 Eastcheap, London, E.C.3, and The Coffee Information Bureau, Williams House, Eastbourne Terrace, London, W.2.

TEA *LE THÉ*

Tea is the name given to the young leaves and leaf buds of the tea plant after they have been specially treated and dried.

Tea is produced in India, Pakistan, Assam, Darjeeling, Ceylon, Java, Sumatra, China, East Africa, Uganda, Kenya, Tanganyika and Nyasaland.

Teas show marked differences according to the country and district in which they are produced and it is usual to blend several types.

China teas have the most delicate flavour of any, but lack 'body'.

TYPES

There area large number of teas on the market and as water in different districts affects the flavour, the only sure way to select a tea for continual use is by trying out several blends, tasting them and then assessing the one that gives the most satisfactory flavour.

BUYING

Tea may be obtained in packs from ½ oz. to 100 lb. so that obviously many factors concerned with the type of business must be considered when deciding how to buy.

The cheapest way of purchasing tea is in 100-lb. chests which are lined with lead or aluminium paper. This is to prevent the tea from absorbing moisture and odours.

STORAGE

Tea should always be stored in dry, clean, airtight containers in a well-ventilated store room.

FOOD VALUE

Tea alone has no nutritional properties, but it is a most refreshing drink. Nutritional value is only supplied by the milk and sugar in the tea.

USE

1. Use a good tea—the ideal recipe is 60 grammes to a 5 litres of boiling water; there should be no guess-work, the tea should be weighed or measured for each brew.
2. Always use freshly drawn, freshly boiled water.
3. Heat the pot—unless this is done the water goes off the boil rapidly, thus preventing the correct infusion of the tea.
4. Take the pot to the boiling water—the water must be as near boiling point as possible to enable the leaves to infuse properly.
5. Allow the tea to brew for 4–5 minutes, and stir well before pouring.

Further information from: The Tea Centre, 22 Regent Street, London, S.W.1.

PULSES

Pulses are the dried seeds of plants which form pods.

	Wholesale		*Retail*	
Types	*Unit*	*Cost*	*Unit*	*Cost*
Beans, Butter	bags			
Beans, Haricot	bags			
Lentils (split)	bags			
Lentils (whole green)	bags			
Peas (blue—small round)	bags			
Peas (marrowfat)	bags			
Peas (green split)	bags			
Peas (yellow split)	bags			

FOOD VALUE

They are good sources of protein and carbohydrate and therefore help to provide the body with energy. With the exception of the soya bean, they are completely deficient in fat and are therefore suitable for serving with fatty foods; e.g. fat bacon or pork.

STORAGE

All pulses should be kept in clean containers in a dry, well-ventilated store.

USE

Pulses are used mainly for soups, stews, vegetables, accompaniments to meat dishes and vegetarian cookery.

Menu examples:	Haricot-bean soup	Purée Soissonnaise
	Lentil soup	Purée de Lentilles
	Green-pea soup	Purée St.-Germain
	Yellow-pea soup	Purée Égyptienne
	Haricot Oxtail, Boiled Belly of Pork and Pease Pudding, Lentil Croquettes	

HERBS *LES HERBES*

Of the thirty known types of herbs, approximately twelve are generally used in cookery. Herbs may be used fresh, but the majority are dried, so as to ensure a continuous supply throughout the year. The leaves of herbs contain an oil which gives the characteristic smell and flavour. They are simple to grow and where possible any well-ordered kitchen should endeavour to have its own fresh herb patch. Tubs or window-boxes can be used if no garden is available.

Dried herbs are obtainable in 1-lb. bags and ¼-oz. packets.

Herbs have no food value but are important from a nutritive point of view in aiding digestion because they stimulate the flow of gastric juices.

These are the most commonly used herbs:

BAY-LEAVES

These are the leaves of the bay laurel or sweet bay trees or shrubs. They may be fresh or dried and are used for flavouring many soups, sauces and stews in which case they are usually included in a faggot of herbs (bouquet-garni).

CELERY SEED

This is dried and used for flavouring soups, sauces and stews when fresh celery is unobtainable. If used in a white soup or sauce it should be tied in a piece of muslin, otherwise it can cause discolouration.

CHERVIL

This plant has small, neatly shaped leaves with a delicate aromatic flavour. It is best used fresh, but may also be obtained in dried form. Because of its neat shape it is employed a great deal for decorating chaud-froid work. It is also one of the 'fines-herbes', the mixture of herbs used in many culinary preparations.

CHIVES

This bright green member of the onion family resembles a coarse grass. It has a delicate onion flavour. It is invaluable for flavouring salads and hors d'œuvre and should be used fresh.

MARJORAM

This is a sweet herb which may be used fresh in salads and when dried, marjoram can be used for flavouring soups, sauces, stews and certain stuffings.

MINT

There are many varieties of mint. Fresh sprigs of mint are used to flavour peas and new potatoes. Fresh or dried mint may be used to make mint sauce or mint jelly for serving with roast lamb. Another lesser known but excellent mint for the kitchen is apple mint.

PARSLEY

This is probably the most common herb in this country and has numerous uses for flavouring, garnishing and decorating a large variety of dishes. It is generally used fresh, but my be obtained in dried form. When garnishing deep fried fish it is customary to fry whole heads of fresh parsley till crisp.

ROSEMARY

Rosemary may be used fresh or dried for flavouring sauces, stews and salads.

SAGE

This is a strong, bitter, pungent herb which aids the stomach to digest rich fatty meat and is therefore used in stuffings for duck, goose and pork.

TARRAGON

This plant has a bright green attractive leaf. It is best used fresh, particularly when decorating chaud-froid dishes. Tarragon has a pleasant flavour and is used in sauces, one well-known example being Sauce Béarnaise. It is one of the 'fines-herbes' and as such is used for omelettes, salads, fish and meat dishes.

THYME

A popular herb in this country which is used fresh or dried for flavouring soups, sauces, stews and stuffings.

FINES-HERBES (FINE HERBS)

This is a mixture of fresh herbs, usually chervil, tarragon and parsley which is referred to in many classical cookery recipes.

BALM, BASIL, BERGAMOT, BORAGE, DILL, FENNEL, SAVOURY, SORREL, TANSY, LEMON THYME

These are used in cookery, but on a much smaller scale.

HARVESTING AND DRYING OF HERBS

1. The shoots and leaves should be collected from the plants just before they bloom.
2. They should be inspected to see that they are sound.
3. They are then tied in small bundles and hung up to dry in a warm but not sunny place.
4. After 24 hours paper bags should be tied over them to keep out dust and to help retain colour in the leaves.
5. When sufficiently dry they should break up easily if rubbed between forefingerand thumb.
6. The leaves have the middle vein removed and they are then passed through a sieve.
7. The sieved herbs must be kept in airtight bottles or tins in order to conserve flavour.

ANGELICA

Although not a herb, angelica is found growing in a herb garden. It has a long bamboo-like stem growing to a height of about 1·5 metres. The stems are bleached, cut into 36 cm pieces and boiled in a green syrup, cooled, then reboiled daily in syrup for five days.

Further information from: Heath and Heather, Herb Specialists, St. Albans, Hertfordshire.

SPICES *LES ÉPICES*

Spices are natural products; they are fruits, seeds, roots, flowers or the bark of a number of different trees or shrubs.

ALLSPICE OR PIMENTO

This is so called because the flavour is like a blend of cloves, cinnamon and nutmeg. It is the unripe fruit of the pimento tree which grows in the West Indies. Allspice is picked when still green and dried; the colour then turns reddish brown. Allspice is ground and used as a flavouring in sauces and sausages. It is one of the spices blended for mixed spice.

CLOVES

Cloves are the unopened flower-buds of a tree which grows in Zanzibar, Penang and Madagascar. The buds are picked when green and dried in the sun, when they turn to a rich brown colour. They are used for flavouring stocks, sauces.

The studded onion (oignon piqué or clouté) is an onion and a bay leaf studded with a clove.

When apples are cooked, in most cases cloves are used as a flavouring. Cloves may be obtained in ground form and as such they are used in mixed spice.

CINNAMON

This is the bark of the small branches of the cinnamon shrub. The inner pulp and the outer layer of the bark are removed and the remaining pieces dried. It is a pale brown colour and is obtained and used in stick or powdered form. It is mainly used in bakery and pastry work. When stewing pears a stick of cinnamon improves the flavour. Doughnuts may be passed through a mixture of sugar and ground cinnamon. Slices of apple for fritters may be sprinkled with cinnamon before being passed through the frying batter. It is another of the spices blended for mixed spice.

NUTMEGS AND MACE

The tropical nutmeg tree bears a large fruit like an apricot which when ripe, splits. Inside is a dark brown nut with a bright red net-like covering which is the part that becomes mace. Inside the nut is the kernel or seed which is the nutmeg. Although the two spices come from the same fruit the flavour is different. Mace is more delicate and is used for flavouring sauces and certain meat and fish dishes. Nutmeg is used in sweet dishes (particularly milk puddings), sauces and some potato dishes. It is also used for mixed spice.

CORIANDER

Coriander is a pleasant spice obtained from the seed of an annual plant grown chiefly in Morocco. It is a yellowish brown colour and tastes like a mixture of sage and lemon peel. It is used in sauces, curry powder and mixed spice.

CARRAWAY

Carraway seeds come from a plant grown in Holland. The seeds are about $\frac{1}{2}$ cm long, shaped like a new moon and brown in colour. They are used in seed cake.

GINGER

This is the rhizome or root of a reed-like plant grown in the Far East. The root is boiled in water and sugar syrup until soft. Ground ginger is used mainly for pastry and bakery work and for mixed spice.

TURMERIC

Turmeric grows in the same way as ginger and it is the rhizome which is used. It is without any pronounced flavour, its main use being for colouring curry powder. It is ground into a fine powder, after which the colour is bright yellow.

SAFFRON

The stigmas from a crocus known as the saffron crocus (grown chiefly in Spain) are dried and form saffron, which is a flavouring and colouring spice. It is used in soups, sauces and particularly in rice dishes, giving them a bright yellow colour and distinctive flavour. Saffron is very expensive as it takes the stigmas from approximately 4000 crocus flowers to yield 30 grammes.

CHILLIES AND CAPSICUMS

These are both from the same family and grow on shrubs. They are bright red and are used in pickles and for red pepper. The larger kind are called capsicums; they are not so hot and, when ground, are called paprika. This is used for a Hungarian type of stew known as goulash.

INGREDIENTS FOR A TYPICAL CURRY POWDER

2 parts bayleaves	2 parts garlic	4 parts cinnamon
3 parts ginger	3 parts carraway	4 parts mace
3 parts chillies	40 parts coriander	4 parts mustard
2 parts nutmeg	3 parts cloves	4 parts pepper
3 parts saffron	3 parts allspice	20 parts turmeric

INGREDIENTS FOR MIXED SPICE

4 parts allspice	4 parts cloves	4 parts cinnamon
4 parts coriander	1 part nutmeg	1 part ginger

CONDIMENTS

SALT — *SEL*

	Wholesale		*Retail*	
	Unit	*Cost*	*Unit*	*Cost*
Dried salt				
Cut lumps				
Cooking salt				
Table salt				

FOOD VALUE

Salt (Sodium Chloride) is essential for stabilising body fluids and preventing muscular cramp.

STORAGE

Salt must be stored in a cool, dry store as it readily absorbs moisture. It should be kept in airtight packets, drums or bins. Block salt must also be kept in a dry place.

PRODUCTION

Salt occurs naturally in the form of rock salt in underground deposits, mainly in Cheshire. It may be mined or pumped out of the earth after water has been introduced into the rock salt. The salt is extracted from the brine by evaporation and it is then purified.

USE

It is used for curing fish such as herrings and haddocks and for cheese and butter making. Salt is also used for the pickling of foods, in the cooking of many dishes and as condiment on the table.

PEPPER — *POIVRE*

Wholesale		*Retail*	
Unit	*Cost*	*Unit*	*Cost*

Pepper is obtained from the berry of a tropical shrub. These berries are black pepper corns. White pepper corns are obtained by removing the skin from the black pepper corn. White pepper is less pungent than the black, and both may be obtained in ground form.

Pepper corns are used whole in stocks, court-bouillons, sauces and dishes where the liquid is passed. They are crushed for reductions for sauces and used in a pepper-mill for seasoning meats before frying or grilling.

Ground pepper is used for seasoning many dishes and as a condiment at the table.

CAYENNE PEPPER

Wholesale		*Retail*	
Unit	*Cost*	*Unit*	*Cost*

This is a red pepper used on savoury dishes and cheese straws. It is a hot pepper which is obtained from grinding chillies and capsicums, both of which are tropical plants related to the tomato.

PAPRIKA

Wholesale		*Retail*	
Unit	*Cost*	*Unit*	*Cost*

This is a bright red mild pepper used in goulash and for decorating hors d'œuvre dishes such as egg mayonnaise.

It is produced from capsicums grown in Hungary.

MUSTARD *MOUTARDE*

Wholesale		*Retail*	
Unit	*Cost*	*Unit*	*Cost*
tins	tins		

Mustard is obtained from the seed of the mustard plant which is grown mainly in East Anglia. It is sold in powder form and is diluted with water, milk or vinegar for table use.

It is used in the kitchen for sauces (e.g. mustard, mayonnaise, vinaigrette), for devilled dishes such as grilled leg of chicken, and in Welsh Rarebit.

Continental mustards are sold as a paste in jars having been mixed with herbs and wine vinegar.

VINEGAR *VINAIGRE*

Wholesale		*Retail*	
Unit	*Cost*	*Unit*	*Cost*
casks			
		bottles	

Malt vinegar is made from malt which is produced from barley. Yeast is added which converts it to alcohol, and bacteria are then added to convert the alcohol into acetic acid. The resulting vinegar is stored for several months before being bottled or casked.

Artificial, non-brewed, pure or imitation vinegars are chemically produced solutions of acetic acid in water. They are cheaper and inferior to malt vinegar, having a pungent odour and a sharp flavour.

Spirit vinegars are produced from potatoes, grain or starchy vegetables, but they have not the same flavour as malt vinegar.

Red or white wine vinegars are made from grapes and are more expensive and have a more delicate flavour than the other vinegars.

All vinegars can be distilled; this removes the colour. The colour of vinegar is no indication of its strength as burnt sugar is added to give colour.

To produce flavoured vinegar the required herbs, usually tarragon, are placed in a jar and covered with good quality vinegar and then stored for at least two weeks and used as required (e.g. Sauce Béarnaise).

USES

Vinegar is used as a preservative for pickles, rollmops and cocktail onions.

As a condiment on its own or with oil as a salad dressing.

It is used in marinades to tenderise meats (beef for braising, hare, venison) before cooking, and in court-bouillons to tenderise the flesh of fish during cooking (crab and lobster).

Vinegar is used for flavouring sauces such as mayonnaise and in reductions for sharp sauces (sauce piquante, sauce diable).

COLOURINGS AND ESSENCES

A number of food colourings are obtainable in either powder or liquid form.

NATURAL COLOURS

COCHINEAL

This is a red colour used in pastry and confectionery work.

GREEN COLOURING

This can be made by mixing indigo and saffron, but chlorophyl, the natural green colouring of plants, e.g. spinach, may also be used. This is used in pastry, confectionery and in green sauce which is sometimes served with salmon.

INDIGO

A blue colour seldom used on its own, but when mixed with red, produces shades of mauve.

YELLOW COLOURING

A deep yellow colour can be obtained from turmeric roots and is prepared in the form of a powder mainly used in curry and mustard pickles.

Yellow colour is also obtained by using egg yolks or saffron.

BROWN SUGAR

Is used to give a deep brown colour in rich fruit cakes; it also adds to the flavour.

BLACKJACK OR BROWNING

This is usually made in the kitchen by lightly burning sugar, then diluting it with water; this gives a dark brown, almost black, liquid. Blackjack is used for colouring soups, sauces, gravies, aspics and in pastry and confectionery.

CHOCOLATE COLOUR

This can be obtained in liquid or powder form, and is used in pastry and confectionery.

COFFEE COLOUR

Is usually made from coffee beans with the addition of chicory.

A large range of artificial colours are also obtainable; they are produced from coal tar and are harmless. Some mineral colours are also used in foodstuffs. All colourings must be pure and there is a list of those permitted for cookery and confectionery use.

ESSENCES

Essences are generally produced from a solution of essential oils with alcohol, and are prepared for the use of cooks, bakers and confectioners.

Among the many types of essence obtainable are:

Almond	Lemon	Orange	Peppermint
Pineapple	Raspberry	Strawberry	Vanilla

They are available in many size bottles.

GROCERY AND DELICATESSEN GOODS

Delicatessen means table delicacies and the word covers a wide range of foods.

ASPIC JELLY

Unit	*Cost*
tins	

This is a clear savoury jelly which may be the flavour of meat, game or fish. It may be produced from fresh ingredients (*Practical Cookery*, page 41) or obtained in a dried form.

It is used for cold larder work, mainly for coating chaud-froid dishes, and may also be chopped or cut into neat shapes to decorate finished dishes.

GELATINE

	Unit	*Cost*
Leaf		
Powdered		

This is obtained from the bones of certain animals; it is manufactured in leaf or powdered form in varying qualities.

Gelatine is used for setting foods such as jellies and aspics, and sweets, e.g. bavarois.

EXTRACTS (Meat and Vegetable)

Unit	*Cost*
tins	

Extracts are highly concentrated forms of flavouring used in some kitchens to strengthen stocks and sauces. They are also used for making hot drinks, e.g. Bovril, Marmite, Maggi.

CONTINENTAL SAUSAGES

A large variety of these are imported from European countries.

SALAMI

This is a very popular sausage imported chiefly from Italy and Hungary. It is usually made from pork, beef and bacon; highly seasoned and coloured with red wine it is then well dried and cured so as to keep for years.

It is thinly sliced and eaten cold; usually as part of an hors d'œuvre.

MORTADELLA

This large, oval-shaped, cooked sausage is imported from Italy. Mortadella is made from pork and veal and has pieces of pork fat showing. It is thinly sliced and eaten in the same way as salami.

CERVELAT BEEF OR PORK SAUSAGE

These sausages are chiefly imported from Germany; they are dried, smoked and eaten raw.

FRANKFURT OR VIENNA SAUSAGE

There are several varieties of these small sausages which are made from ham or pork. They are dried then smoked and are boiled before being used. Frankfurters are obtainable in tins. They should be served as part of the garnish to Sauerkraut, e.g. Choucroûte Garni.

LIVER SAUSAGE

This is produced in large quantities in this country and may be made from pigs' or calves' liver mixed with lean and fat pork and highly seasoned. It is sliced and served cold usually as part of an hors d'œuvre. Liver sausage is also used in sandwiches, and it may be served with other cold meats. This needs to be kept in a refrigerator.

HAMS

A ham is the hind leg of a pig cured by a special process which varies according to the type of ham. One of the most famous English ham is the York ham (6–7 kg) which is cured by salting, drying and sometimes smoking. The Bradenham ham is of coal-black colour and is a sweet-cured ham from Chippenham in Wiltshire. Hams are also imported from Northern Ireland, Denmark, Czechoslovakia (Prague hams 2–4 kg).

All the above hams should be soaked in cold water for several hours before being boiled or braised. Ham may be eaten hot or cold in a variety of ways. Continental raw hams, Bayonne and Ardenne from France and Parma from Italy are cut in thin slices and served raw, usually as part of hors d'œuvre.

FOIE GRAS

This expensive delicacy is obtained from the livers of specially fattened geese and is produced mainly in Strasbourg. It is obtainable either plain or with truffles in tins of various sizes and at certain times of the year is also obtained in round pastry cases (foie gras en croûte). Foie gras is a classic first course for any lunch, dinner or supper menu. It is also used as a garnish, e.g. Tournedos Rossini, and is included in the rice stuffing for certain chicken dishes.

TRUFFLES

The truffles chiefly used in this country are imported in tins of varying sizes. Truffles are a fungus and many varieties are found in many parts of the world. The black truffle found in the Périgord region of France is the most famous.

Because of the jet black colour truffles are used a great deal in the decorating of cold buffet dishes, particularly on chaud-froid work. Slices of truffle are used in the garnishing of many classical dishes such as Sole Cubat, Tournedos Maréchale, Poulet Sauté Archiduc.

Truffles are considered to be a delicacy and are extremely expensive.

PÂTÉ MAISON

This is a highly seasoned cooked preparation of fat pork, lean pork and liver.

BRAWN

This is a preparation made from the boiled, well-seasoned head of a pig. After being cooked the meat is picked off the bones, roughly chopped or minced, then set in a mould with some of the cooking liquor. When cold and set it is carved in thick slices and served as a cold meat.

GALANTINE

This is a cooked meat preparation made from well seasoned finely minced chicken, veal or other white meat. A first class galantine is stuffed with strips of fat pork, tongue, chicken or veal, truffles and pistachio nuts, then rolled in thin fat pork, tied in a cloth and boiled. When cold, galantines are coated with chaud-froid and masked with aspic and served on cold buffets (see page 187, *Practical Cookery*).

BOAR'S HEAD

This is a combination of a brawn and galantine, prepared from the head of the boar. It is moulded back in the skin of the head in its original shape and coated with a dark reddish-brown aspic and decorated with piped butter. Boars heads are used on cold buffets.

HAGGIS

This popular Scottish dish is made from the heart, lungs and liver of the sheep, mixed with suet, onion and oatmeal and sewn up in a stomach bag. It is boiled and served with mashed potatoes.

COCKSCOMBS AND KIDNEYS

These are dressed and preserved in bottles and are used for garnishing certain dishes, e.g. Financière.

ROLLMOPS—BISMARK HERRINGS

These are fillets of herring which are rolled, well spiced and pickled then served cold, usually as an hors d'œuvre.

SMOKED HERRING FILLET

These are preserved in oil and used as hors d'œuvre.

SNAILS (ESCARGOTS)

These edible snails are raised on the foliage of the vine. They are obtainable in boxes which include the tinned snails and the cleaned shells. The snails are replaced in the shells with a mixture of butter, garlic, lemon juice and parsley then heated in the oven and served in special dishes as a first course.

FROGS' LEGS (GRENOUILLE)

The flesh of the hindquarters of a certain species of green frog are esteemed as a delicacy in certain continental restaurants. They are cooked in various ways.

TINNED SOUPS

Most soups are obtainable in tins. The classic ones are: Turtle Soup, Lobster Soup, Vichyssoise, etc.

POTTED SHRIMPS

These are the peeled tails of cooked shrimps, which are preserved in butter and are usually served as an hors d'œuvre. They must be refrigerated.

PICKLES

These are vegetables and/or fruits preserved in vinegar or sauce and include

RED CABBAGE

Which can be served as part of hors d'œuvre and may also be offered as an accompaniment to Irish Stew.

GHERKINS

Are a small, rough-skinned variety of cucumber, the size of which should not exceed the size of the small finger. Gherkins are used for hors d'œuvre, tartare sauce, charcutière sauce, certain salads and for garnishing some cold dishes, and as an accompaniment to Bœuf Bouilli à la Française.

OLIVES

These are the fruit of the olive tree and there are three main varieties:

(*a*) *Manzanilla*—the small green olive used for cocktail savouries, hors d'œuvre and garnishing many dishes such as Escalope de Veau Viennoise. These olives may also be obtained stuffed with pimento.

(*b*) *Spanish Queens*—the large green olives used for hors d'œuvre and cocktail savouries.

(*c*) *Black Olives*—used for hors d'œuvre and certain salads.

COCKTAIL ONIONS

These are the small queen or silver skin onion used for cocktail savouries and hors d'œuvre.

WALNUTS

Are pickled when green and tender before the shell hardens. They are used for hors d'œuvre, salads and garnishing certain dishes such as Canapé Ivanhoe.

CAPERS

These are the pickled flower buds of the caper plant. They are used in Caper Sauce, Tartare Sauce, Piquant Sauce and for garnishing many hot and cold fish dishes such as Truite Grenobloise, Mayonnaise de Homard.

MANGO CHUTNEY

This is a sweet chutney which is served as an accompaniment to curried dishes.

TOMATOES

Are obtainable: (*a*) peeled whole in tins of various sizes; (*b*) in tins of various sizes and of different strengths; (*c*) paste form in tubes and tins.

All types are used a great deal in the preparation of many soups, sauces, egg, fish, farinaceous, meat and poultry dishes.

CÈPES

A species of French mushroom obtainable as Cèpes au Naturel or Cèpes à l'Huile.

They are usually sold in tins or bottles or in dried form. They are used in many French-style dishes.

CHOW-CHOW

(*a*) A Chinese or pidgin English word for a mixture. It is the name given to oriental fruits preserved in syrup which is served with curry.

(*b*) The name also of a fleshy fruit obtainable at Christmas time.

SALTPETRE

This is a natural product (nitrate of potash) which may also be produced artificially. It is used for pickling, and is one of the chief ingredients in a brine-tub for pickling meats.

HORSERADISH

Is obtainable in sauce or cream form in jars or bottles; either may be served with hot or cold roast beef.

WORCESTER SAUCE

Is a thin, highly seasoned, strong-flavoured sauce used as an accompaniment at table and in flavouring certain sauces, meat puddings and pies.

ANCHOVY ESSENCE

Is a strong, highly seasoned commodity used for flavouring certain fish sauces and fish preparations such as anchovy sauce or fish cakes.

BOMBAY DUCK

Are dried fillets of a fish found in Southern Asia. They are lightly cooked, usually by grilling and served as an accompaniment to curry dishes of meat and poultry. Bombay duck are purchased in packets of 12 fillets.

POPPADUMS

Are thin round biscuits prepared in India from a mixture of finely ground pigeon peas (dhal) and other ingredients. When lightly cooked, either by frying or grilling, they are also served as an accompaniment to curry dishes. Poppadums are obtainable in tins of 50 pieces.

CONFECTIONERY GOODS

MARRONS GLACÉS

Are peeled and cooked chestnuts preserved in syrup. They are used in certain large and small cakes, sweet dishes and as a variety of petit fours.

FONDANT

Is a soft white preparation of sugar. It is made by boiling sugar and glucose to a temperature of about 102°C, allowing it to cool slightly, then working it to a soft cream. Fondant has many uses in pastry and confectionery work, chiefly for coating petit fours, pastries and gâteaux. Fondant is generally made by pastry cooks; it may also be obtained as a ready-made preparation.

COCKTAIL CHERRIES

Are bright red cherries preserved in a syrup often flavoured with a liqueur known as Maraschino. They are obtainable in jars and bottles of various sizes. In addition to being used for cocktails they are also used to give colour to grapefruit and grapefruit cocktails.

PIPING JELLY

Is a thick jelly of piping consistency obtainable in different colours and flavours. It is used for decorating pastries and gâteaux and cold sweets. Piping jelly is obtainable in large tins.

HONEY

Is a natural sugar produced by bees working upon the nectar of flowers. It is generally used in the form of a preserve and as such it may be offered on breakfast and tea menus. Honey is obtainable in 1-lb. jars and 7-lb. tins.

JAM

Is a preserve of fruit and sugar which is obtainable in 1-oz., 1-lb. and 2-lb. jars and 7-lb. tins. Raspberry and apricot jams are those mostly used in the pastry.

MARMALADE

Is a preserve of citrus fruits and sugar, which is used mainly for breakfast menus and for certain sweets.

RED-CURRANT JELLY

Is a clear preserve of red currants used as a jam and also in the preparation of savoury sweet sauces such as Réforme and Cumberland sauce. Red-currant jelly is also used as an accompaniment to Roast Saddle of Mutton and Jugged Hare (Civet de Lièvre).

MINCEMEAT

Is a mixture of dried fruit, fresh fruit, sugar, spices, nuts, etc., chiefly used for mince-pies. A recipe for mincemeat is on page 291 in *Practical Cookery*. It can also be obtained in 1-lb. and 2-lb. jars and 6-lb. tins.

GUM TRAGACANTH

Is a soluble gum used for stiffening pastillage; only a very clear white type of gum tragacanth should be used.

PASTILLAGE

Is a mixture of icing sugar and gum tragacanth which may be moulded into shapes for set pieces for cold buffets and also for making baskets, caskets, etc., for the serving of petits fours.

RENNET

Is a substance obtained from the stomach of calves, pigs and lambs. It is prepared in powder, extract or essence form and is used in the production of cheese and for making junket.

CHOCOLATE VERMICELLI

Is a ready-made preparation of small fine chocolate pieces used in the decorating of small and large cakes and some chocolate flavoured sweets. Chocolate vermicelli is obtainable in 7-lb boxes.

MARZIPAN

Is a preparation of ground almonds, sugar and egg yolks used in the making of petits fours, pastries and large cakes. Marzipan is freshly made by pastry cooks; it is also obtainable as a ready-prepared commodity.

CAPE GOOSEBERRIES (PHYSALIS)

A tasty, yellow-berried fruit resembling a large cherry. Cape gooseberries are often dipped into fondant and served as a petit four.

ICE CREAM

Is a frozen preparation of a well-flavoured, sweetened mixture which can be made in many ways and in many flavours. Ice cream may be bought ready prepared, usually in 5 litre cans which are suitable for deep-freeze storage. The storage temperature for ice cream should not exceed −19°C. A large number of sweets can be prepared using ice cream as a base mixed with various fruits, nuts, sauces and cream. Many variations of semi-hot sweets of the 'omelette surprise' type have ice cream as one of the chief ingredients. Other sweets are made from an enriched ice-cream mixture and frozen in specially shaped moulds which give their names to the sweets, e.g. a heart-shaped mould—cœur glacé; a bomb-shaped mould—bombe glacé.

WAFERS

Are thin crisp biscuits of various shapes and sizes usually served with ice cream. They are obtainable in large tins of approximately 1000 and half-tins of approximately 500 wafers.

9. Preservation of Foods

Unless foods are preserved they deteriorate; therefore, to keep them in an edible condition it is necessary to know what causes food spoilage. In the air there are certain micro-organisms called moulds, yeasts and bacteria which cause foods to go bad.

Moulds

These are simple plants which appear like whiskers on foods, particularly sweet foods, meat and cheese. To grow, they require warmth, air, moisture, darkness and food; they are killed by heat and sunlight. Moulds can grow where there is too little moisture for yeasts and bacteria to grow, and will be found on jams and pickles.

Although not harmful they do cause foods to taste musty and to be wasted. Example: the top layer of a jar of jam would be removed if it had mould on it.

Correct storage in a dry cold store prevents moulds from forming.

Not all moulds are destructive, some are used to flavour cheese (Stilton, Roquefort) or to produce antibiotics (penicillin, streptomycin).

Yeasts

These are single-cell plants, or organisms larger than bacteria, which grow on foods containing moisture and sugar. Foods containing only a small percentage of sugar and large percentage of liquid, such as fruit juices and syrups, are subject to yeasts. Although they seldom cause disease yeasts do increase food spoilage; foodstuffs should be kept under refrigeration if they may be spoiled by yeasts. Yeasts are also destroyed by heat.

Bacteria

Bacteria are minute plants, or organisms, which require moist, warm conditions and a suitable food to multiply. They spoil food by attacking it, leaving waste products or by producing poisons in the food.

Their growth is checked by refrigeration and they are killed by heat. Certain bacteria (spores) are more resistant to heat than others and require higher temperatures to kill them.

Pressure cooking destroys heat resistant bacteria provided the food is cooked for a sufficient length of time, because increased

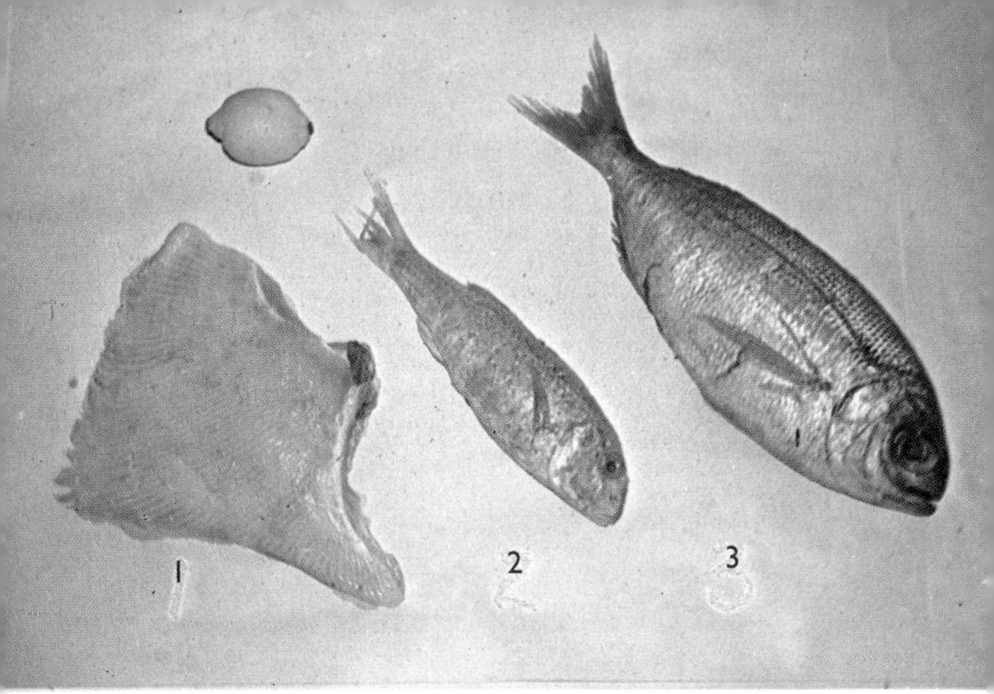

Plate 7. 1. Wing of Skate. 2. Red Mullet. 3. Bream.

Plate 8. Carcass of Lamb.

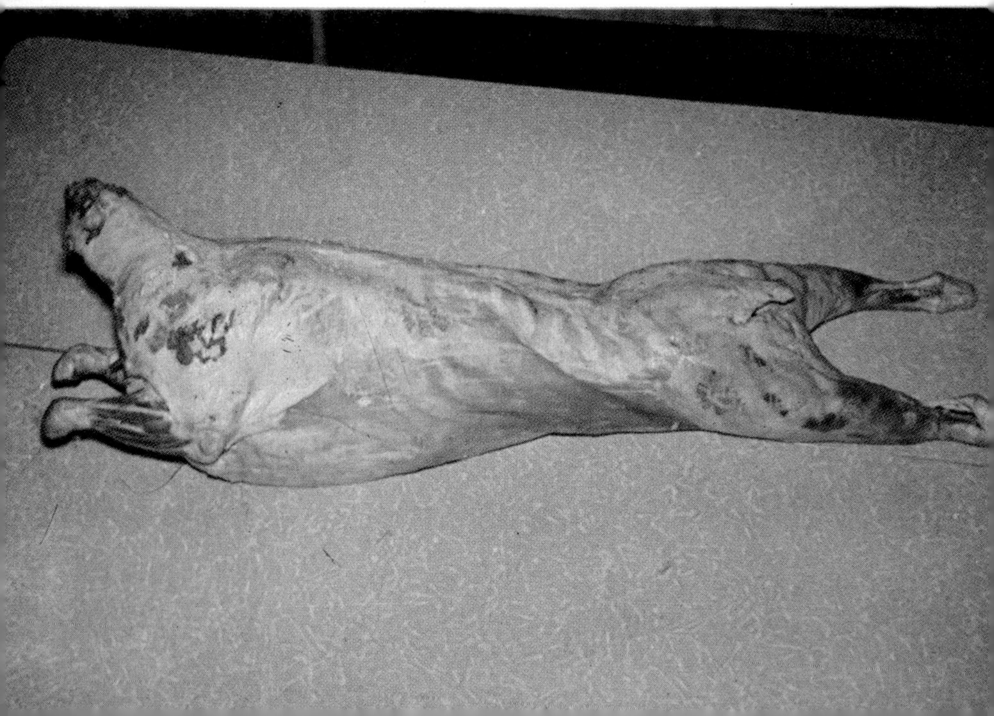

pressure increases the temperature, therefore heat resistant bacteria do not affect canned foods. Acids are generally capable of destroying bacteria—for example, vinegar in pickles.

Dehydrated foods and dry foods do not contain much moisture and provided they are kept dry, spoilage from bacteria will not occur. If they become moist then bacteria can multiply for example, if dried peas are soaked and not cooked they will be attacked by bacteria.

Other Causes

Food spoilage can occur from other causes, such as by chemical substances called enzymes, which are produced by living cells. Fruits are ripened by the action of enzymes; they do not remain edible indefinitely because other enzymes cause the fruit to become over-ripe and spoil.

When meat and game are hung they become tender; this is caused by the enzymes. To prevent enzyme activity going too far, foods must be refrigerated or heated to a temperature high enough to destroy the enzymes. Acid retards the enzyme action; for example, lemon juice prevents the browning of bananas or apples when they are cut into slices.

PRESERVATION

may be achieved by several methods:

(*a*) By removing the moisture from the food, e.g. drying, dehydration.
(*b*) By making the food cold, e.g. chilling, freezing.
(*c*) By applying heat, e.g. canning, bottling.
(*d*) By radiation, using X- or Y-rays.
(*e*) By chemical means, e.g. salting, pickling, crystallising.

Food may be preserved by the following ways:

1. Drying
2. Dehydration
3. Chilling
4. Freezing
5. Canning
6. Bottling
7. Pickling
8. Salting
9. Smoking (curing)
10. Chemical
11. Gas storage
12. Radiation

DRYING AND DEHYDRATION

This method of preserving is achieved by extracting the moisture from the food, thus preventing moulds, yeasts and bacteria from growing. This was done by drying foods, such as fruits, in the sun; today many types of equipment are used, and the food is dried by the use of air at a regulated temperature and humidity.

Accelerated Freeze Drying

This is a process of dehydration whereby food requires no preservation or refrigeration yet when soaked in water regains its original shape and flavour. It can be applied to every kind of food. The food is frozen in a cabinet, the air is pumped out and the ice vaporised. This is called Accelerated Freeze Drying and it is the drying of frozen foods by sublimation under conditions of very low pressure. Sublimation is the action of turning from solid to gas without passing through a liquid stage; in this case it is ice to steam without firstly turning to water.

The food when processed in this way does not lose a great deal of its bulk, but it is very much lighter in weight. When water is added the food gives off its natural smell.

Advantages of Drying

(*a*) If kept dry, food keeps indefinitely.

(*b*) Food preserved by this method occupies less space than food preserved by other methods. Some dried foods occupy 10% of the space required when fresh.

(*c*) Dried foods are easily transported and stored.

(*d*) The cost of drying and the expenses incurred in storing are not as high as other methods of preservation.

(*e*) There is no waste after purchase, therefore portion control and costing are simplified.

Foods preserved by Drying

Vegetables: Peas, onions, beetroot, beans, carrots, lentils, cabbage, mixed vegetables, potatoes.

Herbs

Eggs

Milk

Fruits: Apples, pears, plums (prunes), apricots, figs, grapes (sultanas, raisins, currants).

Meat

Fish

Vegetables

Many vegetables are dried; those most used are the pulse vegettables: beans, peas and lentils which are used for soups and vegetable purée. Usually potatoes are cooked, mashed and then dried. The other dried vegetables are used as a vegetable, e.g. cabbage, onions.

Pulse vegetables are generally soaked in water before use, then washed before being cooked. Vegetables which are dehydrated (having a lower content of water as more moisture has been extracted) are soaked in water.

Potatoes which are dehydrated are in powder form and are reconstituted with water, or milk, or milk and water.

Herbs

Herbs are tied into bundles and allowed to dry out in a dry place.

Fruits

Sultanas, currants and raisins are dried grapes which have been dried in the sun or by hot air. Figs, prunes, apricots, apples and pears are also dried by hot air. Apples are usually peeled and cut in rings or dice and then dried.

All dried fruits must be washed before use and fruits such as prunes, figs, apricots, apples and pears are cooked in the water in which they are soaked.

Little flavour or food value is lost in the drying of fruits.

Milk

Milk is dried either by the roller or spray process. With the roller method the milk is poured on to heated rollers which cause the water to evaporate, the resulting powder is then scraped off. With the spray process the milk is sent through a fine jet as a spray into hot air, the water evaporates and the powder drops down. The temperature is controlled so that the protein in the milk is not cooked.

Use. Milk powder may be used in place of fresh milk mainly for economic reasons and is used for cooking purposes such as custard, white sauce, etc.

Eggs

Eggs are dried in the same way as milk and although they have a food value similar to fresh eggs, dried eggs do not have the same aerating quality. When reconstituted the eggs should be used at once; if left in this state in the warm atmosphere of the kitchen bacteria can multiply and food poisoning may result because the heat used in the drying process is insufficient to kill the bacteria present in the original egg.

Use. Dried eggs are mainly used in the bakery trade.

CHILLING AND FREEZING

Refrigeration is a method of preservation where the micro-organisms are not killed; they are only prevented from multiplying. The lower the temperature the longer foods will keep. Refrigerators kept at a temperature between 0°C–7°C prevent foods from spoiling for only a short time; most frozen foods can be kept at −17°C for a year and at −28°C for two years. Foods must be kept in deep freeze until required for use.

Cold storage of fresh foods merely retards the decay of the food; it does not prevent it from eventually going bad.

If frozen slowly, large uneven crystals are formed in the cells of food. The water in each cell contains the minerals which give flavour and goodness to food; if frozen slowly the minerals are separated from the ice crystals which break through the cells; on thawing, the goodness and flavour drain away. Quick-freezing is satisfactory because small ice crystals are formed in the cells of food; on thawing, the goodness and flavour are retained in the cells.

The following graph shows how only small ice crystals are formed when the temperature falls rapidly through zone, whereas in the second curve, the slower fall results in larger ice crystals.

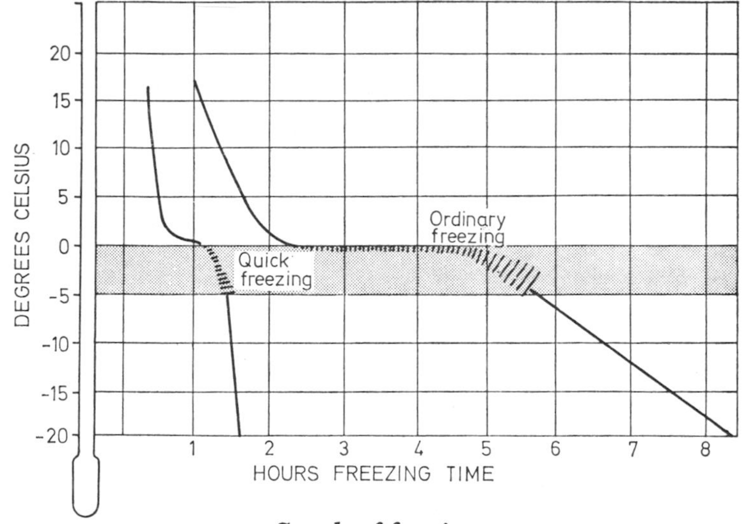

Speeds of freezing.

MEAT

Chilling

Meat which is chilled is kept at a temperature just above freezing-point and will keep for up to one month. If the atmosphere is controlled with carbon dioxide the time can be extended to ten weeks. Beef from the Argentine takes about three weeks for the journey and is chilled, not frozen. Meat from Australia is frozen because the journey takes about twelve weeks.

Freezing

Mutton and lamb carcasses are frozen; beef carcasses are not usually frozen because owing to the size of the carcass it takes a long time to freeze and this causes ice crystals to form which, when thawed, affect the texture of the meat. Frozen meat must be thawed before it is cooked.

QUICK FREEZING

To quick-freeze, trays of foods are placed on hollow shelves through which passes a refrigerant having a very low temperature. The foods stay in the freezing chamber for 60–90 minutes according to size.

Foods which are frozen

A very wide variety of foods are frozen, either cooked or in an uncooked state.

Examples of cooked foods. Whole cooked meals; braised meat; vol-au-vents; éclairs; cream sponges; puff pastry items.

Examples of raw foods. Fillets of fish; fish fingers; poultry; peas; French beans; broad beans; spinach; sprouts; broccoli; strawberries; raspberries; blackcurrants.

With most frozen foods, cooking instructions are given; these should be followed to obtain the best results.

Fillets of fish may be thawed out before cooking; vegetables are cooked in their frozen state. Fruit is thawed before use and as it is usually frozen with sugar the fruit is served with the liquor.

Advantages of using Frozen Foods

(*a*) Frozen foods are ready-prepared, therefore there is a saving of time and labour.

(*b*) Portion control and costing are easily assessed.

(*c*) Foods are always ‘in season’.

(*d*) Compact storage.

(*e*) Additional stocks to hand.

(*f*) Guaranteed quality.

Further information from: Education Department, Unilever House, Blackfriars, London, E.C.4.

CANNING AND BOTTLING

Bottled and canned foods are sealed in airtight bottles or tins and heated at a high enough temperature for a sufficient period of time to destroy harmful organisms.

Dented cans which do not leak are safe to use, but blown cans, that is those with bulges at either end, must not be used.

Tinned hams are canned at a low temperature and therefore should be stored in a refrigerator and consumed soon after purchase. Other tinned foods are kept in a dry, cool place and the following table indicates the advised storage time:

Fruit	up to 12 months
Milk	up to 12 months
Vegetables	up to 2 years
Meat	up to 5 years
Fish in oil	up to 5 years
Fish in tomato sauce	up to 1 year

Foods are canned in tins of various sizes, e.g.:

Size	*Approx. weight*	*Use*
	142 g	Baked beans, peas
	227 g	Fruits, meats, vegetables
A 1	284 g	Baked beans, soups, vegetables, meats, pilchards
14 Z	397 g	Fruits, vegetables
A 2	567 g	Fruits, vegetables, fruit and vegetable juices
A 2½	794 g	Fruit, vegetables
A 10	3079 g	Fruit, vegetables, tongues

The advantages of canned foods are similar to those of frozen foods.

Further information from Canned and Packaged Foods Bureau, 37 Baker Street, London, W.1.

PRESERVATION BY SALT AND BY SALTING AND SMOKING

Micro-organisms cannot grow in high concentrations of salt. This method of preservation is used mainly to preserve meat and fish and the advantage lies chiefly in the fact that a wider variety of dishes with different flavours can be put on the menu.

Meats

Meats which are salted or 'pickled' in a salt solution (brine) are brisket, silversides of beef, ox tongues, legs of pork.

A Recipe for Brine is:

4 litres cold water	$\frac{1}{2}$–1 kg salt
22 g saltpetre	

Boil the ingredients together for 10 minutes, skimming frequently. Strain into a china, wooden or earthenware container. When the brine is cold, add the meat. Immerse the meat for up to 10 days.

Pork used for bacon and for hams, is first salted and then usually smoked. The addition of saltpetre gives an attractive pink colour as well as acting as a preservative.

Joints are smoked by being hung over burning oak or beech sawdust, this process adds to the keeping qualities of the meat.

Fish

Fish is usually smoked as well as being salted and include: salmon; trout; haddock; herrings; cods' roes.

The amount of salting varies. Bloaters are salted more than kippers and red herrings more than bloaters.

The salt added to butter and margarine and also to cheese acts as a preservative.

PRESERVATION BY SUGAR

A high concentration of sugar prevents the growth of moulds, yeasts and bacteria. This method of preservation is applied to fruits in these forms: jams, marmalades, jellies, candied, glacé and crystallised.

Jams are prepared by cooking fruit and sugar together in the correct quantities to prevent the jam from spoiling. Too little sugar means the jam will not keep.

Jellies such as red-currant jelly, are prepared by cooking the juice of the fruit with the sugar.

Marmalade is similar to jam in preparation and preservation, citrus fruits being used in place of other fruits.

Candied—the peel of such fruit as orange, lemon, grapefruit and lime and also the flesh of pineapple are covered with hot syrup, the syrup's sugar content is increased each day until the fruit is saturated in a very heavy syrup, then it is allowed to dry slowly.

Crystallised. After the fruit has been candied it is left in fresh syrup for 24 hours. It is then allowed to dry slowly until crystals form on the fruit. Angelica, ginger, violet and rose petals are prepared in this way.

Glacé. The fruit, usually cherries, is first candied, then dipped in fresh syrup to give a clear finish.

PRESERVATION BY ACIDS

Foods may be preserved in vinegar which is acetic acid diluted with water. In this country malt vinegar is the one most used, although distilled or white wine vinegar is used for pickling white vegetables such as cocktail onions and also for rollmops (herrings).

Foods usually pickled in vinegar are: gherkins, capers, onions, shallots, walnuts, red cabbage, mixed pickles, chutneys.

PRESERVATION BY CHEMICALS

Certain chemicals are permitted by law to be used to preserve certain foods such as sausages, fruit pulp, jam, etc. For domestic fruit bottling, Campden preserving tablets can be used.

PRESERVATION BY RADIATION

Foods subjected to certain rays, for example X-rays or Y-rays, are preserved and research is being carried out on this method of preserving food.

PRESERVATION BY GAS STORAGE

Gas storage is used in conjunction with refrigeration to preserve meat, eggs and fruit. Carbon dioxide added to the atmosphere surrounding the foods increases the length of time they can be stored. Without the addition of gas these foods would dry out more quickly.

10. Storekeeping

A clean, orderly food store, run efficiently, is essential in any catering establishment for the following reasons:

1. Stocks of food can be kept at a suitable level, so eliminating the risk of running out of any commodity.

2. All food entering and leaving the stores can be properly checked; this helps to prevent wastage.

3. A check can be kept on the percentage profit of each department of the establishment.

A well-planned store should include the following features:

(*a*) It should be cool and face the north so that it does not have the sun shining into it.

(*b*) It must be well ventilated and free from dampness (dampness in a dry store causes it to be musty, and encourages bacteria to grow and tins to rust).

(*c*) It should be in a convenient position to receive goods being delivered by suppliers and also in a suitable position to issue goods to the various departments.

(*d*) A good standard of hygiene is essential, therefore the walls and ceilings should be free from cracks, and either painted or tiled so as to be easily cleaned. The floor should be free from cracks and easy to wash. The junction between the wall and floor should be rounded to prevent the accumulation of dirt.

(*e*) Shelves should be easy to clean.

(*f*) Good lighting, both natural and artificial, is very necessary.

(*g*) A counter should be provided to keep out unauthorised persons, thus reducing the risk of pilfering.

(*h*) The storekeeper should be provided with a suitable desk.

(*i*) There should be ample, well-arranged storage space, with shelves of varying depths and separate sections for each type of food. These sections may include deep-freeze cabinets, cold rooms, refrigerators, chill rooms, vegetable store bins and container store. Space should also be provided for empty containers.

(*j*) Efficient, easy-to-clean weighing machines for large and small scale work should be supplied.

STORE CONTAINERS

Foods delivered in flimsy bags or containers should be transferred to suitable store containers. These should be easy to wash and have tight-fitting lids. Glass or plastic containers are suitable for many foods, such as spices and herbs, as they have the advantage of being transparent, therefore it is easy to see at a glance how much of the commodity is in stock.

Bulk dry goods (pulses, sugar, salt, etc.) should be stored in galvanised bins with tight-fitting lids. These bins should have wheels so that they can be easily moved for cleaning. All bins should be clearly labelled or numbered.

Sacks or cases of commodities should not be stored on the floor; they should be raised on duckboards so as to permit a free circulation of air.

Some goods are delivered in containers suitable for storage and these need not be transferred. Heavy cases, bags and jars should be stored at a convenient height to prevent any strain in lifting.

SPECIAL STORAGE POINTS

1. All old stock should be brought forward with each new delivery.

2. Commodities with strong smells or flavours should be stored as far away as possible from those foods which readily absorb flavour. For example, strong-smelling cheese should not be stored near eggs.

3. Bread should be kept in a well-ventilated container with a lid. Lack of ventilation causes condensation and encourages moulds. Cakes and biscuits should be stored in airtight tins.

4. Tinned goods should be unpacked, inspected and stacked on shelves. When inspecting tins, these points should be looked for:

(*a*) Blown tins—this is where the ends of the tins bulge owing to the formation of gases either by bacteria growing on the food and producing gases or by the food attacking the tin-plate and producing gases. All blown tins should be thrown away as the contents are dangerous and the use of the contents may cause food-poisoning.

(*b*) Dented tins—these should be used as soon as possible not because the dent is an indication of inferior quality but because dented tins if left will rust and a rusty tin will eventually puncture.

(*c*) Storage life of tins varies considerably and depends mainly on how the contents attack the internal coating of the tin which may corrode and lay bare the steel. See Preservation of Food, page 244.

(*d*) Cleaning materials often have a strong smell, therefore they should be kept in a separate store. Cleaning powders should never be stored near food.

Storage Accommodation

Foods are divided into two groups for the purpose of storage: dry foods and perishable foods.

(*a*) *Dry stores* include: Cereals, pulses, sugar, flour, etc.; bread, cakes; jams, pickles and other bottled foods; canned foods; cleaning materials.

(*b*) *Perishable foods* include: Meat, poultry, game, fish; dairy produce and fats; vegetables and fruit.

THE COLD ROOM (see also Refrigeration, page 242)

A large catering establishment may have a cold room for meat, with possibly a deep-freeze compartment where supplies can be kept in a frozen stage for long periods. Poultry is also stored in a cold room. Fish should have a cold room of its own so that it does not affect other foods. Game, when plucked, is also kept in a cold room.

CHILL ROOM

This keeps foods cold without freezing, and is particularly suitable for those foods requiring a consistent, not too cold, temperature, such as dessert fruits, salads, cheese, etc.

REFRIGERATOR

This gives cold-room and chill-room conditions and is ideal for storing fats.

Use of Refrigeration

1. All refrigerators, cold rooms, chill rooms and deep-freeze units should be regularly inspected and maintained by qualified refrigeration engineers.

2. Defrosting should occur regularly, according to the instructions issued from the manufacturers. Refrigerators usually require to be defrosted weekly; if this is not done, then the efficiency of the refrigerator is lessened.

3. While a cold unit is being defrosted it should be thoroughly cleaned, including all the shelves.

4. Hot foods should never be placed in a refrigerator or cold room because the steam given off can affect nearby foods.

5. Peeled onions should never be kept in a cold room because the smell can taint other foods.

VEGETABLE STORE

This should be designed to store all vegetables in a cool, dry, well-ventilated room with bins for root vegetables and racking for other vegetables. Care should be taken to see that old stocks of vegetables are used before the new ones. This is important as fresh vegetables and fruits deteriorate quickly. If it is not convenient to empty root vegetables into bins they should be kept in the sack on racks off the ground.

ORDERING OF GOODS WITHIN THE ESTABLISHMENT

In a large catering establishment the stores carry a stock which for variety and quantity often equals a large grocery store. Its operation is similar in many respects, the main difference being that requisitions take the place of cash. The system of internal and external accountancy must be simple but precise.

THE STOREKEEPER

The essentials which go to making a good storekeeper are:

1. Experience.
2. Knowledge of how to handle, care for and organise the stock in his charge.
3. A tidy mind and sense of detail.
4. A quick grasp of figures.
5. Clear handwriting.
6. A liking for his job.
7. Honesty.

There are many departments which draw supplies from these stores—kitchen, still room, restaurant, grill room, banqueting, floor service. A list of these departments should be given to the storekeeper, together with the signatures of the heads of departments or those who have the right to sign the requisition forms.

All requisitions must be handed to the storekeeper in time for him to order the goods and have them delivered on the appropriate day. Different coloured requisitions may be used for the various departments if desired.

TYPES OF BOOKS USED IN STORES CONTROL

(*a*) *Bin Card.* There should be an individual Bin Card for each

BIN CARD

PRICE ....

UNIT (lbs., Tins, etc) .... MAX. STOCK........

COMMODITY.............................. MIN. STOCK........

DATE	RECEIVED	ISSUED	STOCK IN HAND	

item held in stock. The following details are found on the Bin Card:

1. Name of the commodity
2. Issuing unit
3. Maximum stock
4. Minimum stock
5. Date goods are received or issued
6. From whom they are received and to whom issued
7. The quantity received
8. The quantity issued
9. The balance held in stock

(*b*) *Stores Ledger*. This is usually found in the form of a loose-leaf file, giving one ledger sheet to each item held in stock. The following details are found on a Stores Ledger Sheet:

1. Name of commodity
2. Classification
3. Unit
4. Maximum stock
5. Minimum stock
6. Date of goods received or issued
7. From whom they are received and to whom issued
8. Invoice or requisition number
9. The quantity received or issued and the remaining balance held in stock
10. Unit price
11. The cash value of goods received and issued and the balancing cash total of goods held in stock

BIN No. DESCRIPTION CLASSIFICATION CODE UNIT MAXIMUM MINIMUM

Date	DETAIL	Invoice or Req. No.	QUANTITY			UNIT PRICE	VALUE		
			Received	Balance	Issued		Received	Balance	Issued

Every time goods are received or issued the appropriate entries should be made on the necessary stores ledger Sheets and bin cards. In this way the balance on your bin card should always be the same as the balance shown on the stores ledger sheet.

(*c*) *Departmental Requisition Book*. One of these books should be issued to each department in the catering establishment which finds it necessary to draw goods from the store. These books can either be of different colours or have serial numbers denoting to which department they belong. Every time goods have to be drawn from the store a requisition must be filled out and signed by the necessary head of department. This applies whether one item or twenty items are needed from the store. When the storekeeper issues the goods he will check them against the requisition and tick them off. At the same time he fills in the cost of each item. In this way the total expenditure over a period for a certain department can be quickly found. The following details are found on the Requisition Sheet:

1. Serial number
2. Name of department
3. Date
4. Description of goods required
5. Quantity of goods required
6. Unit
7. Price per unit
8. Issue, if different
9. Quantity of goods issued
10. Unit
11. Price per unit
12. Cash column
13. Signature

DEPARTMENTAL REQUISITION BOOK

Date................ Class...........................

Description	Quan.	Unit	Price per Unit	Issued if Different	Quan.	Unit	Price per Unit	Code	£	

(*d*) *Order Book*. This is in duplicate and has to be filled in by the storekeeper every time he wishes to have goods delivered. Whenever goods are ordered, an order sheet must be filled in and sent to the supplier. On receipt of the goods they should be checked against both Delivery Note and Duplicate Order Sheet. All order sheets must be signed by the storekeeper.

Details found on an Order Sheet are as follows:

1. Name and address of catering establishment
2. Name and address of supplier
3. Serial number of Order Sheet
4. Quantity of goods
5. Description of goods to be ordered
6. Date
7. Signature
8. Date of delivery, if specific day required

(*e*) *Stock Sheets*. Stock should be taken at regular intervals of either one week or one month. Spot checks are advisable about every three months. The stock check should be taken where possible by an independent person, thus preventing the chance of 'pilfering' and 'fiddling' taking place. The details found on the Stock Sheets are as follows:

1. Description of goods
2. Quantity received and issued and balance
3. Price per unit
4. Cash columns

The stock sheets will normally be printed in alphabetical order.

All fresh foodstuffs such as meat, fish, vegetables, etc., will be entered in the stock sheet in the normal manner, but as they are purchased and used up daily a NIL stock will always be shown on their respective ledger sheets.

COMMERCIAL DOCUMENTS

Essential parts of a control system of any catering establishment are Delivery Notes, Invoices, Credit Notes and Statements.

Delivery Notes are sent with goods supplied as a means of checking that everything ordered has been delivered. The Delivery Note should also be checked against the duplicate order sheet.

Invoices are bills sent to clients, setting out the cost of goods supplied or services rendered. An Invoice should be sent on the day the goods are despatched or the services are rendered or as soon as possible afterwards. At least one copy of each invoice is made, and used for posting up the books of account, stock records and so on.

Invoices contain the following information:

(*a*) The name, address, telephone numbers, etc. (as a printed heading), of the firm supplying the goods or services.

(*b*) The name and address of the firm to whom the goods or services have been supplied.

(*c*) The word INVOICE.

(*d*) The date on which the goods or services were supplied.

(*e*) Particulars of the goods or services supplied together with the prices.

(*f*) A note concerning the terms of settlement (e.g. 'Terms 5% one month'), which means that if the person receiving the invoice settles his account within one month he may deduct 5% as discount.

Credit Notes are advices to clients, setting out allowances made for goods returned or adjustments made through errors of overcharging on invoices. They should also be issued when chargeable containers such as crates, boxes, sacks are returned. Credit Notes are exactly the same in form as invoices except that the word CREDIT NOTE appears in place of the word Invoice. To make them more easily distinguishable they are usually printed in red, whereas invoices are always printed in black. Credit notes are always made out in red ink. A credit note should be sent as soon as it is known that a client is entitled to the credit of a sum with which he has been previously charged by invoice.

Statements are summaries of all invoices and credit notes sent to clients during the previous accounting period, usually one month. They also show any sums owing or paid from previous accounting periods and the total amount due. A statement is usually a copy of a client's ledger account and does not contain more information than is necessary to check invoices and credit notes.

When a client makes payment he usually sends a cheque, together with the statement he has received. The cheque is paid into the bank and the statement may be returned to the client duly receipted.

Cash Discount is a discount allowed in consideration of prompt payment.

At the end of any length of time chosen as an accounting period (e.g. one month) there will be some outstanding debts. In order to encourage customers to pay within a stipulated time, sellers of goods frequently offer a discount. This is called Cash Discount. By offering cash discount the seller may induce his customer to pay more quickly, so turning debts into ready money. Cash discount varies from 1¼% to 10%, depending on the seller and the time, e.g. 2½% if paid in 10 days; 1¼% if paid in 28 days.

Simple Discount Table

Percentage	*Part of £1*
2½%	2½p
5%	5 p
10 %	10 p
12½%	12½p
15 %	15 p
20 %	20 p
25 %	25 p

Trade Discount is discount allowed by one trader to another.

This is a deduction from the catalogue price of goods made before arriving at the invoice price. The amount of trade discount does not therefore appear in the accounts. For example in a catalogue of kitchen equipment a machine listed at £70 less 20% trade discount shows:

Catalogue price	£70
Less 20% Trade Discount	14
Invoice price	£56

The £56 is the amount entered in the appropriate accounts.

In the case of purchase tax on articles, discount is taken off *after* the tax has been deducted from list price.

Gross Price is the price of an article before discount has been deducted.

Nett Price is the price after discount has been deducted; in some cases a price on which no discount will be allowed.

STORES CONTROL

INVOICE

Phone: SOU 1133
Telegrams: SOUT

No. 03957
Vegetable Suppliers Ltd.,
5 Warwick Road,
Southall,
Middlesex

Messrs. L. Moriarty & Co.,
597 High Street,
Ealing,
London, W.5.

Terms: 5% One month

Your order No. 67		Dated 3rd September, 19....	£	
19....				
Sep. 26th	25 kg	Potatoes at 10p per kg	2	50
	2 kg	Sprouts at 20p per kg		40
			£2	90

STATEMENT

Phone: SOU 1133
Telegrams: SOUT

Vegetable Suppliers Ltd.,
5 Warwick Road,
Southall,
Middlesex

Messrs. L. Moriarty & Co.,
597 High Street,
Ealing,
London, W.5.

Terms: 5% One month

19....		£
Sep. 10th	Goods	3.48
17th	Goods	1.20
20th	Goods	2.32
26th	Goods	57
		7.57
28th	Returns Credited	76
		£6.81

DAILY STORES ISSUE SHEET (QUANTITY)

Commodity	*Unit*	*Stock in hand*	*Monday*		*Tuesday*		*Wednesday*		*Thursday*		*Friday*		*Total purchases*	*Total issues*	*Total stock*
			In	*Out*	*In*	*Out*	*In*	*Out*	*In*	*Out*	*In*	*Out*			
Butter	kg	27		2						3				5	22
Flour	Sacks	2		1			1						1	1	2
Olive oil	Litres	8		1						½				1½	6½
Spices	30g packs	8		4			8						8	4	12
Peas, tin	A10	30		6						3				9	21

THE DAILY STORES ISSUE SHEET

This may be made out to check daily the quantities of goods received and issued.

.....................CANTEEN Week Ending........... No. Meals Served........ Cost per Meal........

Commodity	*In hand B/F*	*Stock Received During Week*						*Stock Used During Week*											*Stock in hand C/F*
		M.	*Tu.*	*W.*	*Th.*	*F.*	*Total*	*M.*	*Tu.*	*W.*	*Th.*	*F.*	*S.*	*Total*	*@**	*Cost**			
Apples, Canned																			
Apples, Dried																			
Apricots, etc.—Dried																			
Baking Powder																			
Baked Beans																			

The cost of stock used can also be checked by using two extra columns.*

In conclusion, the following list gives the duties of a storekeeper.

DUTIES OF A STOREKEEPER

1. To keep a good standard of tidiness and cleanliness.
2. To arrange proper storage space for all incoming foodstuffs.
3. To keep up-to-date price lists of all commodities.
4. To ensure that an ample supply of all important foodstuffs is always available.
5. To check that all orders are correctly made out, and despatched in good time.
6. To check all incoming stores—quantity, quality and price.
7. To keep all delivery notes, invoices, credit notes, receipts and statements efficiently filed.
8. To keep a daily stores issue sheet.
9. To keep a set of bin cards.
10. To issue nothing without receiving a signed chit in exchange.
11. To check all stock at frequent intervals.
12. To see that all chargeable containers are properly kept, returned and credited—that is, all money charged for sacks, boxes, etc., is deducted from the account.
13. To obtain the best value at the lowest buying price.
14. To know when foods are in or out of season.

CASH A/C

The following are the essentials for the keeping of a simple cash account.

1. All entries must be dated.
2. All moneys received must be clearly named and entered on the left-hand or debit side of the book.
3. All moneys paid out must also be clearly shown and entered on the right-hand or credit side of the book.
4. At the end of a given period—either a day, week or month or at the end of each page—the book must be balanced—that is, both sides are totalled and the difference between the two is known as the balance. If, for example, the debit side (money received) is greater than the credit side (money paid out), then a credit or right-hand side balance is shown, so that the two totals are then equal. A credit balance then means cash in hand.
5. A debit balance cannot occur because it is impossible to pay out more than is received.

General Rule:

Debit moneys coming in
Credit moneys going out

Example:

Make out a cash account and enter the following transactions:

Oct.	1	Paid for repair to stove	£20·52½
	2	Paid to grocer	15·47½
	3	Received for lunches	30·52
	4	Received for teas	10·52½
	5	Received tax rebate	25·25
	6	Paid to butcher	10·54
Oct.	8	Paid to fishmonger	7·50
	9	Received for sale of pastries	15·47½
	10	Paid for fuel	10·50
	11	Paid tax	25·00
	11	Received for goods	32·83½
	12	Paid to greengrocer	14·36½
Oct.	15	Received for teas	16·52½
	17	Received for pastries	14·69½
	19	Paid to butcher	5·30½
	21	Paid to grocer	7·17½
	24	Received for goods	15·18½
	26	Received for goods	14·19½
	29	Received for goods	10·51½

Dr. *First Week* Cr.

Date	*Receipts*	£	*Date*	*Payments*	£
Oct. 3	To Lunches	30·52½	Oct. 1	By Repairs	20·52½
4	,, Teas	10·52½	2	,, Grocer	15·47½
5	,, Tax Rebate	25·25	6	,, Butcher	10·54
				,, Balance c/fwd	19·76½
		£66·29½			£66·29½

Dr. *Second Week* Cr.

Date	*Receipts*	£	*Date*	*Payments*	£
Oct.	To Balance b/fwd	19·75½	Oct. 8	By Fishmonger	7·50
9	,, Sale of Pastries	15·47½	10	,, Fuel	10·50
			11	,, Tax	25·00
11	,, Goods	32·83½	12	,, Greengrocer	14·69½
				,, Balance c/fwd	10·37
		£68·06½			£68·06½

Dr. *Third Week* Cr.

Date	*Receipts*	£	*Date*	*Payments*	£
Oct.	To Balance b/fwd	10·37½	Oct. 19	By Butcher	5·30½
15	,, Teas	16·52½	21	,, Grocer	7·17½
17	,, Pastries	14·36½		,, Balance c/fwd	68.67
24	,, Goods	15·18½			
26	,, Goods	14·19			
29	,, Goods	10·51			
		£81·15			£81.15

11. Kitchen Organisation

The organisation of kitchens will vary, due mainly to the size and the type of the establishment. Obviously, where a kitchen has 100 chefs preparing for banquets of up to 1000 people and a lunch and dinner service of 300–400 customers with an *à la carte* menu, the organisation will be quite different from a small restaurant doing thirty table d'hôte lunches or a hospital diet kitchen preparing diets.

Even when there are two kitchens of a similar nature the internal organisation may vary as each chef de cuisine will have his own way of running his kitchen. It has been found most satisfactory in organising the work of a kitchen to divide it into 'parties' or corners.

The number of parties required will depend on the size of the establishment. The organisation on page 263 could be for a large hotel, that on page 262 for a medium-sized establishment.

The Head Chef — *le Chef de Cuisine*

The duties of the Chef de Cuisine or Head Chef are mainly administrative; only in small establishments would it be necessary for the chef to be engaged in handling the food. His function is—

to organise the kitchen
to compile the menus
to order the foodstuffs
to show the required profit
to engage the staff
to supervise the kitchen (particularly at service time)
to advise on purchase of equipment
and in many cases to be responsible wholly or partially for the stores, still room and the washing up of silver, crockery, etc.

The Second Chef — *le Sous Chef*

The Second Chef relieves the head chef when he is off duty. He is the chef's right-hand man, whose main function is to supervise the work in the kitchen so that it runs smoothly and according to the chef's wishes. In large kitchens there may be several sous chefs with specific responsibility for separate services such as banquets, grill room, etc.

The Chef de Partie

The Chef de Partie is in charge of a section of the work in the kitchen. Usually the chef in charge of the sauce 'partie' is next in status to the sous chefs, and the larder chef being responsible for the perishable foods is often considered of a higher status than the other chefs except the pastry chef. This is the job of the specialist. The chef de partie organises his own section, delegates the work to his assistants and is in fact the 'backbone' of the kitchen.

ORGANISATION OF MEDIUM-SIZED KITCHEN

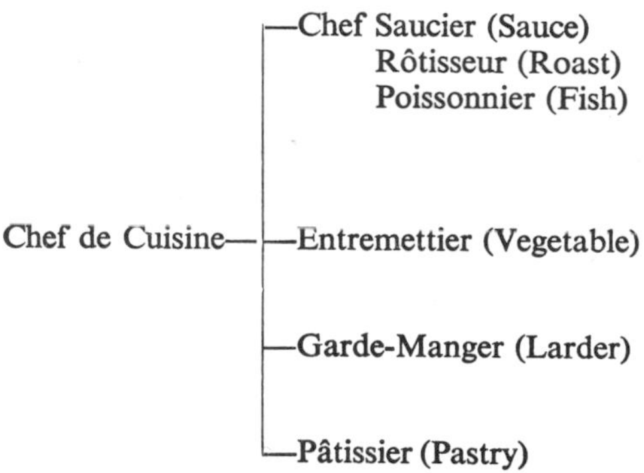

The Assistant Cooks *Commis Chefs*

The chef de partie is assisted by commis or assistants, the number varying with the amount of work done by the party, e.g. the vegetable party is larger than the fish party, due to the quantity of work to be prepared, so there are more assistants on that party. The first commis is usually capable of taking over a great deal of the responsibility, and in some cases will take charge of the party when the chef is off duty.

The Apprentice *l'Apprenti*

The apprentice is learning his trade and is moved to each of the parties to gain knowledge of all the sections in the kitchen.

The Work of the Chefs and their Parties

The Sauce Party (*Head: le Chef Saucier*). The sauce cook prepares the entrées; that is to say all the meat, poultry and game dishes which are not roasted or grilled. This includes all made-up dishes such as, vol-au-vents, stews, braised, boiled, poêled and sautéd dishes. The sauce cook will prepare certain garnishes for these dishes and make the meat, poultry and game sauces.

THE ORGANISATION OF A KITCHEN

THE KITCHEN STAFF (LA BRIGADE DE CUISINE)

Head Chef (Chef de Cuisine)
|
Second Chef (Sous Chef)
|

- Sauce Cook (le Chef Saucier) — Assistant Sauce Cook (Commis Saucier)
  - Apprentice (l'Apprenti)
- Roast Cook (le Rôtisseur)
- Fish Cook (le Poissonnier)
- Vegetable Cook (l'Entremettier)
- Soup Cook (le Potager)
- Larder Cook (le Garde-Manger)
  - Cold Work Chef (le Chef du Froid)
  - Hors d'Œuvre Cook (le Hors d'Œuvrier)
  - Butcher (le Boucher)
- Pastry Cook (le Pâtissier) — Ice Cream Cook (le Glacier)
- Baker (le Boulanger)
- Relief Cook (le Chef Tournant) — Assistant Relief Cook (le Commis Tournant)
- Night or Duty Cook (le Chef du Nuit ou le Chef de Garde)
- Breakfast Cook (le Chef du Petit Déjeuner)
- Staff Cook (le Communard)
- Carver (le Trancheur)
- Grill Cook (le Grillardin)

The Roast Party (*Head: le Chef Rôtisseur*). All roasted and grilled meat, poultry and game are cooked by the roast cooks. All grilled and deep-fried fish and other deep-fried foods, including potatoes, are cooked by this party, as well as many savouries. The only deep-fried foods which may not be cooked by the roast party are cooked in the pastry. The work of the rôtisseur includes the garnishing of the grills and roasts; he therefore grills the mushrooms and tomatoes and makes the Yorkshire pudding and roast gravy.

The Fish Party (*Head: le Chef Poissonnier*). Except for grilled and deep-fried fish, all the fish dishes and fish sauces and garnishes are cooked by this party, as well as béchamel, sauce hollandaise and melted butter. The preparation of the fish is usually done by a fishmonger in the larder.

The Vegetable Party (*Head: le Chef Entremettier*). All the vegetables and potatoes, other than deep fried, and the egg and farinaceous dishes are the responsibility of the vegetable party as well as the vegetable garnishes to the main dishes. Such things as savoury soufflées and in some places pancakes will be cooked by this party.

The Soup Party (*Head: le Chef Potager*). In large establishments there will be a separate party to make the soups and their garnishes. In some brigades, the eggs and farinaceous dishes will be the responsibility of this party.

The Larder Party (*Head: le Chef Garde-manger*). The larder is mainly concerned with the preparation of food which is cooked by the other parties. This includes the preparation of poultry and game and in smaller establishments the preparation of meat. The fish is prepared by a fishmonger in the larder by cleaning, filleting and portioning.

All the cold soup, egg, fish, meat, poultry and game dishes are decorated and served by this party. This work is done by the chef du froid and will entail a certain amount of cooking.

The sandwiches and certain work for cocktail parties such as canapés and the filling of bouchées is done here.

The hors d'œuvres and salads are made up by the hors d'œuvrier in his own place which is near to the larder.

All cold sauces are prepared in the larder.

The oysters, cheeses and the dessert fruits may also be served by a person in the larder.

The Pastry Party (*Head: le Chef Pâtissier*). All the sweets and pastries are made by the pastry cooks, also items required by other parties, such as vol-au-vents, bouchées, noodles, etc., as well as the covering for pies.

Ice cream and petits fours are also made here. Formerly, a glacier was employed to make all the ice creams, but the majority of ice cream is now produced in factories.

The bakery goods such as croissants, brioche, etc., may be made by the pastry when there is no separate bakery.

The Butcher *le Boucher*

Usually the butcher works under the direct control of the chef or sous chef and he dissects the carcasses and prepares all the joints and cuts ready for cooking.

The Baker *le Boulanger*

The baker will make all the bread, rolls, croissants, etc., but few hotels today employ their own bakers.

The Relief Cook *le Chef Tournant*

The chef tournant usually relieves the chefs of the sauce, roast, fish, and vegetable parties on their day off. The first commis in the larder and pastry usually relieves his own chef. In some places a commis tournant will also be employed.

The Duty Cook *le Chef de Garde*

The chef de garde is employed where split duty is involved and this chef is on guard to do any orders in the kitchen during that time when most of the staff are off duty and also for the late period when the other staff have gone home. Split duty hours involve a break from approximately 2.30 p.m. to 5.30 p.m. Usually a commis will be on guard in the larder and pastry.

The Night Cook *le Chef de Nuit*

A chef de nuit is employed to be on duty part of the night and all night if necessary to provide late meals.

The Breakfast Cook

The breakfast cook will prepare all the breakfasts and often in smaller establishments will do additional duties, sometimes working until after lunch.

Staff Cook

The staff cook provides the meals for the employees who use the staff room; these are the wage-earning staff and includes uniformed and maintenance staff, chamber maids, etc. This applies in large hotels.

The Grill Cook *le Grillardin*

The Carver *le Trancheur*

In places where there is call for a large number of grills and roast joints a grill cook and a carver will be employed in many cases in the dining room or grill room.

SUBSIDIARY DEPARTMENTS UNDER THE CONTROL OF THE CHEF

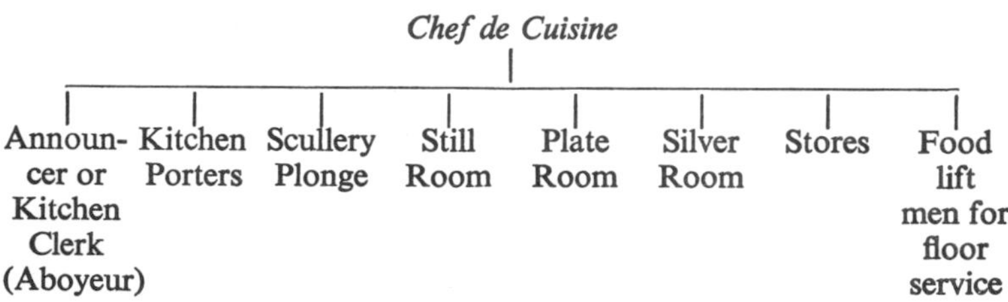

Kitchen Clerk and Aboyeur

These two duties are usually performed by one person.

The kitchen clerk is responsible for much of the chef's routine clerical work and is in fact secretary to the chef.

During service time he will often call out the orders from the hot plate. Aboyeur means barker, caller or announcer.

Kitchen Porters

Kitchen porters are responsible for general cleaning duties.

Larger parties such as the pastry, larder, and vegetable parties may have one or more porters to assist the chefs. They may prepare breadcrumbs, chop parsley, peel vegetables and carry food from one section to another.

When several porters are employed one is usually appointed head porter and he may be responsible for extra duties, e.g. changing laundry, etc.

Scullery

The sculleryman or 'plongeur' is responsible for collecting, washing and returning to the appropriate place in the kitchen, all the pots and pans.

Stillroom

In the stillroom are prepared and served all the beverages, e.g. tea, coffee, chocolate, etc., also the bread and butter, rolls and toast. Simple afternoon teas are also served from the stillroom.

Plate Room (Silver)

All silver dishes and cutlery are cleaned and polished in the plate room. The kitchen is supplied from here with clean silver ready for service.

China Pantry

Here the used crockery and glass are returned, washed and stored ready for service.

Food-lift Men

Where food is served to customers in their rooms, lift men are employed to send it to the floors by a food lift.

Stores

The storekeeper is in charge of the stores, and is responsible for checking all inward delivery of goods. In some places he will not be responsible for checking perishable foodstuffs; these will go direct to the kitchen and be checked by the chef or sous chef.

The storeman will be responsible for the issuing of food to the separate parties.

More details of the stores and the storekeepers duties will be found in the section on 'Storekeeping'.

KITCHEN SERVICE

To help understand the organisation of the kitchen it is best to follow what happens from the time the customer gives his order to the waiter to the time he receives his meal. This will vary from place to place.

If the customer orders:

Cauliflower Soup

Grilled Rump Steak
Fried Potatoes   Stuffed Tomatoes

Strawberry Ice Cream

Coffee

then the waiter makes out his order in triplicate and this is the procedure:

1. A copy is taken to the kitchen hot plate.
2. It may then be stamped with the time, so that if the customer reads on his menu that he will have to wait, for example, 20 minutes for his steak to be cooked, then if he is kept waiting longer or if the waiter wishes to collect the steak too soon, the kitchen have proof of how long and at what time the steak should be ready.
3. The aboyeur will call out for the soup and the main course and vegetables.
4. The soup will be sent immediately to the hot plate by the soup cook.
5. The aboyeur will tick his check as he gives it to the waiter so that he knows it has gone to the customer.
6. The roast cook on hearing the order for a rump steak orders it from the larder, or the butcher, and it is sent out to be cooked. The roast cook puts it on to cook.
7. When the waiter is ready he returns and the roast cook will be asked by the aboyeur for the steak.
8. The vegetable cook will be asked for the vegetables.
9. The aboyeur passes them on to the waiter and he ticks off his check. If he keeps a note of the various main dishes served he will mark off his chart so that he knows how many portions have been sold.
10. When the waiter requires the sweet he takes a separate check to the pastry in exchange for which he receives the ice cream.
11. When he is ready for the coffee he takes another check to the stillroom. (See also Chapter 12.)

12. *Kitchen French*

SOME TERMS USED DURING SERVICE

Le service commence or le service va commencer	Service begins
Ca marche, deux couverts	Warning order that an order for two covers is to be announced
Faites marcher	Begin to cook
Envoyez	Send up
Supplément	Another portion
En vitesse or vite	Quickly, with all speed
Annulez	Cancel the order
Arrêtez	Stop the order
Soigné	Carefully done (for a special customer)
Très soigné	Very carefully (for a very special customer)
Soignez la commande	The order to be done with care
Ils passent à table	The customers are now going to the table
Couvert	Cover or person
Un couvert	One person
Deux couverts	Two persons
Dix couverts	Ten persons
Deux fois deux	Twice two covers
Trois et deux fois deux de Soles frites	Three and two twos of fried soles
Poissonnier, faites marcher, deux Soles Meunière	Fish cook, start to cook two Sole Meunière
Saucier, envoyez quatre Escalopes de Veau Viennoise, soignèes, pour les ètages	Sauce cook, send up four carefully done escalopes of veal viennoise for the floors (this would be for floor or room service in a hotel)
Entremettier, envoyez une omelette aux champignons en vitesse	Vegetable cook, send up one mushroom omelet as soon as possible
Le parti de vingt-cinq couverts passe à table	The party of twenty-five customers is going to the table

Rôtisseur, faites marcher deux entrecôtes doubles, une bien cuite et une saignante	Roast cook, prepare two double entrecôte steaks, one well cooked and one under-done
Pâtissier, envoyez deux fois, deux crème caramel	Pastry cook, send up twice two caramel creams
Garde-manger, envoyez un saumon froid supplément	Larder cook, send another portion of cold salmon
Envoyez les pommes et légumes	Send the potatoes and vegetables
Arrêtez le merlan frit	Stop the fried whiting
Argentier, envoyez les saucières	Silverman, send some sauceboats
Plongeur, envoyez les sauteuses	Sculleryman, more sauteuse wanted

LISTS OF WORDS IN COMMON USE

Numerals

one	*un*	five	*cinq*	eight	*huit*
two	*deux*	six	*six*	nine	*neuf*
three	*trois*	seven	*sept*	ten	*dix*
four	*quatre*				

Days of week

Monday	*Lundi*	Thursday	*Jeudi*	Saturday	*Samedi*
Tuesday	*Marai*	Friday	*Vendredi*	Sunday	*Dimanche*
Wednesday	*Mercredi*				

THE GRAMMAR OF KITCHEN FRENCH TERMS

'The' in French is translated by different words according to the gender and number of word used.

If the noun is masculine and it is singular 'the' is *le*:

le sucre *le jambon* *le saumon*

If the noun is feminine and singular 'the' is *la*:

la farine *la plie*

If the singular noun begins with a vowel or in many cases an *h* then the *e* or *a* is lost and an apostrophe takes its place:

eau (*f.*)	*l'eau*	the water
ail (*m.*)	*l'ail*	the garlic
hôtel (*m.*)	*l'hôtel*	the hotel

Many words begin with *h*, but the le or la is not altered, e.g.:

homard (*m.*) *le homard*

In the dictionary these words are usually marked with an asterisk.

When the noun is plural—that is, when more than one item is considered—the French for 'the' is *les*:

les saumons *les homards* *les hôtels*

When using *le*, *la* or *les* on the menu before a cut, part or joint then the gender used is that of the cut, part or joint, not the food of which it is a part:

la darne de	*la selle de*
le tronçon de	*le cœur de*
le suprême de	*le ris*
le délice	*les goujons*
la paupiette	*le filet*

The method of cooking the cut or piece must also agree with the cut or piece:

les filets de sole frits *la selle d'agneau rôtie*
le gigot d'agneau rôti

Verbs are often used to describe the cooking method. In the dictionary the verb is given in the infinitive, e.g. *brouiller*—to scramble; *sauter*—to toss. On the menu they are given in the past tense and follow the noun:

sauter to toss; *sauté* tossed. (*Pommes sautées.*)
flamber to set alight; *flambé* set alight. (*Pêche flambé.*)
concasser to cut roughly; *concassé* cut roughly. (*Tomates concassées.*)

It will be seen that the form of the verb with the accent acute agrees with the noun it is describing.

With a masculine singular noun the verb is left alone, e.g. *saumon fumé.*

With a masculine plural noun add *s*, e.g. *champignons grillés.*

With a feminine singular add *e*, e.g. *anguille fumée.*

With a feminine plural add *es*, e.g. *pommes persillées.*

Most verbs to do with cooking end in *er*, but some end in *ir*, *re* or *ire* and these take a different spelling in the past tense, for example:

frire	to fry	*frit*	fried
fondre	to melt	*fondu*	melted
bouillir	to boil	*bouilli*	boiled
farcir	to stuff	*farci*	stuffed

The agreement rule still applies:

Cabillaud (masculine, singular)	*Cabillaud frit*
Pommes (feminine, plural)	*Pommes frites*
Beurre (masculine, singular)	*Beurre fondu*
Bœuf (masculine, singular)	*Bœuf bouilli*
Tomates (feminine, plural)	*Tomates farcies*

Some words end in *e*, but they are not verbs and the agreement does not take place, e.g.:

condé; dugléré

à has several meanings, but on the menu the usual meanings are 'with' and 'in'.

Changes in the translation of 'with the' or 'in the' take place according to the gender and number of the noun used. All the following translate 'in the' or 'with the':

à le becomes *au*
à la is not changed
à l' is not changed
à les becomes *aux*

Therefore 'tart with apples' (*tarte à les pommes*) must be written:

Tarte aux Pommes

'Skate with black butter' (*raie à le beurre noir*) must be written:

Raie au Beurre Noir

Homard à la Américaine becomes *Homard à l'Américaine*
Crêpes à le Citron becomes *Crêpes au Citron*
Chou-fleur à la Grecque remains *Chou-fleur à la Grecque*

Nouns—e.g. as used below: apple, butter, chocolate—following the name of the main ingredient of a dish can be singular or plural:

raie au beurre noir *profiteroles au chocolat*
tarte aux pommes

If taken from a quantity, e.g. butter, the singular form is used; if separate objects, e.g. apples, the plural form is used. If a quantity is indefinite the singular is required, e.g. some butter.

de means of, and the *e* is replaced by an apostrophe before words beginning with a vowel or *h*, except, for certain words, as with *le* and *la*:

Gigot de agneau	becomes *Gigot d'agneau*
Table de hôte	becomes *Table d'hôte*
Râble de lièvre	is unchanged
Longe de veau	is unchanged
Filet de bœuf	is unchanged
Bisque de homard	remains *Bisque de homard*

On the menu the term 'of' = *de* or 'with' = *au* is used to describe the composition of a dish. If the main ingredients of the dish is described, *de* is used:

beignets de pommes
salade de tomates

If the item is only part of the dish *au* is usually used:

crêpes au citron *dinde aux marrons*
omelette au jambon

á la mode meaning 'in the style of' or 'fashion' is often left out of the name of a dish, but the word following which describes the fashion must agree with the noun *la mode* which is feminine:

Petits pois à la mode française becomes *petits pois à la française*

The shortening of the phrase is even taken to the stage that it is not written, but understood:

Chou-fleur à la mode polonaise becomes *Chou-fleur polonaise. Polonaise* is feminine because it is describing *mode* which is feminine; it is not describing *chou-fleur* which is masculine.

en used on the menu means 'in'. E.g.:

en tasse —consommé en tasse	consommé in a cup
en branche—épinard en branche	leaf spinach
en goujons—sole en goujons	sole in small strips
en colère —merlan en colère	curled whiting (with tail in mouth

Pommes purée is written in this way because the full name would be *Pommes de terre en purée.* The *purée* remains singular because it is not an adjective but a noun.

Care should be taken to ensure that 'various hors d'œuvres' is translated by '*hors d'œuvre variés*'.

Months of Year

January	*Janvier*	May	*Mai*	September	*Séptembre*
February	*Février*	June	*Juin*	October	*Octobre*
March	*Mars*	July	*Juillet*	November	*Novembre*
April	*Avril*	August	*Août*	December	*Décembre*

Seasons of Year

Spring	*le Printemps*	Autumn	*l'Automne*
Summer	*l'Été*	Winter	*l'Hiver*
Christmas	*la Noël*	Easter	*les Paques*

VERBS USED IN THE KITCHEN

ajouter	to add
apporter	to bring
arrêter	to stop
arroser	to baste as with roast joints
assaisonner	to season

barder	to cover with a slice of fat bacon (on game)
blanchir	to blanch
bouiller	to boil
braiser	to braise
brider	to truss poultry and game
casser	to break
chauffer	to warm
chaufroiter	to mask with sauce as in cold larder work
chemiser	to line a mould, e.g. with jelly
ciseler	to shred
concasser	to roughly chop (as for tomatoes and parsley)
couvrir	to cover
cuire	to cook
débarrasser	to clear away
déglacer	to swill out as with the roast gravy
dégraisser	to skim off the fat
ébarber	to remove the beard (oysters, mussels)
écumer	to skim
émincer	to cut into scallops or neat slices
éplucher	to peel or discard outside leaves
farcir	to stuff
flamber	to singe as with game and poultry
fouetter	to whisk
fraiser	to finally mix sweet pastry
frire	to fry
fumer	to smoke, e.g. salmon, ham, etc.
garnir	to garnish
glacer	to freeze
griller	to grill
hacher	to chop
Larder	to insert lardons of fat bacon, e.g. with roast fillet of beef
Laver	to wash
Lier	to bind or thicken
mariner	to souse or pickle
marquer	to prepare for cooking
mélanger	to mix
mijoter	to simmer
monter	to mount (*monter au beurre*)

napper	to mask with a sauce
nettoyer	to clean
paner	to crumb
parer	to trim
peler	to peel
pendre	to hang game or meat
peser	to weigh
pocher	to poach
passer	to pass
rafraîchir	to refresh
râper	to grate
réduire	to reduce
rissoler	to brown or colour
rôtir	to roast
servir	to serve
sucrer	to sweeten
suer	to sweat, e.g. vegetables for soup
tamiser	to sieve
verser	to pour
vider	to empty (or draw poultry)

THE KITCHEN STAFF

The Kitchen Staff	*La Brigade de Cuisine*
head chef	le chef de cuisine
second chef	le sous-chef
party chef	le chef de partie
assistant chef	le commis
apprentice	l'apprenti
the announcer or barker	l'aboyeur
kitchen porter	le garçon de cuisine
kitchen maid	la fille de cuisine
stillroom maid	la fille d'office
stillroom man	le garçon d'office
potman or sculleryman	le plongeur
crockery washer-up	le vaisselier
silver-plate cleaner	l'argentier
store-room clerk	l'économe
kitchen clerk	le controleur

Party Chefs	*Les Chefs de Partie*
sauce cook	le chef saucier
fish cook	le chef poissonnier

roast cook	le chef rôtisseur
vegetable cook	le chef entremettier
soup cook	le chef potager
larder cook	le chef garde-manger
hors d'œuvre cook	l'hors d'œuvrier
butcher	le boucher
cold work cook	le chef du froid
pastry cook	le chef pâtissier
ice-cream cook	le glacier
confectioner	le confiseur
baker	le boulanger
relief cook	le chef tournant
duty cook	le chef de garde
night cook	le chef de nuit
breakfast cook	le chef du petit déjeuner
the carver	le trancheur
the grill cook	le grillardin
the staff cook	le communard

SMALL KITCHEN UTENSILS

*In the following lists those words marked with * are those which are in more general use.*

Small Kitchen Utensils, etc.	*Les Petits Utensils de Cuisine*
*vegetable knife	le couteau d'office
filleting knife	le couteau à filet
chopping knife	le couteau à hacher
boning knife	le couteau à desosser
*carving knife	le tranche lard
palette	la palette
kitchen fork	la fourchette de cuisine
vegetable peeler	l'économe
scissors	les ciseaux (m.)
trussing needle	l'aiguille à brider (f.)
grooving knife	le couteau à canneler
steel	le fusil
sharpening stone	la pierre à aiguiser
vegetable scoop	la cuiller à racine
sardine tin key	la clef à sardine
tin-opener	l'ouvre-boite (m.)
corkscrew	le tire-bouchon
pastry cutters	l'emporte-pièce (m.)
pastry cutters, plain	l'emporte-pièce, uni
pastry cutters, grooved	l'emporte-pièce, cannelé
column cutters	la boîte a colonne
*piping bag	la poche
*piping tubes	la douille

string-box	la boîte à ficelle
salt-box	la boîte à sel
mushroom	le champignon
*skimmer	l'écumoire
*tammy-cloth	l'étamine
*pepper-mill	le moulin à poivre
grater	la râpe
*steel bat	la batte
chopper	le couperet
saw	la scie
pastry pincers	la pince à pâte
pastry cutting wheel	la roulette à pâtisserie
rolling-pin	le rouleau
pastry brush	le pinceau
*ladle	la louche
*whisk	le fouet
*sieve	le tamis
*conical strainer	le chinois
*mandoline	la mandoline
frying basket	le panier à friture
*friture (deep fat frying-pan)	la friture
*frying-pan	la poêle
*saucepan	la russe
*stockpot	la marmite
*braising-pan	la braisière
*fish kettle	la poissonnière
*fish kettle for turbot	la turbotière
*fish kettle for salmon	la saumonière
the steamer	le vapeur
*the cold room	la chambre froide
*the floors	les étages
*the hot plate	la table chaude
*the bain-marie	le bain-marie
*the oven	le four
*the stove	le fourneau
*the grill	le gril

GROCERIES

almond	l'amande (f.)
*salted almonds	les amandes salées
ground almonds	les amand pilées
angelica	l'angéliqu (f).
arrowroot	la marant
beer	la bière
*bayleaf	le laurier
*bread	le pain
baking powder	la poudre à lever

pearl barley	l'orge perlée (f.)
*butter	le beurre
*bacon	le lard
cochineal	la cochenille
caper	la capre
*cheese	le fromage
cinnamon	la canelle
cloves	le clou de girolfe
*coffee	le café
cornflour	la farine de mais
*cream	la crème
*curry	le kari
currants	les raisins de corinthe
coriander	la corinadre
cocoa	le cacao
date	la datte
essence of almond	l'essence d'amande
essence of anchovy	l'essence d'anchois
essence of lemon	l'essence de citron
essence of orange	l'essence d'orange
essence of rum	l'essence de rhum
essence of vanilla	l'essence de vanille
*eggs	l'œuf (m.)
*flour	la farine
*fondant	le fondant
figs	la figue
flageolet *or* dwarf kidney beans	le flageolet
gherkins	le cornichon
ginger	le gingembre
gelatine	la gélatine
glacé cherry	la cerise glacée
*haricot beans	les haricots blancs (m.)
honey	le miel
*ham	le jambon
*jam	la confiture
lard	le saindoux
*lentils	les lentilles (f.)
macaroni	le macaroni
margarine	la margarine
*mustard	la moutarde
*milk	le lait
marmalade	la marmalade
nutmeg	la muscade
*olive	l'olive (f.)
*olive oil	l'huile d'olive (f.)
*peel	le zeste confit
pepper	le poivre
cayenne pepper	le poivre de cayenne

yellow split peas	les pois cassés jaunes (m.)
green split peas	les pois cassés verts (m.)
prune	le pruneau
raisin	le raisin sec
*rice	le riz
sago	le sagou
*semolina	la semoule
*salt	le sel
suet	la graisse de rognon
*sugar	le sucre
castor sugar	le sucre en poudre
granulated sugar	le sucre cristallisé
*spice	l'épice (f.)
sultanas	les raisins de smyrne (m.)
*tea	le thé
tomato purée	la purée de tomate
*vermicelli	le vermicelle
*vinegar	le vinaigre
yeast	la levure

FISH

Fish	*Le Poisson*	*Typical menu examples*
*anchovy	l'anchois (m.)	Anchois sur Croûte
*brill	la barbue	Suprême de Barbue Bonne-Femme
bream	la brèmc	
*cod	le cabillaud	Darne de Cabillaud Poché, Sce Persil
cod (dried *or* salt)	la morue	
carp	la carpe	
dab	le carrelet	Filet de Carrelet Dugléré
eel	l'anguille (f.)	
eel, conger	le congre	
*gudgeon	le goujon	
*haddock	l'aigrefin *or* l'aiglefin (m.)	Filet d'Aigrefin Bretonne
*haddock (smoked)	le haddock *or* l'aigrefin fumé	
hake	la merluche *or* colin	
*halibut	le flétan	Suprême de Flétan d'Antin
*herring	le hareng	Hareng Grillé, Sce Moutarde
John Dory	le St. Pierre	
*mullet	le rouget	Rouget Grenobloise
*mackerel	le maquereau	Macquereau Grillé, Beurre d'Anchois
perch	la perche	
*plaice	la plie	Filets de Plie Frites, Sce Tartare

Fish	*les Poisson*	*Typical menu examples*
pike	le brochet	
*salmon	le saumon	Darne de Saumon Grillé, Sce Vert
*salmon (smoked)	le saumon fumé	Cornets de Saumon Fumé
*salmon trout	la truite saumonée	Suprême de Truite Saumonée Doria
*smelt	l'éperlan (m.)	Éperlans Grillés Maître d'Hôtel
sprat	le sprat	Sprats Frits au Citron
*skate	la raie	Raie au Beurre Noir
*sardine	la sardine	Sardines sur Croûte
*sole	la sole	Sole Meunière
sole, lemon	la limande	Limande Grillé, Sce Diable
sturgeon	l'esturgeon (m.)	
trout	la truite	Truite au Bleu
*turbot	le turbot	Tronçon de Turbot Poché Sce Hollandaise
*young *or* chicken turbot	le turbotin	Suprême de Turbotin Véronique
tunny	le thon	Thon à l'Huile
*whiting	le merlan	Merlan en Colère
*whitebait	la blanchaille	Blanchailles Diablées
*roe	la laitance	Laitances Méphisto
*caviar	le caviar	

Shellfish	*les Crustaces* (m.)	*Typical menu examples*
*crayfish	l'écrevisse (f.)	
*crawfish	la langouste	
*crab	le crabe	Cocktail de Crabe
*lobster	le homard	Salade de Homard
*prawns	la crevette rose	Mayonnaise des Crevettes Roses
*prawns (Dublin Bay)	la langoustine	Langoustines Frites, Sce Tartare
*shrimps	la crevette grise	
*mussel	la moule	Moules Marinière
*oyster	l'huître (f.)	Huîtres Florentine
*scallop	la coquille St. Jacques	Coquille St. Jacques Mornay
coral	le corail	
turtle	la tortue	Tortue Claire
frog	la grenouille	
snail	l'escargot (m.)	

MEAT

Meat	*la Viande*	*Typical menu examples*
*mutton	le mouton	
lamb	l'agneau (m.)	
*leg	le gigot d'agneau *or* de mouton	Gigot d'Agneau Rôti, Sce Menthe
*saddle	la selle d'agneau *or* de mouton	Selle de Mouton Rôti, Sce aux Oignons
*loin	la longe, d'agneau *or* de mouton	Longe d'Agneau Farci
*best-end	le carré d'agneau *or* de mouton	Carré d'Agneau Boulangère
*breast	la poitrine d'agneau *or* de mouton	
*shoulder	l'épaule (f.) d'agneau *or* de mouton	Épaule d'Agneau Froide, Salade Française
*neck	le cou	
*liver	le foie d'agneau *or* de mouton	Foie d'Agneau et Lard
*kidney	le rognon d'agneau *or* de mouton	Rognons Sautés Turbigo
*tongue	la langue d'agneau *or* de mouton	Langues d'Agneau Poulette
*sweetbread	le ris d'agneau *or* de mouton	
*brain	la cervelle d'agneau *or* de mouton	
*heart	le coeur d'agneau *or* de mouton	Cœur de Mouton Braisé aux Légumes
*chop	la chop d'agneau *or* de mouton	Chop de Mouton Grillé
*cutlet	la côtelette d'agneau *or* de mouton	Côtelettes d'Agneau Réforme
*middle-neck cutlets	la basse cote	
*noisette	la noisette d'agneau *or* de mouton	Noisettes de Mouton Fleuriste
*fillet mignon	le filet mignon	

Pork	*e Porc*	*Typical menu examples*
*leg	le cuissot de porc	Cuissot de Porc Rôti, Sce Pommes
*chop	la côte *or* chop de porc	Côte de Porc, Sce Charcutière
*loin	la longe de porc	Longe de Porc Rôti, à l'Anglaise
*belly	la poitrine de porc	

Pork	*le Porc*
*shoulder (hand)	l'épaule (f.) de porc
trotters	le pied de porc
head	la tête de porc
liver	le foie de porc

Beef	*le Bœuf*	*Typical menu examples*
*sirloin	l'aloyau (m.) de bœuf	Aloyau de Bœuf Rôti, à l'Anglaise
*boned-out sirloin	le contrefilet de bœuf	Contrefilet de Bœuf Dubarry
*fillet	le filet de bœuf	Filet de Bœuf Bouquetière
*sirloin steak (boned out)	l'entrecôte de bœuf	Entrecôte Bordelaise
*head of the fillet	le château briand	Châteaubriand Grillé, Sce Bearnaise
*cut from the middle without fat	tournedos	Tournedos à la Portugaise
*ribs	la côte de bœuf	Côte de Bœuf Froide, Salade Panachée
*thin flank	la bavette	Bœuf Bouilli à la Française
thick flank	la tranche grasse	Carbonnade de Bœuf à la Flamande
*rump	la culotte de bœuf	Rump Steak Vert Pré
Topside	la tranche tendre	Paupiettes de Bœuf
silverside	la gîte à la noix	Bœuf Bouilli à l'Anglaise
shin *or* shank	la jambe	Consommé Julienne
*liver	le foie de bœuf	Foie de Bœuf Lyonnaise
*tail	la queue de bœuf	Queue de Bœuf aux Primeurs
*tripe	la tripe	Tripe à l'Anglaise
*marrow	la moelle	Moëlle sur Croûte
*tongue	la langue de bœuf	Langue Braisée au Madère
*heart	le cœur de bœuf	Cœur de Bœuf Braisé

Veal	*le Veau*	*Typical menu examples*
*cutlet	la côte de veau	Côtelette (Côte) de Veau Milanaise
leg	le cuissot de veau	Cuissot de Veau Rôti
*head	la tête de veau	Tête de Veau Vinaigrette
saddle	la selle de veau	Selle de Veau Mercédès
shoulder	l'épaule (f.) de veau	
*cushion	la noix de veau	Escalope de Veau Viennoise
*under cushion	la sous noix de veau	Fricassée de Veau à l'Ancienne
shin	le jarret	Osso Buco
liver	le foie de veau	Foie de Veau et Lard
sweetbread	le ris de veau	Ris de Veau Bonne-Maman

Veal	*le Veau*	*Typical menu examples*
*brain	la cervelle de veau	Cervelle au Beurre Noir
*sausage	la saucisse	Saucisse de Bœuf ou de Porc
bone	l'os (m.)	
suet	la graisse	

POULTRY

Poultry	*la Volaille*	Vol-au-Vent de Volaille
*chicken	le poulet	Poulet Sauté Chasseur
*turkey	la dinde	Dinde Rôtie
*young turkey	le dindonneau	Dindonneau Farci aux Marrons
guinea fowl	la pintarde	Pintarde en Casserole
*duck	le canard	
*duckling	le caneton	Caneton Braisé aux Petits Pois
goose	l'oie (f.)	Oie Braisé aux Navets
gosling	l'oison (m.)	Oison Rôti, Sauce Pommes
pigeon	le pigeon	Pigeon Braisé aux Olives

GAME

Game	*le Gibier*	*Typical menu examples*
*pheasant	le faisan	Faisan Braisé au Céleri
*partridge	le perdreau	Perdreau aux Choux
*woodcock	la bécasse	Bécasse Rôtie
*snipe	la bécassine	Bécassine Rôtie
ptarmigan	la poule de neige	Poule de Neige Rôti
grouse	la grouse	Grouse Rôtie
*wild duck	le canard sauvage	Canard Sauvage à l'Orange
teal	la sarcelle	Sarcelle à l'Orange
plover	le pluvier	Pluvier au Porto
quail	la caille	Cailles aux Raisins
ortolan	l'ortolan (m.)	
venison	la venaison	Roast Haunch of Venison
deer	le chevreuil	Selle de Chevreuil, Sauce Grand Veneur
*hare	le lièvre	Civet de Lièvre
*rabbit	le lapin	Blanquette de Lapin

VEGETABLES

Vegetables	*les Légumes (m.)*	*Typical menu examples*
*artichokes (globe)	l'artichaut (m.)	Artichauts en Branche, Sauce Hollandaise

Vegetables	*les Légumes (m.)*	*Typical menu examples*
*artichokes (Jerusalem)	le topinambour	Topinambours en Purée
*beetroot	la betterave	Salade de Betterave
*broad beans	les fèves (f.)	Fèves Persillées
*broccoli	le brocoli	Broccoli au Beurre
*Brussels sprouts	les choux de bruxelles (m.)	Choux de Bruxelles Sautées au Beurre
*cabbage	le chou vert	Choux Braisés
*red cabbage	le chou rouge	Choux à la Flamande
*carrots	la carotte	Carottes Vichy
*cauliflower	le chou-fleur	Chou-fleur Polonaise
celeriac	céleri rave	Salade de Céleri Rave
*celery	le céleri	Céleri Braisé
*chicory	l'endive	Endive, Belge a l'Étuvée
*cucumber	le concombre	Concombre Farci
*endive	la chicorée	Salade de Chicorée
*egg plant	l'aubergine (f.)	Aubergine Frite
*curly kale	le chou frisé	Chou Frisé Nature
*French beans	les haricots verts (m.)	Haricots Verts
*leek	le poireau	Poireau, Sce Crème
*lettuce	la laitue	Laitue Braisée
*mushroom	le champignon	Champignons sur Croûte
*marrow	la courge	Courge Provençale
*young marrow	la courgette	
*onion	l'oignon (m.)	Oignons Frits à la Française
*pimento	le piment	Piment Farci
*parsnip	le panais	Panais Rôti
*peas	les petits pois (m.)	Petits Pois à la Menthe
*potato	la pomme de terre	Pommes Duchesse
salisfy	le salsifi	Salsifis à la Crème
sorrel	l'oseille (f.)	
*spinach	l'épinard (m.)	Epinard en Branche
sea-kale	le chou de mer	Chou de Mer, Beurre Fondu
shallot	l'echalote (f.)	
*sweetcorn	le maïs	Maïs à la Crème
*swede	le rutabaga	Purée de Rutabaga
*tomato	la tomate	Tomate Farci
*turnip	le navet	Navets au Beurre
*truffle	la truffe	

*lettuce	la laitue
*cos lettuce	la laitue romaine
*radishes	le radis
*watercress	le cresson
corn salad	la mâche

HERBS

Herbs, spices and aromates	*Herbes, épices et aromates*
*bay leaves	les feuilles de laurier
basil	le basilic
cinnamon	la canelle
*chervil	le cerfeuil
*chives	la ciboulette
coriander	la coriandre
cumin	le cumin
clove	le clou de girofle
*curry	le kari
fennel	le fenouil
*garlic	l'ail (m.)
ginger	le gingembre
juniper	le genièvre
mace	le macis
marjoram	la marjolaine
*mint	la menthe
mignonette	la mignonnette
*mustard	la moutarde
*horseradish	le raifort
nutmeg	la muscade
*parsley	le persil
*pepper (white)	le poivre blanc
Pepper (cayenne)	le poivre de cayenne
Pepper (paprika)	le poivre paprika
rosemary	le romarin
saffron	le safron
sage	la sauge
*thyme	le thym
*salt	le sel

FRUITS AND NUTS

Fruits and nuts	*Les fruits (m.) et les noix*	*Typical menu examples*
*almond	l'amande (f.)	
*apple	la pomme	Tarte aux pommes
*apricot	l'abricot (m.)	Bande aux abricots
*banana	la banane	Beignets de bananes
blackberry	la mure de rouce	
blackcurrants	les cassis (m.)	
black grapes	les raisins noirs (m.)	
*cherry	la cerise	Tartelettes aux cerises
*chestnut	le marron	Marrons glacés
*cranberries	les airelles (f.)	Sauce airelles

Fruits and nuts	*Les fruits (m.) et les noix*	*Typical menu examples*
damson	la prune de damas	
*date	la datte	
fig	la figue	
gooseberry	la groseille à maquereau	
*grapefruit	la pamplemousse	Pamplemousse cerisette
grapes	les raisins (m.)	
greengage	la reine claude	
hazelnut	l'aveline (f.) *or* la noisette	
hops	le houblon	
*lemon	le citron	Crêpes au citron
*melon	le melon	Melon frappé
*orange	l'orange (f.)	Pouding soufflé à l'orange
*peach	la pêche	Pêche Melba
*pear	la poire	Poire Hélène
*pineapple	l'ananas (m.)	Ananas Condé
pistachio	la pistache	
plum	la prune	
pomegranate	la grenade	
red currants	les groseilles rouges	

KITCHEN TERMS

A

Kitchen terms etc.	
l'abats (m.)	Offal
l'abbatis de volaille (m.)	Poultry offal (giblets)
l'aile (f.)	Wing of poultry or game birds
à la	In the style of (*à la mode*)
à la française	Dishes prepared in the French way
à l'anglaise	In the English style
à la broche	Cooked on a spit
à la diable	Devilled, a highly seasoned dish
à la carte	Dishes on a menu prepared to order and individually priced
l'aloyau (m.)	Sirloin of beef (on the bone)
anglaise	Beaten egg with oil and seasoning
appareil (m.)	A preparation of one or more ingredients mixed prior to making certain dishes
arroser	To baste as in roasting
aspic (m.)	A savoury jelly
assaisonner	To season
assorti	An assortment, e.g. *Fromage assorti*

au bleu	When applied to meat it means very underdone. When applied to trout it is a specific dish—*truite au bleu*
au four	Cooked in the oven, e.g. *Pomme au four*
au gratin	Sprinkled with breadcrumbs and/or cheese and browned

B

au vin blanc	With white wine
le bain-marie	(*a*) A container to keep foods hot so as to prevent burning (*b*) A shallow pan of water for cooking foods to prevent them burning or boiling (*c*) A deep narrow container for storing hot soup, sauces and gravies
le blanc	A cooking liquor of water, lemon juice and salt slightly thickened with flour and used for cooking artichoke bottoms, calves head, etc.
la blanquette	A white stew cooked in stock from which the sauce is made, e.g. *Blanquette de veau*
les blancs d'œufs	Egg whites
blond	Very slightly coloured, e.g. *Blond roux*
la bombe	An ice cream of different flavours in the shape of a bomb
la bordure	A ring, sometimes of rice or potatoes
bouchées	Small puff-pastry cases
bouillir	To boil
le bouillon	Unclarified stock
le bouquet-garni	A faggot or bundle of herbs, usually parsley stalks, thyme and bay leaf, tied inside pieces of celery and leek
braiser	To braise
la braisière	Braising pan
en branche	A term denoting vegetables, such as spinach, cooked and served as whole leaves
brider	To truss (poultry)
la brioche	A light yeast cake
la broche	A roasting spit
la brochette	A skewer
brouillé	Scrambled, e.g. *Œufs brouillés*
brun	Brown
brunoise	Small neat dice
le buffet	A sideboard of food, or a self-service table

C

le canapé	A cushion of toasted or fried bread on which are served various foods. It is used as a base for savouries. When served cold as canapé moscovite the base may be toast, biscuits or short or puff-paste pieces with the food on top and finished with aspic
le caramel	Sugar cooked until coloured to a certain degree
la carte du jour	Menu, or bill of fare for the day
la casserole	A fireproof dish with a lid
Chantilly	Sweetened whipped vanilla-flavoured cream
la chapelure	Breadcrumbs made from dried stale crusts of bread
la charlotte	Name given to various hot and cold sweet dishes which have a case of biscuits, bread, sponge, etc.
le châteaubriand	The head of the fillet of beef
chaud	Hot
le chaud-froid	A creamed velouté or demi-glace with gelatine or aspic added, used for masking cold dishes
le chinois	A conical strainer
le civet	A brown stew of game, usually hare
clair	Clear
la cloche	A bell-shaped cover, used for special *à la carte* dishes, e.g. *Suprême de volaille sous cloche*
clouté	Studded, as with a clove inserted into an onion (*Oignon clouté*)
la cocotte	Porcelain fireproof dish
la compôte	Stewed fruit, e.g. *Cômpote des poires*
concassé	Coarsely chopped, e.g. parsley and tomatoes
le consommé	Basic clear soup
le contrefilet	Boned sirloin of beef
le cordon	A thread or thin line of sauce
la côte	Rib, e.g. *Côte de bœuf*
la côtelette	Cutlet
coupe	Cut; also ice cream dish
le court-bouillon	A cooking liquor for certain foods, e.g. oily fish, calf's brains, etc. It is water containing vinegar, sliced onions, carrots, herbs and seasoning
la crème fouettée	Whipped cream
la crêpe	Pancake
la croquette	Cooked foods moulded cylinder shape, egg and crumbled and deep fried, e.g. *Croquette de volaille*

la croûte	A cushion of fried or toasted bread on which are served various hot foods, e.g. savouries, game stuffing, etc.
le croûton	Cubes of fried bread served with soup, also triangular pieces which may be served with spinach and heart-shaped ones which may be served with certain braised vegetables and entrees
Crustacés (m.)	Shellfish
la cuisine	The kitchen
la haute cuisine	High-class cooking
le cuisinier	Male cook
la cuisinière	Female cook
la cuisse de poulet	Leg of chicken
cuit	Cooked
culinaire	To do with cooking

D

dariole	A type of mould
la darne	A slice of round fish cut through with the bone, e.g. *Darne de saumon*
le dés	Dice, *coupé en dés*—cut in dice
déglacer	To swill out a pan in which food has been cooked with wine or stock, to use the sediment
dégraisser	To skim fat off liquid
demi glace	Half glaze—reduced espagnole
le déjeuner	Lunch
le petit déjeuner	Breakfast
désosser	To bone out
le dîner	Dinner
doré	Golden
du jour (plat du jour)	Special dish of the day
duxelle	Finely chopped mushrooms cooked with chopped shallots

E

l'eau	Water
ébarber	To remove the beard (from mussels, etc.)
écumer	To skim
émincer	To slice
l'entrecôte (f.)	A steak from a boned sirloin
l'escalope (f.)	Thin slice of meat

espagnole	Brown sauce
estouffade	Brown stock
étuver	To cook in its own juice

F

la farce	Stuffing
farci	Stuffed
la farine	Flour
le feuilletage	Puff paste
les fines herbes	Chopped parsley, tarragon and chervil
flambé	Flamed or lit, e.g. *Poire flambé*
le flan	Open fruit tart
le fleuron	Small crescent pieces of puff paste used for garnishing certain dishes, e.g. fish and vegetable
le foie	Liver
le foie gras	Fat goose liver
le fondant	A kind of icing
les fonds (m.)	The foundation stocks
fondu	Melted
le four	Oven
frappé	Chilled, e.g. *Melon frappé*
les friandises	Petits fours, sweetmeats, etc.
la fricassée	A white stew in which the poultry or meat is cooked in the sauce
frisé	Curled
fumé	Smoked, e.g. *Saumon fumé*
fumet	A concentrated stock or essence

G

la garniture	The trimmings on the dish
le gâteau	Cake
la gelée	Jelly
le gibier	Game
la glace	Ice or ice cream
glacé	Iced
glacer	To glaze under the salamander
le goût	Taste
gratiner	To colour or gratinate under the salamander or in a hot oven using grated cheese or breadcrumbs
le gril	Grill
grillé	Grilled

H

hacher	To chop finely or very finely dice—to mince
les herbes (f.)	Herbs
hors d'œuvre	Preliminary dishes of an appetising nature, some kinds are served hot
l'huile (f.)	Oil

J

le jambon	Ham
le jambon froid	Cold ham
jardinière	Cut into baton
julienne	Cut into fine strips
le jus lié	Gravy thickened with arrowroot or cornflour or fecule
le jus rôti	Roast gravy

K

le kari	Curry

L

le lait	Milk
larder	To insert strips of fat bacon into lean meat
le lardon	Small strip of bacon
la levure	Yeast
liaison	Name given to yolks of eggs and cream when used as a thickening
lier	To thicken
la longe	Loin
losange	Diamond shaped

M

macédoine	(*a*) A mixture of fruit or vegetables, e.g. *macédoine des fruits*—fruit salad (*b*) Cut into 6 mm dice
macérer	To steep, to soak, to macerate
la marinade	A richly spiced pickling liquid for enriching the flavour and tenderness of meats before braising
mariné	Pickled
le madère	Madeira wine
le maître	Master
manié	Kneaded, e.g. *Beurre manié*
manger	To eat
marbré	Marbled

la marmite	Stock pot
marquer	To prepare foods for cooking
masquer	To mask or coat
médaillon	Foodstuffs prepared in a round, flat shape
le menu	Bill of fare
la mie de pain	Fresh white breadcrumbs
mignonette	Coarse ground or crushed pepper
mijoter	To simmer
les mille-feuilles (f.)	'Thousand leaves', a puff-pastry cream slice
à la minute	Cooked to order
mirepoix	Roughly cut onions, carrots, celery and a sprig of thyme and bay leaf
mise-en-place	Preparations prior to service
mollet	Soft, e.g. *œuf mollet*
monter	To mount a sauce, to whip egg whites or yolks or to add butter to a sauce, to add oil to mayonnaise
le moule	Mould
le moulin à poivre	Pepper mill
la mousse	A hot or cold dish of light consistency, sweet or savoury
la moutarde	Mustard
moutarder	To smear with mustard, or to add mustard to a sauce
le mouton	Mutton or sheep
mûr	Ripe, mature
la mûre de ronce	Blackberry
la muscade	Nutmeg

N

napper	To mask
natives (f.)	A menu term denoting English oysters, e.g. *Les huîtres natives*
navarin	A brown lamb or mutton stew
le nid	Nest—imitation nest made from potatoes or sugar, etc.
la noisette *or* noisette	(*a*) A hazelnut used in confectionery (*b*) Small round potatoes cut with a special scoop (*c*) As for noisette butter (*d*) A cut of loin of lamb
la noix	Nut, also the name given to the cushion piece of the leg of veal (*Noix de veau*)
les nouilles (f.)	Noodles, a flat Italian paste

O

l'œuf (m.)	Egg
œuf brouillé	A scrambled egg
œuf en cocotte	Egg cooked in an egg cocotte
œuf à la coque	Egg boiled and served in its shell
œuf dur	A hard-boiled egg
œuf mollet	A soft-boiled shelled egg
œuf poché	A poached egg
œuf sur le plat	Egg cooked in an egg dish
œuf à la poêle	A fried egg
l'oignon	Onion
l'olive farcie	Stoned and stuffed olive
l'olive tournée (f.)	A stoned olive
orge (f.)	Barley
l'os (m.)	Bone
oseille (f.)	Sorrel

P

les pailles (f.)	Straws (*Pommes pailles*)
les paillettes de fromage (f.)	Cheese straws
le pain	Bread
panaché	Mixed
e panade	A flour composition used for binding
pané	Crumbed
panier	Basket
papillote	Foods cooked en papillote are cooked in greased greaseproof paper in their own steam in the oven
parer	To trim
passer	To strain or pass
la pâte	A dough, paste, batter, pie or pastie
la pâte à frire	Frying batter
la pâtisserie	Pastry department
la paupiette	A strip of fish, meat or poultry stuffed and rolled up
paysanne	To cut into even thin triangles round or square pieces
le pilon	Pestle for use with a mortar, name given to the drumstick of a leg of chicken
le piment	Pimento
piquant	Sharp flavour
piqué	Studded

poêler	A method of cookery (pot roasting)
la pointe d'asperge	Asparagus tip
la praline	Chopped grilled almonds or hazel nuts or crushed almond toffee
primeur	Early vegetables
printanière	Garnish of spring vegetables
profiteroles	Small balls of choux paste for garnishing soups or as a sweet course
la purée	A smooth mixture obtained by passing food through a sieve

Q

la quenelle	Forcemeat of poultry, fish or game or meat, pounded, sieved and shaped then usually poached

R

le râble	The back, e.g. *Râble de lièvre*—the back of a hare
le ragoût	Stew
le ravioli	An Italian paste, stuffed with various ingredients including meat spinach and brains
rechauffer	To reheat
réduire	To reduce, to concentrate a liquor by evaporating
le risotto	Italian rice stewed in stock
le ris	Sweetbread
rissoler	To fry to a golden brown
rôtir	To roast
roux	Flour and fat cooked together for thickening

S

le sabayon	Yolks of eggs and a little water cooked till creamy
la salamandre	A gas or electric grill under which food is cooked or completed
sauter, sauté	To toss in fat or to turn in fat; also a specific meat dish
soubise	An onion purée
le soufflé	A light dish, sweet or savoury, hot or cold. Whites of egg are added to the hot basic preparation and whipped cream to the cold
le suprême	When applied to poultry it means a whole wing and half the breast of the bird (there are two *suprêmes* to a bird). For other foods it is applied to a choice cut

T

table d'hôte	A meal of several courses, which may have a limited choice, served at a fixed price
le tamis	Sieve
la terrine	An earthenware utensil with a lid. A terrine also indicates a pâté cooked and served in one
tomaté	Preparations to which tomato purée has been added to dominate the flavour and colour
tourner	To turn, to shape (barrel or olive shape)
la tranche	A slice
le tronçon	A slice of flat fish cut with the bone, e.g. *Tronçon de turbot*

V

le velouté	(*a*) Basic sauce (*b*) A soup of velvety or creamy consistency
vert	Green, e.g. *Sauce vert*
la viande	Meat
voiler	To veil or cover with spun sugar
la volaille	Poultry
le vol-au-vent	A puff-pastry case

For further information: Senn, *Dictionary of Foods* (Ward Lock).

13. *Menu Planning or Menu Compilation*

A menu or a bill of fare is a list of prepared dishes of food which are available to a customer.

The compiling of a menu is one of the most important jobs of a caterer and there are a number of factors that must be taken into consideration before any menu is written.

1. THE KIND OF MENU

It must be clearly understood what kind of menu is required, whether a special party menu, table d'hôte or à la carte.

(*a*) *Special party menu*—these are menus for banquets and parties of all kinds.

(*b*) *Table d'hôte*—this is a set menu forming a complete meal at a set price. A choice of dishes may be offered at all courses; the choice and number of dishes will usually be limited.

(*c*) *A la carte*—this is a menu with all the dishes individually priced. The customer can therefore compile his own menu. A true à la carte dish should be cooked to order and the customer should be prepared to wait for this service.

Examples of luncheon menus suitable for a medium-sized hotel:

A. SPECIAL PARTY (AT A SET PRICE)

Luncheon Menu

Hors d'Œuvre

Poached Scotch Salmon Hollandaise Sauce

Roast Saddle of Mutton
Garden Peas New Potatoes

Strawberries and Cream

B. TABLE D'HÔTE (AT A SET PRICE)

Déjeuner

Pamplemousse Cerisette
Melon Frappé
Hors d'Œuvre

Consommé Royale
Minestrone

Omelette Espagnole
Raviolis au Jus
Coquille St.-Jacques Mornay

Filets de Sole Frits, Sauce Tartare

Queue de Bœuf Printanier
Emincé de Volaille Duchesse
Epaule d'Agneau Boulangère

Buffet Froid

Choux Verts	*Pommes:* Persillées
Petits Pois	Sautées
Carottes Vichy	Frites

Salade de Saison

Gâteau Praliné
Pouding Soufflé Saxon
Compôte Assorties
Glace Panachée
ou
Fromage

C. A LA CARTE (ALL DISHES INDIVIDUALLY PRICED)

A la Carte Luncheon Menu

Hors d'Œuvre:
Oysters; Smoked Salmon; Pâté Maison; Parma Ham; Prawn Cocktail Smoked Trout, Potted Shrimps; Assorted Sausage; Hors d'œuvre

Soups:
Pea; Tomato; Onion; Vegetable; Petite Marmite; Turtle; Minestrone; Double Consommé

Eggs:
Omelettes (Ham, Mushroom, Tomato, Cheese)
Poached Egg Washington; Scrambled Eggs with Shrimps; Eggs in Cocotte with Cream

Pastes:
Spaghetti Bolognaise; Risotto with Cheese; Noodles with Cheese; Raviolis

Fish:
Sole Colbert; Sole Meunière; Fried Sole; Grilled Sole; Sole Bonne-Femme; Boiled Turbot with Hollandaise Sauce; Devilled Whitebait; Lobster Mornay; Grilled Herrings with Mustard Sauce

Entrées:
Calf's Head Vinaigrette; Chicken Sauté Chasseur; Braised Tongue with Sherry; Curried Beef and Rice; Pork Chop Normande; Veal Escalope Viennoise

Roasts:
Best End of Lamb; Aylesbury Duckling; Surrey Chicken; Game (in season)

Grills:
Rump Steak; Entrecôte Steak; Minute Steak; Fillet Steak; Lamb Cutlets; Lamb Chop; Mixed Grill; Sheep's Kidneys

Cold Buffet:
Chicken; Turkey; Ham; Tongue; Galantine; Pressed Beef; Pork; Dressed Crab; Cold Lobster

Salads:
Lettuce, Tomato, Beetroot, French, Japanese

Vegetables:
Peas, French Beans, Leaf Spinach, Vichy Carrots, Cauliflower, Hollandaise sauce, Brussels Sprouts, Braised Celery
Potatoes (Creamed, Allumettes, Lyonnaise, Marquise, Soufflé)

Sweets:
Peach Melba; Fruit Salad; Lemon Pancakes; Cream Caramel, Jam Omelette; Stewed Fruits; French Pastries; Assorted Gâteaux; Assorted Ices

Savouries:
Welsh Rarebit; Welsh Rarebit with Mushrooms; Mushrooms on Toast; Scotch Woodcock; Soft Roes on Toast; Sardines on Toast

Cheese:
As available

Coffee:
Cona; Turkish; Irish

KIND OF MEAL

It is necessary to know if the menu is required for breakfast, luncheon, tea, dinner, supper or for a special function.

KIND OF ESTABLISHMENT

The type of establishment will have to be considered. Menus will vary for the following examples:

Luxury-class hotel
First-class restaurant
Medium-priced hotel
Medium-priced restaurant
Country hotel
School meal
Directors' room in an industrial canteen
Female workers' dining-room in an industrial canteen
Heavy manual workers' dining-room in an industrial canteen
Hospital

THE SEASON OF THE YEAR

If menus have to be compiled a long time in advance of the actual date of production, the season of the year should be considered—

(*a*) Because of the weather; it may be hot, cold or mild and certain dishes which would be acceptable in hot weather would be most unsuitable in cold weather and vice versa.

(*b*) Because foods in season, e.g. strawberries, should be included in menus where possible, as they are usually in good supply, of good quality and a reasonable price.

(*c*) Special dishes for certain days or a time of the year should be considered. For example, pancakes on Shrove Tuesday and Turkey at Christmas.

THE CAPABILITIES OF KITCHEN STAFF

The capabilities of the cooks should be considered. There are many excellent cooks, male and female, whose training is such that they can cope with simple dishes but who might be at a loss if asked to produce highly complicated foreign fare. On the other hand, if a staff of well-trained cooks, capable of a good standard of international cookery, is available, they should be given a chance to produce dishes that can express their skill and pride of craftsmanship.

SIZE AND EQUIPMENT OF KITCHEN

The type of kitchen should be considered—how large? how small? And what large-scale equipment is available such as stoves, steamers, hot plates, etc. A good cook will usually manage to produce a required meal somehow in spite of any shortcomings of space or equipment. Nevertheless, the writer of menus should be aware of such deficiencies and be wary of putting on dishes that might be difficult to produce because of shortages. Care should be taken to see that the method of cooking is not repeated, otherwise certain pieces of equipment can be overloaded; for example, steamer, friture.

CAPABILITIES OF SERVING STAFF

The person who serves the meal should be considered. If the standard of the waiter or waitress is of the highest order then a high standard of well-dressed and garnished dishes can be used because the caterer can be sure that the prepared food will be correctly shown to the customer and that it will be transferred to the customer's plate in a neat, presentable fashion. If the waiters, waitresses or servers are untrained, care should be taken in the selection of dishes and only those dishes suitable for easy serving selected.

SIZE AND EQUIPMENT OF DINING-ROOM

The type of dining-room and its equipment have sometimes to be taken into account. The china in some catering establishments needs to be considered, particularly if it is coloured or highly patterned, as either factor can affect the appearance of certain foods.

The size of silver dishes needs to be considered when planning menus. This is important when a well-garnished dish such as Filet de Bœuf Bouquetière is planned which, if dressed on dishes that are too small, would risk losing its presentation value.

The amount of china and silver must be taken into account if a menu of several courses is required. Operating a five-course menu with only sufficient china and silver for three courses can raise problems which would upset the smooth running of the meal.

PRICE OF THE MENU

The proposed charge per head is obviously an important factor to consider when selecting food for any menu. When the caterer is asked to produce, for example, a meal to sell at 35p per head he cannot consider expensive foods such as oysters, fresh salmon, game, asparagus, etc. Similarly, if asked to produce a meal for a good price, say over two pounds, then he should offer good value for the price charged. A useful working rule with regard to the cost of food for a meal is to see that the food cost does not exceed 40% of the selling price. For example, if the cost of the food per head for a meal is 20p, then the suggested selling price would be $\frac{20p \times 100}{40} = 50p$.

This point is explained further in the section on costing.

TYPE OF PEOPLE

The type of guests to be present at a meal, particularly at special parties, can sometimes affect the choice of foods. For example, the caterer may be asked to produce a dinner menu for a special party of:

Young people attending a twenty-first birthday party
Heavy steel workers attending a celebration
Elderly ladies attending a conference
Old-age pensioners attending at Christmas
Polish refugees
American Air Force officers and their wives

In each of the above groups of people there are certain foods which would suit one group but not necessarily the others.

2. SUPPLIES

When considering foods for a menu, it is sound policy to think of any in season. Although in these days of deep-freeze storage many foods are available all the year round there are still items which, when in season, are plentiful, of good flavour and a reasonable price, for example strawberries, asparagus, herrings, scallops.

If large stocks of food are held, care should be taken, where possible, to use foods on the menu which are already in store, before ordering fresh supplies. This can help to avoid wastage of food and, of course, money.

The cold room or refrigerator should be inspected to see if there are any cooked foods that may be incorporated into menus. This is an important point and one that the experienced caterer makes full use of, as there are many ways in which cooked foods can be used to produce or help to produce attractive dishes. For example, a good hors d'œuvrier can use almost any item of cooked food. The use of cooked foods is to be found in the section on rechauffé dishes.

Foods selected for a menu should be easy to obtain locally. Special foods are sometimes difficult to obtain at certain times of the year in some parts of the country. It is bad practice to offer customers particular dishes before checking that they are readily available.

If the customer has any special wishes, the good caterer should always do his best to comply with them.

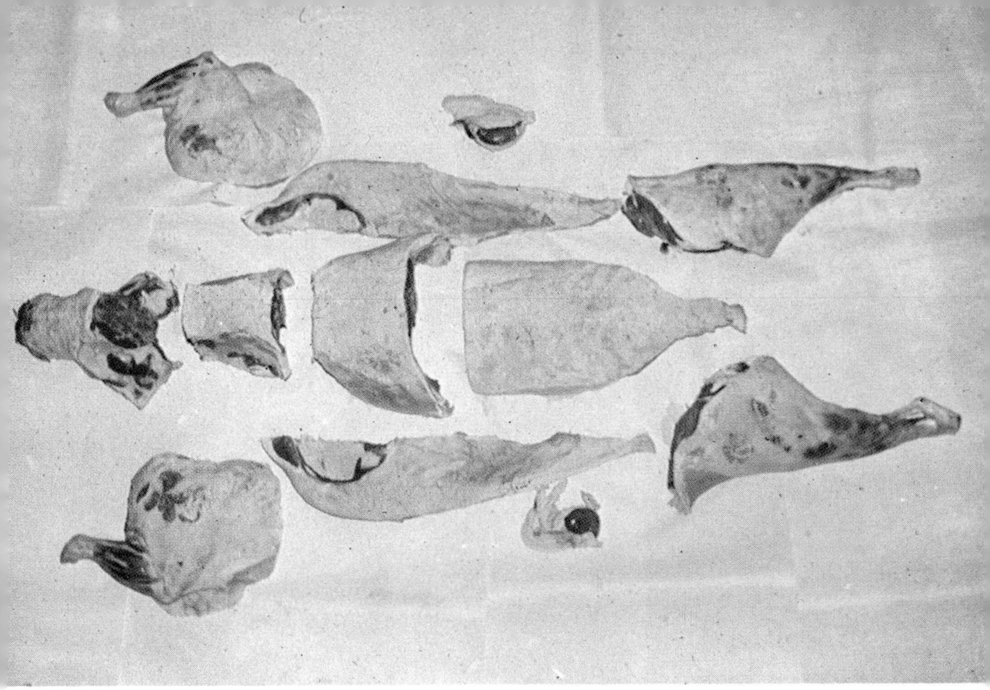

Plate 9. Joints of Lamb.

Plate 10. Lamb prepared for cooking.

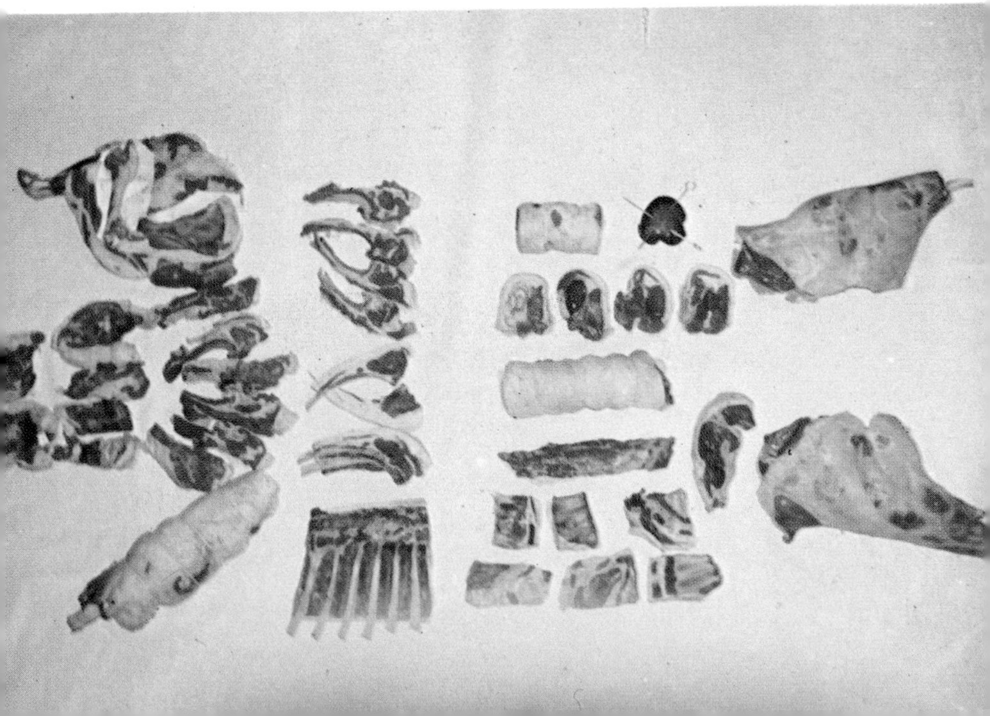

3. BALANCE

This is particularly important when compiling special party menus, and the following points should be considered:

(*a*) *Repetition of Ingredients*

Never repeat the basic ingredients on one menu.

For example, if mushrooms, tomatoes, peas, bacon, etc., are used in one course of a menu then they should not reappear in any other course on the same menu. Examples:

Mushroom Soup
Fillet of Sole Bonne-Femme
Casseroled Chicken Grandmère
Mushroom and Bacon Savoury
(repetition of Mushroom)

Tomato Salad
Steak Pie
Brussels Sprouts; Sauté Potatoes
Dutch Apple Tart
(repetition of Pastry)

(*b*) *Repetition of Colour*

Where possible avoid repetition of colour. Examples:

Celery Soup
Fricassée of Veal
Buttered Turnips; Creamed Potatoes
Meringue and Vanilla Ice Cream

Tomato Soup
Goulash of Veal
Vichy Carrots; Marquise Potatoes
Peach Melba

Examples of a menu with repetition of both an ingredient and colour:

Purée St. Germain (Peas)
Darne de Saumon: Grillé Sauce Vert
Noisette d'Agneau Clamart (Peas)
Gooseberry Fool

(*c*) *Repetition of Words*

Avoid repeating the same words on a menu. Examples:

Crème Portugaise
Carré d'Agneau à la Menthe
Purée d'Epinards à la *Crème*
Pommes Boulangère
Fraises à la *Crème*

Hors d'Œuvre
Bœuf *Braisé* aux Nouilles
Endive *Braisé*
Profiterolles au Chocolat

Oysters
Fried *Fillet* of Sole
Grilled *Fillet* Steak
Parsley Potatoes; Cauliflower
Apple Pie

(*d*) *Overall Balance of a Menu*

If many courses are to be served, care should be taken to see that they vary from dishes of a light nature to those of a more substantial nature and finish up with light dishes. In the case of a meal consisting of two or three meat courses, a rest may be made in the middle of the meal when a sorbet (a well-flavoured, lightly frozen water-ice designed to cleanse the palate) can be served; then a fresh start to the meal can be made with the roast. Example:

Dîner

Melon Frappé
Consommé Royale
Filets de Sole d'Antin
Escalope de Ris de Veau aux Pointes d'Asperges
Filet de Bœuf Bouquetière
Sorbet au Grand Marnier
Caneton d'Aylesbury Rôti
Salade Mimosa
Soufflé Vanille
Paillettes au Parmesan

(*e*) *Texture of Courses*

Regard should be given to the texture of courses; some food should be soft, some should require chewing, crunching, biting, some should be swallowed and so on.

Example of varied texture menu:

Crème Dubarry
Escalope de Veau Viennoise
Petits Pois au Beurre; Pommes Marquise
Flan aux Pommes

Examples of bad menus:

Cauliflower Soup
Irish Stew
Buttered Peas; Mashed Potatoes
Semolina Pudding

Salami
Fried Scallops
Veal Escalope
Fried Aubergine; Sauté Potatoes
Apple Fritters

(*f*) *Seasonings*

If strong seasonings like onion, garlic or pungent herbs such as thyme, sage or bay leaf are used, ensure that they are not repeated in more than one course.

(*g*) *Sauces*

If different sauces are served on one menu the foundation of the sauces should vary, e.g. demi-glace, velouté, tomato, butter thickened, arrow-root or cornflour thickened.

(*h*) *Garnishes*

Garnishes should be correct and they should not be repeated. Potatoes should only be named on a menu once, but they may be used in moderation on other courses; for example, pommes duchesse may be piped around a dish of fish. Pommes parisienne, noisette or olivette may be used to help lightly garnish an entrée or light meat course on a menu where two or three meat courses are being served.

(*i*) *Food Values*

When a customer selects from an à la carte or table d'hôte menu the composition of the meal is the customer's own responsibility. When a set meal is offered for a special party or banquet the menu is usually more than adequate to fulfil the nutritional needs. Special attention should be paid, however, to the nutritional balance of meals for people engaged in light or heavy work. The manual worker will require more substantial food than the office worker. Meals served to schoolchildren, meals served in hospitals, hostels, homes for invalids or homes of the aged all need thought on nutritional balance. It is usual to prepare such menus a week or two in advance, and it is necessary to see that the food provided over the period is satisfactory from the point of food value.

Further information on food value will be found in Chapter 7, on elementary nutrition.

4. COLOUR

This is a most important factor to consider in the presentation of food. The sensible use of colour will always help the eye-appeal of a dish. If it is sometimes necessary to use a little artificial colouring in order to finish certain foods correctly, care must be taken to see that these colours are used in moderation. Deep vivid colouring of any food should be avoided; the aim should be to use natural tints.

If a drab-looking main dish is being served, the careful use of a colourful garnish can greatly improve the presentation.

Plate appeal is a term which refers to the appearance of a course when it is served on a plate. The attractive appearance of each course is essential to the successful meal, and foods such as carrot, tomato, peas, watercress, parsley, truffle, oranges, cherries, etc., can give colour to the dullest coloured dishes. For example, a spring of watercress with a dish of roast beef and Yorkshire pudding; chopped parsley on sauté potatoes; paprika on egg mayonnaise; turned vegetables and peas with a brown lamb stew; orange salad with roast duck are but a few examples of how important colour is in the presentation of a dish and in the planning of a menu.

WORDING OF MENUS

When all the previous points have been considered then the menu can be written. Many errors can occur in the writing of menus and the following are examples which should be noted.

1. Consider the customer to be fed, and select language which will be easily understood.

2. It is customary in first-class establishments to use French for menu writing. A sensible thing to do is to give an English translation as a simple description under or by the side of each dish.

3. Having selected a language for the menu avoid using a mixture of languages on the same menu except in the case of certain national dishes which are best kept in the language of the country of origin. For example: in a first-class hotel or restaurant on a table d'hôte menu which may be of the highest order and written in French, dishes such as Irish Stew, Lancashire Hot Pot, Steak and Kidney Pie should appear in the language of the country of origin not as

Ragoût Irlandaise or Irish Stew aux Légumes, Casserole Lancashire, Pie à la Biftek et Rognon.

Certain menu terms such as Hors d'œuvre, Mayonnaise, Hollandaise, Bonne-Femme, Chasseur, Consommé, should not be translated into English.

Where the place of origin of a food is known it may be used on the menu: Roast *Aylesbury* Duckling; Grilled *Dover* Sole; *Vale of Evesham* Asparagus; Minted New *Jersey* Potatoes; *Kentish* Strawberries with *Devonshire* Cream; *York* Ham with *Belgian* Chicory Salad.

When writing a menu in French, care should be taken to see that the spelling is correct and that the accents are included.

The words used to describe a dish on a menu must agree in gender and number (also see page 270). For example:

A fillet of sole	Le filet de sole
Two fillets of sole	Deux filets de sole
Two fried fillets of sole	Deux filets de sole frits
Lamb	Agneau (masculine)
Lamb cutlet	La côtelette d'agneau
Two lamb cutlets	Deux côtelettes d'agneau
Grilled lamb cutlet	Côtelette d'agneau grillée
Two grilled lamb cutlets	Deux côtelettes d'agneau grillées

It will be noticed that the agreement is made with the cut or joint.

The definite article, *le* or *la*, if used with one dish should be used on all dishes, for example:

Le Saumon Fumé
La Selle d'Agneau Rôtie
Le Chou-fleur; Sauce Hollandaise
Les Pommes Parisienne
La Pêche Melba

and not

Le Saumon Fumé
Selle d'Agneau Rôtie
Le Chou-fleur; Sauce Hollandaise
Les Pommes Parisienne
Pêche Melba

Care should be taken over the use of the term *à la* which means 'in the *or* after the style of'. This means that it can be used when a dish is prepared in the style of a certain place, town or country, for example:

Hors d'Œuvre à la Grecque
Filets de Sole Frits à la Française
Poulet Sauté à la Portugaise
Petits Pois à la Flamande

When a dish of food is named after a person or place the name usually follows the food.

Pêche Melba, named after Madame Melba
Crème Dubarry, named after Madame Dubarry
Salade Waldorf, named after Waldorf Astoria Hotel

When using classical garnish names, see that any vegetable which is included in the garnish is not repeated as a vegetable. For example: Chou-fleur Mornay would not be put on the menu as a vegetable to be served with Selle d'Agneau Dubarry.

The list which follows includes some of the terms used on a menu, which signify that a specific item of food will be served. For example: parmentier indicates that potatoes will be used; therefore Purée Parmentier is potato soup; Omelette Parmentier is an omelet garnished with potatoes.

Dubarry	Cauliflower	Lyonnaise	Onions
Bruxelloise	Brussels sprouts	Florentine	Spinach
Clamart	Peas	Portugaise	Tomatoes
Doria	Cucumber	Princesse	Asparagus
Provençale	Tomato and Garlic	Washington	Sweetcorn

SOME MEAT AND POULTRY GARNISHES WITH SUITABLE MENU EXAMPLES

Name of garnish	*Composition of garnish*	*Use of garnish*	*Menu term: example using garnish*
Boulangère	Onions and potatoes	For roast lamb joints	Gigot d'Agneau Boulangère
Bouquetière	Artichoke bottoms, carrots, turnips, peas, French beans, cauliflower, château potatoes	For roast joints, usually beef	Filet de Bœuf Bouquetière
Bourgeoise	Carrots, onions, dice of bacon	For large joints	Bœuf Braisé Bourgeoise
Bruxelloise	Braised chicory, brussels sprouts, château potatoes	For large joints	Noix de Veau Bruxelloise
Clamart	Artichoke bottoms filled with peas à la française. Or purée of peas and château potatoes	For large joints	Carré d'Agneau Clamart
Dubarry	Small balls of cauliflower mornay, château potatoes	For large joints	Contrefilet de Bœuf Dubarry
Fermière	Paysanne of carrots, turnips, onions, celery	For large joints	Poulet en Casserole Fermière
Fleuriste	Tomatoes filled with carrots, turnips, peas, French beans; château potatoes	For tournedos and noisettes	Noisette d'Agneau Fleuriste
Henri IV	Pont-neuf potatoes and watercress	For tournedos and noisettes	Tournedos Henri IV
Jardinière	Carrots, turnips, French beans, flageolets, peas and cauliflower coated with Hollandaise Sauce	For joints	Selle d'Agneau Jardinière
Judic	Stuffed tomatoes, braised lettuce, château potatoes	For joints	Longe d'Agneau Judic
Mascotte	Quarters of artichoke bottoms, cocotte potatoes, slices of truffle	For joints and poultry	Pculet Sauté Mascotte
Mercédès	Grilled tomatoes, grilled mushrooms, braised lettuce, croquette potatoes	For joints	Selle de Veau Mercédès

SOME MEAT AND POULTRY GARNISHES WITH SUITABLE MENU EXAMPLES

Name of garnish	*Composition of garnish*	*Use of garnish*	*Menu term: example using garnish*
Parmentier	1 cm dice of fried potatoes	For tournedos, noisettes and poultry	Poulet Sauté Parmentier
Portugaise	Small stuffed tomatoes, château potatoes	For tournedos, noisettes and poultry	Tournedos à la Portugaise
Printanier	Turned carrots and turnips, peas, dice of French beans	For entrées, stews	Navarin d'Agneau Printanier
Réforme	Short batons of beetroot, white of egg, gherkin, mushroom, truffle and tongue	For lamb or mutton cutlets	Côtelette d'Agneau Réforme
Sévigné	Braised lettuce, grilled mushrooms, château potatoes	For tournedos, noisettes and joints	Carré de Veau Sévigné
Soubise	Onion purée or sauce	For cuts of mutton	Côte de Mouton Soubise
Tyrolienne	French fried onions, tomate concassé	For small cuts of meat	Noisette d'Agneau Tyrolienne
Vert Pré	Straw potatoes and watercress	For grilled meats	Entrecôte Vert Pré
Vichy	With Vichy carrots	For entrées	Blanquette de Veau Vichy
Washington	Sweetcorn	For eggs and poultry	Poularde Poêlé Washington
Duxelle	Finely chopped shallots and chopped mushrooms	This is a basic culinary preparation with many uses—for example, stuffed vegetables, sauces, etc.	

A LIST OF SOME OF THE NAMES USED IN FISH COOKERY TO INDICATE CERTAIN GARNISHES OR METHODS OF COOKING AND SERVING

Name of garnish	*Composition of garnish*	*Menu example*
Bercy	Poached with chopped shallots, parsley, fish stock and white wine; finished with white wine sauce and glazed	Filets de Sole Bercy
Bonne-Femme	As for Bercy, with the addition of sliced mushrooms, glazed	Suprême de Turbot Bonne-Femme
Bréval or d'Antin	As for Bonne-Femme, with the addition of chopped tomatoes, glazed	Suprême de Barbue Bréval
Véronique	Poached with white wine and fish stock; coated with white wine sauce; glazed and garnished with grapes	Sole Véronique
Dieppoise	Poached; coated with white wine sauce, garnish mussels, shrimps tails and mushrooms	Suprême de Carrelet Dieppoise
Dugléré	Poached with chopped shallots, parsley, tomatoes, fish stock; coated with a sauce made from the cooking liquor	Filet d'Aigrefin Dugléré
Mornay	Poached; coated with cheese sauce and glazed	Coquille de Cabillaud Mornay
Florentine	Poached; dressed on a bed of leaf spinach; coated with mornay sauce and glazed	Suprême de Turbotin Florentine
Hollandaise	Plain boiled; served with hollandaise sauce and plain boiled potatoes	Tronçon de Turbot Hollandaise
Meunière	Shallow fried on both sides; garnished with slice of lemon; coated with nut-brown butter, lemon juice and parsley	Truite de Rivière Meunière
Belle Meunière	As for meunière, with the addition of grilled mushroom, a slice of peeled tomato, and a soft herring-roe (passed through flour and shallow fried) all neatly dressed on each portion of fish	Sole Belle Meunière
Doria	As for meunière, with a sprinkling of small, turned, cooked pieces of cucumber	Suprême de Flétan Doria

A LIST OF SOME OF THE NAMES USED IN FISH COOKERY TO INDICATE CERTAIN GARNISHES OR METHODS OF COOKING AND SERVING

Name of garnish	*Composition of garnish*	*Menu example*
Grenobloise	As for meunière, with the lemon in peeled segments and capers	Rouget Grenobloise
Bretonne	As for meunière, with picked shrimps and sliced mushrooms	Filet d'Aigrefin Bretonne
Princesse	Poached; coated with white wine sauce; garnished with asparagus heads and slices of truffle	Délices de Sole Princesse
Saint-Germain	Filleted white fish dipped in butter; breadcrumbed; grilled; served with béarnaise sauce and noisette potatoes	Filets de Plie St.-Germain
Orly	Deep fried and served with tomato sauce	Filet de Cabillaud à l'Orly

A LIST OF SOME OF THE NAMES USED IN SWEET DISHES TO INDICATE THE USE OF A PARTICULAR INGREDIENT

	Composition	*Menu example*
Chantilly	Whipped, sweetened, vanilla-flavoured cream	Meringue Chantilly
Glacé	With ice cream	Meringue Glacé Chantilly
Meringuée	Finished with piped meringue and glazed	Flan aux Pommes Meringuées
Normande	With apple	Crêpes Normande
Rubané	With different flavours and colours	Bavarois Rubané
Montmorency	With cherries	Coupe Montmorency
Condé	With rice	Poire Condé
Moka	Coffee flavour	Glace Moka
Suchard	Chocolate flavour	Profiteroles, Sauce Suchard
Praliné	With chopped almond and hazel-nut toffee	Gâteau Praliné
Melba	With vanilla ice cream and raspberry purée or sauce	Pêche Melba
Cardinal	With strawberry ice cream and raspberry sauce, sliced almonds	Fraises Cardinal
Hélène	Vanilla ice cream, hot chocolate sauce	Poire Hélène
Jamaïque	Rum flavour	Coupe Jamaïque

BREAKFAST MENUS

A Breakfast Menu can be compiled from the following foods:

1. *Fruits:* Grapefruit, orange, melon, apple.
   Fruit juices: Grapefruit, orange, tomato, pineapple.
   Stewed fruit: Prunes, figs, apples, pears.

2. *Cereals:* Cornflakes, shredded wheat, etc., porridge.

3. *Eggs:* Fried, boiled, poached, scrambled; omelets with bacon (streaky, back or gammon) or tomatoes or mushrooms or sauté potatoes.

4. *Fish:* Grilled herrings, kippers or bloaters; fried sole, plaice or whiting; fish cakes, smoked haddock, kedgeree.

5. *Meats (hot):* Fried or grilled bacon (streaky, back or gammon), sausages, kidneys, calves' liver, with tomatoes or mushrooms or sauté potatoes or potato cakes or bubble and squeak.

6. *Meats (cold):* Ham, bacon, pressed beef with sauté potatoes.

7. *Preserves:* Marmalade (orange, lemon, grapefruit, ginger), jams, honey.

8. *Fresh fruits:* Apple, pear, peach, grapes, etc.

9. *Beverages:* Tea, coffee, chocolate.

10. *Bread:* Rolls, croissants, brioche, toast.

Points to consider when compiling a Breakfast Menu:

(*a*) It is usual to offer three of the above-mentioned courses. For example:

Fruit or Cereals
Fish, Eggs or Meat
Preserves, Bread, Coffee

(*b*) As large a menu as possible should be offered, depending on the size of the establishment, bearing in mind that it is better to offer a smaller number of well-prepared dishes than a large number of hurriedly prepared ones.

(*c*) A choice of plain foods such as boiled eggs or poached haddock should be available for the person who may not require a fried breakfast.

Breakfast menus may be table d'hôte or à la carte; a continental breakfast does not include any cooked dish. A typical continental breakfast consists of:

Rolls and Butter, Croissant, Toast
Preserves
Tea or Coffee

Examples of Breakfast Menus:

TABLE D'HÔTE

Full Breakfast

Shredded Wheat   Porridge   Wheat Flakes

or

Stewed Fruit

****

Omelette Maison   Scrambled Eggs with Mushrooms

or

Fried Fillets of Fish   Finnan Haddock   Kipper

or

Bacon and Fried Egg   Bacon and Mushrooms

or

Grilled Bacon   Grilled Sausage

Rolls and Butter   Croissant   Toast
Preserves   Honey
Tea   Coffee   Chocolate

CONTINENTAL BREAKFAST

Rolls and Butter   Croissant   Toast
Preserves   Honey
Tea   Coffee   Chocolate
Ovaltine   Cocoa

BREAKFAST MENU

A LA CARTE

Porridge, Rolled Oats, All Bran, Grapenuts, Shredded Wheat, Quaker Wheat Flakes, Weetabix

Post Toasties . . . .

Croissants . . . .

Stewed Fruit

Stewed Prunes, Figs, Pears, Apples, Plums . .

Fish

Fried Fillets of Sole . . . . .

Fried Fillets of Plaice . . . . .

Grilled Turbot . . . . . .

Smoked Haddock . . . . . .

Fried Whiting . . . . . .

Kippers (pair) . . . . . .

Grilled Herrings (pair) . . . . .

Egg Dishes

Scrambled Eggs with Mushrooms . . .

Omelette with Mushrooms . . . .

Omelette with Tomatoes . . . . .

Fried Eggs (2) . . . . . .

Poached Eggs (2) on Toast . . . .

Grill

Ham . . . .

Grilled Ham and Egg . . . . .

Bacon and Kidney . . . . . .

Sausages and Mushrooms . . . .

Bacon and Mushrooms . . . . .

Bacon and Tomatoes . . . . .

Sausages and Tomatoes . . . . .

Bacon and Fried Egg . . . . .

Sausages (2) . . . .

Fresh Fruit

Grapefruit (half) . . . . . .

Grapefruit Cocktail . . . . .

Oranges Grapes Melon Peaches
Apple Pear

Fruit Juices

Orange (Fresh) . . . . . .

Apple . . . .

Orange . . . .

Grapefruit . . . .

Pineapple . . . .

Tomato . . . .

Beverages

Tea, Coffee, Chocolate, Nescafé . . .

Café Filtre . . . .

Yoghourt . . . .

LUNCHEON MENUS

A luncheon table d'hôte menu should include as wide a choice of dishes as possible, depending on the type of establishment. If a special party luncheon menu is required, three or four courses are usually offered, for example:

Luncheon

Grapefruit Cocktail

Fillets of Sole Bonne-Femme
Roast Surrey Chicken
French Beans; Château Potatoes

Sherry Trifle

Luncheon

Hors d'Œuvre

Mixed Grill
Brussels Sprouts; Fried Potatoes

Cream Caramel

Almost all foods are suitable for serving at luncheon. In warm weather cold dishes are popular and as large a cold buffet as possible should be available.

Luncheon menus can be compiled from the following foods:

First Course

(*a*) *Fruit cocktails:* Melon, grapefruit, orange, florida.

(*b*) *Fruits:* Melon, grapefruit, avocado pear.
Fruit juices: Grapefruit, orange, pineapple, tomato.

(*c*) *Shellfish, etc.:* Potted shrimps, prawns, oysters, caviar, snails, seagulls' eggs, crabmeat.
Shellfish cocktails: Lobster, crab, prawn, shrimp.

(*d*) *Smoked:* Salmon, trout, eel, sprats, buckling, mackerel, roe, ham, salami.

(*e*) *Hors d'œuvre.*

Second Course

Soups: Consommé with simple garnish. Cold in summer.
Purée: Parmentier, St. Germain, etc.
Crème: de volaille, de tomates, etc.
Potage: Paysanne, minestrone, Scotch broth.

Third Course

Farinaceous: Spaghetti, macaroni, ravioli, canneloni, gnocchi (Italienne, Romaine, Parisienne), nouilles, risotto.

Fourth Course

Eggs: Scrambled, poached, mollet, en cocotte, sur le plat, omelette.

When served for a luncheon menu these dishes are usually garnished.

Fifth Course

Fish. (Nearly all kinds of fish can be served, but without complicated garnishes. They are usually steamed, poached, boiled, grilled, deep or shallow fried.)

Mussels, scallops, herrings, skate, whiting, plaice, cod, turbot, brill, sole, scampi, trout, salmon trout, salmon, whitebait, kedgeree.

Sixth Course

Entrées. (This is a dish of meat, game or poultry which is not roasted or grilled.)

Brown stews (ragôut de bœuf; navarin de mouton).
Braised steaks, braised beef, civet de lièvre.
Goulash de veau, braised oxtail, salmis of game.
Hot pot, Irish stew.
Meat pies, chicken pies.
Meat puddings.
Boiled meat (French and English style).
Fricassée, blanquette.
Calves' head, tripe, liver, sauted kidneys.
Vienna and Hamburg steaks.
Sausages, minced meat, chicken émincé.
Fried lamb, veal or pork cutlets or fillets.
Fried steaks (entrecôte, tournedos, fillets, etc.).
Veal escalopes, sweetbreads.
Vol-au-vent of chicken or sweetbreads or both.
Sauerkraut, pilaff, kebab, chicken cutlets.

Seventh Course

Roasts: Beef, pork, veal, lamb, mutton, chicken.

Eighth Course

Grills: Steaks (châteaubriand, fillet, tournedos, point, rump).
Porterhouse, entrecote.
Cutlets (single, double).
Chops (loin, chump).
Kidneys, mixed grill, chicken, chicken legs.

Ninth Course

Cold Buffet: Salmon, lobster, crab.
Pâté or terrine.
Beef, ham, tongue, lamb.
Chicken, chicken pie, raised pies.
Pressed beef, duck, aspic dishes.
Ham mousse.

Tenth Course

Vegetables: Cabbage, cauliflower, French beans, spinach, peas.
Carrots, tomatoes, etc.
Asparagus, globe artichoke, sea-kale (hot or cold with a suitable sauce).

Potatoes: Boiled, steamed, sauté, fried, roast, creamed, croquette, lyonnaise, etc.

Eleventh Course

Sweets: Steamed puddings (fruit and sponge).
Milk puddings.
Fruit (stewed, fools, flans, salad, pies, fritters).
Egg custard sweets (baked, bread and butter, cream, caramel, diplomat, cabinet).
Bavarois, savarin, baba.
Charlottes, profiteroles, gâteaux.
Pastries (mille feuilles, éclairs, etc.).
Various ices.

Twelfth Course

Savouries: Simple savouries may also be served; for example, Welsh Rarebit.

Thirteenth Course

Cheese: A good selection of cheese. Biscuits, celery and radishes.

Fourteenth Course:

Dessert: Fresh fruit of all kinds and nuts.

Coffee.

TEA MENUS

These vary considerably, depending on the type of establishment. The high-class hotel will usually offer a dainty menu. For example:

Sandwiches: (Smoked salmon, ham, tongue, egg, tomato, cucumber) made with white or brown bread.

Bread and butter (white, brown, fruit loaf).

Jams, honey, lemon curd.

Small pastries, assorted gâteaux.

Fruit salad and cream, ices.

Tea (Indian, China, Russian, Iced).

The commercial hotels, public restaurants, canteens, will offer simple snacks and cooked meals. For example:

Assorted sandwiches.

Buttered buns, scones, tea cakes, sally lunns, Scotch pancakes, waffles, sausage rolls, assorted bread and butter, various jams, toasted tea-cakes, scones, crumpets, buns.

Eggs (boiled, poached, fried, omelets).

Fried fish; grilled meats; roast poultry.

Cold meats and salads.

Assorted pastries; gâteaux.

Various ices, coupes, sundaes.

Tea; orange and lemon squash.

DINNER MENUS

A list of some of the foods suitable for dinner menus is given below, and both table d'hôte and à la carte menus should offer as wide a choice as possible, depending upon the size of the establishment.

The number of courses on special party menus can vary from three to ten. The occasions for special dinner parties are often very important for the guest attending, therefore the compiling of such a menu is extremely important, calling for expert knowledge and wise judgment on the part of the caterer. The following are some of the foods used:

First Course

(*a*) *Cocktail:* Fruit and shellfish.

(*b*) *Fruit:* Melon, fresh figs, avocado pear.

(*c*) *Delicacies:* Caviar, oysters, snails, potted shrimps, prawns, foie gras.

(*d*) *Smoked:* Salmon, trout, ham, salami, sausages, sprats, eel.

(*e*) *Hors d'œuvre.*

Second Course

Soup: Clear and consommé based, double consommé, petite marmite, croûte au pot, consommé de volaille, turtle soup, bisque de homard, crème de champignons, crème d'asperges, germiny, velouté agnès sorel, soupe à l'oignon, bortsh.

Cold soups: Vichyssoise, consommé, crème de pois.

Third Course

Fish: Boiled salmon, turbot, trout (au bleu).

Shallow poached: sole, turbot, brill, halibut, with such classical garnishes as newburg, américaine, cubat, véronique, bonne-femme.

Hot shellfish: Lobster, mornay, thermidor, newburg, cardinal; scampi, oysters.

Meunière: Sole, fillets of sole—grenobloise, belle meunière.

Fried: Sole, fillets of sole, goujons, scampi.

Grilled: Lobster, sole, salmon.

Cold: Salmon, salmon trout, trout, sole.

Fourth Course

Entrée: Light entrée dishes are used which are small and garnished.

Vegetables are not served with an entrée if it is followed by a rèlevé or roast with vegetables. Examples are:

Sweetbreads, hot mousse of ham or foie gras.

Sauté of chicken, tournedos, noisettes or cutlets of lamb.

Suprême de volaille sous-cloche.

Saddle of hare, filet mignon, vol-au-vent.

Fifth Course

Rèlevé: This is usually a joint which is carved and is cooked by braising or poêler such as:

Poularde poêlée, aux champignons.

Poulet en casserole bonne-femme.

Poulet en cocotte grand'mère.

Selle d'agneau poêlé bouquetière.

Selle de veau poêlé, filet de bœuf poélé, contrefilet de bœuf poêlé.

Braised ham, tongue, duck, pheasant, pigeon.

The rèlevé is served with a good quality vegetable and potato.

Vegetable: French beans, broccoli, asparagus points, peas, broad beans, button brussels sprouts, aubergine, cauliflower, etc.

Potatoes: Parmentier, noisette, olivette, dauphine, nouvelles, rissolées, mireille, duchesse, Byron.

Sixth Course

Sorbet: This a lightly frozen water ice flavoured with a liqueur or champagne and served with a wafer. Russian cigarettes are often served during this course.

Seventh Course

Roast: The roast course should be served with a salad, usually compound, such as lorette, niçoise, française.

Examples of roasts are:

Saddle of lamb or veal, fillet or sirloin of beef.

Poultry or game such as chicken, turkey, duck, goose, grouse, partridge, pheasant, snipe, woodcock, guinea fowl, wild duck, plover, teal, venison, saddle of hare.

Eighth Course

Cold Dish: Such dishes as chicken in aspic or mousse de foie gras or jambon may be served.

Ninth Course

Hot Dish: A hot dish, usually a vegetable such as asparagus, globe artichoke, sea-kale, petits pois à la française, truffles au champagne or a spinach, mushroom or ham souffle, may be served.

Tenth Course

Sweet: Hot soufflés or pancakes are the usual hot sweets to serve for dinner menus:

Iced soufflé, bombes, coupes and biscuits with fruit such as peaches, strawberries, raspberries are used accompanied by petits fours.

Friandises, mignardise or frivolities (these are different names for very small pastries, sweets, biscuits, etc.).

Eleventh Course

Savoury: Any savouries such as canapé diane, anges à cheval, quiche lorraine may be used on dinner menus.

Twelfth Course

Cheese: All varieties may be offered.

Thirteenth Course

Dessert: All dessert fruits may be served.

Coffee

Examples of Dinner Menus (suitable for a medium-sized hotel)

A. TABLE D'HÔTE

Dîner

Hors d'Œuvre
Pamplemousse Rafrâichi
Consommé Madrilène
Crème de Volaille

Filet de Sole Bonne-Femme
Truite de Rivière Meunière

Tournedos Niçoise
Escalopes de Ris de Veau Florentine
Suprême de Volaille Princesse
Jambon braisé au Madère

Petits Pois	Pommes Rissolées
Épinards en Purée	Parisienne
Céleri Braisé	Maître d'Hôtel

Poire Belle-Hélène
Meringue Glacée Chantilly
Bande aux Cerises
Crêpes à l'Orange

B. SPECIAL PARTY

Dîner

Crème de Volaille

Filets de Sole Cardinal

Tournedos Sauté au Madère
Petits Pois fins au Beurre; Pommes Parisienne

Soufflé Arlequin

C. A LA CARTE

Hors d'Œuvre

Foie gras de Strasbourg . . . . .
Escargots de Bourgogne . . . . .
Crevettes Roses . . . . . .
Gulls Eggs . . . .
Coupe Florida . . . . . .
Saumon Fumé . . . . . .
Honeydew Melon . . . . . .
Potted Shrimps . . . . . .

Potages

Bisque de Homard . . . . . .
Soupe à l'Oignon . . . . . .
Vichyssoise . . . .
Consommé Judic . . . . . .
Germiny . . . .
Velouté Agnès-Sorel . . . . .

Poissons

Filets de Sole Caprice . . . . .
Suprême de Turbot Waleska . . . .
Homard Américaine . . . . .
Saumon Poché, Sauce Hollandaise . . .
Scampis Frites, Sauce Tartare . . . .
Truite au Bleu . . . . . .

Entrées

Suprême de Volaille Maréchale . . . .
Tournedos Rachel . . . . . .
Vol-au-Vent de Volaille . . . . .
Escalope de Veau au Marsala . . . .
Côtelettes d'Agneau Réforme . . . .
Poussin en Casserole . . . . .

Rôtis

Poulet de Surrey . . . . . .
Caneton d'Aylesbury . . . . .
Selle d'Agneau . . . . . .
Gibier (en saison) . . . . . .

Grillades

Châteaubriand . . . . . .
Fillet Steak . . . .
Tournedos . . . .
Entrecôte . . . .
Chop d'Agneau . . . . . .
Côtelettes d'Agneau . . . . .

Buffet Froid

Mayonnaise de Volaille . . . . . .
Mayonnaise de Homard . . . . . .
Jambon de York . . . .
Côte de Bœuf . . . .
Langue de Bœuf . . . .
Saumon d'Ecosse . . . .
Chicken Pie . . . .

Salades

Française, Laitue, Romaine, Niçoise, Lorette, Japonaise . . . .

Légumes

Haricots Verts, Endives au Jus, Aubergines Frites, Broccoli, Beurre Fondu, Petits Pois à la Française
Pommes: Frites, Rissolées, Nouvelles, Purée à la Crème, Olivette . . . . . .

Entremets

Pêche Cardinal . . . .
Soufflé Grand Marnier . . . . . .
Biscuit Glacé Praliné . . . . . .
Gâteau au Chocolat . . . . . .
Sabayon au Marsala . . . . . .
Crêpes Suzette . . . .
Ananas Flambé . . . .
Coupe Jacques . . . .

Canapés

Anges à Cheval . . . .
Quiche Lorraine . . . .
Canapé Diane . . . .
Canapé Quo Vadis . . . .
Croûte Windsor . . . .
Canapé Baron . . . .

Les Fromages au Choix

Dessert

Café

SUPPER MENUS

Supper menus are more limited than luncheon or dinner menus and, with the exception of supper balls, the dishes are lighter. Dishes would be selected from the following:

First Course

Shellfish, caviar, snails, smoked salmon, smoked ham, smoked trout.

Consommé, onion soup, turtle soup.

Second Course

Fish: Fried or grilled salmon, lobster, scampi, poached haddock, kippers.

Cold fish such as salmon, salmon trout, lobster.

Entrées: Sautés tournedos, noisettes, cutlets, vol-au-vent, and small birds braised or poêlé.

Roast: Snipe, woodcock, quail or poussin may be served.

Grills: Particularly chicken, kebab and kidneys.

Vegetables: Can be served—they usually garnish the dish. Potatoes are usually fried.

Cold dishes: Cold meats, poultry, mousse, terrines are usually served with a salad.

Third Course

Sweet: Hot soufflées, pancakes and fritters are served.

Various coupes, bombes, biscuits are usually accompanied by petits fours.

Any of the savouries may be served.

Dessert.

Coffee

Example of Supper Menu

A. TABLE D'HÔTE

Consommé au Fumet de Céleri
Sugar Melon
Truite Fumée

Scampis Frites
Poulet Grillé à l'Américaine
Pommes Frites

Pêche Melba
Scotch Woodcock

B. A LA CARTE

Soupe à l'Oignon
Consommé en Gelée
Saumon Fumé
Jambon de Bayonne
Haddock Monte Carlo
Sole Grillée
Suprême de Volaille sous Cloche
Tournedos Rossini
Côtelettes d'Agneau Grillées
Haricots Verts
Pommes Sautées
Biscuit Glacé aux Fraises
Croque Monsieur

C. SPECIAL PARTY

Tortue Claire
Kebab à la Turque
Soufflé à l'Orange

BANQUET MENUS

When compiling banquet menus certain points should be considered:

1. The food which will possibly be for a large number of people must be dressed in such a way that it can be served fairly quickly. Heavily garnished dishes should be avoided.
2. If a large number of dishes have to be dressed at the same time certain foods deteriorate quickly and do not stand storage, even for a short time in a hot plate—for example, deep-fried fish.

Banquet Luncheon Menus

A normal luncheon menu is used, bearing in mind the number of people involved. It is not usual to serve farinaceous dishes, eggs, stews or savouries. A luncheon menu could be drawn from the following courses:

First Course

Soup, cocktail (fruit or shellfish), hors d'œuvre.

Second Course

Fish.

Third Course

Meat, hot or cold, but not a stew or made-up dish. Vegetables and potatoes or a salad should be served.

Fourth Course

If the function is being held during the asparagus season, then either hot or cold asparagus with a suitable sauce may be served as a course on its own.

Fifth Course

Sweet, hot or cold.
Cheese and Biscuits.

Coffee

Example of Luncheon Banquet Menu

Hors d'Œuvre
Fillets of Sole Bonne-Femme
Grilled Chicken and Bacon
Minted Garden Peas   New Jersey Potatoes
Dutch Apple Tart
Devon Clotted Cream
Cheese and Biscuits

Banquet Dinner Menus

Here the caterer has the opportunity to excel, and two menu examples are given here:

(*a*)

Consommé Alexandra
Délice de Sole Newburg
Escalopes de Ris de Veau Maréchale
Filet de Bœuf Bouquetière
Sorbet au Champagne
Caneton Rôti
Salade Mimosa
Omelette Surprise Mylord
Quiche Lorraine

(*b*)

Melon au Porto
Tortue Claire
Darne de Saumon Pochée
Sauce Hollandaise
Sorbet Grand-Marnier
Faisan aux Céleris
Brocolis au Beurre
Pommes Amandine
Coupe Montmorency

FUNCTIONS AND BANQUETS

It will be necessary to know the nature of the function, as special facilities may be required. The type of function could be a wedding breakfast, silver or golden wedding anniversary, coming of age, retirement, presentation, conference, etc.

If there are any special diet requirements of guests, such as fish or eggs in place of meat, then the kitchen should know of them.

The type of meal for functions can vary from:

Buffets: Light, where the food is served or where the guests help themselves
Buffets: Fork, hot or cold
Buffets: Cold
Buffets: Hot

to a formal sit-down meal.

The cost of the menu is agreed with the organiser of the function, and if any of the following are required then they will be charged as extras:

Floral decorations	Place-name cards
Special menu printing	Table plan
Orchestra	Toastmaster or M.C.
Cabaret	Hire of rooms
Invitation cards	Special decorations

LIGHT BUFFETS

(including Cocktail Parties)

Light Buffets can include:

1. Hot savoury pastry patties of lobster, chicken, crab, salmon, mushroom, ham, etc.

2. Hot sausages (chipolatas), various fillings, such as chicken livers, prunes, mushrooms, tomatoes, gherkins, etc., wrapped in bacon and skewered.

3. Savoury finger toast to include any of the cold canapés. These may also be prepared on biscuits or shaped pieces of pastry. On the bases the following may be used: salami, ham, tongue, thinly sliced cooked meats, smoked salmon, caviar, mock caviar, sardine, eggs, etc.

4. Game chips, gaufrette potatoes, fried fish balls, celery stalks spread with cheese.

5. Sandwiches, bridge rolls open or closed but always small.

6. Sweets such as trifles, charlottes, jellies, bavarois, fruit salad, strawberries and raspberries with fresh cream, ice creams, pastries, gâteaux.

7. Beverages, coffee, tea, fruit-cup, punch-bowl, iced coffee.

Fork Buffets

For these functions individual pieces of fish, meat and poultry are prepared so that they can be eaten by the guests standing up and balancing a plate in one hand. Salads should also be sensibly prepared so that they can be easily handled by the guest using only a fork; the lettuce should be shredded and kept in short lengths. Chicken or ham mousse, galantine, terrine, pâté, mayonnaise of salmon, lobster and chicken are all suitable dishes.

FULL BUFFETS

(*a*) *London Hilton*

Coupe Hawaii

Selection of cold cuts of meat to include:
Roast Beef
York Ham
Chicken
Various Mixed Salads

Apple Strudel & Fresh Cream

Coffee

(*b*) *London Hilton*

Cocktail de Fruits de Mer
Saumon Fumé
Truite de Rivière Fumé
Melon de la Saison
Saumon d'Ecosse en Bellevue
Cote de Bœuf Froid 'Belle Jardiniere'
Suprême de Volaille 'Hawaienne'
Jambon et Langue 'Marguerite'

Salads

Russian, Tomato, Cucumber, Lorette, Waldorf

Hot Entrées (in chafing dish)

Petits Kebabs de Bœuf à l'Oriental Riz Pilaw
ou
Goujonettes de Sole Frites, Sauce Tartare

Sauces

Mayonnaise, Tartare, Cocktail, Vinaigrette
Plateau de Fromages

Desserts

Macedoine de Fruits
Babas au Rhum
Tourte mille Feuille
Friandises

Café

PANCAKES

International Selection

Russian Style *(Meat)* Meat Blinza Pancakes Filled with Fresh Minced Beef Steak and Liver Filling 27p

Russian Style *(Cheese)* Pancakes Filled with Sweet and Sour Double Cream Cheese and Lemon 27p

Italian Style Pancake Filled with Chopped Veal Filling and topped with Creamy Cheese Sauce 27p

Spanish Style Pancake Filled with Special Savoury Filling of Tomato, Rice and Mushrooms 27p

★ ★ ★

American Style Savoury Pancakes

Showboat Pancake interlaced with a large helping of Sweetcorn and topped with Rasher of Bacon and Tomato 22p

Kentucky Pancakes topped with Crispy Bacon, Sliced Tomatoes and Special Rich Tomato Sauce 22p

New Orleans Pancakes topped with Chicken in Chef's White Sauce and Crushed Pineapple.. .. .. .. 20p

Uncle Tom Pancakes Filled with Fresh Scrambled Egg and Crispy Rasher of Bacon 27p

Plantation Pancakes with Sliced Frankfurter Sausages and Covered with a Rich Meat Sauce & Sliced Tomato 25p

Mississippi Pancakes Layered with Ham, Tomato and Chef's Special Sauce .. 25p

Florida Pancakes filled with Pure Beef Hamburger and Lettuce topped with Fresh Pancake and ring of Pineapple.. 20p

American Pancakes topped with sliced Chicken and Cranberries 25p

★SWEET PANCAKES ★

Regular Pancakes topped with Whipped Butter and Choice of M Syrup or Strawberry Melba or Chocolate Sauce and topped w Dairy Whipped Cream .. ..

Fresh Delicious Soft Ice Cream 4p Extra.

Five Silver Dollar Pancakes topped with Whipped Cream Morello Cherries and Melba Sauce .. .. ..

Hawaiian Style Pancakes topped with Pineapple, Melba Sauce Whipped Dairy Cream .. ..

With Soft Ice Cream 4p Extra

Cranberry Surprise Fresh Pancakes with a generous portion Cranberry Sauce and Whipped Cream .. .. ..

Banana Pancake topped with Melba Sauce and Whipped D Cream .. ..

Apple Surprise Pancake Chunks of Apple blended into a Hc Cinnamon Syrup and sandwiched between Pancakes .. With Soft Ice Cream 4p Extra

Special Crunch Pancake topped with Maple Syrup and Cara Crunchnut and Whipped Dairy Cream .. .. .. With Soft Ice Cream 4p Extra.

★ ★ ★

American Pancake Pizza Selection

Pizza Neapolitan with Anchovies, Olives Rich Neapolitan Sauce .. ..

Pizza Prosciutto topped with Ham

Pizza topped with Salami .. ..

Pizza Mississippi topped with Ham, Mu rooms, Salami, Olives and Anchovies

Toasted Sandwiches

Cheese and Tomato .. ..

Ham and Tomato .. ..

(Not served between 12 and 2 p.m.)

Double Decker American Club Sandwiches

Sliced Ham, Lettuce, Cheddar Cheese and Sweet Pickle.. .. ..

Double Cream Cheese, Bacon, Lettuce & Tomato .. .. ..

Sliced Chicken Ham, Cranberries and Lettuce .. ..

(All served with Potato Salad)

Waffles •

Freshly Baked Waffle topped with Whipped Butter and Choice of Maple Syrup or Strawberry Melba or Chocolate Sauce, and Whipped Cream

The Above with Soft Ice Cream 4p Extra

Waffles served with Soft Sugar and Whipped Cream

Waffles topped with Ham & Fried Egg

• Beverages

Tea .. ..

Milk and Dash .. ..

Special Old Kentucky Coffee .. .. ..

Special Old Kentucky Coffee with Cream ..

Lemon Tea .. ..

New Orleans French Chocolate topped with Fresh Dairy Cream .. ..

Cola .. ..

Orange Squash .. ..

MINIMUM CHARGE AFTER 6.0 p.m. - 14p

MINIMUM CHARGE 12 p.m. - 2.30 p.m. - 15p

A Speciality Menu

SCHOOL DINNERS

Monday: Brown stew of beef, boiled potatoes, greens; mincemeat tart and custard or jam tart.

Tuesday: Egg, cheese and bacon pie, mashed potatoes, carrots in white sauce; chocolate blancmange.

Wednesday: Roast mutton, gravy, onion sauce, roast potatoes, carrots, mashed potatoes; apple pudding and custard.

Thursday: Cornish pasties, mashed potatoes, greens; sponge trifle, mock cream.

Friday: Lancashire hot pot, boiled potatoes, beans; steamed lemon pudding, lemon sauce.

CANTEEN

Monday: Roast beef, Irish stew, steak and kidney pie, fried fillet of cod, grilled lamb cutlet, bacon, egg and tomato, creamed and chipped potatoes, green peas, baked beans in tomato sauce; steamed sultana sponge and custard, rice pudding, mince pie.

Tuesday: Roast lamb, savoury mince roll, calves' liver and bacon, steak and kidney pudding, cold ham and salad, egg mayonnaise; creamed, baked, chipped potatoes, spring greens, buttered mashed turnips; steamed sponge, syrup sauce, lattice jam tart and custard, apple tart and custard, rice pudding.

Wednesday: Roast beef, fried fillet of haddock, cottage pie, grilled sausages and onions, grilled pork chop and apple sauce, cold ham and tongue and salad, egg mayonnaise; creamed, chipped potatoes, green peas, haricot beans, sliced carrots; damson tart and custard, Bakewell tart and custard, bread and butter pudding, rice pudding.

Thursday: Roast lamb, stewed steak and dumpling, steak toad in the hole, calves' liver and bacon, grilled sausages and onions, cold tongue and salad; creamed, chipped potatoes, green peas, diced carrots, beans in tomato sauce; apple tart and custard, steamed ginger sponge and custard, rice pudding, lattice jam tart and custard.

Friday: Roast beef and Yorkshire pudding, fried fillet of cod, steak and kidney pie, Cornish pasty, cold ham, tongue and salad, cottage pie; creamed, baked, chipped potatoes, green peas, haricot beans, sliced carrots; baked jam roll and custard, steamed sultana roll and custard, damson tart and custard, rice pudding.

INDUSTRIAL FIRM—STAFF CANTEEN

Monday:

Soups: Celery, oxtail.
Fish: Fried fillets of plaice.
Meats: Roast sirloin of beef and Yorkshire pudding.
  Braised kidney jardinière.
  Grilled bacon and mushrooms.
  Grilled pork chop.
  Roast chicken.
Vegetables: Boiled potatoes, savoy cabbage, mashed potatoes, peas.
Sweets: Steamed jam sponge and custard.
  Apple tart and custard.
  Milk pudding.
Cold table:
  Juices: Tomato, pineapple, grapefruit, orange.
  Hors d'œuvre: Sardine, tomato, plain.
  Pickles: Assorted.
  Dishes: Egg and salad.
    Ox-tongue and salad.
    Roast chicken and salad.
    Boiled ham and salad.
    Cold roast meat and salad.
    Cheese and salad.
Cold sweets and Cheese:
  Blancmange and chopped jelly.
  Prunes.
  Jelly and cream.
  Jelly.
  Fruit salad.
  Jelly whip.
  Assorted cold desserts.
  Cheese and biscuits.
  Blue-vein cheese and biscuits.

Tuesday:

Soups: Tomato, hare.
Fish: Fried fillet of plaice.
Meats: Braised liver and onion.
  Braised liver and bacon.
  Individual chicken pie.
  Grilled lamb chop.
  Roast chicken.
  Mixed grill.
Vegetables: Boiled potatoes, haricot beans, mashed potatoes.
Sweets: Steamed Dundee pudding and custard.
  Gooseberry pudding and custard.
  Milk pudding.
Cold table: As on Monday.

Plate 11. Game Birds. 1. Cock Pheasant. 2. Woodcock. 3. Snipe. 4. Wild Duck 5. Grouse. 6. Hen Pheasant. 7. Red Legged Partridge. 8. Partridge 9. Plover.

Plate 12. Vegetables. 1. Chicory. 2. Endive. 3. Red Pepper. 4. Green Pepper. 5. Jerusalem Artichokes. 6. Globe Artichoke. 7. Aubergine. 8. Baby Marrow. 9. Celeriac.

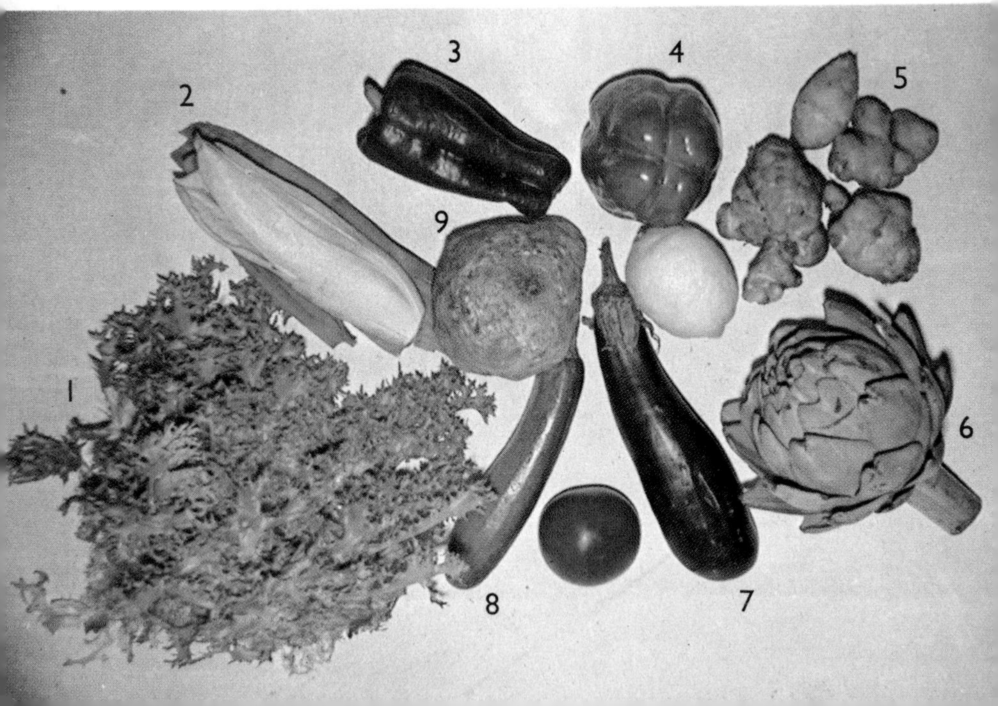

Wednesday:

Soups: Green pea, kidney.
Fish: Fried fillet of plaice.
Meats: Roast leg of pork and apple sauce.
Beef croquettes and tomato.
Grilled bacon and mushrooms.
Baked Virginia ham and Raisin sauce.
Roast chicken.
Roast duck.
Vegetables: Boiled potatoes, savoy cabbage, mashed potatoes, peas.
Sweets: Steamed date sponge and custard.
Bakewell tart and custard.
Milk pudding.
Cold table: As on Monday.
(in addition) Scotch egg and salad.
Vegetable salad.
Cold sweets: As on Monday.
(in addition) Peach velvet cream.

Thursday:

Soups: Oxtail, bean and onion.
Fish: Fried fillet of plaice.
Meats: Individual steak and kidney pudding.
Scotch egg and tomato.
Grilled bacon and mushrooms.
Grilled pork chop and apple sauce.
Roast chicken and seasoning.
Roast duck.
Vegetables: Boiled potatoes, diced carrots, mashed potatoes, peas.
Sweets: Steamed golden sponge and custard.
Raisin tart and custard.
Milk pudding.
Cold table: As on Monday.

Friday:

Soups: Celery, brown Windsor.
Fish: Fried fillet of plaice.
Meats: Cheese and tomato rissoto.
Roast lamb and mint sauce.
Corned beef fritters and tomatoes.
Grilled bacon and sausage.
Grilled ham steak and tomato.
Roast chicken.
Vegetables: Boiled potatoes, mashed potatoes, peas.
Sweets: Steamed Dundee pudding and custard.
Gooseberry pudding and custard.
Milk pudding.
Cold table: As on Monday.

14. Food buying

The purchasing of food is important in any catering establishment. To be able to buy efficiently it is essential to possess a sound knowledge of food and to have a good business sense. Other important points are:

1. Consult up-to-date price lists frequently.
2. When possible see the goods before buying.
3. Give food orders clearly and accurately.
4. When possible order by number and weight, e.g.:

   20 kg plaice could be 80 × ¼ kg plaice
   40 × ½ kg plaice
   20 × 1 kg plaice

It could also be 20 kg. total weight of various sizes and this makes efficient portion control difficult.

5. When goods are delivered see that they are checked for quantity and quality before the delivery note, which signifies acceptance of the order is signed.

PORTION CONTROL

Portion control means controlling the size or quantity of food to be served to each customer. The amount of food allowed depends on:

(*a*) *The type of customer or establishment.* There will obviously be a difference in the size of portions served—for example, to heavy industrial workers and female clerical workers. In a restaurant offering a three-course table d'hôte menu for 50p lunch including salmon, the size of the portion would naturally be smaller than in a luxury restaurant charging £1 for the salmon on an à la carte menu.

(*b*) *The quality of the food.* Better quality food usually yields a greater number of portions than poor quality food, e.g. cheap stewing beef often needs so much trimming that it is difficult to get six portions to the kilo, and the time and labour involved also mean loss of money. On the other hand, good quality stewing beef will often yield eight portions to the kilogramme with much less time and labour required for preparation.

(*c*) *The buying price of the food.* This should correspond to the quality of the food if the person responsible for buying has bought wisely. A good buyer will ensure that the price paid for any item of food is equivalent to the quality—in other words a good price should mean good quality. This should mean a good yield and so help to establish a sound portion control. If on the other hand an inefficient buyer has paid a high price for indifferent quality food then it will be difficult to get a fair number of portions, and the selling price necessary to make the required profit will be too high.

Portion control should be closely linked with the buying of the food; without a good knowledge of the food bought it is difficult to state fairly how many portions should be obtained from it. To evolve a sound system of portion control each establishment or type of establishment needs individual consideration. A golden rule should be 'a fair portion for a fair price'.

PORTION CONTROL EQUIPMENT

There are certain items of equipment which can assist in maintaining control of the size of the portions. For example:

Scoops—for ice cream or mashed potatoes.

Ladles—for soups and sauces.

Butter pat machines—butter pats can be regulated from 7 grammes onwards.

Fruit juice glasses—75–150 grammes

Soup plates—14, 16, 17, 18 cm.

Milk dispensers and tea-measuring machines.

Individual pie dishes, pudding basins, moulds and coupes.

As an example of how portion control can save a great deal of money the following instance is true

1. It was found that ·007 litres of milk was being lost per cup by spilling it from a jug.

32 000 cups = 214 litres of milk lost daily: resulted in a loss of hundreds of pounds per year.

2. When an extra pennyworth of meat is served on each plate it means a loss of £1000 over the year when 1000 meals are served daily.

The following list is of the approximate number of portions that are obtainable from various foods:

Soup: 2–3 portions to the ½ litre.
Hors d'œuvre: 120–180 grammes per portion.
Smoked salmon: 16–20 portions to the kg when bought by the side; 24–36 portions to the kg when bought sliced.
Shellfish cocktail: 16–20 portions to the kg.
Melon: 2–8 portions per melon, depending on the type of melon.
Foie gras: 15–30 grammes per portion.
Caviar: 15–30 grammes per portion.

Fish

Plaice, cod, haddock fillet	8 portions to the kg
Cod and haddock on the bone	6 portions to the kg
Plaice, turbot, brill, halibut, on the bone	4 portions to the kg
Herring and trout	1 per portion (180 g–¼kg fish)
Mackerel and Whiting	¼kg–360g fish
Slip-sole	180g–¼ kg
Sole for main dish	300 g–360 g fish
Sole for filleting	½ kg– ¾ kg best size
Whitebait	8–10 portions to the kg
Salmon (gutted, but including head and bone)	4–6 portions to the kg
Crab or Lobster	¼ kg–360 g per portion

(A ½ kg lobster yields approx. 150 g meat; a 1 kg lobster yields approx. 360 g meat)

Sauces

8–12 *portions to ½ litre*

Hollandaise	Custard
Béarnaise	Apricot
Tomato	Jam
Any Demi-glace sauce	Chocolate

10–14 *portions to ½ litre*	15–20 *portions to ½ litre*
Apple	Tartare
Cranberry	Vinaigrette
Bread	Mayonnaise

Meats

Beef:

Roast on the bone	4–6 portions per kg
Roast boneless	6–8 portions per kg
Boiled or Braised	6–8 portions per kg
Stews, pudding and pies	8–10 portions per kg
Steaks—Rump	120g–¼ kg per one portion
Sirloin	120g–¼ kg per one portion
Tournedos	90–120 g per one portion
Fillet	120–180 g per one portion

Offal:

Ox-liver	8 portions to the kg
Sweetbreads	6–8 portions to the kg
Sheeps kidneys	2 per portion
Oxtail	4 portions per kg
Ox-tongue	4–6 portions per kg

Lamb:	
Leg	6–8 portions to the kg
Shoulder boned and stuffed	6–8 portions to the kg
Loin and best-end	6 portions to the kg
Stewing lamb	4–6 portions to the kg
Cutlet	90–120 g
Chop	120–180 g

Pork:	
Leg	8 portions to the kg
Shoulder	6–8 portions to the kg
Loin on the bone	6–8 portions to the kg
Pork chop	180 g–$\frac{1}{4}$ kg

Ham:	
Hot	8–10 portions to the kg
Cold	10–12 portions to the kg

Sausages are obtainable 12, 16 or 20 to the kg
Chipolatas yield approximately 32, 48 to the kg

Cold Meat	16 portions to the kg
Streaky bacon	32–40 rashers to the kg
Back bacon	24–32 rashers to the kg

Poultry:	
Poussin	1 portion 360 g (1 bird) 2 portions $\frac{3}{4}$ kg (1 bird)
Ducks and chickens	360 g per portion
Geese and boiling fowl	360 g per portion
Turkey	$\frac{1}{4}$ kilo per portion

Vegetables	
New potatoes	8 portions to the kg
Old potatoes	4–6portions to the kg
Cabbage Turnip Parsnips Swedes Brussels sprouts Tomatoes French beans Cauliflower	6–8 portions to the kg
Spinach Peas Runner beans	4–6 portions to the kg

FOOD COSTING

In order to apply Food Costing it is necessary to understand:

1. The *amount* of food required per portion.
2. The *cost* of food.
3. The *price to charge for the food* as a percentage of its cost price.

A rule that can be applied to calculate the food cost price of a dish is: let the dish equal 40% and *fix the selling* price at 100%.

E.g. Cost of dish = 10p = 40%

$$\therefore \text{Selling price} = \frac{10 \times 100}{40} = 25\text{p}$$

Selling the dish at 25p, making 60% Gross Profit above the cost price would be known as 40% Food Cost.

To cost a dish take as example:

Bread and Butter Pudding
(4 portions)

½ litre milk	@ 8p per litre	=	4
3 eggs	@ 2p each	=	6
60 grammes sugar	@ 8p per kg	=	½
30 grammes sultanas	@ 18p per kg	=	½
2 slices buttered bread, Vanilla essence		=	1
			12p

Cost of 4 portions = 12p
Cost of 1 portion = 3p = 40%

$$\text{Selling price at 40\% food cost} = \frac{3 \times 100}{40} = 7{\cdot}5\text{p}$$

The following will help with various food costings:

Food cost	*To find the selling price multiply the cost price of the food by*	*If the cost price of food is £1 the selling price is*	*If cost price is 5p the selling price is*	*Gross profit*
60%	1⅔	£1·66	8p	40%
55%	1¾	£1·75	8½p	45%
50%	2	£2	10p	50%
45%	2²⁄₉	£2·22	11p	55%
40%	2½	£2·5	12p	60%
33⅓%	3	£3	15p	66⅔%

The *Gross Profit* is the difference between the cost price and the selling price.

Overheads are items that must be allowed for and paid out of gross profit. Overheads include heating, lighting, rent, equipment repairs, staff wages. These can account for up to 5/6ths of a gross profit. The remaining 1/6th of the gross profit is the *nett profit*.

Nett Profit is profit remaining after food, costs and overheads have been paid.

E.g. A restaurant takes in a week £250

Cost of Food	£100	
Overheads	125	225
Nett Profit		£ 25

For further reading: Kotas, *An Approach to Food Costing* (Barrie & Rockliff).

15. *Service of Food*

This chapter deals with the service of food from the kitchen, and there are several methods which are employed to enable the customer to receive the meal. The mode of service will depend on the type of establishment, and in some places more than one kind of service will be used, often from one kitchen. The cost of operating these methods varies, but the final objective is the same—that is, the food, when presented to the customer, should look attractive, should be of the right temperature and it should be as ordered.

The kinds of service that are used are:

Waiter or waitress service
Cafeteria service
Hatch and counter service
Snack bar and buffet service

The kind of service to be provided will depend to some extent upon the type of people to be served, the number of people to be served, the dining accommodation, the number of sittings and the amount of time and money to be spent on the meal.

WAITER OR WAITRESS SERVICE

This method of service is the most costly to operate and it is used extensively in all kinds of restaurants. The food ordered by the customer to the waiter or waitress is collected from the hot plate by the waiting staff and served to the customer. (The details of this method are given in the chapter on Kitchen Organisation.)

The points of importance from the kitchen are as follows: the food ordered by the waiter should be ready when it is required. It should leave the kitchen at the correct temperature (hot if it should be hot, cold if it is meant to be cold), so that the food is presented correctly to the customer by the waiter. Orders received from the waiting staff should be dealt with in strict rotation and must go from the hot plate in the same order. Needless to say the waiters should not expect food to be on the hot plate before a reasonable period of time. The correct kitchen accompaniment to dishes should be sent from the hot plate with the appropriate dish, and the vegetables, as ordered, should be ready to go with the main dishes.

Co-operation between the kitchen and restaurant staff is essential for the successful service of food. The teaching of waiting to young people training to work in the kitchen is invaluable, since they are given an opportunity to see beyond the hot plate and to appreciate the waiters' problems. The need to serve portions of equal size becomes more obvious when a customer complains that the person opposite paying the same money has a portion larger than his own. The difficulty of sharing five potatoes between two people or trying to bone an insufficiently cooked sole in front of the customer should cause the kitchen brigade to be careful in the way they serve the food.

Waiting staff will be used for à la carte and table d'hôte menus service (see chapter on menu planning, p. 296), also for banquets and for club service.

In serving food the kitchen staff should remember these points:

1. That it is necessary to dress the dish in such a way that the waiter may effectively transfer the food from the dish to the customers' plate.
2. To serve the food on the correct dish, which should be clean and of the right temperature.
3. The food should be arranged attractively; this is very important.
4. The dish should be clean after the food has been added to it and the correct amount should be placed on the dish.
5. Food which is served on a plate should be arranged neatly.
6. Hot foods (except those which are deep fried and would go limp and soft) should be covered with a lid.

CAFETERIA SERVICE

Cafeteria service is used mainly in popular restaurants, industrial canteens and similar establishments.

The customer proceeds alongside the service counter, choosing food from the selection displayed. The counter contains bains-marie and has sections for hot and cold foods; usually one part is for beverages. The food is served and replenished by counter-hands.

The customer collects his own cutlery, and therefore staff are required only to clear tables. In some places the tables are laid; the customer then has only to choose his food and take it to the table.

When a large number of people have to be fed in a limited time, several counters would be provided, and the customers' meal times in industrial establishments would be staggered so as to reduce queueing.

The advantage of this method of service is speed, and it is therefore necessary for the kitchen to keep the counter supplied with food and not to cause a hold-up in the service by keeping the counter-hands waiting. The arrangement of the food should be such that the cold dishes are collected first and the hot items placed towards the end of the service counter.

HATCH SERVICE

When high-speed service of meals is required this method may be used. Hatches connect the kitchen and dining-room. These hatches will be numbered and the numbers correspond to items numbered on the menu. The customer makes up his mind at the entrance and goes to the appropriate hatch and collects the meal.

Another form of this method of service is to provide the main course at the hatch and for a selection of vegetables to be provided. This of course is a slower method of service because as soon as a choice is provided, service slows down. This type of service is also referred to as counter service.

SNACK BARS

Snack bars usually provide beverages, sandwiches, salads, fruit, pastries and pies which are suitable for people requiring something quickly or something light. Seating accommodation is provided at the service counter as well as in the room.

BUFFETS

Full buffets, where all kinds of foods are used, some requiring carving or skilled service, are usually served from behind the buffet by members of the kitchen staff. The customer will help himself to those foods not requiring the service of the staff. For such functions it is usual for the kitchen to replenish the buffet as required and to keep the buffet tables attractive.

For cocktail parties all the foods are dressed on dishes and the customers help themselves. When hot foods are served they are sent into the room whilst the customers are there so that they are still hot when waiters pass them round or when people help themselves.

AUTOMATIC VENDING

Because of the increased cost of labour there has been a considerable development in the use of vending machines: this is because their use does not require labour to serve, labour is only required to maintain and replenish the machines. Complete meal service can be achieved by using prepared meals held in a refrigerated compartment and used in conjunction with a microwave oven and a vending machine for drinks. This aspect of service can be of considerable importance to catering, particularly to replace or supplement existing catering services.

Some advantages of automation are:

1. Foods are available for 24 hours of the day.
2. Machines can relieve pressure of normal service at peak periods.
3. Staff are not required to serve from machines.
4. Clearing and washing-up are dispensed with as disposable cartons are used.
5. Refreshments are available on the job so reducing tea breaks.

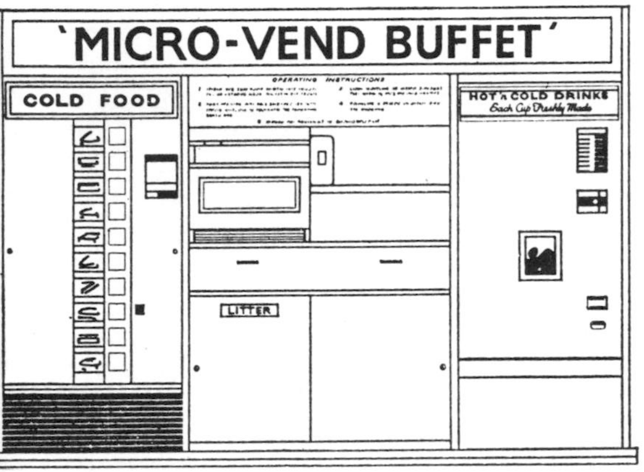

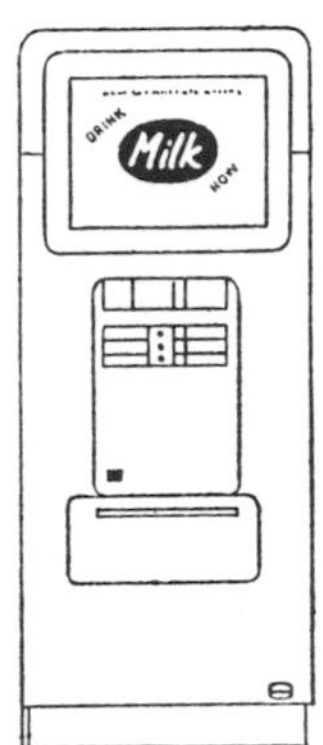

SPECIALITY RESTAURANTS

Mention is made of restaurants serving a limited menu specialising in a particular food or foods. Usually a very good standard is obtained because there is more control and less waste with a limited menu, and the people concerned with cooking and serving a small number of dishes can become very efficient. Certain hotels devote entire dining-rooms to serving a particular item, such as Roast Rib of Scotch Beef or Smorrëbrod. Other examples are Seafood Restaurants, Omelet Bars, Wimpy Bars, Cheese and Grills. See page p. 332 for a menu example.

GANYMEDE DRI-HEAT

This is a method of keeping foods either hot or cold. It is being used in some hospitals as it ensures that the food which reaches the patients is in the same fresh condition as it was when it left the kitchens.

A metal disc or pellet is electrically heated or cooled and placed in a special container under the plate. The container is designed to allow air to circulate round the pellet so that the food is maintained at the correct service temperature.

This is used in conjunction with conveyor belts and special service counters and helps to provide a better and quicker food service.

16. Types of Catering

The provision of food for people of all ages, in all walks of life, at all times of the day or night, and in every situation shows the variety of scope which is to be found in the catering industry.

One thing is common to all—*the need for food to be cooked and served well.* Certain groups of people, however, have special food requirements, for example some old people, due to poor digestion and to the fact that they may have dentures, require foods which are easily digested and need little chewing.

When catering for invalids the following points should be noted:

1. The doctor should be consulted as to the patient's diet, and instructions given should be carefully followed.
2. Only perfectly fresh food should be used.
3. Nourishing foods suitable for the patient should be served.
4. Foods should be those easily digested; in illness the digestive system is sometimes weakened. Do not serve greasy foods.
5. Serve food punctually, in small portions, and pay particular attention to eye appeal.
6. Avoid monotony. If certain foods have to be used, serve them in different ways, in different dishes and if possible with varying flavours.
7. Beef-tea and all meat soups for invalids should be made of fresh meat and not from stock from the stockpot. All fat should be removed from the soup or broth before serving. The addition of milk, eggs or egg yolks to certain soups makes them more nutritious.

Dishes Suitable for Invalids

Consommé
Cream soups
Egg dishes
Steamed, boiled, grilled fish
Kedgeree
Chicken and rabbit dishes
Lamb and mutton dishes
Calf brains and sweetbreads
Vegetable purées
Milk puddings
Fruit purées and fools

Likewise when catering for young people it is particularly important to consider the nutrional needs of those who are still growing. An adequate supply of protein and calcium is essential.

Religious and national requirements are considerations of ever growing importance in a world which, due to increased travel, and better communications, demands an awareness of the social and religious requirements of others.

The various types of catering establishments may be listed as follows:

Hotels	Restaurants
Hospital catering	School meals service
Residential schools, colleges, hostels	Industrial canteens
Luncheon clubs	Aircraft catering
Railway catering	Catering at sea

These may be grouped as: (*a*) Hotels and restaurants; (*b*) welfare and industrial catering; (*c*) transport catering; (*d*) other aspects of catering.

HOTELS AND RESTAURANTS

The great variety of hotels and restaurants is demonstrated when the palatial, first-class, luxury hotel is compared with the small hotel owned and run as a family concern. With restaurants a similar comparison may be made between the exclusive top-class restaurant and the small restaurant which may serve just a few lunches.

Hotels are residential and most of them will provide breakfasts, lunches, teas, dinners and suppers. In some hotels banquets will be an important part of the business.

Restaurants will vary with the kind of meals they serve. Some will serve all types of meals whilst others will be restricted to the service of lunch and dinner or lunch and tea, etc. Again, banqueting may form an important part of the restaurant's service.

In some cases various types of meal service, such as grill rooms, or speciality restaurants which may limit the type of foods served—e.g. smorrëbrod, steaks, eggs, etc.—will be provided.

CLUBS

These are usually administered by a secretary appointed by a management committee formed from club members. Good food and drink with an informal service in the old English style is the requirement in most clubs, particularly of the St. James's area type.

Night clubs usually have the type of service associated with the restaurant trade.

CHAIN-CATERING ORGANISATIONS

There are many concerns having catering establishments spread over wide areas and in some cases over the whole country. Prospects for promotion and the opportunities are often considerable whether it is in a chain of hotels or restaurants. There are the well-known hotel companies and also the restaurant chains of cinema companies, the popular type of restaurant, chain stores and the shops with restaurants. These restaurants often serve lunches, teas and morning coffee and have snack bars and cafeterias.

Several nation-wide, moderately priced chain stores operate cafeterias. These organisations are backed by very progressive managements and one particular example has a very high reputation for cleanliness. In some cases considerable experimental work is carried out to standardise dishes throughout the company's concerns.

Further information can be obtained from: The Hotel and Catering Institute, 191 Trinity Road, London, S.W.17.

WELFARE CATERING

The fundamental difference between Welfare Catering and the catering of hotels and restaurants is that the hotel or restaurant is run to make a profit and provide a service. The object of welfare catering is to provide a service without necessarily making a profit. The standards of cooking should be equally good, though the types of menu will be different.

HOSPITAL CATERING

The object of catering in hospitals is to assist the nursing staff to get the patient better as soon as possible. To do this it is necessary to provide good quality food, to cook it with the minimum loss of nutritional value and to present it to the patient in an appetising manner. When this is done, the catering staff are doing a really worth-while job, which is one of the most important in the industry.

The standard of catering has improved and is improving, as it is now recognised that the provision of an adequate diet is just as much a part of the patient's treatment as careful nursing and skilled medical attention.

Catering Officers

The appointment of Catering Officers, male and female, having suitable qualifications and experience, to be responsible for the feeding of patients, staff and visitors has done much good for hospital catering. The Catering Officer is usually in charge of one hospital or a group of hospitals and will be responsible for organising and controlling the work involved in catering for patients and staff varying from 250–3000. The menus are planned by the Catering Officer who also obtains the food and supervises its preparation, cooking and service. He also engages his staff.

Assistant Catering Officers

Assistant Catering Officers are employed in larger hospitals to assist catering officers. A knowledge of nutrition is desirable and personnel holding recognised dietetic qualifications receive an additional salary allowance.

Kitchen Superintendents and Head Chefs

These positions are divided into two grades:

Grade I, where there is no Catering Officer in charge of a kitchen serving over 350 persons.

Grade II, where there is a Catering Officer in charge of a kitchen serving over 500 persons.

The Grade I person is responsible for controlling the kitchen, planning menus and requisitioning stores, and is paid more than Grade II, who is responsible for the control of one or more kitchens.

Cooks

The standard week of 44 hours applies to cooks and head chefs; overtime is paid with additional pay for Sundays and night work. They are granted two weeks' holiday with pay, and two months' full pay and two months' half-pay are allowed for sick leave. Regular hours are worked, though many hospital kitchens are open 24 hours a day for seven days a week. Cooks are graded, and additional pay is given to holders of suitable certificates.

Butchers, bakers and pastry chefs are employed in the larger hospitals. Training is provided for those who wish to improve their position and the conditions in most hospital kitchens are good and the tempo of work is not so fast as in a hotel kitchen.

Dietician

In most hospitals a qualified dietician is responsible for all the diets, and there is usually a separate kitchen or a part of the main kitchen set aside for the preparation of diets. In large hospitals the dieticians department is a separate unit and does not come under the control of the catering officer, except for the ordering of stores from the main store. Diet cooks are usually employed in the diet kitchen.

The Main Hospital Kitchen

All food except diets and food cooked in the ward kitchens is cooked here. In this kitchen all meals for patients, doctors, nurses, clerical and maintenance staffs are prepared. In hospitals where a canteen is provided for out-patients and visitors this will come under the control of the catering officer.

Hospital Routine

Hospital catering has its own problems, which often make it very difficult to provide meals correctly served. Wards are sometimes spread over a wide area, or, in a large hospital, where there are long distances for the food to travel, provision of effective, silent trolleys is essential to keep the food hot. Each ward has its own service kitchen from where meals are served; drinks are prepared and such foods as eggs are cooked.

The routine of a hospital is strictly timed and meals have to fit in with the duties of the nursing staff. Usually the night staff wake the patients at 6 a.m. and go round with cups of tea. The day staff take over at 8.30 and breakfast is cleared away and the wards tidied by 9. Lunch is usually at 12.30 p.m., tea at 4 p.m. and supper at 6.30 p.m. Hot and cold drinks are served before lights out, which is usually 9.30 p.m.

Diets

Information about the type of meal or diet(s) to be given to each patient is supplied by the ward sister to the kitchen by 10 a.m. The information will give the number of full, light, fluid and special diets, and with each special diet will be given the name of the patient and the type of diet required.

For breakfast, the porridge and main dishes are sent from the main kitchen, the cereals, bread and butter, preserves and tea are prepared in the ward kitchen. Except for bread and butter or rolls the complete lunch comes from the main kitchen. The tea meals are prepared in the ward kitchen and this is supplemented by cakes or buns prepared in the main kitchen. Supper is also prepared in the main kitchen.

The maximum amount of money the Catering Officer has to spend is stated as so much per head, this varies from £1·75 per week to £2 per week. To provide good, wholesome varied meals on this amount can only be achieved by careful buying and the elimination of waste.

Further information about hospital catering can be obtained from the Hospital Caterers Association, 54 Lyford Road, London, S.W.18, and about dietetics from the British Dietetic Association, 251 Brompton Road, London, S.W.3.

SCHOOL MEALS SERVICE

Local Education Authorities organise the school meals service to provide the lunch meal for children being educated in schools run by the Authority. The details vary from county to county, but one thing is common to all: they are providing a meal of a satisfactory standard from the nutritional point of view. The way this is expressed varies, one council insists on a minimum of 20 grams of protein per meal whilst another had a varying standard according to the age of the child.

Children over 11 years	minimum 800 calories
Children 7–11 years	minimum 650 calories
Children up to 7 years	minimum 500 calories

The weight of the meal may also be taken into account:

Children over 11 years	600 g
Children 7–11 years	450 g
Children up to 7 years	360 g

One council insists that a sample plate of every meal prepared is placed in the refrigerator. Should a case of food poisoning occur, then in all probability the laboratory can trace the cause from the sample plate. Periodically, the sample is collected by the laboratory and the food value of the meal is assessed.

In some cases the menu is made for four weeks, during which the following main dishes are used:

Butchers' meats	15 meals
Tinned meat	2 meals
Bacon	1 meal
Cheese	1 meal
Fish	1 meal

and vegetables:

Green vegetables	10 times
Salad	4 times
Root vegetables	6 times

With children it is most important that they enjoy their food; it must be varied and appetising and if possible a choice of vegetable should be provided. They should be allowed more, or less, food as their appetite demands.

The food is usually obtained by contract through the county supplies department and the cost paid by the children only covers the cost of the food. The overheads and other expenses are paid by the council.

Nearly all the people employed in this service are women, and further particulars can be obtained from the School Meals Organiser of the Local Education Authority.

RESIDENTIAL ESTABLISHMENTS

Under this heading are included schools, colleges, halls of residence, hostels, etc., where all the meals are provided. It is essential that in these establishments the nutritional balance of food is considered, as in all probability the people eating here will have no other food. It is important that food cooked for the residents should satisfy all the nutritional needs. Since many of these establishments cater for students and the age group which leads a very energetic life, these people usually have large appetites, and are growing fast. All the more reason that the food should be well cooked, plentiful, varied and attractive.

Further particulars of employment in this type of establishment can be obtained from the Institutional Management Association, 324 Gray's Inn Road, London, W.C.1.

CATERING FOR INDUSTRY

The provision of canteens for industrial workers has given opportunities to many catering workers to be employed in first-class conditions. Apart from the main lunch meal, tea trolley rounds are part of the service. In some cases a 24-hour canteen service is necessary and it is usual to cater for the social activities of the workers. Not only are lunches provided for the manual workers but the clerical staff and managerial staff will in many cases have their meals from the same kitchen. There is ample scope for both men and women, and in this branch of the industry there are more top jobs for women than in any other.

Many industries have realised that output is related to the welfare of the employees. Well-fed workers produce more and better work and because of this a great deal of money is spent in providing first-class kitchens and dining-rooms and in subsidising the meals. This means that the workers receive their food at a price lower than its actual cost, the rest of the cost being borne by the company.

Further information on Industrial Catering can be obtained from the Industrial Catering Association, 53/54 King William Street, London, E.C.4.

LUNCHEON CLUBS

Clerical staffs in large offices are provided with lunching facilities, usually called a luncheon club or staff restaurant. These are usually subsidised and in some instances the meal is supplied without charge. The catering is frequently of a very high standard and the kitchen or kitchens will provide meals for the directors, which will be of the best English fare or French cuisine.

Business lunches are served in small rooms so that there is privacy; the standard of food served will often be of the finest quality since the company will probably attach considerable importance to these functions. The senior clerical staff may have their own dining-room, whilst the rest of the staff will in some cases have a choice of an à la carte menu, a table d'hôte menu, waitress service or help-yourself and snack-bar facilities.

The kitchens in most places are modern and the conditions of work are excellent and there is opportunity for both men and women.

Luncheon clubs are provided by most large offices belonging to business firms, such as insurance head offices, petroleum companies, banks, etc. When luncheon facilities are not provided many firms provide their employees with luncheon vouchers.

Large stores also provide lunching arrangements for their staffs as well as the customers' restaurants.

TRANSPORT CATERING

Aircraft

Aircraft catering is concerned with the provision of meals during flights and this form of catering presents certain problems. Owing to very limited space on the plane special ovens are provided to heat the food, which is frozen. The food is prepared by the aircraft company or by an outside contract and the standard of the meals is very high.

Railway Catering

The function of catering on trains in this country is carried out by British Railways. Breakfast, lunch, tea and dinner are served in restaurant cars, and snacks are served from buffet cars. The space in a restaurant car kitchen is very limited and there is considerable movement of the train, which does not help the staff. However, many interesting menus are served on trains, and railway catering provides a most useful service.

Catering at Sea

The large liners' catering is of a similar standard to the large first-class hotels. Many shipping companies are noted for the excellence of their cuisine. The kitchens on board ship are usually oil-fired and extra precautions have to be taken in the kitchen in rough weather. Catering at sea includes the smaller ship, which has both cargo and passengers, and the cargo vessels and this includes the giant tankers of up to 100 000 tonnes.

OTHER ASPECTS OF CATERING

The Services

Catering in the Army, Navy and Air Force is another form of catering, particulars of which can be obtained from recruitment centres.

Contract Catering

There are many catering concerns who are prepared to undertake the catering for businesses, schools, hospitals, etc., leaving these establishments free to concentrate on the business of educating or nursing or whatever may be their main concern. By employing contract caterers they are using the services of people who have specialised in catering, thus relieving themselves of the worry of entering a field outside their province. Contract catering is employed by nearly every branch of catering, including the armed forces. The arrangements made will vary. The contractor may meet certain operating costs or receive a payment from the company employing the contractor. Often the cost of food, wages and light equipment is the responsibility of the contractor, whilst the cost of fuel, heavy equipment and maintenance is borne by the company.

Outside Catering

When functions are held where there is no catering set-up or where the function is not within the scope of the normal catering routine then certain firms will take over completely. Considerable variety is offered to people employed on these undertakings and often the standard will be of the very highest order. A certain amount of adaptability and ingenuity is required, especially for some outdoor jobs, but there is no chance of repetitive work. The types of function will include garden parties, agricultural and horticultural shows, the opening of new buildings, banquets, parties in private houses, etc.

REHEATED FOODS *RECHAUFFÉ*

In the interests of economy a sound knowledge of handling leftover food is necessary. Many tasty dishes can be prepared, but care must always be taken to see that the food is thoroughly and carefully reheated. If care is not taken then food poisoning can result (see page 19). Only sound food should be used ('if in doubt, throw it out').

After each meal service all unserved food should be cleared away in clean dishes, cooled quickly in the larder and placed in a cold room or refrigerator.

A good hors d'œuvrier can make interesting dishes out of left-over meats, poultry, fish and certain vegetables by mixing them with foods such as rice, gherkins, tomatoes, chives, parsley and a well-seasoned dressing such as mayonnaise or vinaigrette.

Trimmings and bones of meat, game and poultry should be used for stock. Trimmings of meat fat cooked or uncooked should be minced and rendered down for dripping.

FISH

Cooked kippers and haddock may be turned into savouries if freed from skin and bone, and finely minced or pounded with anchovy essence and a little butter and used as a spread on toast.

Cold fish may be used in many interesting dishes. For example:[1]

Coquille de poisson mornay
Curried fish
Fish cakes
Fish cutlets or croquettes
Fish pie
Fish kedgeree
Fish salad

VEGETABLES

Cold cooked vegetables such as peas, beans, cauliflower, haricot beans, potatoes, may be left and mixed with vinaigrette or mayonnaise and used for salads. Cold boiled potatoes can be used for potato salad or for sauté potatoes. Cold mashed potatoes may be used for fish cakes or potato cakes.

MEAT

Left-over cooked items such as bacon, ham, tongue, kidneys or liver may be mixed with mince of any meat and used to give extra flavour to croquettes[1], rissoles[1].

Cold meats can be used for a number of dishes. For example:[1]

Minced for Cottage Pie
Minced lamb or mutton
Cornish pasties
Miroton of beef
Durham cutlet
Kromeski
Salad

Left-over poultry, such as chicken, if cut into joints can be reheated carefully in a curry sauce.

[1] The recipes may be found in the authors' *Practical Cookery* (Arnold).

If the skin and bone are removed the poultry can be used for

Salad[1]
Mayonnaise[1]
Cutlets or croquettes[1]
Vol-au-vent or bouchees[1]

RICE, SPAGHETTI, MACARONI can be turned into mixtures for hors d'œuvre with items such as chopped onion, chives, tomatoes, beetroot, cooked meat, haricot or French beans and a dressing of vinaigrette or mayonnaise.

BREAD

Trimmings of crusts, etc., should be kept until dry, lightly browned in the oven, then passed through a mincer to make browned bread crumbs (chapelure) which may be used for crumbing cutlets, croquettes of fish, etc.

Stale bread can also be used for bread pudding as follows:

Bread Pudding

1 kg stale bread
120 g sugar
120 g currants or sultanas
¼ teaspoonful mixed spice
60 g lard or margarine

1. Soak the bread in cold water until soft.
2. Squeeze bread dry and place in a bowl.
3. Mix in 60 g sugar and rest of ingredients.
4. Place in a greased baking tray.
5. Sprinkle with 60 g sugar.
6. Bake in a hot oven for approximately 30 minutes.

Stale sponge cake can be utilised for:
Trifles[1]
Cabinet pudding[1]
Queen of puddings[1]

CHEESE

Left-overs of cheddar cheese can be grated or chopped and used for Welsh Rarebit.[1]

SANDWICHES

Sandwiches are one of the most varied types of food produced. They may be made from every kind of bread, fresh or toasted, in a variety of shapes and with an almost endless assortment of fillings.

[1] The recipes may be found in the authors' *Practical Cookery* (Arnold).

Types of bread	*Types of filling*	
White	Ham	Tomato
Brown	Tongue	Cucumber
Caraway seed	Beef	Cress
Rye	Chicken	Lettuce
	Smoked fish	Watercress
	Tinned fish	Egg
	Fish and meat paste	

Examples of Combination Fillings

Fish and lettuce
Cheese and tomato
Cucumber and egg
Apple and chutney

Seasonings to Flavour Sandwiches

Mayonnaise (egg, salmon, etc.)
Vinaigrette (crab, lobster, fish, egg)
English mustard (ham, beef)
French mustard (cheese, tongue)
Chutney (cheese, tinned meat)

Where sandwiches are required in large quantities the usual method is to use large sandwich loaves, remove the crusts from three sides and one end. The bread is then cut in thin slices across the loaf, using a sharp carving knife (the modern type of serrated knife will be found ideal). (The bread may be buttered before being cut.)

The slices of bread are stacked neatly, one on top of the other, resting on a crust of bread. When the bread is cut it is then buttered (unless this has been done) and the prepared fillings are added quickly and efficiently and the complete loaf is made into long sandwiches. If they are to be kept for any length of time the crusts are replaced and wrapped in clean cloth or greaseproof paper. When required for service the sandwiches are easily and quickly cut into any required size or shape, neatly dressed on a doily on a silver flat dish and sprinkled with washed and drained mustard and cress. A typical set of fillings for a loaf could be, ham, tongue, smoked salmon, tomato, cucumber, egg.

Toasted Sandwiches

These are made by inserting a variety of savoury fillings between two slices of hot, freshly buttered toast, e.g. scrambled egg, bacon, fried egg, scrambled egg with chopped ham.

Club Sandwich

This is made by placing between two slices of hot buttered toast a filling of lettuce, grilled bacon, slices of hard-boiled egg, mayonnaise and slices of chicken.

Bookmaker Sandwich

This is an underdone minute steak between two slices of hot buttered toast.

Double-decker and Treble-decker Sandwiches

Toasted and untoasted bread can be made into double-decker sandwiches, using three slices of bread with two separate fillings. Treble- and quadro-decker sandwiches may also be prepared. They may be served hot or cold.

The Open Sandwich or Scandinavian Smorrëbrod

This is prepared from a buttered slice of any bread garnished with any type of meat, fish, eggs, vegetables, salads, etc.

The varieties of open sandwich can include some of the following:

1. Smoked salmon, lettuce, potted shrimps, slice of lemon.
2. Scrambled egg, asparagus tips, chopped pimento.
3. Grilled bacon, cold fried egg, tomato sauce, mushrooms.
4. Cold sliced beef, sliced tomato, fans of gherkins.
5. Shredded lettuce, sliced hard-boiled egg, mayonnaise, cucumber.
6. Cold boiled rice, cold curried chicken, chutney.
7. Minced raw beef, anchovy fillet, raw egg yolk, chopped horse radish, onion and parsley.
8. Pickled herring, chopped gherkin, capers sieved, hard-boiled egg.

When serving open sandwiches it is usual to offer a good choice. Care should be taken with finishing touches, using parsley, sliced radishes, gherkins, pickles, capers, etc., to give a neat clean look to the dish. Presentation is important.

BEVERAGES

Tea

There are five rules for making good tea:

1. Use a good quality tea, carefully measure each brew 45–60 grammes to 5 litres.
2. Always use freshly drawn, freshly boiled water.

3. Pre-heat the pot or container. This is done to make sure that when the boiling water is added to the tea in the pot it keeps at a high temperature for as long as possible, thus making an efficient infusion.

4. Take the pot to the water, never the water to the pot, and use as short a pour as possible, so that when the water enters the tea-pot it is actually boiling.

5. Allow the tea to stand for 3–5 minutes to infuse and so draw out the full flavour, after which it should be used at once, otherwise tannin is extracted, giving strong over-infused tea with a bitter taste.

Quantities required for tea service:

$\frac{1}{2}$ litre milk	=15–20 cups of tea
$\frac{1}{2}$ kilo sugar (cube)	=approximately 100 cubes
$\frac{1}{2}$ kilo sugar (granulated)	=approximately 50–60 teaspoons
1 tea cup	= $\frac{1}{6}$ litre
1 breakfast cup	= $\frac{1}{4}$ litre

Coffee

The following are the rules for making good coffee:

1. Use good coffee which is freshly ground.
2. Use freshly drawn, freshly boiled water.
3. Measure the quantity of coffee carefully (300–360 grammes).
4. After the coffee has been made it should be strained off, otherwise it will acquire a bir taste.
5. Milk, if served with coffee, should be hot but not boiled.
6. All coffee-making equipment must be kept scrupulously clean, washed thoroughly after each use and rinsed with clean hot water (never use soda).
7. The various methods for making coffee are as follows:

Instant Coffee: Boiling water is added to soluble coffee solids.

Jug or Saucepan Method: Boiling water is poured on to the coffee grounds in a jug or a saucepan, allowed to stand for a few minutes then strained.

Percolator: When the water boils it rises up through a tube and percolates through the coffee grounds.

Cona Coffee: The water is boiled in a glass globe then it passes up a tube to a glass cup which contains the ground coffee. Here it infuses and as it cools it drops as liquid coffee into the bottom of the glass globe.

Still Set: This consists of a container into which the ground coffee is placed. Boiling water is passed through the grounds and the coffee is piped into an urn at the side.

Espresso: This method involves passing steam through coffee grounds and infusing under pressure.

Filter Method: Boiling water is poured into a container into which the ground coffee has been placed. The infusion takes place and the coffee drops into the cup below.

Cocoa

To make cocoa:

1. Measure the amount of cocoa and liquid carefully 30g cocoa; 60g sugar; 1 litre milk or milk and water).
2. Mix the cocoa with a little of the cold liquid.
3. Bring the remaining liquid to the boil, add the cocoa, stirring all the time.
4. Return to the pan and bring to the boil, stirring until it boils, then add the sugar.

Lemonade or Orangeade 16–24 servings

5 litres water
360 grammes–½ kg sugar
12–16 lemons or oranges

1. Wipe the fruit and remove the zest thinly with a peeler.
2. Squeeze the juice from the fruit and strain so as to remove pips.
3. Place the rind, juice and sugar in jug or basin and add boiling water.
4. Cover, allow to cool and then strain.

THE COOKING OF SUGAR

Sugar is boiled for a number of purposes—in pastry work, bakery and sweet-making. Loaf (lump) sugar is generally used, placed in a copper saucepan or sugar boiler and moistened with sufficient cold water to melt the sugar (approx. ⅛ litre per ¼ kg) and allowed to boil steadily without being stirred. Any scum on the surface should be carefully removed, otherwise the sugar is liable to granulate. Once the water has evaporated the sugar begins to cook and it will be noticed that the bubbling in the pan will be slower. It is now necessary to keep the sides of the pan free from crystallised sugar; this can be done either with the fingers or a piece of damp linen. In either case the fingers or linen should be dipped in ice water or cold water, rubbed round the inside of the pan and then quickly dipped b ck into the water.

The cooking of the sugar then passes through several stages which may be tested with a special sugar thermometer or by the fingers (dip the fingers into ice water, then into the sugar and quickly back into the ice water).

DEGREES OF COOKING SUGAR

Small thread (104°C). When a drop of sugar held between the thumb and forefinger forms small threads when the finger and thumb are drawn apart. Used for stock syrup.

Large thread (110°C). When proceeding as for small thread the threads are more numerous and stronger. Used for crystallising fruits.

Soft ball (116°C). Proceeding as above, the sugar rolls into a soft ball. Used for making fondant.

Hard ball (121°C). As for soft ball, but the sugar rolls into a firmer ball. Used for making sweets.

Small crack (140°C). The sugar lying on the finger peels off in the form of a thin pliable film which sticks to the teeth when chewed. Used for meringue.

Large crack (153°C). The sugar taken from the end of the fingers when chewed breaks clean in between the teeth, like glass. Used for dipping fruits.

Caramel (176°C). Cooking is continued until the sugar is a golden brown colour. Used for crème caramel.

Black-jack. Cooking is continued until the sugar is deeply coloured and almost black. Water is then added and the black sugar is allowed to dissolve over a gentle heat. Used for colouring.

To prevent the granulating of sugar a tablespoon of glucose or a few drops of lemon juice per lb. may be added before boiling.

17. Examinations

In the sphere of examining there is considerable change occurring in the techniques and methods used to assess students.

Examining bodies such as the City and Guilds of London Institute are constantly adapting their examining methods to keep abreast of modern developments. But as teachers are always made aware of any changes in advance of the examinations students should not find this a problem.

Apart from examinations set by external bodies, teachers no doubt will continue to set internal examinations and the following observations may be helpful.

Why do we have examinations?

Their purpose is to find out the extent of knowledge or practical ability of a student. The object of learning is to enable a person to become a more useful member of society, and in catering this usually means a better craftsman. To achieve this, it is necessary for the practical worker to understand the theory and those subjects related to the practical work.

Practical Examinations

The student puts into practice the knowledge gained from experience in practical and theory classes and from reading.

Theory Examinations

This is putting on paper knowledge gained from theory and practical classes.

Theory cannot be separated from practice, as both are necessary to obtain good results.

Learning

Learning requires effort and hard work; best results can be achieved by:

1. Studying in a quiet place (the local library's reading-room is ideal).
2. Studying when not tired.
3. Rewriting carefully, lesson notes.
4. Answering previous examination questions.
5. Studying all the time, not cramming just before the examination.

Hints on Examinations

A problem which has to be faced by many people is nerves; these may only be controlled to a certain degree according to each individual.

Confidence in one's own ability helps, and this confidence comes from knowledge, and provided the candidate has done his utmost to learn, there need be no excessive nervousness.

The practical examination can be quite an ordeal, mainly because an examiner may be present. Try to forget (within reason) the examiner and concentrate on the work in hand.

To be confronted with a menu containing a dish which the candidate has not done can be disconcerting. Should this happen the examiner can be told, or, if the recipe is in the recipe book, common sense and the recipe book should be used to solve the problem.

Most candidates' nerves disappear as soon as they start writing in the theory examinations. Some people, however, find their minds go blank; in this case it may help to concentrate on one small part of the question, particularly questions on practical cookery. The student who may not have learnt a particular recipe by heart can often, by thinking hard of the practical preparation, arrive at a sufficiently sound answer to satisfy the examiner.

PRACTICAL EXAMINATIONS

Object

The object of the practical examination is to find out if the candidate can cook to a required standard, in a clean manner within a specified time.

The examiner will expect the candidate to work as if it was a normal working day and will be looking at the following:

1. The candidate.
2. The way the candidate works.
3. The manner in which the food is presented.

To assist the candidate to do well in practical examinations the following points may be considered:

Personal Appearance

1. The candidate should appear professional, capable and confident (not over-confident or flustered).
2. Whites should be clean and worn correctly.
3. Knives should be clean and sharp.
4. Clean cloth or cloths and a clean swab are essential.

Order of Work

The purpose of an order of work is to enable the candidate to sit down and think out the order in which the menu is to be prepared. The main thing to consider is that those items needing the longest time must be done first; for example, puff paste, meat pudding. The order of work for many menus will be a matter of opinion. The examiner has a copy of the order of work, and should the candidate wish to alter it the examiner must be informed.

Example of an Order of Work for the following Menu:

Grapefruit Cocktail

Steak and Kidney Pudding

Parsley Potatoes Mixed Vegetables

Pancakes with Lemon

It is necessary to prepare the steak and kidney pudding first, therefore the making of the suet paste and preparation of the steak head the order of work, because of the time required to cook this dish. From an examination of the rest of the menu it is discovered that the pancake batter will need to stand, therefore it should not be left to the last. The grapefruit should be served cool, and once prepared can be put out of mind when in the cold room or refrigerator.

All the vegetables are best prepared at the same time and the table cleared of peelings. This leaves the small jobs such as chopping the parsley and cutting the lemons.

The order of work, then, may look like this:

1. Check ingredients and clear table.
2. Make suet paste and line basin.
3. Prepare the steak and kidney.
4. Finish the pudding and place in pan of boiling water (or steamer) to cook.
5. Make the pancake batter and allow to rest.
6. Peel the vegetables and potatoes.
7. Cut the vegetables and potatoes.
8. Cut the grapefruit, dress and place in refrigerator.
9. Cook the vegetables.
10. Chop the parsley and cut the lemons.
11. Cook the potatoes.
12. Serve the grapefruit.
13. Finish the potatoes and vegetables.

14. Serve the pudding.
15. Serve the vegetables and potatoes.
16. Cook and serve the pancakes.

The order of work should be brief and only the important points included. For most menus 16–20 well-thought-out points should be sufficient, because time spent doing this means there is less time available in the kitchen. The time of serving courses should be known before the commencement of the order of work.

Method of Work

The way in which the candidate sets about the work is very important, and the following points can be borne in mind:

1. Perishable foods should be placed in the cold room.
2. Tables should be cleared ready to start work.
3. Only gases required at once should be lit.
4. Apart from the food which is being prepared the only other things on the table should be a triangle, board and knives.
5. Care should be taken to weigh foods accurately.
6. Trays or containers for rubbish, swill and trimmings should be kept.
7. Washing-up should be kept down.
8. Correct knives should be used for the job and wiped after use.
9. The candidate should work cleanly, quickly and correctly.
10. Should something go wrong, for example the blind flan burn, and if there are sufficient ingredients available, the candidate should start again and if possible produce the dish.
11. Should something be spoiled at the last moment it does not mean that all is lost, because the examiner will have seen the work prior to the accident.

Service of Food for Examinations

1. Food should be served on time.
2. Hot dishes should be hot, cold dishes cold.
3. All dishes should be clean.
4. Food must be correctly seasoned and
5. Served in the right dishes.
6. The exact number of portions should be in the dish.
7. Appropriate accompaniments must be served.

Hygiene

The candidate must work cleanly all the time. Stove, table and floor area should be kept clean, and at the end of the examination all pans used placed on the table for checking.

General Points

1. Candidates should be courteous to the examiner.
2. Only necessary questions should be asked.
3. When runners are available they should only be used to obtain anything the candidate may require.
4. All items of equipment in the kitchen are available for use, not just those laid out on the table.
5. If the candidate thinks the menu is difficult it should be remembered that the examiner is an experienced person and will give all the more credit for a difficult job well done.
6. In an examination where a student may have complete or limited choice in selecting dishes these points should be considered.

(*a*) The dishes chosen should be at the appropriate level of the course. (*b*) Do not attempt work of too difficult a nature. (*c*) Do not select work of an easy nature below the level of the course.

Where time is allowed prior to the practical examination to complete certain items such as selection of menu, costing, etc., then it is usual, as with practical examinations, to use any books, notes or lists that may be of assistance.

THEORY EXAMINATIONS

The object of a theory examination is to find out if the candidate knows the answers. Provided the facts have been learnt the candidate must now convey the information to the examiner and these points should be considered.

With the increased use of objective (short answer) type questions it is essential to carefully read the instructions and to pay particular attention to the instructions on how to change an answer if you change your mind after having made the necessary mark on the paper.

Whilst it may seem difficult to select the right answer say from a choice of four, provided the subject has been learnt well, the student should be quite capable of selecting the correct answer. However it is important to emphasise the need for the student to *carefully* read the question before he decides on his answer.

1. *Writing*.

This must be readable. The easier it is to read, the more favourable impression is given of the paper.

2. *Spelling*.

The facts are what the examiner wants, but if there are many words spelt wrongly an unfavourable impression is given. French words should be correct. It is better to use correctly spelt English words than misspelt French words.

Extra care must be taken not to misspell words which are similar in French and English, e.g. filet and fillet, carotte and carrot.

Simple words are often spelt wrongly, such as gravy, plaice, gherkin, lettuce, etc.

3. *Answering Questions.*

1. The meaning of the answer must be clear to the examiner.
2. The question should be understood and answered to the point.
3. The answer should be precise, with no padding.
4. No essential facts should be omitted from the answer.
5. All parts of a question should be answered.
6. Avoid using first person singular, e.g.: 'Braising is a nice method of cooking, but I like fried steak'.
7. Avoid slang expressions and terms which are not good English.
8. Avoid vagueness and inaccurate phrases, e.g.: 'Spot of water'.
9. Use correct terms and words. E.g.: Sugar is not *diluted*, but dissolved. Gelignite does not go into bavarois.
10. Use accepted abbreviations for weights and measures, but avoid marge, veg., fridge.
11. Answer only the number of questions asked for. No extra marks will be gained if more are answered, but be certain to answer the required number of questions.
12. Answer questions in any order, but number them clearly.
13. Re-read the answers carefully when the paper is completed.

4. *Layout*

A paper laid out clearly creates a favourable impression. The following points perhaps may be helpful:

1. Leave a good margin.
2. Tabulate answers where suitable.
3. If an essay form answer is necessary give an introduction and have a good concluding paragraph.
4. Name the recipe, underline the heading.
5. Where diagrams can be used these should be drawn carefully.

Summary

It is necessary to know the facts to present them clearly. The writing must be legible, the English and spelling correct, the layout neat and the information to the point.

BIBLIOGRAPHY

General Reference

Repertoire de la Cuisine. L. Saulnier. (Bailey)
Guide to Modern Cookery. A. Escoffier. (Heinemann)
Professional Knowledge. W. Bachman. (MacLaren)
Progressive Catering. J. Morel. (Barrie and Rockliff)
Classical Recipes of the World. H. Smith. (Barrie and Rockliff)
Larousse Gastronomique. (Hamlyn)
I.C.I. Catering Manual. (I.C.I.)
Complete Pâtissier. J. Kollist. (Maclaren)
Practical Larder Work. O. Cêtre. (Pitman)
Dictionary of Food. H. Senn. (Ward Lock)
Elementary Science of Food. Hildreth. (Allman)
Practical Cookery. Ceserani and Kinton. (Arnold)
Hering's Dictionary of Classical and Modern Cookery. (Mills and Boon)
The Kitchen in Catering. Walley. (Constable)
The Larder Chef. Lets and Bode

General Reading

Kitchen Prelude. Pierre Hamp.
Cesar Ritz. Marie-Louise Ritz.
Pinch of Pound Notes. J. Dingle. (Hart-Davis)
Imperial Palace. A. Bennett
Café Royale. P. Deghy. (Hutchinson)
Hotel Splendide. L. Bemmelman. (Hamish Hamilton)
Cooking with the French Touch. A. Maurois. (Hamish Hamilton)
Escoffier. E. Herbodeau
Meet Me at the Savoy. J. Nicol. (Museum)
The Royal Chef. G. Tshumi. (Kimber)
Chez Pavan. R. Llewellyn. (Michael Joseph)
The Story of Prunier. Mme. Prunier.

Special Topics

HYGIENE

Clean Catering. (H.M.S.O.)
Hygienic Food Handling. Betty Hobbs. (St. John Ambulance Association)
Food Poisoning and Food Hygiene. Betty Hobbs. (Arnold)
Food Hygiene Codes of Practice. (H.M.S.O.)

SCIENCE

Understanding Cooking. Ceserani Lundberg and Kotschevar (Arnold)

SERVICES AND EQUIPMENT

General

Practical Maintenance and Equipment for Hoteliers. D. Gladwell. (Barrie & Rockliff)
The Kitchen. J. Walley. (Constable)

Gas

Gas Council's Catering Handbook
Gas in the Home. (Education Productions Ltd.)

Water

Water in the Home. (Education Productions Ltd.)

Electricity

Electricity in the Home. (Education Productions Ltd.)

NUTRITION

Manual of Nutrition. (H.M.S.O.)
Human Nutrition. Mortram. (Arnold)
Food and Its Functions. Cameron. (Arnold)

COSTING

Catering Calculations. A. Grattidge. (Pitman)
An Approach to Food Costing. R. Kotas. (Barrie & Rockliff)

KITCHEN ORGANISATION

Chef's Manual of Kitchen Management. J. Fuller. (B. T. Batsford)

KITCHEN FRENCH

French. W. Philpin. (Pitman)
Dictionary of Cuisine French. S. Coombes. (Barrie & Rockliff)

PRESERVATION OF FOOD

Accelerated Freeze Drying. (H.M.S.O.)

BOOKS ON COMMODITIES

Law's Grocers Manual. W. Copsey. (Clowes)
Commodities. Beeches College, Bourneville
Distinguishing Features of Fish. (Fishmongers Hall)
The Caterer's Potato Manual. Potato Marketing Board. (Pitman)
Student's Egg Book. Egg Marketing Board
Cheeses of the World. S. Simon. (Faber)

FURTHER INFORMATION

Safety

Royal Society for the Prevention of Accidents, 52 Grosvenor Gardens, London, S.W.1

First Aid

St. John Ambulance Association, 10 Grosvenor Crescent, London, S.W.1

Gas

Gas Council, 1 Grosvenor Place, London, S.W.1

Water

Local Water Board

Electricity

British Electricial Development Association, 2 Savoy Hill, London, W.C.2

Electricity Council, Winsley Street, London, W.1

C.S. Services Ltd., 5 Carlos Place, London, W.1

Nutrition

British Dietetic Association, 251 Brompton Road, London, S.W.3

Nutrition Information Centre, Beecham House, Great West Road, Brentford, Middlesex.

Food Information Centre, 36 Park Street, Croydon, Surrey.

Meat

National Federation of Meat Traders, 29 Lingfield Lane, Redhill, Surrey

Argentine National Meat Board, 1/11 Hay Hill, London, W.1

New Zealand Lamb Information Bureau, Williams House, Eastbourne Terrace, London, W.2

Bacon

Bacon Information Council, Williams House, Eastbourne Terrace, London, W.2

Poultry

British Turkey Federation, The Bury, Church Street, Chesham, Bucks.

British Chicken Association, High Holborn House, High Holborn, London, W.C.1

Chicken Information Council, 12 Hay Hill, London, W.1

Fish

White Fish Authority, Lincolns Inn Chambers, 2/3 Cursitor Street, London, E.C.4

Unilever Education Section, Unilever House, London, E.C.4

Vegetables

Potato Marketing Board, 50 Hans Crescent, London, S.W.1

Fruit

Fruit Trade Association, 9 Russell Chambers, Covent Garden, London, W.C.2

Eggs

British Egg Marketing Board, Wingate House, Riverside House, Hough Street, S.E. 18.

National Milk Publicity Council, 5 John Princes Street, London, W.1.

Milk

National Diary Council, Melbourne House, Aldwych, London, W.C.2

Fats

Unilever Education Section, Unilever House, London, E.C.4

Van der Berghs, Kildare House, Dorset Rise, London, E.C.4

Margarine Manufacturers Association, 4 Lygon Place, London, S.W.3

Butter Information Council, Salisbury House, London Wall, London, E.C.2

Cheese

English Cheese Bureau, 148 Charing Cross Road, London, W.C.2.

Cereals

Flour Advisory Bureau, 21 Arlington Street, London, S.W.1

Baking Powder

Baking Powder Information Bureau, Orchard House, Orchard Street, London, W.1

Tea

Tea Centre, 22 Regent Street, London, S.W.1

Coffee

Coffee Information Bureau, Williams House, Eastbourne Terrace, London, W.2

Cocoa

Cadbury Bros. Ltd., Bourneville, Birmingham

Sugar

Sugar Board, 52 Mark Lane, London, E.C.3

Index

aboyeur, 266
absorption, nutrition, 105
  refrigeration, 71
accelerated freeze drying, 240
accidents, 1
aerated gas burner, 43
allspice, 222
almonds, 186
alphabets, 204, 206
alternating current, 56
aluminium, cleaning of, 18
ampères, 57
anchovy, 157
  essence, 234
angelica, 222
animal fats, 196
  infection, 27
apples, 182
apricot, 178
arrowroot, 210
artichoke, globe, 173
  Jerusalem, 173
artificial respiration, 5
ascorbic acid, 115
asparagus, 173
aspic jelly, 229
aubergine, 173
automatic boiler, 98
automatic vending, 344
avocado pear, 182

bacon, 131, 139
bacteria, 21-25
bain-marie, 93
baking powder, 211
balanced diet, 126
ball valve, 77, 78
banana, 183
barley, 207
basal metabolism, 120
bay leaves, 220
beans—
  broad, 173
  butter, 219
  French, 173
  haricot, 219
  runner, 173
beef—
  food value, 131
  French, 282
  preservation, 131
  storage, 130
  uses, 133
beetroot, 174
bel paese, 202
beverages, 358-360
bin cards, 250
birds, entry of (kitchen hygiene), 30
blackberries, 178
blackcurrants, 178
blackjack, 215, 228
boar's head, 232
boiling pans, 93
Bombay duck, 235
bottling, 244
brains, 144
brawn, 231
Brazil nuts, 186
bread pudding, 356
bream, 161
brie, 203
brill, 159
brine-tub, 245
British Thermal Unit, 40
broad beans, 173
broccoli, 174
browning, 228
Brussels sprouts, 174
buffets, 331-346
burns, prevention of, 2
burst pipes, 86
butchers' blocks, 96
butter, 194
buying, 336

cabbage, 174
  red, 174
  Savoy, 174
Caerphilly, 202
cafeteria service, 343
calcium, 116
calorie requirement, 120
calories, 119
Camembert, 203
canning, 244
canteens, 352
Cape gooseberries, 237
capers, 233
capons, 147
cappicums, 224
carbohydrates, 110
Carolina rice, 208
carraway, 223
Carrè de l'est, 203
carrots, 174
cash account, 259, 260
  discount, 254
cast aluminium, 102
cauliflower, 174
cayenne, 226
celeriac, 174
celery, 174
  seed, 220
Central Council for Health Education, 36
cèpes, 234
cereals, 204
  breakfast, 210
Cheddar, 201
cheese, 198-204
chemical food poisoning, 19
cherries, 178
  cocktail, 235
chervil, 220
Cheshire, 202
chestnuts, 186
chicken, 145, 146
chicory, 174
chillies, 224
chilling, 242
china, cleaning of, 18
chippers, 98
chives, 221
chocolate, 216
choppers, 97
chow-chow, 234
chutney, 234
cinnamon, 223
citrus fruits, 183
clostridium botulinus, 27
clostridium Welchii, 27
clothing, hygiene, 12
cloves, 223
club sandwich, 358
clubs, 347, 352, 353
coal gas, 39
cochineal, 228
cocoa, 215, 360
cockroaches, 29
cockscombs, 232
coconut, 186
cod, 161
coffee, 216, 217, 359
cold water systems, 77
colourings, 228
conduction, 38
conger eel, 158
contact grills, 95
contract catering, 354
condiments, 225, 226
convection, 38
cooking fat, 194
copper equipment, 18, 101, 102
coriander, 223
corn on the cob, 175, 207
cornflour, 207
cosmetics, 12
crab, 165
cranberries, 184
crawfish, 165
crayfish, 164
cream, 193
credit notes, 253
cross contamination, 27
crystalised foods, 181
cucumber, 174
currents, electric, 56
curry powder, 224
custard powder, 208
cuts, prevention of, 1

daily stores issue sheet, 256, 257
damsons, 178, 182
Danish blue, 204
dates, 185
deep fat-fryers, 93
dehydration, 239
delicatessen goods, 229
delivery note, 253
demi-sel, 199
digestion, 105
direct current, 56
discount, 254
  table, 254
dishwashing machine, 99
double Gloucester, 202
drainage of water, 84
dripping, 196
drying of foods, 239
Dublin Bay prawn, 164
duck, 147
  wild, 152
dust, 30

earthenware, cleaning of, 18
Edam, 198
eel, 158
eggs, 187-190
electrical cookers, 68
  Development Association, 74
  equipment, large, cleaning of, 19
  fuses, 63-64
  plugs, 65-67
  shock, 5
  terms, 57
  water heating, 69-70
Emmental, 202
essences, 229
examinations, 362
extracts, 229

fats, 109, 194
feet, 11
figs, 185
filberts, 186
fines-herbes, 222
finger-nails, 10
fire extinguishers, 6
fire precautions, 5-6
first aid, 4-5
fish, composition, 123
  food value, 156
  French names, 153-154
  garnishes, 311
  preservation, 156
  seasons, 153-154
  storage, 155
  uses, 157
fitness, 12, 13
floor, 16
flour, 204
flushing systems, 78
foie gras, 231
fondant, 235
food-borne diseases, 33
  buying, 336
  choppers, 97
  costing, 340
  hygiene, 19
    Regulations, 33-35
    Summary, 35-36
  mixers, 97
  poisoning, 19-21
  preservation, 238, 245, 246
  slicers, 97
  storage, hygienic, 31
  waste disposers, 99
Frankfurt sausage, 230
freezing, 242
French—
  fish, 279-280
  fruit, 285-286
  game, 283
  groceries, 277-279
  herbs and spices, 285
  kitchen staff, 275, 276
  kitchen terms, 286-295
  meat, 281-282
  nuts, 285-286
  poultry, 283
  service terms, 269-270
  simple grammar, 270-273
  utensils, 276-277
  vegetables, 283-284
  verbs, 273-275
frogs' legs, 232

fruit—
  food value, 180
  French names, 178-179
  preservation, 180-181
  purchasing unit, 178-179
  quality, 180
  season, 177-179
fruit—
  storage, 180
fry plates, 95
fuels, comparison of, 87-90

galantine, 231
game, 149
garnishes, 309-312
gas, bills, 40
  explosions, 4
  instantaneous heater, 47
  meter, 40, 41
  storage, 48
gelatine, 229
gherkins, 233
ginger, 224
glucose, 111
goose, 147
gooseberry, 182
Gorgonzola, 203
Gouda, 198
grapefruit, 183
grapes, 184
greengage, 179
green vegetables, 172
griddle plate, 95
grills, 94
grocery goods, 229
groundnut oil, 197
grouse, 151
Gruyére, 202
gudgeon, 161
guinea fowl, 148
gum tragacanth, 236

haddock, 161
haggis, 232
hair, 10
hake, 161
halibut, 160
hams, 230
hands, 9
hard water, 75
hare, 150-151
hazel nuts, 186
heads, calves', 144
health, 12
hearts, 142
herbs, 220
herrings, 158
honey, 235
horseradish, 234
hospital catering, 348-350
hot cupboards, 93
  water, boiler, 81
    instantaneous, 83
    storage water heater, 82
    systems, 81
hotels, 347

ice cream, 237
infection, sources, 27
  spread, 28
insect infection, 29
invalid cookery, 346
invoices, 255
iodine, 117
iron equipment, 100
  (mineral), 117

jam, 236
jelly bag, 104
  piping, 235
  red currant, 236

Kale, 174
kidney, 141
kitchen clothing, 13
  French, 269
  hygiene, 15
  lighting, 15
  organisation, 261
  premises, 15
  service, 269
  staff, 275
  terms, 286-295
  utensils, 276

lactose, 111

lamb, French, 281
  quality, 130
  uses, 136
Lancashire cheese, 202
lard, 196
leek, 174
lemon, 179, 183
lemonade, 360
lentils, 219
lettuce, 174
lifts, food, 17
lighting, kitchen, 15
liver, 140
liver sausage, 230
lobster, 164
locker, 12
luncheon clubs, 352-353

mackerel, 158
mace, 223
macaroni, 204, 206
maize, 207
  oil, 197
maltose, 111
mandarine, 179
mandolins, 103
mango chutney, 234
marble, cleaning of, 18
marzipan, 237
marmalade, 236
marrow, 174
  beef, 144
marjoram, 221
marrons glacés, 235
margarine, 195
masher, hand or electric, 98
meat, composition, 123
  French, 281-283
  garnishes, 309, 310
  preservation, 131
  storage, 130
melon, 184
metabolism, 120
meter reading, 41, 42
menu balance, 303
  banquet, 328-330
  breakfast, 313-317
  colour, 306
  dinner, 321-327
  functions, 330
  light buffets, 331
  luncheon, 318-321
  planning, 296-308
  supper, 327-328
  supplies, 302
  tea, 321
  wording, 306-308
milk, 191-192
mincemeat, 236
mincers, 97
mineral elements, 116
mint, 221
mixed spice, 224
mixers, 97
mortadella, 230
moulds, 101
mouth, 11
mullet, 162
mushrooms, 174-175
muslin, 18, 104
mussels, 166
mustard, 226
mutton, French, 281
  quality, 130
  uses, 136

niacin, 115
nicotinic acid, 115
noodles, 204, 206
nose, 11
nutmegs, 223
nutrients, 105
nutrition, fats, 109
nuts, 185

oatmeal, 206-207
oats, 206-207
offal, 140
ohms, 58
oils, 196-197
oily fish, 157-158
olive oil, 197
olives, 233
onions, 175
orangeade, 360

oranges, 179
order book, 252
outside catering, 354
ovens, 92
oxtail, 144
oysters, 165-166

pans, 101-103
paprika, 226
Parmesan, 202
parsley, 221
parsnips, 175
partridge, 151
pastillage, 236
patna rice, 208
peaches, 179, 182
pear, 182
  avocado, 182
pearl barley, 207
peas, fresh, 175
  green split, 219
  marrowfat, 219
  yellow split, 219
pepper, 225
  (pimentos), 175
personal hygiene, 9, 14, 15
pheasants, 151
phosphorous, 117
physallis, 237
pickling, 173
pigeon, 148
pimentos, 170, 175
pineapple, 183
piping jelly, 235
  bag, cleaning of, 18, 104
pistachio, 185-186
plaice, 160
plastic, cleaning of, 18
plate room, 267
plover, 151
plumbing, kitchen, 16
plums, 179
pommel, 203
Pont l'éveque, 202
poppadums, 235
pork, French, 137
  quality, 131
  uses, 137
portion control, 336
  equipment, 337
potato, 175
  flour, 210
  peelers, 96
potted shrimps, 233
pots, 101-103
poultry, garnishes, 309-310
  quality, 146
  storage, 146
  types of, 145
  uses, 146-147
poussin, 146
practical examinations, 363
prawns, 164
preservation of food, 238, 245-246
pressure governor, 46
protein, 107
pulses, 219

quail, 152
quick freezing, 243

rabbit, 150-151
radiation, 38
radishes, 175
raising agents, 211
raspberries, 179, 182
redcurrants, 178, 182, 183
refrigerants, 74
refrigeration, 71
refrigerators, absorption, 73
  compression, 72
  maintenance, 96
reheated food, 354-356
rennet, 236
requisition book, 251
restaurants, 347
rhubarb, 184
riboflavin, 115
rice, 208
ring circuit system, 62
roe, 157, 167
rollmops, 232
root vegetables, 168, 171-172
Roquefort, 203
rosemary, 221

safety, 1
saffron, 224
sage, 221
sago, 209
St.-Paulin, 202
salamander, 94
Salami, 230
salmon, 158
  trout, 159
salmonella, 25
salt, 225
salting, preservation, 244
saltpetre, 234
salsify, 175
sandwiches, 356-358
sardine, 159
sausage, 230
saute pan, 101
sauteuse, 101
Savoy cabbage, 169, 174
saws, 18
scalds, prevention of, 2
scallops, 166
scampi, 164
school meals service, 350-351
scratches, prevention of, 1
scullery, 266
scakale, 175
semolina, 204, 206
service of food, 342
  terms, 269-270
shallots, 175
shellfish, food value, 163
  French, 162
  seasons, 162
  storage, 163
shrimps, 163
shock, 5
silver room, 267
sinks, 95
skate, 160
sleep, 12
smelt, 162
smoking, hygiene, 12
  preservation, 244
snack bars, 347-348
snails, 232
snipe, 151
sodium, 117
soft fruit, 182
sole, 160
spaghetti, 204, 206
speciality restaurants, 345
spices, 222
spinach, 175
spitting, 12
sprats, 159
spring greens, 175
stainless steel equipment, 103
  cleaning of, 18
staphylococci, 27
starch, 111
statements, 253, 255
steamers, 92
stillroom, 267
Stilton, 203
stock sheets, 252
stone fruits, 182
stopcock, 80
storekeeper's duties, 258
storekeeping, 247
  ledger, 251
stores, 247-249
  cleaning, 247
sucrose, 111
suet, 144, 196
sugar, 214
  cooking of, 360
swedes, 175
sweetbreads, 143
sweetcorn, 175

tables, 95
tammy cloth, cleaning of, 18, 104
tangerine, 179
tapioca, 209
taps, 79-80
tarragon, 221
tea, 228, 377
teal, 152
teeth, 11
temperature, 23
theory examinations, 362
thermostats, 44
thiamine, 115
thyme, 221

tin, cleaning of, 18
tinned foods, 244
  steel equipment, 100-101
tomatoes, 185, 234
tongues, lambs, 142
  ox, 142
trade discount, 254
transport catering, 353
tripe, 144
tropical fruits, 183
trout, 159
truffles, 176, 231
tunny, 159
turbot, 160
turkeys, 148
turmeric, 224
turnips, 176
types of catering, 346

value of foods in diet, 121
veal, garnishes, 135
  joints, 135
  quality, 130
  uses, 135
vegetables—
  composition, 124-125
  food value, 171-172
  French, 169-170
  preservation, 172-173
  purchasing, 169-170
  quality, 172
  season, 169-170
  storage, 172
  uses, 173-176
venison, 150
ventilation, kitchen, 15
vermicelli, 204, 206
vinegar, 227
vitamins, 113
vitreous enamel, 18
volts, 57

walls, kitchen, 16
washing up, 30
water boiling appliances, 98
  taps, 79-80
watercress, 176
watts, 57
walnuts, 186
welfare catering, 348
Wensleydale, 203
wiring of plugs, 67
white bait, 159
white fish, 153
whiting, 162
wholemeal flour, 205
wood, cleaning of, 18, 103
woodcock, 151
wood pigeon, 149
wooden equipment, 18
working methods, 7
works study, 7-8

yeast, 212-213
yeasts, 238

zinc, 18